FRONTIERS OF CAPITAL

FRONTIERS OF CAPITAL

ETHNOGRAPHIC REFLECTIONS ON THE NEW ECONOMY

Edited by MELISSA S. FISHER and GREG DOWNEY

Duke University Press   Durham and London   2006

© 2006 Duke University Press
All rights reserved
Printed in the United States
of America on acid-free paper ∞
Designed by Amy Ruth Buchanan
Typeset in Minion by Keystone
Typesetting, Inc.
Library of Congress Cataloging-in-
Publication Data appear on the last
printed page of this book.

CONTENTS

ACKNOWLEDGMENTS

The editors would first like to acknowledge one another's effort in working on the volume. We would also like to acknowledge the Program on the Corporation as a Social Institution at the Social Science Research Council (SSRC, with funds provided by the Alfred P. Sloan Foundation) and the Business Institutions Initiative, also of the SSRC, for funding the 2001 Workshop on the New Global Economy. In particular, we owe special thanks to Craig Calhoun, president of the SSRC and professor of sociology at New York University, and Doug Guthrie, program director of the Corporation as a Social Institution at SSRC and professor of sociology and management at NYU, for their enthusiastic support of the workshop. The conference was graciously hosted by the Goizueta Business School at Emory University. In addition, Ken Wissoker, our editor, and Courtney Berger, both of Duke University Press, have each had an important hand in the volume's development, for which we are very grateful.

Siobhán O'Mahony, Paul Silverstein, Daniel Walkowitz, and two anonymous reviewers all offered insightful suggestions for the introduction. We are grateful to all the authors for their contribution to the anthropology of the New Economy. In addition, Melissa wishes to thank Sherry Ortner, Alice Kessler-Harris, Wendy Mackenzie, Saskia Sassen, and Daniel Walkowitz for their support. She also wishes to acknowledge the support of the Department of Sociology and Anthropology at Georgetown University. Greg wishes to acknowledge the research and technical assistance of Jake Weiler and the support of the Department of Anthropology at the University of Notre Dame.

Greg Downey and Melissa S. Fisher

INTRODUCTION: THE ANTHROPOLOGY
OF CAPITAL AND THE FRONTIERS OF
ETHNOGRAPHY

For a brief moment in the late 1990s, journalists, business gurus, politicians in the United States, and even sober observers abroad talked enthusiastically about a "New Economy." Advances in information and communication technology (ICT), management and production techniques, and global integration, some proponents alleged, had irrevocably changed fundamental economic dynamics. Workplace models emphasizing flat corporate structures and a bohemian approach to work became the hallmark of start-up companies created by the new digital economy (Ross, 2003). In the halcyon days of the New Economy, optimists contemplated a world without business cycles, where technology, ever-increasing productivity, and globalization were to usher in unprecedented prosperity and unrelenting expansion. At the very least, venture capitalists, start-up entrepreneurs, and other investors began to think that the numbers would always go their way: the indexes would continually rise in defiance of old rules for stock valuation. To be fair, careful observers always noted countervailing trends, and pessimists pointed to cracks in the consensus, immiseration in the midst of the boom, and rumblings of crises brewing around the world. However, the robustness of the U.S. economy and the excitement generated by the Internet helped to drive the global expansion of ICT as well as the spread of the "Washington consensus" of neoliberal economic policies.

In January 2000, the Dow Jones Industrial Average reached a peak of 11,723, in spite of some troubling indicators; by October 2002, the average had fallen to 7,286—losing about 38 percent—the slide dashing exuberant dreams of the Dow vaulting over 30,000. The correction of the NASDAQ average, home to many of the most well-known technology and Internet stocks, was even more brutal. From September 2000 to October 2002, the index lost over 70 percent of its value, plummeting from a historic high of 5,132 to as low as 1,108. Trillions of dollars in paper wealth vanished in fluctuating markets.[1] At the end of the millennium, dot-coms turned into "dot-bombs," downsizings and layoffs became frequent as the brisk market in initial public stock offerings (IPOS) for technology firms dried up, and millenarian hopes for endless expansion and transcendence of the business cycle through technology suddenly seemed, not just hollow, but possibly a cynical fraud.

Star corporate performers of the 1990s—WorldCom, Enron, Global Crossing, Adelphia, Arthur Andersen, Merrill Lynch, Tyco, Qwest, Long-Term Capital Management, Credit Suisse First Boston, Martha Stewart Living, mutual funds, Parmalat, even such staid players as Freddie Mac—turned out to have been puffed up on dicey accounting, regulatory dodges, and old-fashioned corruption, albeit accomplished on a staggering scale with sophisticated new digital tools. Productivity gains started to look less like purely technical achievements and more like a combination of ICT with social factors, such as financial chicanery and hyperexploitation. Workers bullied with threats of their jobs fleeing overseas put in longer hours and greater exertion in a slow labor market. Simultaneously, cities such as Chicago witnessed a boom in flexible, short-term, temporary, low-paying employment (Peck and Theodore, 2001), and youngsters bribed with promises of stock options delayed compensation that evaporated when the markets turned.[2] Breathless futurism and nationalist triumphalism gave way to white-knuckle reports from the Wall Street roller coaster, the IPO market sank beneath the waves, and financial crashes around the globe started to look intrinsic to an increasingly unstable regime of hot money.

The New Economy looked like an old story: speculator hype driving a stock market bubble. The United States slid into a stubborn recession and threatened (and still threatens) to drag down a global economy already buffeted by currency crises, overextended debt, sluggish demand, and regional recessions. There was no New Economy, if that term meant the dawn of an age without business contractions, where the cyclical laws of the economy had been repealed. The events of September 11, 2001, made the heady optimism seem incomprehensibly distant; if there was talk of a new age in the United States after the destruction of the World Trade Center and the attack on the Pentagon, it was a dawning of open-ended war and doubts about security.

So why assemble a volume of ethnographic studies around the New Economy if it was equal parts speculative bubble and collective delusion? Why discuss a myth debunked by myriad failures and decisively wiped out by the massive violence of competing, uncompromising fundamentalisms? Are these ethnographic dissections of a bogus imaginary, a kind of intellectual autopsy or sheepish reassessment of an overheated mass self-deception?

In fact, we contend that the New Economy was a revelatory moment. Clearly, ICT will have lasting effects on economic productivity.[3] And sudden fears about computer security and the permeability produced by globalization, heightened in the wake of September 11, are unlikely to reverse completely these trends. But the immediate expansion and contraction, the premature surge of expectations ahead of realized applications for ICT, provide abundant opportunities to perceive the cultural and social underpinnings and reworkings of radical economic and technological change. The New Economy moment, as Ash Amin and Thrift (2004, x) suggest, demonstrates that "the social and the economic are woven together as a single and inseparable fabric." An overly quick dismissal of the New Economy concept, because it became the banner of hyperbolic techno-optimists, squanders a chance for gaining intellectual leverage on longer-standing relations between society and technology, how people understand technological change as they experience it (and how this understanding shapes the unfolding change), and the cultural foundation of "business as usual." All were thrown into high relief by such rapid acceleration and sudden, bone-jarring deceleration, by the manifest gap that arose between capitalist fantasy and material reality, and by the harried renegotiations of meaning and social relations on the frontiers of economic change.

The economic reorganization produced by shifts in late capitalism may not have rewritten the laws of economic cycles, but these shifts occurred alongside profound cultural and symbolic change, as well as social upheaval. As Nigel Thrift (2000, 674) suggests, "Something new is happening to Western capitalism—not as new as some of its more evangelical proponents would argue, no doubt—but not just business as usual either."[4] This volume, taken as a whole, makes the case that many sorts of change were afoot, some more apparent than real.[5] The inability to render all the blooming and buzzing confusion into a coherent master narrative is not a failure of vision. Rather, the uneven spread of innovative forms of value and symbols, the unstable alchemy of new technology and local social relations, quite simply produced radically different phenomena in different locations.

In the process of debunking many New Economy myths, Doug Henwood (2003, 67) writes what might serve as a concise agenda for this collection:

"Trying to quantify the contributions of computers and other high-tech stuff to economic growth is probably a symptom of statistical fetishism at its most advanced. A lot less energy should be devoted to such imprecise and dubious pursuits and a lot more to asking the kinds of qualitative questions that economists rarely ask." One need only turn on the television news or open a magazine to witness the extent to which aspects of the New Economy occupy our minds and imaginations. E-mail, Internet dating, chat rooms, downloaded media, cell phones, and mailing lists have become a pervasive part of quotidian life for many people, not only in the wealthiest classes and countries. New techniques of just-in-time manufacturing, integrated design and production, globalized firms, and long-term financial planning have insinuated themselves into the subterranean, opaque spaces that underwrite our lived worlds. The New Economy also produced a spate of new anxieties about terrorists with high technology, hackers and virus writers attacking the electronic infrastructure of the developed world, and the precariousness of a financial future turbocharged on fiber-optic transfers. As Jean Gadrey (2003, 20) writes, "The progress of this information economy lies less in the growth of units produced than in the impact of these ICTs on the functioning of other technical and human systems."

This volume collects reports from the frontiers of transformation, where new technologies, shifting economic patterns, and novel symbolic systems have helped to convince people that they live on the cusp of a new age—whether that future is utopian or dystopian. Eschewing Panglossian optimism or blanket pessimism, the authors in this collection use ethnographic and anthropological tools to unravel some of the complex local relations in sites looked to as harbingers of epochal change. In particular, the contributors explore the mutually constituting relations between technology and social change, the cultural foundations of the economic "material," and the subtle ways that social relations affect business both at the helm as well as the frontiers of the New Economy.

TECHNOLOGY AND SOCIAL CHANGE

The New Economy was an episode of collective euphoria sparked when people witnessed real changes and many mistakenly assumed (or fraudulently asserted) that shifts in everyday life would necessarily translate seamlessly, quickly, into economic opportunity. Every substantial technological advance under capitalism—the steam engine, the telegraph, railroads, electricity, the automobile, telephones, air travel—has produced speculative "irrational exuberance," to borrow from Alan Greenspan.[6] Investors invariably overestimate immediate business opportunities to be wrung from new technologies. In the long run, these inventions have indeed brought about large-scale systematic change to people's everyday lives (e.g., C. Fischer, 1992; Schivelbusch, 1986). But they have never ended economic cycles, as contemporary optimists invariably predicted. Capitalism since the Industrial Revolution has depended as much on a changing foundation of fantasies, desires, and dreams as on shifts in technology or material relations (Campbell, 1987).

Talk of a New Economy was an entirely predictable way that observers identified an era of turbulence as rapid cultural, organizational, and social change proceeded with unknown economic consequences. Innovative forms of organization emerged, new technologies were integrated (sometimes haltingly) into everyday life, management struggled to reorganize corporate life (sometimes to take advantage of new opportunities and sometimes to meet raised expectations for short-term profitability), and financiers invented new conceptual models and forms of value to understand and manipulate the world around them. These novelties may not have been unprecedented, but there were sharp discontinuities, sudden reversals, and rapid transformations.

Ethnographic study at sites of the New Economy helps to undermine accounts of change that privilege technology as the sole, driving causal agent. Some social theorists conceive technological development as though it were subject to its own unfolding logic—or an unpredictable course determined entirely by the creative "genius" of heroic innovators.[7] Ironically, many anthropologists who would vigorously deny this position do not include technology in their analyses. Leaving technology out of analyses of culture has the unintended implication that it is an autonomous realm of human activity. By leaving technology out of discussions of culture, they hold open the possibility that technology is an uncaused cause, unaffected by culture, social relations, or even economic considerations. By default, technology becomes external to social development (see Barry and Slater, 2002, 179).

Close ethnographic study, as in the cases explored by several contributors to this volume, shows that even in the sectors archetypal of the New Economy, engineers could not foresee or determine how innovation would be taken up or understood by social actors. Caitlin Zaloom, for example, examines the use of electronic trading systems. Whereas the designers of electronic trading systems sought to "purify" prices of social connotations, disentangling numbers from social interactions in the pits, the traders who use these systems attempt to breathe more robust significance back into simplified indicators (see Abolafia, 1998). The interface engineers had an idealized vision of how markets operated, treating traders like the rational actors of economic theory. Traders, in contrast, explicitly eschewed calculation in guiding their actions in the pits, arguing that reading the market's mood from the physical presence of crowds, other traders' facial expressions, and the volume of shouted bids and asks was a superior way to anticipate immediate price movements. New "information technology" of electronic trading, ironically, cuts them off from the overpowering sensory environment that once informed their decisions. Working before computer screens and shouting between their cubicles, traders read numbers, tell stories, and make exploratory trades for hints of the social processes that were previously obvious in the bodies of other traders—even attributing agentive power to the numbers themselves in an attempt to anticipate market trends. As Zaloom (this volume) suggests, "[Screen-based] traders mine the crevices of the technology" for additional information about other actors and social forces hidden beneath the supposedly transparent numbers before them.

Over time, social and cultural constraints often proved resilient obstacles to some forms of New Economy innovation, one reason that anthropologists became increasingly important actors in corporations (as we explore later). People typically adopted and adapted technology in ways that reinforced their identities or incrementally improved the relations they already enjoyed, often refusing to use technology that might undermine their positions. When they did embrace technology, they often put it to unanticipated uses and profit, reflecting local conditions and forms of reason, so that technology followed channels unforeseen by its engineers.

Aihwa Ong, Paul Silverstein, AbdouMaliq Simone, and Greg Downey, for example, examine how New Economy ideas and technologies expanded into various economic peripheries. What is most intriguing about the sites they examine is not just the surprising reach of technological change, but the unexpected ways that peripheral players enthusiastically integrated these new developments into their everyday lives. Technological-determinist accounts of New Economy changes anticipated the dawn of virtual spaces of elective communities and the spreading instrumental logic that would erase local identities, place, embodiment, and prior forms of social solidarity. These accounts clearly cannot explain the peculiar adaptations of these technologies in local projects. Paul Silverstein, for example, suggests that North African youth in French suburbs seek out and explore particular sorts of distant contacts and adopt technologies and aesthetics as they fight the encroachment of the French government into their communities and subcultures.

Simply focusing on products, people, or symbols out of place—rap in France, CD production in a ghetto, Internet cafés in Africa, or graduates of American business schools with Francophile tastes in East Asian cafés—suggests that New Economy culture is a boundaryless jumble. In fact, ICT creates very particular connections, and users are selective about the technology, commodities, and ideas that they seek out, thus pointing to the importance of examining ethnographically the production, circulation, and receivership of knowledge and "things" in particular communities of interpretive practice. In the case of the *Ultimate Fighting Championship*, a series of "no-holds-barred" fighting tournaments broadcast on cable television explored in this volume by Greg Downey, a network of athletes largely invisible to outsiders uses commoditized sport and technological tools to extract embodied knowledge of fighting techniques. The technology enabled a heightened attention to mimetic learning and bodily knowledge.

On closer examination, then, New Economy discourse was a vision of complex technological, economic, social, and psychological change (see Löfgren, 2003). Internet entrepreneurs were well aware that technological advances in isolation would not propel start-ups into profitability. Entrepreneurs preached about the social transformations that their technologies would produce, hoping that changes in lifestyle would ensure that innovative products did not lie unused. Some social theorists, "techno-optimists" like Manuel Castells (1996, 1997, 1998) and columnists in New Economy dream factories such as *Fast Company, Red Herring*, and *Business 2.0*, assumed that obstacles to the adoption of innovation would evaporate before engineering savvy. Talk about innovation-driven "necessity" was equal parts forecasting and sales pitch. As Nigel Thrift (2001, 414) suggests, New Economy rhetoric "was an attempt at mass motivation, which, if successful, could result in a new kind of market culture—or a spiritual renewal of an old one." The extraordinary glut of fiber-optic capacity in the U.S. communications industry is stark testimony to the fallacy of this perspective; just because technology is built does not guarantee it will be used. Nor does design determine use.

CULTURAL FOUNDATIONS OF THE "ECONOMIC"

Some academic fields treat economic relations unproblematically as the material dimension of social life. But economic facts such as "value" are also a social achievement, contingent on cultural as well as material processes (see Callon, Méadel, and Rabeharisoa, 2004). Moreover, social actors cannot define products, markets, and clients without extensive forms of cultural knowledge (Slater, 2002). As Leyshon and Thrift (1997, xv) demonstrate in their detailed exploration of money, the economic sphere presumes and works on shared cultural norms, bonds of trust, and standards for predictable social practices. The point of recognizing this cultural foundation of the economic, according to du Gay and Pryke (2002b, 2), is not merely to show, as sociologists typically have argued, that markets and corporations are "embedded" in a social context or "socially constructed." Rather, a cultural study of economic institutions and activities demonstrates how technical and organizational discourse literally "make them up" (see Callon, 1998).

The boom and bust of the New Economy laid bare the cultural foundations of economic "fundamentals." The constitutive role of hybrid academic-professional disciplines—especially the fields of accounting, marketing, law, finance, and economics—became more apparent, for example, when scandal and sudden market reversals forced a rapid retreat from some of their newest fictions. The cultural underscoring was especially pronounced when intangibles such as "risk," "innovation," or "the future" were factored into value, as they were on the frontiers of new economic activity in securitization.[8] For instance, the ability of specialized trusts to transform and repackage various forms of debt, such as mortgages, credit card balances, and car loans—illiquid social relations between individual parties—into liquid securities helped to heat up the New Economy financial market, allowing finance to bypass traditional intermediaries such as banks (see Kendall, 1996). Securitization required that investors accept standardized ratings as substitutes for evaluating the specific risks associated with individual loan relationships; it also depended on models of behavior, such as repayment schedules, that were transparently fabricated and liable to systematic breakdown (Baron, 1996; Ranieiri, 1996, 35).

The New Economy was not unusual because economic activity was premised on cultural notions of value, but it was a moment when the norms underlying economic activity became unsettled. The links between knowledge production, social standards, and the economy had not yet been established in productive sectors and services created by ICT; new activities forced the renegotiation of cultural consensus on economic fundamentals. The stock market bubble of the late 1990s, for example, resulted in large part from the widespread hope that a new standard for value had arisen, one that subsequently unraveled (see Aglietta and Breton, 2001).

The authors in this volume, then, do not specifically analyze New Economy discourse as construct, myth, aesthetic, or realm of the imaginary, although it could be treated as any one of these (see, e.g., Gadrey, 2003; Löfgren, 2003, 245).[9] Nor are we arguing that the economy is becoming more "culturalized" than it once was, as the fields of marketing, branding, information services, and entertainment play increasing roles in the global economy (see Allen, 2002; du Gay and Pryke, 2002a; Lash and Urry, 1994; Leadbeater, 1999). Rather, contributors explore how cultural consensus was reached (or not) at intersections of disparate regimes of economic understanding or at moments of sudden change. Following theorist Michel Callon (1998), contributors such as Annelise Riles, Aihwa Ong, and Douglas Holmes and George Marcus ask under what conditions economic calculation and "reasoning" might be possible, especially in innovative markets or shifting economic conditions, and show the cultural labor necessary to produce social consensus. Classical economic models assume that market mechanisms invariably create agreement through open price negotiation, that information is widely available and transparent, and that modes of rational calculation are universal. These traditional economic notions, however, look especially fraught with unwarranted assumption in light of the New Economy bust and under the scrutiny of the ethnographic gaze. Indeed, Benjamin Lee and Edward LiPuma (2002, 191–192) note that understanding cultures of circulation, with their distinctive "forms of abstraction, evaluation, and constraint," is one of the central tasks of an anthropology of the New Economy.

The boom in derivatives markets offers a particular case study in how new cultural fictions came to be in a sector considered a hallmark of fast capitalism. A derivative is a financial asset whose price is derived from, or based on, the performance of other equities or commodities, first used to hedge against future currency exchange rate risks, but increasingly traded speculatively for profit in the 1980s and 1990s (Hull, 1997; see Riles, this volume; Zaloom, this volume). One of the most basic forms of a derivative is a currency swap, in which two banks agree to "swap" sums of different currencies at a later date, one paying a smaller price at present for this future, much larger transaction. The simple swap serves as a hedge against future changes in exchange rates. During the heyday of the New Economy, a surging market in progressively more arcane derivatives arose as new techniques for calculating risk allowed portions of financial uncertainty to be spun off into separate products, and these fractions combined into more complex, hybrid financial paper.

Typically, the evolution of these financial fictions is written as a narrative of innovation. Sophisticated mathematical modeling, new product design, and raw computational power allegedly overcame stodgy forms of "business as usual," such as long-standing social networks among brokers or relations between market analysts and the industries they studied. Formal mathematical modeling supposedly replaced intimate personal knowledge of particular firms, industries, and actors.

In 1998, however, Long-Term Capital Management (LTCM), a high-flying, heavily leveraged hedge fund specializing in derivatives, nearly toppled some of the most august institutions on Wall Street when it imploded spectacularly. The threat of bankruptcy was both a terrifying jolt to elite investors and an opportunity to glimpse the fragility of cultural fictions on the frontiers of capital (see Lowenstein, 2000). The boom in derivatives arose from both social and technical roots; large numbers of mathematicians, physicists, and other sophisticated modelers were recruited into financial offices on Wall Street, and the ICT tools necessary to manage complex synthetic securities became widely available. But market participants also had to reach some working agreement on the risks involved in this uncharted territory if they were to produce a coherent market in derivatives. Liquidity in exotic derivatives, like that in mortgage-based securities described by Carruthers and Stinchcombe (1999, 357), was "a matter of how to create a public consensus about value" (see Pryke and Allen, 2000). The Black-Scholes formula, a method for pricing exotic financial papers, provided the opportunity to achieve this cultural consensus among traders.

The Black-Scholes formula circulated as an item of faith among students of Nobel prize–wining economists Myron Scholes and Robert Merton, their collaborator Fischer Black, and the trio's disciples.[10] Traders trained to use the formula and its corollaries were hired up and down Wall Street to establish offices in derivatives, a raucous riptide in fast capitalism. When traders throughout these markets used the same equations to price them, their assumptions appeared rational. As Benjamin Lee and Edward LiPuma (2002, 192) point out, just as novels and newspapers circulate within an interpretive community equipped to understand them, exotic financial creations like equity-based derivatives and currency swaps depend on and presuppose a community that invests them with value. The Black-Scholes option pricing equation had what Donald MacKenzie (2003) describes as a "performative" potency: it became "more real" over time, as specialists in the field deployed it consistently to fix option prices. The spectacular failure of LTCM proved that derivatives' values were grounded in cultural assumptions about social realities that might easily change, not unbending economic law.

The Black-Scholes formula treated price changes as random and risk as normally distributed. Under stress, these assumptions about price volatility proved unfounded. As both booms and crashes demonstrate, although normal price changes can appear random, more volatile movements may follow enduring rules of mob psychology, such as "When everyone is about to panic, it pays to panic first" (Hahnel, 1999). Although the formula was thought to describe reality, it was, in effect, a way to reach consensus on value, especially when coupled with consistent hiring patterns, dense social networking, institutional innovations, and the enormous symbolic prestige of academic departments of economics and Nobel prize winners.

Experts are often acutely aware of how ambiguous and uncertain objectified measures of business are, whether they are accounting fictions at the level of the firm (Carruthers, 1995) or macroeconomic economic indicators, as Douglas Holmes and George Marcus reveal in this volume in the case of Alan Greenspan. Not surprisingly, Greenspan's faith that technological innovation could bring higher rates of growth indefinitely, without an increase in inflation, led to monetary policies that aided and abetted the speculative expansion. The closer we look at sites like this, the more the New Economy appears built on cultural innovation, a shift in how observers understood economic forces to work, rather than a change in material relations. In the case of Greenspan, Holmes and Marcus argue, the production of a kind of economic self-knowledge by experts in the Federal Reserve resembles the knowledge-producing practices of ethnographers. This recognition suggests that experts' "para-ethnographic" practices pose distinctive challenges for scholars exploring this realm of economically efficacious meaning production in an era of fast capitalism. The New Economy, even as a myth, entered the constellation of forces propelling unprecedented economic development, speculation in securities, and some profound changes in organizational form.

Not all that is new in the New Economy is actually novel, of course, and it is also not purely economic. But the expansion and contraction allow us to more readily see the cultural production of a society's, a community's, and even a person's self-knowledge. Agents act on their assumptions, so that the economic imaginary is recycled into the material realm. Leyshon and Thrift (1997, 345–346) suggest, for example, that with massive amounts of information readily available, the difficulty for participants is not in acquiring information, but in understanding how to interpret the flood of data. Far from the Information Age making economic realities transparent, greater access to information makes strong hermeneutical techniques and models essential to understanding fast capitalism, as Holmes and Marcus's case demonstrates.

Because expert actors are aware that their economic spheres of action are dependent on consensus, they often have the opportunity to engineer them intentionally. The "Big Bangs" in global financial sites, such as London and Japan, provided an ideal opportunity to observe a compressed, self-conscious structuring of markets and subjectivities because innovative products demanded new forums for trade, old rules had to be applied to new trading environments, and expanded demand for skilled financial workers drew new populations—such as young, brash, American business school–educated financiers—into these fields.

In this volume, Annelise Riles examines the legal engineering necessary to buttress a nascent market in over-the-counter derivatives in Japan. Financial and legal experts in Japan self-consciously served as architects for a system that supported commercial transactions in currency swaps. Experts saw the market in derivatives not as the natural outcome of a propensity to truck and barker, according to Riles, but as a "fragile entity" that they simultaneously had to produce and promote. To make Japanese derivatives attractive on a global market, defenses against bankruptcy were imported, specifically a legal fiction known as "netting out," in which transactions in derivatives were treated as if they were part of a massive, industrywide single transaction rather than individual agreements. Her Japanese informants insisted, however, that their system was not really liable to the types of failure that netting out could defend against, so the legislation was a culturally efficacious sign of compliance with the aesthetic of "transparent" markets, rather than a pragmatically necessary change in legal architecture. The form of the market—its rules, norms, and accepted behaviors, as well as a style of arguing for those standards—is of central concern to all participants because form legitimates its transactions. Moreover, participants derive aesthetic satisfaction from their role in helping to engineer this sector of the New Economy, rather than just the daily drudgery of "papering the transactions" to enact trades in the resulting market.

Similarly, Aihwa Ong finds a range of creative actors on the frontiers of new economic opportunities in Shanghai, where they must negotiate disparate cultural standards for social behavior and individual subjectivity. The gaps between familiar and unfamiliar subject positions and social expectations are at least as jarring as the economic and legal changes taking place in that country for many middle-level managers. Ong finds that various expert actors use "Americanized" management and human resource technologies to "reengineer" corporate subjectivity among Chinese knowledge workers, sometimes with only limited success. In addition, cultural entrepreneurs, many of them returning expatriates who have been educated overseas, seek to fashion a distinctive Shanghai cosmopolitanism in the clubs, publications, and other institutions that serve the hybrid elite of foreign managers and upwardly mobile young people. As Ong points out, drawing attention to management technologies in the New Economy in China brings into sharper focus the peculiarities of the subjectivities that have sprung up in various locations. Reflective management techniques force participants to act on their own behaviors, refashioning themselves, but not necessarily into a homogeneous character, as local innovations and compromises accumulate into widespread change in a corporation's character and its workers.

Ong's work also points out that technocentric accounts of innovation and cultural change leave out the very specific social institutions and relations that form conduits for the spread of New Economy practices. Business consulting firms, hiring practices that put managers from Taiwan or Hong Kong in charge of Chinese workers, and sojourns at overseas universities are the concrete connections that undergird what appears to be a diffuse globalization when researchers leave an ethnographic scale of analysis. How these social networks and relations affect the configuration of the New Economy at specific sites is the third theme of this volume.

SOCIAL STRUCTURES OF ECONOMIC ACTIVITY

Traditional economic analysis and thought tends to reify and naturalize market structures. However, in recent interdisciplinary studies of cultural economy, writers such as Michel Callon (1998) have drawn attention to the way that market "mechanisms" are constructed of social relations and cultural calculation. Too often, qualities such as liquidity and price volatility are attributed to markets, masking the social interactions and actors that underlie the abstractions. Some observers of the New Economy envisioned ICT allowing actual markets to approach the ideals imagined as economic models,[11] rendering social relations, space, and embodiment irrelevant to commercial interaction. Bill Gates (or his ghost writers), for example, suggested that technology might create "friction-free" capitalism, a virtual plane of electronic transactions where capital could shed the encumbering peculiarities of the material realm.

Ethnographic research in sites of the New Economy demonstrated that social relations, far from being made obsolete by ICT technology, may have actually become more important in such business sectors as financial services and Internet start-ups. Leyshon and Thrift (1997, 349), for example, argue that the "informational frenzy" in London in the 1980s intensified interaction practices and the importance of forms of "face work," especially as the growing demand for management and technical skills drew diverse workers into financial firms. Without prior social ties developed through a shared background in private schools and select universities, New Economy workers found that networking was as much an ongoing face-to-face activity as a virtual one, and vital to their success. Insider rumors and information, social access to other players, and quick responses to changing conditions were at a premium, so, not surprisingly, ethnographers found that participants were determined to create a wealth of personal contacts at many sites of the New Economy (see Abolafia, 1998; Holmes and Marcus, this volume; Ong, this volume; Pryke and Lee, 1995; Zaloom, this volume).

In her studies of women's networked organizations on Wall Street, for example, Melissa Fisher finds a consistent focus on maintaining social-professional ties, even as the occupational profiles and business milieus of participants changed dramatically over time. Shifting social relations, professional skills, and legal standards led to substantial changes in the sorts of professional roles that women fill in Wall Street firms, and recent upheavals in the industry associated with the New Economy and its deflation threw many from the upward career trajectories they expected (and left those still in place feeling more anxious about their status). As women's occupations multiplied and shifting employment practices threatened their job security, some sought to use technology, particularly cyberspace, to knit together a virtual network of personal ties that they might use to move between firms and to multiply their skills. These attempts to create community required the women to define a coherent subjectivity that they might share, in part, by excluding those who do not belong to their community. As they press against occupational frontiers and glass ceilings, Wall Street women strive self-consciously to construct social networks, using both new virtual tools and old-fashioned organization building, in a style that Alexis de Tocqueville might recognize. They hope these social networks might speed their professional ascent—or arrest a sudden fall.

Likewise, AbdouMaliq Simone finds that development officials and international nongovernmental organizations (NGOs) see the introduction of ICT into Africa as creating an unprecedented set of opportunities. He traces the concrete gains made in the spread of ICT, as well as the technical obstacles in the path of this monumental task. But when he turns from the level of macroeconomic indicators and NGOs' reports to the ethnographic level of practice, he finds that ICT allows individuals and groups to produce and maintain social ties. Many technology users in Africa follow familiar strategies for social solidarity, especially when they find other ties under attack from myriad forces, some due to the expansion of state or corporate power and others to the decline of economic opportunity or the ravages of HIV.

Migrants use ICT to buttress far-flung kin relationships as a buffer against local crises, but they also experiment with new types of coordination. Far from ICT creating a transparent, open society of shared information, Simone finds new forms of clandestine organization and subterfuge alongside attempts to rebuild communities.

Some of the distinguishing phenomena associated with the New Economy, although they may have seemed to outside observers to be purely technological or economic achievements, were, in fact, built on substantial social change. These shifts included legal reforms in property law, new administrative procedures in corporations, altered accounting standards, and organizational restructuring (Aglietta and Breton, 2001; see P. Miller, 1998). Carruthers and Stinchcombe (1999) catalogue the specialist actors, institutions, knowledge, standardized practices, and even government interventions that are necessary to create liquidity in financial markets. The reorganization of firms, including aggressive acquisitions and cold-blooded downsizing, arose, in part, because of a shift in management understandings of the nature of corporations (Carruthers, 1995, 319).

Technological advances also allowed experiments with new forms of organization and sociality (cf. Whittel 2001). ICT technology intensified management surveillance, at the same time that it enabled employees to work from home. John Boies and Harland Prechel (2002), for example, chart the increasing complexity of multilayered corporations as they used communications and computing power, modifications in accounting standards, legislative rollbacks of New Deal–era regulations, and new techniques for financial management to spin out subsidiary structures of unprecedented scale. Because subsidiaries, unlike divisions, are legally defined under U.S. law as separate property-holding entities, this shift in a social nexus of law, technology, and financial techniques allowed managers to raise additional capital, offload debt, shield themselves from risk, quarantine troubled units, and engage in virtual social relationships between subsidiary corporate actors. In one of the most notorious cases, Enron listed 5,000 subsidiaries, "special purpose entities," and other business units when it declared bankruptcy at the end of 2001 (see Benston and Hartgraves, 2002). As Boies and Prechel (2002, 308) explain, "In response to rapidly changing economic conditions, competition and globalization, corporations attempted to establish social structures that facilitated flexible accumulation" (see Antonio and Bonanno, 1996; Harrison, 1994). The collapse of Enron should not merely be taken as a cautionary tale of greed, corruption, and cronyism; it should also be a clarion call to us that the corporate form itself, increasingly innovative and experimental, is a field of arcane social structures ripe for anthropological analysis (Garsten and Lindh De Montoya, 2005; Marcus, 1998b; E. Martin, 1995).

Siobhán O'Mahony provides an equally illuminating example in this volume, showing how the networked cooperative programming community responsible for Debian Linux, one of the archetypes of New Economy collaboration held up by techno-optimists, "scaled" virtual social relations around the globe. In the process, however, the group had to negotiate instabilities that arose from its very structure. Some of the most technically savvy and creative programmers are still concerned, as one Internet posting put it, to "close the loop between hand and eye." Although they were on the frontiers of a number of New Economy phenomena—networked social relations, virtual work spaces, advances in software engineering, and new forms of property—O'Mahony suggests that the open source programming community demonstrated parallels with prior generations of voluntary organizations, drafting documents and developing practices to constitute their collective, assure leadership succession, meet face-to-face, and create a corporate persona. Even virtual organizations among virtuoso computer programmers turn out to be constituted in large part of social practices and shared norms.

The contagious collapses of chains of economic players that heralded the end of New Economy optimism itself, whether East Asian currency markets, mammoth hedge funds like LTCM, new age corporations like WorldCom and Enron, or the NASDAQ index, illustrate the social nature of economic entities. Circulations of hot money (capital invested for very short-term, incremental gain) created dependent networks of reciprocal recognition, trust, even faith among economic players, some of them also complex cultural inventions (corporations, banks, exchanges, states, etc.). When liquidity crises suddenly caused the rewinding of chains of debenture, these vital social entities, so central to the global economy in finance, started to dissolve. Such fragility is hardly a hallmark of chains of material production; rather, it is symptomatic of complex, crosscutting social bonds of reciprocity and mutual support. Deprived of their trust and unfolding quality in time—that is, forced to retract quickly to discover where each participant stood with all reciprocal relations rescinded (exactly the danger that Riles's Japanese informants sought to forestall)—these ties evaporated as elaborate social fictions.

Ironically, more and more of material production depends on these fragile, frenetic relations of reciprocity. Without continual financial circulation, material production quickly halts, not out of necessity but because of the shallowness of operating capital. Just-in-time finance and sprawling networks based on faith in credit mean that the most basic exchanges depend on higher-order functions of economic trust: a superorganic faith in the dollar, the NYSE, the new standards for valuation, the Black-Scholes equation, the future. Payrolls cannot be met, deliveries are stuck in warehouses, and store shelves rapidly empty. Capital has been spread thinly through material production. Any available surplus is placed into hyperactive networks to ensure that minimal capital is "wasted" and little left stationary that might be earning more if unlocked from stasis and allowed to dart about maniacally in virtual forms.

Technological innovations have also had unpredictable consequences when they filter through real social relations and worsening economic conditions for those marginalized in the global economy, especially the young. One can attribute some of the excitement about dot-com firms, as well as the fear of hackers, crackers, and virus writers, to generational dynamics. The young are often better able to keep pace with technological change than their elders; intergenerational relations, then, can be severely disrupted by the explosive combination of youth disenfranchisement and ICT technology, as Jean and John Comaroff, Paul Silverstein, and AbdouMaliq Simone recognize in their contributions to this volume (also see Barlow, 1996). The story is not that technology changes family or community structure, but that familial, economic, and technological dynamics interact in unpredictable ways, affecting the forms that all subsequently take.

One fascinating dimension of New Economy change was the sense that, if children were able to master new technologies, they must be relatively easy to use, and yet, they also seemed to allow young people to leverage technical knowledge into substantial power. Apocryphal urban legends, some based in front-page news items, told of high school students making small fortunes by manipulating stock prices from their bedrooms with fraudulent insider tips and of young crackers shredding electronic defenses around vital institutions as childish pranks. In their review of ethnographic material from a wide geographic range, Jean and John Comaroff discuss a pervasive sense in the current moment that youth are in crisis, coming of age just as older social structures slump in exhaustion. The young become the ideal foot soldiers for a range of high-risk endeavors, both illicit and aboveboard. One could argue that the very enthusiasm with which many talented young people threw themselves into dubious New Economy ventures, start-ups, and industries that quickly proved faddish was a symptom of economic desperation, a sign that older professional dreams of secure employment in a corporate family and being embraced by the parental state had been definitively debunked.

During the past decade, an unprecedented number of cultural anthropologists have been hired by companies to work as consultants in consumer,
design, and workplace research.[12] Indeed, by the late 1990s, Sapient, the once
self-proclaimed "Architects of the New Economy," boasted an employee ros-
ter of anthropologists with Ph.D.s from some of the most prestigious universities (Cefkin, 2003). Even when anthropologists began receiving pink slips
from Sapient and other high-tech companies during the dot-com bust, the
practice of bringing anthropologists into the corporate fold did not wane.
Instead, in the first decade of the new millennium, increasing numbers of
anthropologists work for transnational companies such as IBM, Intel, and
BBDO, and the discipline is fast becoming part of the business landscape.

How can we begin to account for the migration of anthropologists out of
academia into business? Has the increasing demise of tenure-track jobs in the
discipline forced academics to look elsewhere for employment? Was a new
generation of anthropologists lured into business by the hyperbole of the
New Economy? What promise does anthropology hold for business? And
what does the increasing affinity between anthropologists and corporate
actors mean for anthropology as a discipline that has traditionally defined
itself as outside and intellectually independent of the major institutions of
capitalism (Marcus, 1998b, 8)?

The idea that some anthropologists stung by the relative lack of tenure-
track jobs have gone in search of work and financial success in the corporate
arena may have some validity. However, we argue that the rise in the popularity of business anthropology, particularly the recent corporate enchantment
with cultural anthropology's two iconic symbols—culture and ethnography
—must be understood within more widespread developments in the New
Economy. Specifically, we link the phenomenal growth in business anthropology to three dimensions of the New Economy discussed in this volume.
First, the interest that anthropology holds for commercial enterprise can be
viewed in relation to a crisis, emerging in the 1990s, in the scientific validity
of the quantitative and statistical techniques traditionally used in market
research (Baba, 2003, 204). Anthropology's signature method—ethnography
—was seen by business as a new, improved way to understand contemporary
consumer behavior, culture, and lifestyle (Zukin, 2004, 109–110). Second, the
emergence of anthropology as a marketing technology must be understood
in terms of the New Economy's intensified investment in branding. Here,
executives believe that anthropology provides a deeper understanding of

the ways consumers invest their fantasies, dreams, and hopes in particular brands. Finally, some anthropologists' ability to engage in "parachute anthropology," to borrow a phrase from Ulf Hannerz (2004, 11), rapidly form cultural analyses of findings, and quickly develop strategies to package images for consumers places them ideally to respond to the increasing emphasis put on the production of fast, creative, and innovative knowledge practices and workers (Thrift, 2000). The anthropologist, in short, is valorized as the quintessential New Economy managerial subject.

Let us first turn to the figure of anthropologist as methodological savior. The New Economy, as we have argued, was a moment when the cultural norms underlying economic activity became unsettled. Corporate actors increasingly found themselves faced with the arduous task of deciphering a flood of data and the sense that somehow their traditional forms of knowledge had failed them (Holmes and Marcus, Riles, and Zaloom, this volume). In marketing, this crisis was experienced as the failure of normative scientific data-gathering practices—surveys and focus groups—to adequately make sense of the consumer. Thus, as reported by the press, the emergence of ethnography was linked to the slow demise of firms' faith in conventional market research methods. For example, in an article published on July 21, 2003, in *Brandchannel.com* titled "Taking a Closer Look at Your Customers," reporter Edwin Colyer quotes Richard Elliot, a professor of marketing and consumer research at Extern University in the United Kingdom, explaining the ethnographic turn. According to Elliot, "A lot of marketing management felt that the tools they were taught didn't really cut it anymore. Life and choices were more complicated than the models they were taught. They needed deeper information from desperation."

Notably, the emergence of anthropology in business is not cultural "anthropology itself—if by that we mean all the heterogeneous, contested realities of theorizing and practice . . .—but anthropology figured as a form of commodity" (Suchman, 2003, 2). Indeed, the corporate hijacking of anthropology does not sample contemporary debates about cultural theory or the epistemological dilemmas of ethnography, but instead draws on an earlier period in the discipline: the Geertzian interpretive turn. For example, the executives in marketing and advertising that hire anthropologists for branding purposes presume that an objective distance exists between anthropologists and the consumers they study. They also generally believe that culture is not only very "real" but does provide the key to understanding the underlying needs, motivations, and behavior of consumers. Furthermore, they tend to assume that the traditional use of ethnography to access the "primitive other" can be easily transferred to observe and understand consumers in contemporary society (3). They are, as Timothy Malefyt and Brian Moeran (2003, 9) describe in their volume on advertising, ethnography, and anthropology, "true to the anthropologist's conception of ethnographic work which is triggered by estrangement or defamiliarization." In other words, corporate anthropologists are no longer necessarily engaged in determining the rules or meaning of Balinese cockfights and the like, thereby making the strange familiar. Instead, they have turned their gaze to unveil and make strange the underlying cultural principles that shape the familiar: consumers' shopping games (Fisher, 2005). Whereas this had once been a source of anthropology's power to critique taken-for-granted assumptions in quotidian life, the defamiliarizing perspective can now produce saleable information and insight. Given this particular set of understandings of the anthropological process by business, fieldwork, not surprisingly, tends to be fetishized in the corporate arena. Both mysterious and fascinating to anthropologists' corporate clients, fieldwork holds out the promise that it can plumb the fickle hearts of consumers, at once so close and so shrouded by enigma. No longer just "cool hunters" stalking exotic urban subcultures and young taste makers for hip consumables (Klein 2000, 72), corporate anthropologists are also lurking in suburban bathrooms, cyber cafés, and corporate boardrooms, trying to wring more knowledge commodities out of their systematic encounters with everyday life.

The corporate turn toward anthropology's signature concepts—culture and ethnography—however, must not only be understood in relation to the failure of conventional forms of knowledge production and the valorization of fieldwork as method. It must also be viewed in terms of how corporations define their commodities. Specifically, one hallmark of the New Economy is that many corporations' business has shifted from manufacturing products to marketing brands (Moore, 2003). As Lucy Suchman (2003, 3) points out, "A crucial element of brand-building in an age of mass production and competitive marketing is the manufacturing of difference, based less in products than in the packaging of products and their association with recognizable images." Indeed, the search for "brand essence," Naomi Klein (2000, 7, cited in Suchman, 2003, 3) proposes, moved companies progressively away from individual products and their attributes "towards a psychological/ anthropological examination of what brands mean to culture and to people's lives."

Finally, the increasing preoccupation of business with anthropology derives from the belief that ethnographic methods provide the fastest means to get the pulse of particular markets and their participants. In this way, anthropology is viewed as particularly well suited to a speed-up of business in the New Economy, chiefly because of the increasing use of information technology. Firms are forced to launch new products and brands more frequently. Managers are, as a result, under growing pressure to produce rapid and continuous innovation (Thrift, 2000). Under these conditions, ethnographic labor has come to be seen as a technique to rapidly acquire consumer knowledge.

Anthropologists trained to engage in in-depth, lengthy fieldwork may find the business pacing and practice of parachute ethnography a particularly hard pill to swallow. However, what we are witnessing in the New Economy is an ongoing production of fast new managerial subjects, of which, we argue, the business anthropologist is now an exemplar. Notably, one of the particular characteristics of contemporary corporate anthropology is the use of teams. Specifically, business anthropologists rarely, if ever, work individually. Instead, clients often accompany anthropologists out in the field. Both individuals may speak to various market subjects. Moreover, the client typically engages, in some way or another, in the actual analysis of consumers' use of particular products.

Notably, this new type of corporate anthropologist differs considerably from his or her Geertzian ancestors in terms of both position and practice in the field. He or she is not completely distant from informants, and research objectives may not necessarily include ascertaining the deep underlying rules of the cultural game of players (Fisher, 2005). Rather, the corporate anthropologist finds himself or herself embedded in what Holmes and Marcus (this volume) define as para-ethnographic work. In other words, the questions, motives, and purposes that project anthropologists into this type of fieldwork arise from engagement with counterparts and actors—managers, account planners, consumers—already defined in the field. A corporate anthropologist enters the field at the behest of the natives.

When the boundaries are blurred between disciplines, as well as between subjects and objects, anthropologists are often unable to construct a position of social and cultural critique fully outside the domain of corporate capitalism, especially when they are implicated in it (Marcus, 1998b, 11). This lack of critical distance on the part of the anthropologist may be disturbing to scholars trained in academic anthropology. However, we argue that the predicament facing business anthropologists is actually shared by many anthropologists engaged in ethnographic research in the New Economy (Ortner, 1999). Indeed, we have entered into a new period of the discipline. As Ulf

Hannerz (2004, 3) points out in his ethnography of foreign correspondents, the anthropologist is engaged in a "case of studying sideways: not so much as a matter of power or rank, but rather as a matter of engaging with a craft that in some ways parallels [his] own."

Anthropologists working within and on the New Economy are thus faced with the task of creating a critical position, all the while finding themselves operating in the engine rooms of twenty-first-century capitalism, especially as corporations and business agendas increasingly invade universities. In other words, as one anonymous reviewer of this volume aptly pointed out, "We have reached a point (of the near-total imbrication of the commodity form in social life, of insides all the way down) where critical distance itself is being reconfigured or reimagined." An emerging challenge in the ethnography of the New Economy, then, as Riles, O'Mahony, Ong, and Holmes and Marcus describe, is that academic models are increasingly part of the self-conscious subjective construction of the actors we study. Daniel Miller (1998; see Callon, 1998; Carrier, 1998) has gone so far as to argue that hyperabstract models borrowed from academic disciplines—he specifically discusses economics, but one could place accounting, law, sociology, network analysis, area studies, and anthropology in the same category—are being used to interpret and structure behavior and institutions in various realms of human activity, a process he calls "virtualism." The contributors to this volume find this happening in environments as diverse as cooperative communities, overseas business schools, the Federal Reserve, and even sporting arenas.

THE IMPORTANCE OF ETHNOGRAPHY

For all these reasons, anthropologists may be better situated than economists to understand the distinctiveness of the New Economy, and ethnographers may be in a privileged position to observe the real changes in lived practices wrought at the interface of the cultural, social, and technical. The extraordinary flows of virtual capital in financial markets, for example, especially in currency trading, derivatives, and mergers and acquisitions, creates the impression of prodigious economic activity by some traditional measures. The total face value of derivatives or the daily flow of currency exchange, for instance, *far* exceeds the volume of traffic in the "real" economy of products. (Already in 1998, the trade in derivatives had a face value ten times greater than total global production.) As skeptics point out, the hyperactive shuttling of virtual value among offshore accounts, when viewed from above—the perspective of aggregate numbers—seems monumental, but it also appears to have only an indirect effect on productive processes, except in moments of crisis.

An ethnographic approach to these flows would necessarily draw attention to the social ties created by the circulation, real and virtual, of goods and value, and to the particular sites where individuals make sense of these phenomena in the process of trying to wring profits from them. Although market rhetoric and the participants' own descriptions might paint these spaces as realms where pure rational calculus dominates, closer examination invariably reveals that humans build social relations and cultural understandings within them (see Knorr Cetina and Breuger, 2002a; Fisher, Holmes and Marcus, and Zaloom, this volume). Ethnographic investigations may counteract New Economy ideology, both optimistic and pessimistic, that Peter Armstrong (2001, 525) warns often erases detail in an attempt to find "simple plot-lines and bold solutions"; these essays help to restore some of this detail, providing greater resolution but less clarity.

This ethnographic approach can complement some of the most important accounts of technoeconomic economic change, for example, Manuel Castells's (1996, 1997, 1998) exploration of an "information economy," Michael Hardt and Antonio Negri's (2000) Deleuzian description of "empire," and David Harvey's (1989) analysis of the transition to "post-Fordism."[13] If the writers in this volume tend to the ethnographic, many other theorists engage in what might be called an "ethnological" approach to understanding. In ethnology, an anthropologist examines a single domain of human activity, such as religion, child care, initiation rituals, or technology, across diverse contexts and cultures to better understand human variation within this domain. In many ways, the ambitious accounts of Hardt and Negri, Castells, and Harvey engage in this sort of survey, examining in great detail the changing relationship of technology to political power, economic systems, social relations, or cultural self-consciousness.

In contrast, our authors are engaged in ethnographic theorizing, substituting the intensive study of a single site for the comparative approach used by these other theorists. The resulting portrait, although idiosyncratic and bound to the particular setting, often reveals a more complex web of causal connections, multivalent effects, and incomplete transformations. The contrast, then, is not between producing theory and working with empirical data; rather, an ethnological approach tries to perceive broader patterns across multiple sites, whereas an ethnographic perspective ideally yields a more complex, holistic portrait of potential interrelations among realms of human action at a single site. Both may yield generalizations, new hypotheses, and theory, but theorizing proceeds from different foundations with distinctive, complementary contributions to offer.

We do specifically take issue with some of the arguments made by Castells; in spite of his explicit claims that his approach is dialectical, we find his provocative account of social change in the Information Age to be a model in which technological developments are the driving force. Castells's search for a single new social morphology, the network, may have led him to overlook other social configurations or to fail to recognize when emergent networks—commodity traders, open source computer programmers, business executives, hip hop producers—demanded that their social relations, identities, and collectives behave in ways that were not networked. An ethnographic mode of theorizing reveals that these new organizations and institutions are often heterogeneous, fashioned out of face-to-face interaction, group identities, shared experiences, large gatherings, and highly charged places, as well as long-distance relations of information exchange.

One thing that emerges from an ethnographic mode of theorizing is a greater awareness of intermediate-level factors—institutions, legal standards, technical limitations, social alliances, supply chains of particular commodities or knowledge, subcultural identities, communities of shared skills—in the adaptation of technology to human use. This may be ethnography's distinctive contribution to theorizing the New Economy: a greater appreciation of the many factors that *may* affect the sites of the New Economy but that do not necessarily impact them all. An ethnographic sensibility reveals that there is not a single New Economy, but a range of network societies and an internally divided information economy.

For example, many of the more sweeping theorists of millennial change in the global economy and observers of the New Economy alike have claimed that it would dissolve the significance of place; Deleuze and Guattari (1972/ 1983) claim that capitalism brought about deterritorialization. More sensitive, ethnographically situated accounts, however, show that deterritorialization is not inevitable, any more than virtual interaction necessarily eclipses face-to-face social relations. Although technological, political, and economic changes have reinscribed and reshaped spaces and technology has made some knowledge workers more mobile, they have also produced a whole new set of mythical locales, spatial segregations, and geographies of power, including global cities (Sassen, 2001). In his contribution to this volume, Neil Smith shows that although abstract models of the New Economy may suggest that emplacement becomes increasingly irrelevant, global competition between cities to attract multinational corporations has led to aggressive partnerships between public and private sectors to gentrify urban centers and invest heavily in space, producing escalating "geo-bribes" for companies, as Smith calls them. Far from being deterritorialized, the New Economy helps to consolidate one stage in an ongoing process of reallocating urban real estate.

One of the ironies in Smith's account is the degree to which discussions of the New Economy, such as current gentrification proposals, efface the existence of the working class, seeming to suggest that blue-collar workers can be conjured away by technology. Gentrification projects at the close of the twentieth century provided public subsidies for middle- and upper-middle-class incursions into working-class neighborhoods, diverting public resources to facilitate the transfer of territory. Smith suggests that projects to reconfigure urban space under a new regime of gentrification are even more ambitious than earlier plans for urban renewal, proceeding increasingly through public-private partnerships that mark the end of liberal urban policy. The editors of this volume find assertions that place is increasingly irrelevant in the New Economy especially dubious in light of this reconfiguration of forces to divert property, both public and private, into the hands of developers.

This volume, then, is not a collection about globalization, the central rubric of much recent anthropology on economic change (see Beynon and Dunkerley, 2000; Canclini, 2001; Haugerud, Stone, and Little, 2000; Inda and Rosaldo, 2001; Lewellen, 2002). Concern about globalization in our discipline is no surprise, as anthropologists have long considered the local—exactly the ecological niche that appears imperiled—to be their intellectual habitat and raison d'être. Although some of our contributors find the term useful, they suggest, as others before us have, that what is "global" is not the same everywhere. Perhaps more intriguing, they locate the local at the center of processes that are hallmarks of the global: trading pits, Japanese law offices, Wall Street corridors, Fed conference calls, networks of computer programmers, global marketing firms, international consultants battering down "Chinese walls," and the rhetoric of those who reform urban centers. Not unexpectedly, they find "culture" at these economic centers: capitalist cosmologies, local rivalries that ripple down through technological and financial structures, and alternative forms of value and social calculation (see Burawoy et al., 2000). But, when studying up to examine elite or expert actors, ethnographers find structural spaces where local logics are leveraged for larger-scale effects.

Too often, it seems to us, studies of globalization mystify individual actors, specific processes, concrete connections, and sites that bind together disparate places or social relations. In discussions of globalization, David Graeber (2002, 1223) suggests, "increasingly the tendency is to detach these processes from any subject entirely and to speak of the struggle of some local community to deal with what are figured as impersonal global 'flows' (e.g., capital flows, flows of consumer goods or media images) treated veritably as natural phenomena." In anthropology, the tendency is perhaps worst when addressing economic phenomena. Many of the writers in this volume have identified some of the sites and agents responsible for what appear elsewhere as anonymous flows or natural forces. Taken together, the essays combine perspectives on New Economy processes from many points of the compass, both geographically and socially.

By uniting these works under the rubric of the New Economy, rather than globalization, we seek to denaturalize these processes, to dispel the sense that there is an irreversible, grand unified globalizing tendency, and to highlight the interdependence of cultural and economic realms. The instantly anachronistic tenor, the almost embarrassing hubris of the concept New Economy, in our opinion, foregrounds the creative nexus between culture, business, and technology. The New Economy moment was at once a cultural myth, a social movement, an economic achievement, a historic moment, and a technological transformation (see Barry and Slater, 2002, 189; Ross, 2003). Far from privileging any one of these factors as the cause of the others, the fragility of the New Economy vision highlights the harmonic convergence that occurred among them all.

THE ORIGIN AND ORGANIZATION OF THIS VOLUME

In April 2001, an interdisciplinary group of scholars came together at the Goizueta Business School of Emory University for a conference, "Workshop on the New Global Economy." The meeting, organized by Melissa Fisher (then of Columbia University) and Doug Guthrie (New York University) and sponsored by the Social Science Research Council, brought together scholars from a wide range of academic disciplines. The workshop presented many opportunities to talk about the sorts of activities that were dominating the business news in those heady days: the Internet, commodity trading, property law, new media, information technology, derivatives, securitization, and wobbles in the stock market. The wide-ranging discussions provoked many of the participants to think outside the boundaries of their disciplines, to consider how changing business practices, technology, economic processes, and symbols were interacting.

After the dust had settled on the conference, and the size of the stock market crash and economic downturn became increasingly apparent, the organizers of this volume, two anthropologists, reflected on the more ethnographic contributors to the discussions. So much of the literature on the New Economy seemed bent on passing judgment (e.g., Alcaly, 2003; Brenner, 2002; Frank, 2000; Pohjola, 2002; Temple, 2002), judging the causes and consequences of the boom, comparing this expansive cycle to others to see whether it was quantitatively greater, ascertaining whether or not the populace had been taken for a ride or led to the gates of a new Eden, or simply skewering the boom's more excessive self-promotion (e.g., McEachern and O'Brien, 2002). We felt that this historic moment needed to be considered more carefully, in part to see what might be learned from it, and in part to ask what specific social and cultural changes may have more lasting effects than the inflation of stock values. Nigel Thrift (2001, 430) similarly cautions against hasty dismissal, suggesting that "new practices might have arisen from this frenzy of capitalist experiment."

Another motive for assembling this collection is to add to the emerging literature reinvigorating discussions of economic questions in the social sciences, specifically anthropology and other fields concerned with culture (see Ash Amin and Thrift, 2004). In the introduction to *The Laws of the Markets*, editor Michel Callon (1998) calls sociologists to radically reconsider their relationship with economics. The editors feel that the New Economy offers an ideal provocation and entry point for anthropologists to do the same, to explore what Annalise Riles has called "the problem of the mundane" in contemporary societies.

Because so many themes tie together these essays into a variety of overlapping discussions, they are divided simply into two sections: the essays in the first address global production, circulation, and interpretation of new forms of knowledge; those in the second explore how such knowledges, technologies, and circuits of information shape new subjects and novel kinds of sociality. More often than not, however, the editors have found that our contributors end up addressing both strands of thought while developing one dimension in more depth and breadth.

Part 1, "Circuits of Knowledge," is concerned predominantly with the ways various elites—bankers, traders, lawyers, academics, and professional athletes—have developed new knowledge practices. Information and communication technology has allowed these actors to find and trade information in unprecedented ways, but it has also deluged them with data, forcing them to develop powerful hermeneutical schemes to sift through the cacophony and discern the data that they need. The authors in these five essays focus particular attention on the social context of knowledge production, including the shifting relations between anthropologists and expert informants in the production process. They also highlight the role that intuition, feeling, sentiment, and aesthetic judgment play in acquiring and circulating knowledge in various global markets and local settings. By focusing an ethnographic lens on different sites of the New Economy, these writers shift the emphasis in the phrase "knowledge economy" from the former to the latter term, noticing how local economies profoundly affect the impact and significance of circulating information. These essays, in a sense, make clearer the social and cultural dimensions of knowledge, emphasizing that this term is not synonymous with a context-neutral notion of information.

Part 2, "New Subjects, Novel Socialities," focuses on the consequences of a range of new technologies and knowledge practices for shaping subjects and social relations. The authors in this section explore various sites—cities, corporations, and cyberspace—at which actors create innovative forms of New Economy sociality, identity, and self-understanding. These new spaces for producing subjectivity demand fresh research techniques and agendas; an openness to imagining the social relations through which these fugitive forms of knowledge might circulate, not only among the people we study, but among us all in this emerging reality. Perhaps some of the most profound changes in the New Economy are not technological, but social; new technologies allow experiments in collective reorganization, facilitate the rise of competing principles for social organization, or undermine long-standing institutions, such as property and the corporation. In other cases, our contributors find technological change running headlong into resilient systems of relations or self-understandings. Adoption of technology winds up being channeled by preexisting motives and relations, definitively demonstrating the failure of models of the New Economy that assume all change is technologically driven. But the New Economy also allows, even demands, that some hierarchies seek to reinforce themselves, casting old relations of domination in new media and rhetoric. That advances in ICT and other technologies do not overdetermine how institutions or groups will develop is one of the central lessons of the New Economy.

The volume concludes with an afterword by Saskia Sassen that addresses the future of an anthropology of the New Economy, an anthropology that foregrounds modern knowledge practices, organizations, and subject making. Our commentator suggests that the various contributions to this volume, although they do not typically make methodological reflection a central point, demonstrate how one might engage in research on the cultural and social dimensions of information and communication technologies. Sassen reflects on the intersections between the other contributors' essays and her long-standing interest in how technical knowledge is culturally embedded, how blurred actors combine technology and social skills, and how physical space enables virtual projection. A number of shared themes, according to Sassen, recur throughout the volume, especially how the digital and nondigital are intimately woven together, how ICT ruptures relations of social and geographic scale, and how "cultures of use" affect the reception of ICT. These offer a distinctly ethnographic contribution to ongoing conversations about the New Economy. Sassen's closing comments point the way not only to a more robust anthropology of technological and economic change, but also to a distinctly anthropological and ethnographic perspective with which to engage a much broader discussion of the links between technological, economic, social, and cultural change in a hyperactive age.

NOTES

1 By a very basic measure of price-to-earnings ratio for the entire stock market—the ratio of corporate equities to total corporate profit after taxes—the bubble was $9 trillion above what it should have been if this economywide price-to-earning ratio had been at the historic average. Following these sorts of long-term indicators, some economic historians still argue that U.S. equities are overvalued and corrections may continue.

2 Peter Armstrong (2001, 543–544), for example, notes that many of the "start-ups" of the 1990s were older workers driven into business when their jobs disappeared. In this frightening labor market, many of these reluctant entrepreneurs engaged in severe self-exploitation, struggling to fend off insolvency in a saturated service market.

3 The debate about the sources and significance of productivity gains during the late 1990s in the United States, whether or not they can be attributed to ICT, is discussed in a range of articles. See, for example, Brenner (2002), Henwood (2003), Jorgenson (2001), and Pohjola (2002).

4 Thrift (2000, 674) goes on to argue that what is new is a condition where firms live in a "permanent state of emergency."

5 Löfgren (2003, 245), for example, suggests that accelerated speed and a transformed sense of spatiality became aestheticized and integrated into such pervasive and banal material as workplace decoration, furniture construction, and the design of office supplies.

6 As *Left Business Observer* editor Doug Henwood (2003, 194–195) points out, in the heady year 2000, of the 8,000 recommendations made by brokerage house analysts on stocks composing the Standard & Poor's 500, the year of the market peak, just twenty-nine (0.36 percent) were to sell (2003, 194–195).

7 See MacKenzie and Wacjman (1999) for a more thorough critique of "technological determinism." The present work differs from many in the social studies of science by focusing on anthropological concerns—meaning, culture, imaginaries—and by assuming that there is no single form of society with which technology interacts, only particular cultures.

8 Callon (1998, 6–7) also highlights the difficulty of achieving market coordination due to "uncertainties on the states of the world." He argues that proposing shared standards or expectations as a solution to the problem of coordination is inadequate and offers his own variant of network theory. Although Callon's criticisms are well taken, the editors believe that an ethnographic focus on the actual achievement of economic rationality obviates the need to pose such a stark analytical contrast between social networks and cultural consensus, as many of our authors show how both contribute to coordinate expectations.

9 In addition to other things, "fast capitalism" is (was?) a performance, with roles, rites, aesthetics, and imaginaries all its own (see Thrift, 2000). The New Economy, in this sense, could be seen as a style of corporate self-presentation. As M. J. Cooper, Dimitrov, and Rau (2001) report, even adding ".com" to a firm's name could increase its perceived value at one point.

10 The discussion of circulating formulas in finance as a cultural foundation for market bubbles in derivatives was inspired by the work of Vincent-Antonin Lépinay (2002). See also Mitchel Abolafia (1998) and Donald MacKenzie (2003).

11 Daniel Miller (1998) refers to the attempt to bring reality into line with models of reality "virtualism." Similarly, Michel Callon (1998) discusses the troubled but productive relationship between economics, the academic discipline, and the economy, the realm of production and commercial transactions.

12 Our discussion of business anthropology focuses primarily on the consumer side of ethnographic research.

13 We have an anonymous reviewer of the manuscript to thank for pointing out this important comparison to the agenda orienting this volume.

PART I

CIRCUITS OF KNOWLEDGE

Douglas R. Holmes and George E. Marcus

FAST CAPITALISM:
PARA-ETHNOGRAPHY AND THE
RISE OF THE SYMBOLIC ANALYST

The social theorist's oscillation between the market as the artifact of knowledge and as evidence of its limits finds powerful expression in the events now shaping the financial world. In the aftermath of the Asian Financial Crisis and the consciousness of so-called "systemic risk" amplified, the failure of the economic models that were the source of central bankers' expertise to offer useful predictions or fine-tuned policy solutions to recent market problems, and current efforts by global banks to do away with the regulation and management of the market by state actors altogether . . . the central bankers at the Bank of Japan . . . were both amazed at what they imagined as their own creation—a global market of seemingly infinite scale and complexity—and fearful of their own powerlessness vis-à-vis their creation. In particular, these central bankers' sense of powerlessness took the form of a heightened awareness of the contradictions in their role as creators and guardians of the global market.
—Riles, "Real-Time: Governing the Market after the Failure of Knowledge"

Annelise Riles's acute insight locates anxieties infiltrating the work of central bankers, but we believe these fears also imbue the outlook of actors across numerous domains of expertise. These figures share the apprehension that their distinctive analytical endeavors have been compromised, that in some deep way their knowledge is in doubt. As Riles notes, central bankers are in a particularly important position in this regard insofar as their anxiety, their sense of powerlessness, is the direct outcome of their own analytical enterprise: the institutional shaping and management of global financial markets. This predicament, faced paradigmatically by central bankers, is the starting point for what we have termed "para-ethnography," the intellectual response to a retreat of those forms of technical knowledge—whether in arts, science, business, finance, politics, government, or law—that have been underwritten and contextualized historically by the nation-state. In the shadow of this failure of technical knowledge is an alternative form of knowledge creation that has integrity in its own right, integrity with which anthropologists have a keen familiarity.

We begin with a discussion of a series of decisions made by the Federal Open Market Committee (FOMC), the key policymaking body of the U.S. Federal Reserve System, and how these decisions reveal distinctive intellectual practices that, we believe, have unusual methodological significance. We then turn to a historical account, informed by the work of David Westbrook, that describes the creation of a global *polity*—the "City of Gold," as he terms it—integrated constitutionally by supranational markets. In this brief assessment, we look at the historical circumstance that reciprocally gave birth to this global polity and brought to an end the era of the nation-state as the preeminent institutional context defining our lives together. We do this in terms of two key figures, John Maynard Keynes and Jean Monnet, who engineered this historical transformation through the Bretton Woods and European institutions, respectively, and whose analytical endeavors help us understand the role of technocratic knowledge in shaping a radical politics of our time: a politics that is not simply congruent with or reducible to the precepts of neoliberalism. This discussion also helps us assess the emergence of "symbolic analysts," a class of technocrats and political figures who, though appointed or elected in nation-states, designed supranational institutional realms in which they became key actors (Reich, 1992).

Fast capitalism thus designates the circumstances under which knowledge is created and effaced as the communicative space of the nation-state is eclipsed and our subjects and we, too, must think and act within a communicative space mediated increasingly by supranational markets. In the broadest terms, we are interested in what kind of intellectual practices are plausible, what kind of methodological innovations are necessary under the sway of contemporary political economy. For us, a reflexive ethnography is key for addressing these challenges and for investigating global assemblages constituting themselves in our midst (Agger, 1989; S. Collier and Ong, 2005; Holmes, 2000; Holmes and Marcus, 2005b; Maurer, 2005; Rabinow, 2003; Westbrook, 2003).[1]

We recapitulate in this text our discussions in which we sought to work out for the first time our conceptualization of the para-ethnographic. This initial exercise has since become the basis of a far broader reappraisal of the character of anthropological ethnography in which we are currently engaged that encompasses what we have termed a "refunctioning" of ethnography (Holmes and Marcus, 2005a, 2005b). Our discussion turns on the postulation of the para-ethnographic as an orienting object of study and a key component in the construction of multisited research designs. Such a notion derives from the long-established anthropological interest in "the native point of view," with its representation being, in generic terms, the goal of ethnographic description. Of course, there have been many means and ways to this goal in the history of anthropology. In the framework of a specifically critical anthropology that is interested in the histories and processes by which distinct peoples and populations have contended with the encroachments of world historical systems, particularly Western ones, in the forms of colonialism, capitalism, and now globalization, this representation of native points of view has been as much about the resistance, accommodation, and resilience of such peoples in the face of these historic encroachments. This kind of study has developed recently along with the strong, critically reflexive examination by anthropologists of their own discipline. In this intersection is the conception that the traditional subjects of study have developed something like an ethnography of both their own predicaments and those who have encroached on them, and that their knowledge practices in this regard are in some sense parallel to the anthropologist's and deserving of more consideration than mere representation in the archive of the world's peoples that anthropologists have created. It is an idea that has been expressed from time to time but has not been fully examined, especially for its implications with regard to the forms, norms, and methods of ethnography (Marcus, 1995, 1998a, 1999a, 1999b, 1999c, 2002a, 2002b).

As we have argued, our postulation of a para-ethnographic dimension to the worlds of meaning constructed by our subjects of study is perhaps a radical investment in this not yet fully examined idea that circulates currently in the production of ethnography. We do so, however, within a fully conceived ethnography of modernity where anthropologists have become accustomed to defining objects of study that are no longer on the border between the encroaching West and the transforming traditional, but are fully located within the shared, but differently situated and located, predicaments of contemporary life. In such a frame, the affinity between the effort to define the contemporary in composing ethnography and the same effort locatable in embedded discourses and practices among subjects is not at all a radical idea, but a necessary one (Boyer, 2003; Maurer, 2002a, 2002b; Miyazaki, 2003; Miyazaki and Riles, 2005; Riles, 2004b).

Thus, the illustrative account of decision making of the FOMC that follows provides the raw material, so to speak, out of which our conception of ethnography constitutes itself by demonstrating how embedded para-ethnographic practice is found in the scene of fieldwork, logically giving rise to the multisited terrain and problematic of contemporary fieldwork.

The impetus for the analysis that follows grew out of a rather focused discussion on the nature of ethnographic data, in particular, the role of "thin" data in shaping ethnographic analyses in what we term cultures of expertise, professional settings in which some form of research function is integral. We were preoccupied with how highly refined, technical documents —thin data—can serve as the material, so to speak, out of which we can create contexts and preconditions for "thick" description (Holmes and Marcus, 2005a; Marcus, 1999b). Coincidently, during this discussion, Holmes was involved in the preliminary research for his current project on central banking, which entailed reviewing enormous volumes of this kind of austere technocratic data, scrutinizing precisely those artifacts that Bruno Latour (1988, 54; quoted in Riles, forthcoming) describes as "the most despised of all ethnographic subjects." In the midst of this survey he encountered a dissonant term, literally a single word that altered our discussion fundamentally. This term was "anecdotal," as in a short, informal description or narrative account. This dissonant usage recurred in transcripts when senior officials of the U.S. Central Bank invoked the notion of "anecdotal data" during crucial deliberations that became the basis of a dramatic change in monetary policy. As we pursued the significance of this usage, we found that it not only provided a means to move between thick and thin description, but, more significant, it marked a breach in technocratic knowledge that opened the way for realigning the relationship between ethnography and political economy.[2]

THE FED

On January 3, 2001, the Federal Reserve Board instigated a surprise reduction in the discount rate of a full half percent (50 basis points, from 6.5 to 6 percent). The announcement came between the Federal Reserve Board's regular Open Market Committee meetings, when these decisions are normally taken, suggesting a marked anxiety about the state of the economy at the end of 2000. Subsequent data, as we now know, confirmed these apprehensions.

The FOMC meets formally eight times a year in Washington, D.C., with telephone consultations and other meetings when needed. The Committee is composed of seven members of the Board of Governors of the Federal Reserve System and five of the twelve presidents of the Federal Reserve district banks. The president of the New York Reserve Bank is a permanent member, and the other reserve bank presidents serve one-year terms on a rotating basis. All twelve presidents of the district banks participate in the FOMC discussions, but only the five presidents who are members of the Committee participate in policy decisions. The Committee is charged under law "to oversee open market operations, the principal tool of national monetary policy" (Board of Governors of the Federal Reserve System, 1994, 12–13). This legal authority over the management of monetary policy, exercised primarily through the setting of interest rates, makes the Committee perhaps the most powerful institution governing the global economy (see Blinder, 1998, 2004; Meyer, 2004). Hence, the social behavior of its members is of unusual significance, and the events of 2000–2001 are particularly intriguing.

The year 2000 had opened strongly, but by late spring problems began to surface at the heart of the New Economy, the technology sector, along with broader problems gripping manufacturing in general. A savage, though widely predicted, correction in equity prices of Internet-related companies unfolded through midyear, and these problems leached into the pricing of chipmakers and related technology companies. The consensus opinion held by the governors and presidents of the district banks of the Federal Reserve during most of 2000 was that the economy was still strong; weakness in the technology sector, outside of Internet-based companies, was understood to involve a short-term inventory correction. By the last few days of the year, the perception had shifted markedly, suggesting that a far broader and more precipitous downturn was looming, with a growing risk of recession. This change in perception impelled the rate cut in early January 2001.

So something happened during the fifteen-day period from the December 19, 2000, regularly scheduled FOMC meeting to the unscheduled telephone conference meeting on January 3 that altered significantly the judgment of the members of the FOMC about the state of the U.S. economy (http://www .federalreserve.gov/fomc/minutes/20001219.htm# jan3minutes). What transpired during this brief period intrigued us because it reveals decisively the operation of the para-ethnographic in a culture of expertise committed to a technocratic ethos predicated on the management of vast amounts of quantitative data. The imperative here for deploying the para-ethnographic is the acute need to interpret the "contemporary" in a meaningful fashion to inform decision making.

In the expert culture of the Federal Reserve System, the structure of the contemporary has a twofold manifestation that its members and staff must act within and on. On the one hand, it takes form as a skein of information—typically, highly refined quantitative data—that is constantly being generated and analyzed. On the other, it has a keen discursive character whereby information is endowed with social perspective and meaning. It is in this latter, rather oblique form of knowledge practice, typically glossed as anecdotal, that the para-ethnographic takes form, and it is under these conditions that key cultural practices of expert subjects converge with our own analytical endeavors as ethnographers. In other words, our subjects are doing something that approximates ethnographic labor to represent the *social* nature of the contemporary, within which they and we pursue our expert practices. The figures we have been looking at summon these narratives to conceptualize the contemporary financial world for a particular purpose: to anticipate the future, to capture shifting configurations of expectations and sentiment. As Westbrook (2003, 145) eloquently puts it, making "the future a task that must be confronted now, and on the terms determined by capital," has a deeply unsettling effect.

> In helping us to secure ourselves from, or at least ameliorate, the dangers that lurk in the middle distance, finance robs us of the ability to enjoy the present. The expectation of the near future, the time of finance, is built up and yet obscures the reality of the present. As a result, we experience the present as quite literally surreal, as something somehow built on top of reality. . . . Surrealism portrays us situated among conventions that we understand to have no foundations, to be arbitrary and quite possibly impossible, and that yet stand because no other basis for tomorrow is historically or otherwise imaginable.

Thus, we have argued that the para-ethnographic is not merely an aspect of expert practice, but is inlaid in the architecture of a future-oriented contemporary; it is the means by which the contemporary is reproduced socially (Holmes and Marcus, 2005b).

The Fed is disarmingly frank to the point of deadpan about the imperfection of its own knowledge and its power to manage the economy:

> In practice, monetary policymakers do not have up-to-the-minute, reliable information about the state of the economy and prices. Information is limited because of lags in the publication of data and because of later revisions in data. Also, policymakers have a less-than-perfect understanding of how the economy works, including knowledge of when and to what extent policy actions will affect aggregate demand. (Board of Governors of the Federal Reserve System 1994, 24)

The irony of this declaration is that the Fed's own technocratic agenda has served to accelerate the pacing of what we are calling here fast capitalism, rendering analysis of economic performance increasingly refractory. Indeed, it is precisely this conundrum that makes the U.S. Central Bank such an intriguing object of study (Miyazaki and Riles, 2005).

Alan Greenspan, former chairman of the Federal Reserve Board, whose role in creating the New Economy has been celebrated widely, illustrates some of the underlying rationale for para-ethnography. Greenspan's technical innovation centered on his conviction that the U.S. economy could grow sustainably at a higher rate, roughly in excess of 2.5 percent per year, than previously thought possible without unleashing the perils of inflation. His insight that inflationary constraints on the economy can be circumvented by growth in productivity—impelled by technological dynamism—has distinguished his management of the U.S. Central Bank. What Greenspan embraced is referred to as "the economy's productivity-enhanced potential" as underwritten by new technologies. Indeed, this is the theoretical position that has been at stake in the unfolding drama that continues to reverberate through the U.S. economy and is echoed in the meetings of the FOMC.

If we return to the January 3 event, the reportage attributed the decision almost exclusively to the personal acumen of Chairman Greenspan, in particular his "intuition," his "instinct," his "feel" about what was "really" happening in the U.S. economy. What this meant was that the enormous range of quantitative data tracking the performance of the economy available to the Fed chairman was inconclusive: it suggested that some kind of change was clearly taking place within the economy, but its significance was ambiguous, hence the need for an alternative means of judgment that draws on experience. In other words, to enter analytically "the contemporary," the chairman had to move from science to art; crucially, he needed an "ethnographic" narrative to think and act in something that approximates "real time" (see Riles, this volume). Para-ethnography, thus, first surfaces here under the ambiguous guise of "intuition," as essentially a structure of feeling. There is, however, far more intriguing evidence of this kind of knowledge practice in the transcripts of the FOMC meetings.[3]

The importance of para-ethnography was, in fact, alluded to at critical points in the discussions of the FOMC meeting of December 19. In this case, the para-ethnography appears not as "a structure of feeling," but as "anecdotal evidence." At those points in the FOMC minutes when serious concern is registered about the state of the economy, "anecdotal reports" rather than quantitative data are invoked. Here, then, the pretext for a dramatic change of Central Bank policy is established using something other than the formidable authority of the massive quantitative measures available to the FOMC (http://www.federalreserve.gov/fomc/minutes/20001219.htm#jan3minutes). Indeed, it is through these anecdotal reports, which are reported publicly only in summary form in the so-called Beige Book, that the space of para-ethnography is marked (Holmes and Marcus, 2005a).

ANECDOTES

What are these "anecdotal reports"? Rather than informal observations and casual asides, as the term "anecdotal" might suggest, these reports constitute a sophisticated means of tracking and interpreting the economy and endowing it with social context and meaning. Each member on the FOMC, as well as the senior officers of the Federal Reserve's twelve district banks, cultivates highly developed social networks with human interlocutors who oversee daily transactions in strategic spheres of the economy. More formally, each of the twelve Reserve Banks has its own nine-member board of directors appointed for three-year terms who are specifically charged with gleaning precisely these kinds of finely tuned anecdotal accounts of very detailed facets of the U.S. economy and society.

Indeed, the directors are classified in terms of the character of their situated knowledge. Three directors of the nine-member district banks, designated Class A directors, represent the stockholding member banks in the region and are typically senior bank executives. The three Class B (appointed by the district bank) and three Class C (appointed by the Board of Governors of the Federal Reserve System) directors are chosen as representatives of the public, and they are *not* permitted to be officers, directors, or employees of any bank; rather, they are chosen "with due, but not exclusive, consideration of the interests of agriculture, commerce, industry, services, labor and consumers" (http://www.federalreserve.gov/generalinfo/listdirectors/about .htm). Apart from formal oversight responsibilities managing the operation of the twelve district banks, these figures serve as strategically positioned interlocutors who report on a regular basis on the conditions of key sectors and often geographically localized aspects of the economy.

The range of informants is impressive. For example, in District 11-Dallas (the district that covers Texas, northern Louisiana, and northern New Mexico), directors serving in 2004 included among the B and C Classes the president of the Texas Iron Workers Union, the CEO of an architectural firm in Austin, the owner of a cattle and land company in Van Horn, a real estate developer in Houston, the founder of the USA/Mexico Alliance in El Paso, and the provost of New Mexico State University. In District 9-Minneapolis (the district covering Minnesota, Montana, northern Michigan, North Dakota, and South Dakota), the Class A directors are bank executives of a small farmers' bank in Victor, Montana, and two commercial banks in Fairfax, Minnesota, and Sioux Falls, South Dakota. The B and C directors included the executive administrator of the Twin City Pipe Trades Service Association in Saint Paul; the former director of the Museum of the Rockies in Boseman, Montana; and the CEO of a health care business in Minneapolis. The deliberations of each of these twelve boards, whether they are composed of a professor at the Harvard Medical School, the CEO of Citigroup, or the director of the Arizona Department of Housing, not only draw on their technical proficiency, but evoke the deep social nature of their diverse expertise and their interrelated predicaments.

These interlocutors are informants—bankers, manufacturers, retailers, educators, union leaders, representatives of governmental and nongovernmental agencies—who transact loans, book orders (and cancellations), track store sales, hire and terminate employees, solicit charitable contributions, and follow the price of wheat and pork bellies minute to minute, hour to hour. They operate in a continuously unfolding present, providing the closest approximation to a contemporaneous engagement with the economy. These men and women, typically senior managers, not only have access to an extraordinary range of quantitative data, but they are constantly in conversations with clients, customers, and colleagues: auto executives walk showroom floors talking to potential car purchasers; bank executives converse with prospective borrowers about the state of their businesses and their outlooks for the future; manufacturers discuss with their customers their future needs in order to plan capital expenditures; union leaders appraise the labor market as they negotiate contracts. By gleaning knowledge from these interlocutors, the Fed gains access to those profound and elusive forces guiding the economy: expectations and sentiments as they take form across an intricate, geographically diverse analytical tableau.

It is not merely that these reports provide a means to overcome the inevitable lag attendant with quantitative data; rather, it is their inherently social character that provides these anecdotal reports with an agile purchase on the contemporary. And these reports would have little force if it were not for the fact that these actors speak from an intimate sense of situated business practices and predicaments. These anecdotes are not just a different kind of supplementary data; they have cogency in their own right in that they represent "a native point of view" mediated through an implicit ethnographic imaginary. These intricate exchanges that report on the economy in something that approximates real time constitute fully formed paraethnographies extending over a vast multisited scene (Holmes and Marcus, 2005b; Riles, 2005).

What makes these reports persuasive is the experience of these interlocutors, their judgment, their feel. Above all, what these interlocutors struggle with is the creation of a semiotics of contemporary capitalism intimately linked to the integrity of their own expert practices (and perhaps even to their own unfolding existential struggles). The accounts of these situated actors are powerful as anecdotal interventions because they subtly compensate for, or even shore up, cracks in a technocratic ethos (exposed as "less than perfect knowledge") whereby the statistical mode of analysis that sustains the authority of institutions like the Fed is compromised by the speed and the unpredictability of supranational markets.

"AFTER THE FACT"

One of the most basic reports gauging the state of the economy is the quarterly gross domestic product (GDP) statistics. The rule of thumb is that two consecutive quarters of declining GDP numbers constitutes the onset of a recession.[4] This means that the events of January 3 would gain full coherence only sometime after July 2001, at which point it would be possible to determine definitively whether or not a recession had in fact commenced. Of course, the bind here for the FOMC is that by July, effective intervention to alter any decline would in all likelihood be too late to avoid significant damage to the economy.

The contemporary thus emerges as the lacuna, as the lag during which events are fundamentally uncertain, when information has yet to confer a conventionalized empirical account of the phenomenon. This is a highly dynamic contemporary on which new information continually encroaches. With each passing week as new data are released, increasingly secure inferences about whether or not a recession has materialized may be drawn. Yet, as the data on the economy are given an increasingly precise longitudinal representation, certain forms of analysis and action are foreclosed (Miyazaki, 2003).

The minutes of the January 30–31, 2001, FOMC meeting are more measured than those of December 19 and January 3, even though the committee approved another major discount rate reduction of 50 basis points. The only reference to anecdotal reports comes when the Committee refers back to their action of January 3. The discussion opened with the tabling of a report on the consequence of the precipitous decline in the U.S. debt (which was subsequently radically reversed) on the Fed's ability and latitude for developing policy. This was followed by an overall summary of the state of the U.S. economy. Then, toward the end of the January 30–31 meeting, there is the following, rather offhand statement:

> Several members observed that the evolving nature of the domestic economy, including the ongoing improvements in inventory management and the increase in managerial flexibility to alter the level and mix of capital equipment, associated in part with the greater availability of information, appeared to have fostered relatively prompt adjustments by businesses to changing economic conditions. As a consequence monetary policy reactions to shifts in economic trends needed in this view to be undertaken more aggressively and completed sooner than in the past. (http://www.federalreserve.gov/fmoc/minutes/20011013i.htm)

This aside was in all likelihood intended as an oblique justification or explanation of the action taken at the January 3 meeting. Yet there is also a theoretically significant assertion conveyed in this laconic prose. The pacing and the behavior of the economic system, which the Fed and members of the FOMC have had a major role in creating, means that their own expert practices, based on the management of enormous amounts of quantitative data, have been undercut. The world they must regulate is far more opaque and unpredictable by virtue of the new accelerated pacing of economic transformation. These experts can no longer always wait for the data to come in to calibrate their action. They can no longer take action "after the fact." They participate directly in the continuous generation of a contemporary, constructed out of information over which they have increasingly tenuous analytical purchase. Under these circumstances, which demand observation and action in real time, ethnography provides the modality of access for the expert and the anthropologist alike, access predicated on socially mediated observation.

By late spring of 2001, a formidable retrospective critique began to take hold regarding critical assumptions about the nature of the New Economy and the Fed's husbandry of it. This critique also marked an important stage by which the complex nature of the contemporary was reconciled with a theoretical narrative. Again, the fundamental issue was the role of technologically induced increases in productivity in transforming the overall economy as well as analytical techniques that we use to understand it. In the evangelical words of John T. Chambers, the chief executive of Cisco Systems, articulated just before the downturn, the technologically driven productivity gains allowed companies to "reduce costs, generate revenue in new ways, empower employees and citizens and provide the agility needed for the Internet economy's rapid pace" (quoted in Norris, 2001). Faith in the acceleration of productivity growth, as suggested earlier, had become, at least in part, the basis for the Fed's policy decisions and expectations about the economy's growth potential. Questions about the nature and the scale of productivity gains thus have far-reaching implications. There are three basic questions: Did government statistics exaggerate productivity gains? Were the gains in productivity narrowly concentrated in high-tech companies? How did faith (and/or hype) in the New Economy itself influence investment and consumption? By the late summer of 2001, these questions were given new force by the release of revised economic statistics. Productivity figures were recalculated for the period 1996 to 2000, revealing gains of 2.5 percent rather than 2.8 percent that had been previously reported (*Economist*, August 13, 2001).

Clearly, members of the Fed did act, to a greater or lesser degree, as if the world had entered a new era of economic possibility and that faith did influence policy decisions. And if it can be shown that the Fed was wrong, if it had in fact exaggerated the scale and the breadth of the productivity surge during the 1990s and its impact on the economy, then the Fed itself was in part responsible for underwriting a speculative bubble. If credit supplied to the market had not sustained balanced programs of investment in an ever more productive high-tech economy, but rather speculative excesses, then the Fed had pursued policy that was ultimately destructive to the economy.

This is one of a number of stories that marks the beginning of the process by which the events of 1999–2001 were given clarity via a retrospective narrative.

But what is lost analytically through this process? What interests us is not whether this critique of the New Economy is right or wrong but how it forecloses certain kinds of analysis. This is a classic bind; the narratives that are employed to conventionalize the events are drawing on the categories, measures, perspectives, and language that are still more or less predicated on the political economy of the nation-state. By endowing events with this kind of narrative framing, we believe, the contemporary is effaced and access to inchoate processes foreclosed. By invoking these retrospective narratives, we inevitably draw on theoretical frameworks that are allied with an eclipsed political economy. The authority of the ethnographic present is typically overridden via an analytical treatment and representational techniques that tether the action of subjects to convention, to tradition, and to the past, obscuring emergent practices and processes. What we are arguing here is that by interleaving our ethnography and the para-ethnography of our subjects, we can create a means to circumvent this bind, to engage a semiotics of society interpretable from experience.

Uncertainty continued to hang over the FOMC meeting of June 26–27, 2001, as the prospect of economic troubles loomed:

> In the Committee's discussion of current and prospective economic developments, members noted that by some measures the overall economic activity remained at a reasonably high level. However, recent data indicated that growth of spending and output was quite sluggish and below the pace many members had anticipated at the time of the previous meeting. . . . Continuing softness in the expansion of economic activity was mirrored in anecdotal reports of business conditions in much of the nation. Typical regional reports referred to slowing increases in economic activity from an already reduced pace to the persistence of sluggish business activity and generally downbeat business sentiment. Manufacturing continued to display particular weakness. (http://www.federalreserve.gov/fmoc/minutes/ 20010627.htm)

The danger, too, was becoming clearer, though shrouded in the flat prose of the Committee's minutes. There is also a marked sense that conditions had deteriorated since the FOMC meeting just a month earlier.

> It was noted, however, that the unique characteristics of the current cyclical experience, including the heavy concentration of weakness in business

expenditures and manufacturing output, increased the uncertainty that surrounded any forecast. Most of the members believed that the risks to the expansion, notably for the nearer term, remained to the downside of the current forecasts. Potential sources of shortfalls included the effect of possible further increases in unemployment or consumer and business confidence; the risks of disappointing business earning that could damp investment and, through lower equity prices, consumption; and the growing indications of weakness in foreign economies could limit demand for exports. (http://www.federalreserve.gov/fomc/minutes/20010627.htm)

A plausible scenario for steep economic decline was taking shape, given the data available to the Committee. What was becoming clearer was how a series of more or less discrete problems in the economy could converge to create an escalating deterioration that spread across the entire system. The likelihood that an accelerating weakness would materialize was still perceived as modest, but the threat was becoming conceivable, if not precisely measurable. There is also an added anxiety that this kind of alarming convergence was possible globally, that similar kinds of weaknesses were surfacing beyond the FOMC's statutory control in foreign economies.

The notion of "foreign" economies is, of course, analytically disingenuous. The members of the FOMC know well how the growing integration of national economies has made their jurisdiction and influence fully global. Their anxieties were, no doubt, focused on something like a repeat of the Asian financial crisis of 1997, in which a confluence of supranational market forces amplified "systemic risk" in a manner that could challenge not just the analytical authority of policymakers, but their power and their ability to intervene. These fears of some ill-defined and unexpected crisis expressed in the FOMC in the early summer were, as we know too well, fully defined on the morning of September 11.

The material world, even in Manhattan, was for the most part intact on the afternoon of September 11, but the structures of sentiment and expectation were profoundly transformed. Obscure global struggles became intimate psychological realities. The personnel of the New York District branch of the Federal Reserve, located two blocks from the Twin Towers, found themselves literally in the midst of the disaster. The research staff had just completed its summary on the state of the regional economy on September 10 intended for the regularly scheduled edition of the Beige Book. For the next two weeks, the New York District offices were closed; within hours of the disaster an expanded research staff began working from their homes, calling their networks of interlocutors to assess the impact of the horrific day on the economy. At this moment, when virtually all quantitative data were rendered irrelevant, para-ethnography became the means for gaining analytical purchase on the radically changed conditions of the world. An internal document, compiled using essentially the same method as the Beige Book, though with this larger staff, was generated within a few days and served as a starting point for assessing the disaster and thus served as the briefing document for the meeting of the FOMC on September 17 (Holmes and Marcus, 2005a).

On September 17, the FOMC responded by lowering its target for the federal funds rate by 50 basis points, and then again on October 2 the Committee lowered the target another 50 basis points to 2.5 percent while adding unusually large volumes of liquidity to the financial markets. This ninth cut in interest rates in 2001 reduced the discount rate to its lowest level in almost forty years; two more interest cuts ensued in 2002, reducing the discount rate to an emergency level of 1 percent, where it remained until June 2004. A recession was at hand. The anxieties that the Fed sought to negotiate revolved around how to restore confidence, if not optimism, to American consumers so that by virtue of their proclivity to spend they might redeem the global economy. And, as we now know, that is precisely what they did: liquidity provided by the Fed fueled heroic purchases of ever more extravagant homes, automobiles, and the like.

CONSTITUTION OF MARKETS

We turn now to an illustrative scenario in the form of a historical outline, of the origins of the contemporary globalization in which new, critical forms of knowledge production were spawned. We do this from the standpoint of key actors—symbolic analysts—who created this system and endowed it with an abiding moral urgency and a future-oriented practice. Their decisive technical innovation of establishing supranational markets as *political* instruments is the foundational achievement defining our era (Westbrook, 2003). Among other things, this discussion also helps us understand why central banks play such a significant role in defining and regulating our lives together (Blinder, 2004).

John Maynard Keynes, working with Harry Dexter White, and Jean Monnet, working with Robert Schuman, while seeking to resolve the most fundamental questions of nation-states—war, trade, and debt—arrived at solutions that yielded two radically subversive projects with a global reach: Bretton Woods and European institutions.

Both Monnet and Keynes experienced World War II from within the bureaucracies and ministries that managed, supplied, and financed the war efforts. They were aware of one another's work; Keynes is reputed to have credited Monnet's skill in orchestrating the Allies' (supranational) logistical efforts with shortening the duration of the war by a year. Both figures understood the inner operations of the *Leviathan*; they knew how to manage the *Wealth of Nations*. Both were in fundamental ways economic nationalists and liberal internationalists, and, to say the least, they both had a critical understanding of the workings of financial markets. What they sought, however, was a deployment of markets to achieve a profound historical transformation. Through the European and Bretton Woods institutions, they sought to create an integrated world economy that, to paraphrase the now famous words of the Schuman Declaration establishing the European project, would make war between nation-states not merely unthinkable, but materially impossible. In other words, they used supranational markets as a *political* tool to eviscerate the nation-state of its economic sovereignty and hence what they understood to be its most rapacious proclivities, as personified by Adolf Hitler (Westbrook, 2003). In its place, they created a politics of a distinctive sort, a politics that for very intriguing reasons never gained expression as a wide-ranging political rhetoric; rather, it operated as a deeply subversive technocratic discourse that transformed the world in the second half of the twentieth century. Their veiled efforts were aimed at achieving, in Keynes's words, "a new order," "a realizable utopia" (Lipgens, 1985; Monnet, 1978; Skidelsky, 2000, 208).

The birth of the new order arose from a technical problem, one that was negotiated at an unlikely time and in an unlikely context. In 1941, Keynes faced a problem posed by a troublesome provision of the Lend-Lease Agreement with the United States. The famous agreement is known for allowing the Roosevelt administration to provide aid to the British in the form of aging and surplus warships against the backdrop of strong American isolationism prior to Pearl Harbor. Inserted in the agreement was a provision, Article VII, that the British found profoundly irksome, if not humiliating, and that bound the parties to an agenda that would define the future status of international trade in the postwar world, a world in which the British would be debtors and the Americans creditors. This obscure provision of a diplomatic treaty amounted to a fait accompli in which the American side betrayed the obvious: that they had the financial might to determine the rules governing the postwar economic order. But it went further, demanding implicitly an end to the economic relations that sustained the twentieth-century remains of the British Empire.

Article VII became part of wide-ranging debates within the British Treasury and the Bank of England already under way in 1941 on planning for the postwar British economy and, more broadly, the structure of international trade. Keynes played a pivotal role in these discussions, particularly in the debate on the relative merits for the British of planned trade, based on the illiberal Schachtian system of bilateral managed trade relations developed by Hitler's banker and economics minister Hjalmar Schacht and Walther Funk, who succeeded Schacht as economics minister, and the laissez-faire approach of "non-discrimination in trade" or "Hullism" espoused by the American secretary of state Cordell Hull (Skidelsky 2000, 179–232). The former arrangement, at least in theory, would have perpetuated the "imperial preferences" of the Commonwealth; the latter would have decisively ended the political economy of empire.

Over a long weekend in September 1941, Keynes drafted two papers as rejoinders to Article VII, "Post War Currency Policy" and "Proposal for International Currency Union," that Robert Skidelsky (2000, 208), Keynes's biographer, described as "the most important he ever wrote in terms of their direct influence on events." In many respects, these were incomplete, ambiguous, and rather messy documents, yet together they constituted a major "fragment of a Grand Design" that was to be fully realized in the Bretton Woods agreements in 1946 (ibid.). At the center of this technical design were the mechanisms of an International Central Bank (ICB) that would, as Keynes fatefully put it, "[make] a beginning at the construction of the future government of the world" (quoted in Skidelsky, 2000, 223). "The challenge with which Article VII faced Keynes was to devise a plan to lock the USA into a system which would maintain balance of payments equilibrium between all countries without trade discrimination but also without forcing deflation, unemployment or debt-bondage on the deficit countries. He met it with the experience of the inter-war years and his economic theories, which were largely commentaries on experience" (182).

The negotiations over this plan first within the British government and then crucially in response to the plan drafted by Harry Dexter White, a New Deal–appointed assistant to Treasury Secretary Henry Morgentheau, yielded the now famous tripartite Bretton Woods institutional arrangement for global financial integration. What is most significant for our purposes is how these complex negotiations defined the space of technocratic intervention predicated on monetary issues. Skidelsky (2000, 181) comments on the prosaic conditions that made possible this kind of technocratic intervention that circumvented conventional political scrutiny:

> It might seem odd that planning for economic disarmament started on the monetary rather than on the trade side, and made faster progress. After all, Article VII was about trade, not money. But it made sense logically and politically. World trade had broken down in the 1930s because the gold standard had disintegrated. So the way to start unblocking the channels of trade was to unblock the flow of money by which traded goods were paid for. . . . It also seemed a lot easier for Britain and America to reach agreement about money. Money was too esoteric and boring to engage interests, passions, and prejudices. So technicians had a chance to make much more progress on money before their plans attracted political attention.

At stake in these negotiations were issues of highest national concern to the two parties, inspiring potentially divisive political confrontation.

> It must not be supposed that the technicians, as they were somewhat contemptuously called, operated in a historical or political vacuum. They brought to their work different understandings of what had gone wrong with the old gold standard; and different national experiences and interests. Above all the British and American plans came from two countries which expected to be very differently situated in the post-war world. The British expected to emerge from the war stripped of trade and assets and burdened with debts; the Americans in the opposite position. Keynes's therefore was a debtor's, White's a creditor's, perspective. The British wanted a scheme which would enable them to borrow without strings; the Americans one which would lend with strings. This difference was reinforced by another. The British plan came from a banking tradition, the American one from a legal tradition. The British wanted a scheme based on prudential maxims; the Americans one based on legal rule. (182)

Yet the translation of these highly fraught political issues into technical terms opened the way to, though did not guarantee, Keynes's "realizable utopia." What this translation entailed was a conceptualization of the supranational as a sphere of theory, analysis, and intervention.

The technical debates were not merely a cover for national self-interest. Keynes and White were both interested in theory, and in finding technical solutions to technical problems. Economics often enables political conflicts which seem intractable if carried on in the language of politics to be bypassed by assuming (or the cynic would say pretending) that they can be reduced to the technical, and imposing a language of debate consistent with that assumption. As the technicians from both sides got to know each other better, a genuine camaraderie developed *contra mundis*—against the politicians, bankers, vested interests on both sides waiting in the wings to sabotage both the Keynes and White Plans. (Skidelsky, 2000, 182)

This conceptualization of a supranational institutional framework also defined the role of a new class of actors, symbolic analysts, whose interests were no longer fully aligned with or reducible to those vested interests that defined the nation-state. These actors were no longer constrained by its theories, methods, and histories; indeed, by virtue of their institutional projects, they sought to render the intellectual apparatus underwriting the nation-state increasingly irrelevant.

Within a decade (by May 9, 1950), Jean Monnet and Robert Schuman engineered in a remarkably similar fashion the founding of the European institutions. The European project was orchestrated procedurally through diplomatic treaties that established complex technocratic agendas that created a supranational space in which a new class of functionaries could operate. An explicit technocratic ethos and practice was embraced by the founders of the European Union that entailed a comprehensive rejection of the nation-state as an instrument for managing human affairs and the development of an expert method—an administrative science of the supranational—that would impel the political integration of Europe.

Jean Monnet made a decisive discovery about the communicative possibilities (and limitations) constituted by supranationalism, a discovery that he relentlessly exploited and built into the fabric of the European project. Commenting on the journalists covering the announcement of the Schuman Declaration, Monnet (1978, 304) notes their bafflement: "They were still uncertain about the significance of the proposal, whose technical aspects at first sight masked its political meaning." It is precisely this bafflement that allowed one of the most important political projects of the twentieth century to develop in plain sight with little, if any, serious public scrutiny. In other words, the inscrutability of the European project and, even more so, the Bretton Woods project was not merely the outcome of public inattention, but a consequence of how these projects displaced fundamental historical realities that endowed events with coherence.

Inspired by Conrad Adenauer, first postwar chancellor of the Federal Republic of Germany, drafted by Robert Schuman, French prime minister, and Jean Monnet with a small group of aides, the founding document of the European Union explicitly aimed to end the possibility of war in Europe via comprehensive and wide-ranging market integration, starting with the production of coal and steel. Monnet was struck at the press conference announcing the Schuman plan that the journalists failed to grasp its significance; the elite French intellectual community lacked a framework and language to understand what the document represented. Monnet expresses in his memoir initial disappoint with this tepid response to this remarkable declaration, but then, one guesses, he realizes what a remarkable asset this public indifference could be: he could build Europe in plain sight without serious public scrutiny. He was free to pursue this staggering project because the journalists, the intellectuals, the political elite of France and Europe would be unperturbed; they operated within intellectual purviews and critical political agendas that were seamlessly tied to histories and theories from which his supranational ambitions were largely inscrutable. Like Keynes, he had discovered the tightly defined communicative character of supranationalism: its technical language and its goal of market integration. Monnet, one of the shrewdest minds of the twentieth century, recognized almost instantaneously that with the Schuman Declaration a vast political space was created that was virtually invisible and inaccessible from the standpoint of conventional political ideology and practice.

An explicit ethos and practice, designed by Monnet, was embraced by the founders of the European Union and used to fill this technocratic space of Europe. At its philosophical core were a comprehensive rejection of the nation-state as an instrument for managing human affairs and the development of an expert method—an administrative science of the supranational—that would impel the political integration of Europe. The founders of the EU were emphatic that their goal was to escape the blighted history of the European nation-state and to create a new grammar and semiotics of society (Haas, 1964, 1968; Herzfeld, 1993, 1997; Lipgens, 1985).

Thus, the dynamism of this new regime incites change that unfolds largely outside the conceptual ambit and political control of actors within the nation-state, change that transpires largely unobserved (and unmeasurable) from the perspectives of conventionally situated politicians, journalists, academics, and intellectuals. Ulrich Beck, Anthony Giddens, and Scott Lash (1994) have characterized the resulting condition as "reflexive modernization" by which, as the director of research at the Atlanta District branch of the Fed averred, "systems, instruments, and markets are evolving faster than the political entities can bring their various rules and regulations into harmony" (quoted in Riles, this volume). This world of fast capitalism that presents itself as structurally inscrutable is, as we have argued here, nonetheless susceptible to meaningful and to manifold scrutiny through the creative assimilation of socially mediated observation, what we have termed para-ethnography.

One additional analytical move enhances this possibility: a move by which the fundamental nature of contemporary capitalism, as shaped by Bretton Woods and European institutional transformations, is restated in explicitly political terms. David Westbrook's (2003) remarkable text, *The City of Gold*, performs this critical intellectual labor.[5]

Westbrook has persuasively argued that a particular appropriation of the market mechanism as a constitutional instrument has yielded a new type of *polity*, what he terms the City of Gold. By shifting our theoretical preoccupations about capital markets, from conceptualizing them in relationship to those commercial transactions organizing production, distribution, and consumption to conceptualizing markets as *constitutional* devices, he provides analytical purchase on the forces giving social form and cultural content to the contemporary world.[6] He distills the constitutional logic governing the City's operation and establishes criteria for a reflexive politics of the contemporary by which we can appraise, as he puts it, the truth, beauty, justice, and tyranny of our time:

> To understand the way we now live rests therefore, on a restatement of politics as it appears in the context of supranational capital, legitimated through our faith in the institutions of money and property, as opposed to the modern nation state, legitimized through the familiar mechanisms of the liberal republic. . . . The communicative space formed by financial markets is the object of political thought in our time, as the nation state was for most political thought during the time we still regard as modern, the pope, king, or emperor were the protagonists of the medieval political imagination, and the *polis* was the context of classical Greek thought. This book uses urban imagery and self-consciously revives the old Marxian personification, "capitalism," in order to solidify the understanding of financial markets as the grammar through which much contemporary political thought should take place. (2003, 12–13)

The predicament we face thus can be stated as a problem of meaning, and specifically, the shifting conditions of its social mediation.

The market's grammar, the dialectic between property and money, does not express many things important to being human. Capitalism is therefore radically impoverished as a system of politics. Insofar as we long for community, we necessarily experience life in capitalism as a sort of exile. . . . The construction of markets—the creation and alienation of property rights—involves the destruction of meaning, and in longing for that meaning, we complain not only about the market before us, but about the arrangement of social affairs through markets per se. (164)

Like our subjects, we, too, are legatees of a theoretical apparatus that conventionalizes data by drawing on the categories, measures, perspectives, and language that are still aligned fundamentally with those key concepts that animated nineteenth-century political economy and social theory. We are arguing here for a method that we can creatively pursue with our subjects, which circumvents this bind to encompass a semiotics of society interpretable from experience. We have sketched out in this essay a very preliminary rendering of this method and its historical relationship to and position within the communicative space of supranationalism. The great potential of this intellectual practice is that it can position the ethnographer within a fraught contemporary, a position from which he or she can delineate and address the questions of our time.

In our version, among other possible versions of this formulation of the object of ethnography, what gives rise to the para-ethnographic are the predicaments of a world of fast capitalism that engenders a constant task to produce the contemporary and in so doing to rethink, reobserve, and represent the categories of society in order to reproduce one's own identity and familiar contexts of agency and meaning. Although this may not apply to everyone everywhere today, it certainly applies, we argue, to the production of the discourses of politics and political interest in their official and displaced forms, and certainly to many other milieus and institutional arenas that anthropologists are increasingly interested in studying these days. The para-ethnographic is that side of diverse discourses and practices that represents the social ground for specific purposes and goals and done thickly or thinly with considerable consequences for events and action. This is an ethnographic process of knowledge creation, what anthropologists do, albeit in a more explicit and committed way. The question of what anthropologists will make of this affinity, how they will shape from it a tradition of research beyond the thick description of situated native points of view, remains in development.

1 One of our students, setting out for her own research on venture capitalists in Korea, presented an interesting gloss on this alternative project of contemporary ethnography in her comments on a candidate for an anthropology faculty position, defined as a specialist in the interdisciplinary field of science and technology studies:

> In some way, he is already recognizably someone like us, existing as he does between two scholarly worlds that produce their own separate sets of expert discourses. I imagine our department to be pioneers of that kind—to re-imagine and put into practice the kind of ethnography that deals with the production of contemporary knowledge. So the emphasis is on the leaving behind of lifeworlds not simply by saying that we are all "connected" somehow, but to actually look at how other knowledge makers make the common "facts" around and on which we build the routines of our understanding and shape the structures of feeling and arcs of expectations.

See Marcus (1995, 1998a, 1999a, 1999b, 1999c, 2002a, 2002b) on these manifold predicaments of contemporary ethnography.

2 This is a propitious moment to work in the anthropology of finance, central banking, and, more generally, contemporary configurations of capitalism given the vibrant scholarship that is currently defining the field. Two superb papers by Mitchel Abolafia (2004, forthcoming) demonstrate the possibilities of reconstructing the context and the processes of decision making at the Fed. We also have superb insider accounts by former senior officials of the Fed that we can draw on that have a strong para-ethnographic dimension (Blinder, 1998; Meyer, 2004). We have wonderful ethnographic work by Annelise Riles on the Bank of Japan (2004b, this volume) that not only provides acute comparative analysis but also serves as rich and creative examples of ethnographic experimentation in this formidable research setting. In addition, there are distinguished ethnographic treatments of traders and the financial markets in which they operate by Hiro Miyazaki (2003) and Caitlin Zaloom (2005, this volume) and outstanding examples, notably by Bill Maurer (1995, 1999, 2002a, 2002b), of how to address the theoretical issues at stake within distinctive configurations of global finance. Michel Callon and Koray Caliskan (2005) have compiled a comprehensive summary of the literature in economic sociology, with particular emphasis on the study of markets, as well as a provocative argument for reconstituting economic anthropology.

3 The crucial work that both legitimates intuition as a method of knowing and connects it to an essentially ethnographic, or cultural historian's, sensibility is Carlo Ginzburg's 1980 essay, "Morelli, Freud and Sherlock Holmes: Clues and Scientific Method."

4 Officially, a private organization, Business Cycle Dating Committee of the National Bureau of Economic Research, is responsible for declaring the onset and duration of a recession. See Abolafia (forthcoming).

5 We have struggled to do justice to Westbrook's magnificent text, to simply gloss what it is about, and we have repeatedly failed. Broadly, the text is about political economy, and insofar as it works out the economic logic and legal conventions defining con-

temporary political economy, it is absolutely essential, but it is much more. Perhaps broader still, it is about the at times excruciating and at times exhilarating possibilities of intellectual life in our time. What follows is just one example of his technique of analysis and of argumentation. In this case, it is concerned with the character of social criticism available to us in the City of Gold and the difficult task of creating an "authentic," as he would put it, basis of political and moral inquiry in which we are all implicated.

And here we come to a weakness that seems entailed in the doing of social criticism, and that therefore infects the criticism of monetization, and so this apology. Social critics depict ruin in part because they are social critics. As already suggested, social criticism attacks developments that are seen to be contrary to life as we have come to understand it, not so much our actual life as our current ideals. Social criticism tells stories, always already begun, which if continued will destroy the meaning we have constructed. A coming must also be a going—to say that a situation has come to mean something is also to say that the same situation no longer means what it once did . . . Insofar as we are fond of the way of life in which we grew up—and because it made us who we are, we have to have a certain respect for it, whatever might be said against it from the outside—then we will tend to view such change as a bad thing, and we may even speak of dehumanization. Social criticism thus tends to rest, if only implicitly, on a sense of dislocation, a sense of losing a pattern of meaning, along with the past in which such meaning was formed. Social criticism is always, at bottom, a charge of impiety, betrayal, leaving home.

Money (like technologies and wars) dehumanizes because it changes patterns, destroys meanings that human life has built up so far. Capitalism, in its relentless commitment to the future, remakes home, for better and worse. And yet there are reasons that capital is attractive, that people choose to treat themselves and others as slaves. Any successful impiety has its attractions, which ideology presumes to state in general terms. Money provides, if in the abstract, the realization of our will, which most of us conceive to be happiness, and what could be more tempting? The dramatic expression of destructive conflicts between goods, such as old meanings and new temptations, is tragedy.

It is also important to remember, however, that humans are resilient. People make meaning all the time. Culture reconstitutes itself. While people leave and die, they also find one another and babies are born. As an intellectual matter, however, it is much harder to say much about things which have not yet come together, about meanings as yet unconceived. So the narrative structure of social criticism—the effort to understand this moment inevitably in terms of a past that we suspect we are losing (indeed, that is a condition of our mortality)—fosters the sense that things are falling apart, and that one ought to be alienated. Social criticism tends to spring from a partial vision, a formal, analytical, and ultimately tragic perspective, as opposed to an intimate, synthetic, and comic perspective. Knowing when one or the other perspective is appropriate would be wisdom. (2003, 285–286)

6 This constitutional process that defines the City can be observed in the technical negotiations over China's membership in the WTO or the recently completed negotiations by which Cyprus, the Czech Republic, Estonia, Hungary, Latvia, Lithuania, Malta, Poland, Slovakia, and Slovenia each gained membership in the EU. Through intricate diplomatic treaties, these countries became integrated into the global system of trade under the jurisdiction of supranational markets that increasingly superseded the regulative role and thereby the economic sovereignty of the nation-state.

Caitlin Zaloom

TRADING ON NUMBERS

On the corner of Walbrook and Cannon Streets, in the heart of the City of London, stands a bronze cast of a man. Erected in 1997, the figure poses legs spread, one arm flung out and head cocked toward a now outsized cell phone. Two badges are pinned to his coat, one a security pass for the trading floor of the London International Financial Futures Exchange (LIFFE) and the other a three-letter identification tag. His loosely fitted trading jacket is permanently spread against the wind that streams through the glass and stone funnel of London's financial district.

This statue commemorates the pit traders of the LIFFE, whose open-outcry markets based in multitiered pits opened in 1982. In the pits the traders would scream out orders, cut deals with their buddies, scribble out completed trades on note pads, and verbally abuse the clerks who checked their trades. The clerks, knowing that many successful traders had begun on the lowest echelons of the hierarchy, hoped that someday they, too, would have the connections or the capital to climb into the pits. Knowledge of the social environment of the pit and the physical strategies of trading were key elements of their economic practice.

In the spring of 1998, the signals that electronic markets were undermining the dominance of open-outcry technology became undeniable. The Parisian open-outcry markets buckled under the pressure from a competing electronic system. Later that year, the all-electronic German DTB exchange reclaimed the contract in German Bunds from the control of London markets. In response to losing control of their most heavily traded contract, the LIFFE reorganized both its corporate structure and the technologies of its markets to compete under the new regime of electronic trading. The last LIFFE pit closed in November 2000, and with its demise came the end of open-outcry financial futures in London.

The demise of the pit trader marks a transformation in futures trading technologies from face-to-face auctions that thrived on the controlled chaos of the pits to electronic futures markets that link traders in a neatly networked web of dealing rooms dispersed throughout the world. In the new online trading networks that are replacing the pits, market transactions are played out not in shouts and frenetic hand gestures but through the boldface type of constantly changing numbers on a graphic user interface. Rather than standing shoulder to shoulder and back to back, scanning the pit for changes in the market and listening for the pitches of alarm and bravado in the voices of traders calling out their bids and offers, the electronic trader spends his days sitting uncomfortably in front of a computer terminal, eyes trained on the image inside a glass and plastic box. Leaving behind the intense sensory cues of the pit, traders now receive the most important market information in the form of digital data streams.

In this essay, I analyze the production of economic rationality at two sites in global financial markets, each operating under a different technological regime: the Chicago Board of Trade (CBOT) and a London futures dealing firm that I call Perkins Silver where many of the traders are LIFFE veterans.[1] I conducted fieldwork on the financial trading floor at the CBOT and in the digital dealing room of Perkins Silver. Working as a clerk at the CBOT, I arrived at work each morning at 6:45 and participated in the heat of trading throughout the day. I learned to understand the markets, as most CBOT traders do, by working within them.

I continued my apprenticeship in financial markets in London, arranging to join Perkins Silver as a new recruit among ten new traders. Along with my fellow trainees, I studied formal trading techniques in a classroom and, on the trading floor, adjusted them to my own risk-taking proclivities. After the training, I traded German Treasury bond futures on a Perkins Silver account. I interpreted the market relying on my new skills and gained the direct experience of risking money that is central to traders' experience of their own work. To supplement my work and observations in these arenas of exchange, I interviewed officials at the exchanges and technology companies and attended meetings on the reorganization of the industry.

Information technologies underpin traders' daily practices of economic judgment by shaping the available informational resources. For traders, this shift from face-to-face to screen-based technologies has transformed the relationship between trading skill and exchange technology.[2] For anthropologists, this transition makes financial futures markets instructive sites in which to examine the tensions between ideals of technological rationalization and the norms and practices of contemporary financial capitalism.[3] This essay examines the changing nature of trading strategies and the composition and quotidian practice of financial reason. The technological platform on which traders work is changing, but techniques of economic action carry over and transmute in interesting ways.

Futures traders on both technologies enact a specific form of modern economic rationality that combines technological acumen with financial interpretation. Their actions are based in a form of reasoning that is far from strict calculation. Futures traders act under highly uncertain and rapidly changing conditions using techniques that focus on creating fragile scenarios and account for the constant shifts in the market. These scenarios identify the specific social information within the bid and offer numbers for financial contracts.[4]

Financial markets and information technologies have come to occupy important places in contemporary social theories and the anthropology of globalization. The futures traders discussed here act within and on what Appadurai (1996) calls "financescapes" and Castells (1996) names "the space of flows." The amplified pace of transactions, heightened flows of capital, and expansion of global market interconnections made possible by new information technologies have spurred scholarly concern over the cultural effects of speed and linkage in capital circuits (Hutton and Giddens, 2001). Indeed, these financial markets now work "in real time on a planetary scale" (Castells, 1996). Whereas the relationship between technology and finance is a critical component of globalization (Held, McGrew, Goldblatt, and Perraton, 1999; Sassen, 1996), the consequences of this technological change for the specific forms of economic action and the fine grain of financial practice have not been fully explored (Boden, 2000).

A group of scholars working within a social studies of science framework has begun to make inroads in this area. Some focus on the objects used in calculation and the shaping of financial technologies by economic theory and professional actors (Callon, 1998; MacKenzie, 2001; MacKenzie and Millo, 2001; Muniesa, 2002), and others analyze the new forms of sociality made possible by information technologies (Knorr Cetina and Breugger, 2000, 2002a; Preda, forthcoming). However, anthropologists have only scratched the surface of the vast and complex field of finance and have yet to fully grasp the significance of new information technologies for forms of sociality and knowledge. The technological changes that create the material for global interconnection transform the practice of financial reason. Trading through anonymous networks demands reshaping older techniques of trading for the screen, the new arena of competition. An anthropological approach that examines the practice of finance is well positioned to examine the intersection of technology and financial reason in action.

DOING THE NUMBERS

The task of understanding market action under different technological regimes requires examining the role of numbers in traders' knowledge practices. Traders base their interpretations of financial conditions in the numbers that represent the market. Since the invention of number-based accounting practices such as double-entry bookkeeping, numbers have been a cornerstone of economic calculation, providing the essential tools for rationalized action. Yet the practice of economic judgments in futures markets challenges this representation of economic action and requires a shift in the way we think about numbers. Numbers have often been considered elements of knowledge *production* that increase objectivity and certainty. The fluid numbers of futures markets invite us to examine the *consumption* of numbers more closely. Traders look for clues to the direction of the market by observing the numbers. At the same time, the short time frame of futures trading introduces a fundamental instability and uncertainty into economic judgments based on these numbers. The provisional nature of market numbers and the approximate character of traders' conclusions suggest that their practices are best characterized as interpretation rather than exacting calculation. But scholarly theories of numbers and quantitative representation are insufficient to provide a full reading of the power of numbers in financial futures markets.

As such scholars as Ted Porter (1995), Michael Power (1997), and Mary Poovey (1998) have shown, such numbers act to (1) establish expertise and authority, (2) make knowledge impersonal, (3) portray certainty and universality, and (4) contribute to resolving situations of doubt, conflict, and mistrust. To use Poovey's phrase, numbers perform ideally as representations of *noninterpretive facts*. As stable objects, numerical units resist conjecture and theory and serve in the production of systematic knowledge.

The pace of trading in futures markets undermines this stability. Traders at the CBOT and Perkins Silver practice trading techniques called "scalping" and "spreading" that focus on the profits to be made in the intraday fluctuation of futures markets. In these trading styles, numbers that represent bids and offers for financial contracts are the material traders use to interpret market conditions and orient their profit-making strategies. A bid is a price at which a trader is willing to buy a financial commodity, and an offer, or ask, is the price at which he is willing to sell.[5] These numbers represent the "needs and expectations of hedgers and speculators" (CBOT, 1997).[6] They are not established price facts. Rather, they are temporary assessments of market conditions, momentary markers of approximate valuation.

Bid and offer numbers surge into the market and fade away in instants. The tempo of the market speeds and slows as the number of contracts on bid or offer increases or diminishes and one set of possible trades slides into the next. The trader will not always "get 'em" or be able to turn his evaluation into a completed purchase or sale. Traders may add or withdraw their bids and offers as time alters market conditions. Traders develop styles of interpretation that incorporate the fluidity of numbers at the same time that they construct explanations for market fluctuations.

The technological transition from open-outcry pit to trading screen reconfigures these foundations of market knowledge by reconstituting the bid and offer numbers. Each technology represents the market in numbers, but the numbers are not all alike. The structure and design of the pits and the screen influence the ways that traders apprehend and act within the market, shaping participants' techniques for managing quantitative information, for fashioning their calculations, and for understanding the dynamics of competition and affect that are central to financial action.

INFORMATIONAL TRANSPARENCY

Open-outcry pits and electronic trading screens are information technologies shaped and constructed in alignment with particular ideals of economic information. The representation of market action, whether in the pit or on the screen, relies heavily on the capacity of numbers to convey abstract and objective information. Both trading technologies are founded in highly rationalized techniques of exchange and information delivery. Modern financial markets are predicated on an idea of informational transparency that presents market information as self-apparent facts free from the distortions of social information. By supplying these economic truths, the market technologies lay the foundations for traders' calculations. In 1869 the CBOT introduced the pit to create a unified market space where all participants could see each other and hear all the bids and offers available.[7] About a century and a half later, designers of online trading systems have also used technology as a tool to shape traders' knowledge context. These architects of financial exchange self-consciously distill the economic content of the market by removing the social information so readily available in the pits.[8]

The designers and the market managers that hire them rely on a narrative of rationalization that rests on a particular idea of the way market data are constructed, transmitted, and received. In an ideal competitive arena, market information must have self-evident meaning. For informational transparency, as I call it, to be realized, all information must lie visible on the surface; interpretation would thus be unnecessary because data are objective and clear. In the pit, this information is transmitted through the bodies of traders and received by their colleagues who challenge and help them in face-to-face competition. Yet the numbers shouted in the pit have the same claim to "clean" representation. The designers of electronic dealing systems seek simply to *purify* the transparent representation that already exists in open-outcry.[9] Alan Lind, an ex-official at the German-Swiss Eurex exchange and the designer of the Perkins Silver graphic user interface, championed the connection of technological rationalization and democratizing access to information: "The truth comes out in the electronic world. There are no physical crutches required."[10] On the screen, a trader needs only a set of eyes to read the market and a finger to click.

The presentation of the market as a set of numbers is critical to the production of informational transparency. But the visual and auditory contexts of open-outcry pits create different opportunities and ambiguities from the graphic user interface of a digital exchange. In the transition from face-to-face markets to electronic technologies, the contrasting representations of the market demand that traders develop new strategies for using numbers to understand the market.

In both technological contexts, traders undermine the rationalizing effects of technology. Tensions between rationalized technology and situated action emerge on the trading floor and in the dealing room as the social is displaced and reconfigured.[11] As observations and participation in the market reveal, traders search out social information contained within the bid and ask prices that anchor their knowledge of the market. They interpret the market numbers through the particular framing of each technology and thereby unearth the specific social dimensions of market conditions. Traders bring questions about the social content of the market to their calculations no matter how much software designers try to remove such cues from their programs. Who are the competitors? What are their individual styles? Are they scared, stolid, eager, or anxious? Traders avidly pursue this information, and when they don't have it, they often fabricate it. Social contextualization and interpretation are critical parts of traders' calculations.

What constitutes "the social" differs between face-to-face and face-to-screen contexts. The technological context changes the scope and content of the social in economic life. In the pits, social information is founded in deep knowledge of the local environment. Traders organize dealing strategies with the situations and motivations of their particular competitors and compatriots in mind. On the screen, social information is the landscape of competitors that traders imagine and identify within the changing digital numbers. These competitors are cloaked in the abstracted numbers of the market, but traders assign personalities and motivations to the characters behind them. In the London dealing room where I worked, traders do not construct these visions alone; they reach out to their coworkers to help form an interpretation of the social dimensions of the electronic marketplace. Software designers may attempt to excise social information from their technologies, but traders create new social contexts to replace the ones they have lost.

The profit-making strategies of traders are based on the multivalent nature of market information. Through their particular technological framings, quantitative objects that seem straightforward gain a complexity that conveys information far beyond what they apparently describe.[12] Located in the interaction between the presentation of market data and the technology of exchange, the layered information of market numbers inspires each trader to interpret their meaning.

WHAT TRADERS KNOW ABOUT NUMBERS

In both open-outcry and online markets, traders exploit the informational ambiguities of numerical information.[13] The changing bids and offers of futures markets demand an interpretive agility, and traders learn that numbers have contradictory roles in the market. Between the representation of the market and the decision to buy and sell futures contracts lies what traders "know" about numbers.

The first thing they learn is that *numbers tell very little.* Although the full number of a bond futures price is five digits long, traders use only the last one or sometimes two digits, playing the differences between fractions of a point in the price of a contract. In this sense, numbers are simply placeholders in a sequence leading from 1 to 9. Once a price passes 0, traders refer to their bids and offers as 1s or 9s again, without specifying the larger change. The number is only a symbol in a sequence that could be any other sequential set.

For short-term traders, larger numbers do not indicate potential for profits. Rather than always "going long" or buying contracts anticipating that the price will rise, futures traders play both the rise and fall of intraday volatility. Traders can also profit by "shorting" the market, selling contracts in advance of a drop in price. If their predictions prove correct, they can then buy them back at a lower cost and pocket the difference. Traders have the opportunity for profit as prices both ascend and descend the scale.

Traders know that numbers stand on their own without reference to events outside the immediate bids and offers. Events external to the immediate market, such as rate cuts, election news, economic reports, or the intervention of a large buyer, can storm the market unexpectedly. The immediacy of the market dictates that attention remains on the bid/ask figures that represent the position of the market at that second. Outside news is supplemental to the information available in the bid/ask numbers. Government announcements are some of the most powerful forces that alter market conditions. A surprise intervention that occurred during my time at Perkins Silver shows the attenuated connection between trading in second-by-second markets and the fundamentals of their underlying assets. These traders can act with little information or understanding of the instrument they trade or the economic conditions of the countries that issue them.

On November 3, 2000, the Perkins Silver dealing room was relatively calm. The market was steadily ticking up and down. Suddenly, shouts erupted from behind computer terminals as routine patterns snapped and the market for all European products spiked upward. Traders who had bought contracts rode the move upward. Traders holding short positions cursed as the market pummeled their bearish expectations and forced them to take losses. The market move took only about thirty seconds but reversed the downward trend in bond prices denominated in the ailing European currency that had dropped toward .80 to the U.S. dollar. Once the action ebbed and the traders had regained their composure, they leaned toward their neighbors and asked each other what had caused the move. The first trader to lift himself from his seat and find a terminal with a Reuters wire scrolled down the screen until a headline appeared on the electronic tickertape. It read, "C-bank intervenes in Euro." The traders buzzed about how Citibank had intervened in the euro until an older trader pointed out, nonchalantly, that "c" bank meant *central* bank. This kind of basic misattribution would make any economist squirm, but to these traders who deal in a time frame of seconds, it is immaterial if it is Citibank or the European Central Bank that takes action. The market prints the result before the news comes through the news wires. Knowing the cause is more important for satisfying an after-the-fact curiosity than for organizing market action. The news wire can supply the reason, but it does not necessarily cause the reaction or even precede it. All the necessary information for these second-by-second traders is in the bid/ask numbers.

Traders also learn that numbers have particular personalities and effects on the human mind. This is especially so for traders who practice a technique called technical analysis. This interpretive strategy bases predictions of future market movements in historical trading patterns. Technical analysts are also known as "chartists" for their use of graphs and other visual tools that describe the past movements of the market. In technical analysis, individual numbers gain strength or weakness, positive or negative potential, as points of support and resistance to the overall trend of the market. Numbers that halt a decline in the market are called "support levels," and numbers that "turn back a price advance" are attributed powers of resistance. The numbers in these statements are themselves agents.

According to the book considered to be the bible of chartists, *Technical Analysis of the Financial Markets,* numbers gain further significance for technical analysts because "traders tend to think in terms of important round numbers, such as 10, 20, 25, 50, 75, 100 (and multiples of 1,000), as price objectives and act accordingly" (Murphy, 1999, 64). Traders invest these numbers with both their own psychological significance and the expectation that these numbers are significant to other traders.[14] Numbers develop greater solidity as support or resistance as more traders invest in a particular price area. According to Murphy, "The more trading that takes place in that support area, the more significant it becomes because more participants have a vested interest in the area" (60). The variation around a modal price defines a "trading range." Trades build up around the fair value or modal price. When the market sharply departs from oscillation around the mode, or between points of support and resistance, technical traders call it a "range break" and seize the opportunity to buy into or sell that swing.

But it is not only by watching the investments in certain prices that traders assess the quality of a number. Traders identify the significance of an individual number as the depth of bids or offers builds up around a price. The larger the number of offers, the greater the expectation that the market will begin to decline in price; the greater the number of bids, the more likely that the price will extend upward from there. Weighty numbers create an informational gravity attracting other traders to the price. For short-term traders, the perceived judgments of other market participants contained in the bid/ask hold an opportunity for making money. As critics of technical analysis point out, this continuous evaluation of others' perceptions of the weight of the bid/ask creates a self-fulfilling effect that validates the circular judgment of traders in relation to the numbers they trade.

Because of the multivalent character of numbers in futures markets, numerical information and technological presentation are inextricably bound. Traders mine the crevices of the technology for specific context that will tell more about the numbers than they represent on their own.

IN THE PIT AND ON THE SCREEN

Bodies and Voices

Traders' tactics for delivering and reading unstable numbers change as the pits give way to dealing rooms filled with the glow and hum of computer terminals. On the trading floor of the CBOT, noise and color swamp the senses. A roar from inside the raised octagonal pits follows the electronic screech of the opening bell. Traders stand in tiered pits, each one dedicated to a single contract, some based on the U.S. Treasury bond complex, others on the Dow Jones Industrial Average or other indexes. Individual voices pierce the din shouting "50 at 3," or "5 for 100," indicating the quantity and price they are selling at or paying for futures contracts. Each call indicates how many contracts the individual trader is willing to buy or sell at that price.

These shouts, which represent the key technology of the open-outcry system, are the main mechanisms for conveying bids and offers in the pit. Open-outcry technology in Chicago has relied on the same techniques for 150 years. These face-to-face interactions constitute a technology that delivers market information in orderly, routinized ways even as they are brought to life in the din of the trading floor. The pit creates a physical arena for financial competition.

The tiered steps of the pits organize the physical space of open-outcry trading. Most important, the stepped structures create a unified space of financial competition where each trader can see and hear all the bids and offers in the market.[15] Every bid or offer is legally required to be shouted to the competitive market. In this regime of exchange, shouts are most often accompanied by hand signals, the hands turned toward the body, palms possessively pulling inward to show a desire to buy, and hands thrust forward, palms out, to sell. Numbers from 1 to 5 are shown predictably with the fingers on each hand extended upward and turned sideways to show 6 to 9. Zero is indicated with a closed fist.

In a simple transaction, a trader makes an agreement with another trader by meeting his eye in response to a bid or offer. The selling partner in the operation yells "Sold." The two jot down the price, quantity, and three-letter code of their trading partner on a paper card and hand it over to their clerks, who will hunt down their counterparts and confirm that each party agrees that the trade took place.

By design and by regulation, all trades must enter into the space of competitive bidding and offering. Rules 332.01A and 332.00 of the CBOT handbook state: "Bidding and offering practices on the Floor of the Exchange must at all times be conducive to competitive execution of orders. . . . All orders received by any member of this Association, firm or corporation, doing business on Change, to buy or sell for future delivery any of the commodities dealt in upon the floor of the Exchange must be executed competitively by open outcry in the open market in the Exchange Hall during the hours of regular trading" (CBOT 1993, 12). The accountability and competitiveness of the market is rooted in these shouted quotations. Any trades that happen outside of this arena, either outside of trading time or through whispers of trading neighbors, are therefore illegal. Each bid and offer in the market must be outwardly presented for all participants to see and hear.[16]

Physicality of Market Numbers

Physical strategies for delivering and receiving bids and offers in the pits are part of the traders' financial strategies. For pit traders, both delivering and receiving the bids and offers of the pits are full bodily experiences. The pit requires stamina and strength. Although there is only one former Chicago Bears player on the floor, many traders compete in height and width for his physical presence. Those who don't have the natural stature of a professional athlete can visit the cobbler in the basement of the CBOT who will add lifts to their shoes. Traders from the CBOT and the nearby Chicago Mercantile Exchange can be identified walking the streets of the western Loop not only by the loud oranges, blues, reds, and yellows of their trading coats, but also by the extra inches of black foam affixed to the soles of their shoes.

Traders' physical location in the pit can limit or expand their access to other traders' bids and offers. Traders may have difficulty or ease being seen or heard when they deliver their bids and offers to market. They may have obstructed sightlines, providing them access to only what lies between visual obstacles, or clear angles of vision enabling transactions with a large area of the trading arena.

Because of the physical and emotional information conveyed with numbers, not all bids and offers are fully equal. Every bid or offer that pit traders emit or engage in the day-to-day operations of exchange is received through the voice and bulk of another trader. The information conveyed in these numbers cannot be divorced from the bodies through which they are conveyed and received. The tone of voice, the body language of the trader, who may be steadily and confidently holding his hands forward in engagement with the market or who may be yelling his bids, spittle flying and eyes wide in desperation to get out of a trade, are crucial inflections that traders draw on to form market judgments.

In a pit bursting with six hundred screaming traders, arms slashing the air, strategies for penetrating the physical strains of the arena are crucial to a trader's calculative repertoire. Delivering bids and offers into the market requires acquiring the physical and emotional techniques for transmitting and receiving market information conditioned by the pit. Leo, a trader whose voice is hoarse and scratchy from twenty years of use in CBOT markets, described training himself for the vocal and emotional demands of open-outcry trading: "When I first got in the business, I had to go in front of a full-length mirror every night and practice screaming, looking at myself."

The intricacy of physical strategy in the pit becomes particularly clear when smaller traders must compensate for their stature by manipulating other resources to get the attention of potential trading partners. It is not enough to be on the right side of the market, each trader needs to attract the others' attention—to have another trader *receive* the numbers he shouts into the market. Victor, an ambitious young broker, physically short and narrow, explained how he creates a presence in the pit that will attract attention to his bids and offers:

> Voice is number one. . . . You have to be a controlled loud. You can't be like a panic loud because once the panic comes out of your mouth you're pretty much admitting to whoever wants to assume the other side of the trade with you that that's not a good trade. . . . Tones of your voice are very important. A lot of guys have higher voices . . . and they can really be heard throughout the pit. . . . A lot of it is hand gestures, being able to kind of like offer your hands out at just the right pace to catch people's attention. . . . Sometimes it's jumping up. People watch me sometimes when I start to catch air and they go, Hey, there's Victor, you know, bidding them.

In addition to orchestrating the presentation of bids and offers, timing the delivery is key. Victor described how he attracted the attention of one of the "big dog" traders: "Just at the right time, I mean literally it was within a second, a split second—I literally caught a little pause in his offer where he was just kind of looking in all directions, I just happened to jump and bid and scream at him at literally—I mean I'm not even going to say tenths of a second—I'm going to say hundredths. . . . If I didn't jump and jump a foot and a half off the ground and bid 4s at that guy *just as I did and the way I did it*, he wouldn't have seen me."

The presentation of market numbers in voice forces the traders to cope with the immateriality of the bid or offer. A number is rarely shouted once. Because each bid or offer hangs in the air for only a second, the trader barks the number into the pit repeatedly to make sure he is identified with it. At the same time, the trader holds out his hands extended into numerical signals to bring a concrete visual presence to his bid or offer. The sounds of repeated numbers form the cadence of the market, which can convey urgency or boredom. In receiving the numbers that others bring to the market, traders appeal to "feeling." This word, encompassing all sensory information, is one traders use to characterize their knowledge of the market.

The body is a key interpretive instrument for the pit trader. Listening to rhythms of the numbers as they run in the pits brings on a sensation that leads traders to judge the market as "heavy" or "light," likely to rise or fall according to their sensory estimations. Beyond creating the basis for individual traders' economic judgments, the ambient noise of the pit affects the market as a whole. Economists studying the CBOT pits found that increased sound levels lead to higher trading volumes and foreshadow periods of high volatility in the pits (Coval and Shumway, 1998). But just as numbers cannot be divorced from the bodies that deliver them, noise cannot be divorced from the numerical content that it conveys. Traders monitor the changing bids and offers of the pits, receiving them into their bodies through their eyes and ears. Numbers, in the context of the dense arena of exchange, produce emotional states in the traders that are integral parts of their predictions. Rather than functioning as obstacles to normatively rational decision making, these signals that work on an intuitive level are a central trading tool. They see formal calculation as a hindrance to their job and to their ability to react. In training their bodies as both receiving and delivery instruments of the underlying information of market numbers, the first step is learning *not* to calculate.

Sean, a lawyer by training and a second-generation member of one of the CBOT trading families, assessed the effects of his legal education on his habits of mind and trading practice: "I am prone to get set in my ways. I'll reason to a particular conclusion based on assumptions that I've got built into the market. . . . Just like I'd craft an argument. I'm crafting a plan and then all of the sudden my plan is this and boy, the market had better listen." It rarely did. Sean argued that his deliberative skills led him to conclusions that may be theoretically correct according to the system he has established. But his words suggest that in formulating arguments, he loses the ability to play on the indeterminacy of market movements. Explicit construction of logical systems inhibited his ability to adapt his positions to rapidly changing market conditions. Sean identified the premium on interpretive agility in financial markets by using his own calculative rigidity as a foil. Constructing elaborate systems can hinder a trader's ability to quickly adapt to swerving bids and offers.

In interviews, other traders described the technique of noncalculation:

> In the commodity [futures] business . . . you do the thinking away from the market. . . . If you start thinking too much during the course of the day when the battle is on, it is really a disadvantage. (Leo)

> It's just like you're in there and you know—like sometimes you just don't want to be buying or you don't want to be selling. I presume like you could figure out after trading off the floor for a long time and really watching things and charting—but nothing like knowing—nothing like standing there and having that feeling. (Jack)

The immediacy of the market requires that traders have an interpretation of every present moment. The importance of sensory cues in both delivering and receiving numerical information in the pit makes use of all a traders' wits and physical skill.

Eyes on the Screen

In contrast to the overpowering sensory information of numbers in the pits, screen-based technologies actually narrow the scope of information available to traders. The representation of the market as a set of changing numbers on the screen is the primary source of information for traders in electronic markets. At the same time, traders try to gain contextual clues from their interactions with other traders by calling across the dividers that separate them, offering interpretations of market movements. In addition to drawing contextualizing interpretations from their coworkers, traders search within the numbers to find social reasons for the movement of the market. They craft identities for their competitors and construct motivations for these illusory actors in the online arena. Fashioning a social narrative for abstract information helps traders create understandings of market fluctuations that direct their decisions to enter and exit the market. Traders create stories around the shifting directions of numbers that many economists consider a "random walk."[17]

The E-trader graphic user interface (GUI) is the point of contact between Perkins Silver screen traders and the market. The GUI hones the representation of the market in numbers. In his design, Alan Lind, the creator of E-trader, framed a numerical and visual representation of the market.[18] Fulfilling his role as a "pragmatic technician" of economic rationality, Lind created a design that cleaves to the dictates of informational transparency (Rabinow, 1989). The GUI design presents all market action and information as available in plain sight, introducing the closest thing to a noninterpretive format as possible. The transparency of the GUI design pares market data down to a minimum: boldface numbers in rectangular boxes. Lind's central concern was to use the design to reduce the distance between the trader and the market. For him, this meant assembling the simplest visual cues to represent market action rather than creating a platform for displaying every piece of information or technical trick available. The outward simplicity of the user interface illustrates well its numerically rationalized representation of the market.

The GUI organizes the market for each financial product into a vertical or horizontal strip. The trader can drag each block to drop it where he likes on the screen next to records of his filled orders, a record of all the orders he's placed in the market, and the box that displays profit and loss. A casual glance at a trader's screen can show if he has made or lost money that day. If the numbers in the P&L box are a profitable green, then he is up for the day. If the numbers are red, the trader often slides the box off to the right of the screen so the numbers are invisible to him and to any curious bystanders. The most important information, the bids and offers and the "depth" of the market, how many and the price levels of bids and offers, are shown in black numbers against blue and red backgrounds.

The design crystallizes a form of simplicity that displays the ideals of informational transparency. This spare visual depiction enacts a commitment to reducing the intermediation between trader and market. The engineer's transparent designs mark a commitment to represent the market in simple and unadorned numerical representation. The use of numbers as techniques of transparency draws the trader toward a distilled idea of the market where disembodied actors display supply and demand for futures contracts.

This attempt to suture traders into the market by reducing the interface to bare, numerical representation shapes the traders' informational environment, elevating numbers to the status of the market itself. Numbers gain a synecdochic power in their relationship to the market. On the GUI, numbers that represent the bids and offers are supposed to raise all hidden information to the surface of the screen and deliver the total of market information into the numbers. In a sharp break from the complex information system in the pit, where fathers and sons, friends and allies passed information through tightly controlled networks, the screen displays the market in simple terms available to the eyes of any trader with access to the screen. In addition to facilitating social and physical distance between actors bound into a global network of exchange (T. Porter, 1995), numbers are, in Lind's design, a technology of *proximity* drawing traders toward the market. Lind's strategy endeavors to cast aside the intermediation of the social information of the pits in favor of honing an ideal of "pure" information based in a representation of the market in numbers.[19]

Lind created direct contact between traders and market information through the numbers of his GUI. As he explains, his plan was to "strip down the chassis" of the exchange technology: "[Traders] don't care about German economic status or European economic status. What they're looking at typically are numbers. They're trading numbers, using numbers to make decisions all day long. I would say that it's like a motor racing driver that doesn't look at the scenery as he's doing two hundred miles an hour going down the track. He's looking at the hazy outline of the road. He's looking at the numbers on his dial. That's it. He's focused."

The organization of the trading industry places many intermediaries between participating traders. The mechanisms of exchange are located in the clearing firm, the material technology itself, the CBOT and Eurex and their programs for completing trades. However, in the technological framing of E-trader, these intermediaries become virtually invisible (Brown and Duguid, 2000), producing an experience of direct connection between the trader and the market.

The technology of E-trader holds the informational frame steady while it delivers the constantly changing bids and offers to the trader's eyes fixed inches from his screen. Using these data to form interpretations, the electronic trader can leap into the market with a click of his mouse. Understood in the terms of informational transparency, the design works to eliminate not only institutional intermediaries, but also intervening tools of evaluation. As Lind explains:

[I want to communicate] ultra fast prices. In other words, I want to show you the real market quicker than anyone else so that you can make the decision to trade. I'm not going to give you analytics, fancy recommendations, because my recommendations may need some explanation or they may need to be mathematically complex. . . . The Spartan approach with technology today is still the best one. Keep it down to the absolute minimum; get rid of the stuff you don't ever look at. . . . Only observe the market that you want to.

In E-trader, Lind created a system of information delivery that provides austere data of bids and offers. While reducing the market to a few printed numbers, Alan Lind also opens the possibility of interpretation based on the very simplicity of the GUI presentation of the market.

In the Dealing Room

In the dealing room, Alan Lind's design comes into contact with the training methods of the Perkins Silver managers and daily practices of Perkins Silver traders. To enter the dealing room floor, traders pass through a set of three doors leading from the elevator bank. At each door, they swipe their key cards through a security lock. Swaths of gray dividers partition the space. Each bank of trading desks is split again into four individual workstations, personalized by bits of decoration that are pinned into the fabric walls. Light filters through the cloudy overhang of London's sky, supplementing the blue-tinted glow of the computer screens. A beige, plastic-encased terminal sits centered on each trader's desk. A thin extra layer of glass screwed to the beige box shields the trader from the screen's radiation.

Walking down the lefthand corridor of the dealing room reveals images of soccer club posters, hot cars, baby photos, and girly pictures cut from magazines. Spare copies of Rupert Murdoch's tabloid, *The Sun*, are strewn about the room. The traders joked that the nipples of the topless page 3 girl were sure indicators of daily market direction. Traders program their computers to make noise when Eurex, the German-Swiss futures exchange, has filled their trades. During busy markets, tinny computer speakers attached to the computers fill the room with the simulated sounds of breaking glass and ricocheting bullets.

Despite the raucous atmosphere, the Perkins Silver managers insisted on discipline from their new recruits. The managers required us to keep a journal that showed a running log of observations and trades. Each entry created an abbreviated record of the new trader's reasoning process. Some excerpts from my own trading journal, which document part of a morning's trading activity, show the focus on the patterns and rhythms and the problem of learning to make sense of the numbers:[20]

> Trying to go long the spread at 7 or 8.
> Long at 8.
> Very slow moving—trying to sell 9 now 0 after shift in Bobl.
> Back to 9's, out at 9.
> Looks like the spread is moving down. Bobl moving up again. A steady Schatz.
> Bought 62's.
> Going 1/2/3 seems like upward pressure.
> Scratched.
> Buying the Spread at 61, Spread 0/1/2.
> Bought 9's trying to scratch.
> Bought 0's.

These spare representations of a new trader's learning process show the trader's focus on numbers. The managers tried to supplement the weak sensory information available through the GUI with a program called Market Sound that augments the visual data of the screen. This software replicates the aural dimensions of the pit by recreating ambient noise levels linked to the size of bids and offers in the market. A trader can hook into the program by plugging an earpiece into the speakers on his computer. Yet, despite this software that exists to supplement the thin information of the screen, hardly any of the traders used it. The algorithm that replicates the noise of open-outcry trading recreates only a sliver of the total body experience of the pits. Although there are demonstrated effects of noise on trading activity in the pits, without the context of face-to-face interaction, the noise of Market Sound was more distracting to the screen traders than it was illuminating. The sort of sensory information helpful to pit traders' interpretations was inappropriate to the context of the screen. Instead, the Perkins Silver traders created other cues that oriented them to the direction of the market.

For example, at the same time that the other new traders and I were developing our basic trading skills, we were learning to develop a narrative around the patterns of the market by listening to the calls and responses of the more experienced traders. Market chatter, as I call it, is an important device for forming interpretations about market fluctuations. I use the word "chatter" because of the ephemeral nature of the conclusions that such talk engenders. This background communication is part of the "ecologies of evaluative principles" of the trading room (Beunza and Stark, 2002). The importance of market chatter lies in the collective construction of unstable interpretations. These weak narratives supply interpretive logics for the market's movements.

In my cohort, Jason and Paul were the most prolific chatterers. In a process that was at once competitive and cooperative, they exchanged commentary and tips back and forth across the aisle that separated them. They assessed and reassessed the market's movements in relation to their positions: "I'd get out of there, the bid's about to disappear." "The offer is weak." "The Bund is moving, watch out in the Schatz." They commented on the pace and depth of the numbers, trying to evaluate the forces shaping the rise and fall of the digits. Market chatter does not produce a definitive explanation of the action on the screen. The uncertainty and instability of the commentary paralleled the constant fluctuation of the market.

Comparing positions is a central part of market chatter. Traders compare deals with each other, or simply tell the other traders their positions to confirm their decisions or seek help in recalibrating their interpretations. This information is not usually shouted across the room, but shared between traders at the same desk. At the desk across the aisle from my own, Freddie, a former pit trader, was flailing through the transition to screen-based trading. The three traders who shared his desk were helping Freddie sharpen his skills of interpreting the market. They would identify actors and significant changes in the market. They showed Freddie how to spot big traders in the market by watching how the bid/ask increased or decreased. If a trader changed his opinion of the market's direction and moved his orders, the bid number would drop by a large, round amount, such as 500 contracts. The more experienced traders encouraged Freddie to accumulate knowledge of the strategies of other players in the market by watching the changing quantities. Jason and Paul would pick up on their remarks and discuss it between themselves. The younger traders would most often simply reproduce the interpretations of Martin, the room's most successful trader, as their own. The chatter at the desk assisted Freddie, Jason, and Paul in forming their own interpretative strategies.

Market chatter does not always assist the traders who listen to it. It can also be used as a tactic to undermine the others' confidence. The confinement of an individual to his own screen and the faceless nature of screen-based trading create opportunities for savvy traders to supply misinformation to the room. The trades on the screen are anonymous, so a trader can simply misrepresent his interpretations in chatter to gain information about the others' positions and opinions. Martin, the object of envy for most Perkins Silver traders, fed his coworkers his own exaggerated reactions. He would gasp as if his gains had been decimated by a market move only to reveal minutes later, as he headed triumphantly out the door for the day, that he'd pocketed enormous profits on the trade. He faked panicked reactions to market events, hoping to fluster the other traders into chattering about their own positions. His status in the room meant that his opinions could confirm or cast doubt on the others' abilities to read market action.

Despite hints available from the environment of the Perkins Silver dealing room, the information located within the boundaries of the terminal retained the focus of traders' interpretive energies. This absorption is pronounced in Perkins Silver's Chicago dealing room. Joshua Geller, the head of trader training, called me in, worried that the London room had given a distorted picture of the market chatter and social nature of online dealing. When I arrived at the Chicago office, he led me to the trading floor, where about thirty traders sat in silence staring at their screens. "I try to get them to make some noise," he told me. But their attention remained concentrated on their screens. During my visit, Alan Greenspan was scheduled to speak to Congress, and Geller turned on the trading room television set. The traders shrieked at him to turn it off and then compromised for a lowered volume. The preference of this set of traders was that the informational environment remains restricted to the numbers in front of them. The screen provides the primary source of information for electronic trading.

For both the London and Chicago screen traders, the majority of players with whom the Perkins Silver traders exchanged lay beyond the boundaries of the Perkins Silver room. Traders on the screen are anonymous, as each individual's actions are represented within the aggregate numbers of the bids and offers. This aggregation narrows the opportunities to understand the intentions of other individual traders. There is no access to these individuals' strategies that traders can leverage for their own profits. Yet the social context of competition is crucial for traders to form narratives of market action that offer an explanation for the market's behavior. When denied the social information of competition and strategy so easily available in the pits, the Perkins Silver traders constructed social scenarios to explain the movements of the market.

Who Plays in the Numbers?

The Perkins Silver traders learned to look for key players who hide in the rhythms and the sizes of the changing bids and offers. The traders at Freddie's desk were trying to help him notice and collect this kind of information about the social content of the market. These characters are most often ideal types that traders construct based on trading styles and risk-taking strategies. Traders locate these characters in the swiftly moving bid and offer numbers, creating a conceptual sketch of the market as a field of specific competitors. Drawing this field establishes a narrative space of competition into which they can insert their own strategies.

The most persistent character was called the Spoofer. The Spoofer used large quantities of bids or offers to create the illusion that there was more demand to buy or pressure to sell than the "true" bids and offers represented. The Spoofer manipulated the weight of the numbers to force the market to go in his favor. Traders learned to identify a spoofer by watching changes in the aggregate number of bids or offers on the screen creating a novel strategy for profit. By riding the tail of a spoofer, a small trader can make money on market direction. Traders who dealt in large contract sizes aspired to take out the Spoofer by calling his bluff, selling into his bid and waiting for him to balk. There was great symbolic capital attached to taking out a spoofer by matching wits with this high-risk player. Taking out the Spoofer showed the prowess of a trader in one-to-one combat.

Eliminating the Spoofer has the effect of enforcing the informational transparency of the bid/ask numbers. Although there is nothing illegal about the Spoofer's maneuver of supplementing the numbers with the weight of his bid or offer, the perceived deception of the Spoofer's tactic lies in the fact that he undermines the verisimilitude of the bid/ask representation. The trader who takes out the Spoofer returns the market to the true bid and offer by eliminating the distortion. The Spoofer attempts to post bids and offers to manipulate the market, an intention that disrupts the abilities of other traders to interpret market numbers with their usual tools. With the Spoofer eliminated, traders can once again use their interpretive techniques with confidence.

But the Perkins Silver traders had a special respect for this character who tried to bend the market to his will. One Perkins Silver trader chattered about a figure he believed to be particularly skillful: "The Spoofer knows what he's doing. He's good. He's a real trader. He must be an Essex boy." His statement links skill and an aggressive style of trading to the Spoofer's membership in a group to which most of the Perkins Silver traders belonged: the residents of Essex County. In the 1980s, many newly wealthy traders moved to this region just to the east of London after the City began to open the doors of their trading rooms to working-class men from east and south London. Essex was a locus of identity for Perkins Silver traders who understood their trading prowess to be connected to their social origins.

Traders identified a second set of characters within the bid and offer numbers. These characters were based on the groupings of traders they perceived as their closest competitors. In the market for German bond futures, the groups that the "Essex boys" competed with were "the Germans" and "Chicago." English Essex boys constructed daily nationalist battles with their German and Chicago counterparts. They drew on their own British and urban identities as Essex boys or streetwise London lads to do combat with their Chicago and Frankfurt counterparts on a market that operates on foreign territory: the German treasury bond futures market.

The language that the traders used to identify these groups linked local identities with trading styles. The Germans were closely associated with an imagined set of national qualities such as dishonesty and inflexibility. The Essex boys suspected them of collaborating with their government to gain market advantages, especially in what is perceived as the absence of valued street-smart trading skills. The Perkins Silver traders often griped that the timing of market movements conveyed that the Germans had inside information from the Bundesbank or the banks of the Konsortium, the group that sets rates for German bonds. The Germans were the targets of the Perkins Silver traders' narratives in the morning hours between 7:00 and 1:00 London time, when the Essex boys and the Germans were seen to be the majority of players in the market.

This changed daily at 1:00, when Chicago "wakes up." Unlike the Germans, Chicago was not identified with the national government of the United States. Instead, Chicago traders were identified as a collective, always spoken of as the name of the city where financial futures trading originated. Perkins Silver traders admired the Chicago group for their aggressive style of speculation. Often, the markets were said to be "more interesting" after 1:00. Several of the most successful traders had license to work whenever they wanted as long as they continued to turn in large profits; they opted to arrive shortly before 1:00 and trade in the afternoon until 4:00, when the Essex boys at Perkins Silver and other firms started to leave their trading terminals for the day. These traders claimed that the afternoon hours gave the best opportunities for competition because Chicago brought larger volumes and more skillful trading to the market.

Chicago's involvement in the market also gave clues to the identities and strategies of yet another set of actors in the markets. In the Perkins Silver dealing room, a cable line connected Perkins Silver to the pits in Chicago. When the bond futures pits in Chicago were open for business, a speaker on the Perkins Silver floor funneled the bids, offers, and final prices into the dealing room. A man with a flat-voweled Midwestern accent called out the bids and offers and occasionally the identity of a bank. The Perkins Silver traders derided the predictability of the big financial houses' strategies. When the nasal voice called out "Merrill's a seller," the reaction was jaded. "Did you hear that, Billy, Merrill's selling." Billy then responded in mock surprise, "Yeah, fancy that." In fact, Merrill Lynch's selling became an ongoing joke in the room. This information oriented the Perkins Silver traders to the players in the market and added to the notion that these actors were consistent. These clues helped traders imagine and identify the patterns of action in the market.

The social information that traders construct is not limited to identifying individual actors and their strategies. Traders considered the market as a whole to have convictions and sentiments. They searched within the numbers to understand these states of market affect. For Perkins Silver traders, the first task of the morning was trying to understand the mood of the market. Traders gained access to this information by "testing" the market. They sold into the bid to see how easily the market would absorb their trades. A market with strong conviction would be able to absorb the pressure from the sale without a shift in the bid/ask. The competing traders remained convinced that their interpretation of the market was correct. They were willing to ignore a signal that another trader believed that the market would fall. If the test did not change the composition of the bid/ask, the trader established that there was confidence that the market would rise. He would likely buy contracts in anticipation of this climb. If the traders immediately withdrew from the bid, the Perkins Silver trader discerned that there was only a fragile belief in the interpretation that the market would rise.

Traders took short-term losses to make these tests, but the managers of Perkins Silver valued gaining information about market sentiment with this method. They trusted that the method would help traders make correct interpretations of the market's direction and, therefore, secure profits. Andrew Blair, the Perkins Silver risk manager, said that he is always nervous if he sees that the company is making money in the early hours of any market. Traders must "pay the price of admission" to understand what lies beyond the surface representation of the bid/ask.

Losing money to gain information was not unique to the morning test. A trader who bought a large number of contracts in expectation of a market rise is said to "get run over" when the market reversed its direction. But this loss is also not entirely negative. A loss produced by a strong trend could signal the market sentiment that the contract was overpriced. The trader then had an opportunity to take advantage of this information. In the words of Joshua Geller, a Perkins Silver manager, losing money to the market provides a "free look" at dimensions of the market that are not visible in the market numbers. The market may be skittish or stolid, immediately giving in to pressure to sell or standing firm. This metaphor of sight exposes the contradictions within the ideal of informational transparency. In the methods Joshua taught, traders used the numbers of the market embedded in the technological design to unearth information about the strategies and characters that populate the market. Although the surface of the interface reduces the market to a set of visual cues, traders can use the patterns of the market and strategies for gathering social information to understand more about the bids and offers than the numbers alone can show.

INTERPRETATION AND TECHNOLOGY

Technology shapes the foundations of financial knowledge. The recent transition from pit to screen-based technologies forces futures traders to retool their skills for reading and interpreting the market, for each technology creates a particular informational matrix in which some techniques and strategies of action are more effective than others.

Traders do not passively consume the representations of the market that pit and screen technologies provide. Market representations are shaped within the conflicts and tensions among market ideals, technologies, and the problems of practice. The designers of market systems work to give material form to the ideal of informational transparency by stripping market technologies of social content. Software design and market architects aim to purify the practice of exchange through microlevel market planning. Yet, because traders rely on their knowledge of competitors to create profit-making strategies, they search out specific information about the other actors in the market. These can be their neighbors in the pit, the Chicago and German traders whom London speculators imagine in the numbers, or the market itself as an actor with affect and intention. The form of technology defines not only where traders look for this social information, but also what they can find in the numbers.

Tensions between technological rationalization and situated action are fertile ground for ethnographers. These intersections contain the materials for a more grounded approach to the analysis of technological influence and reach. But there are dangers in this kind of investigation. Narratives of progressive rationalization from social theory fit neatly with the ideals and aims of technology designers and financial exchange managers. There is reason to be suspicious of this neat fit. A close examination of traders' practices and information technologies can break down the analytical complicity with native discourses of rationalization, illustrating instead how technologies and forms of creative action animate economic life.

At the same time, discourses and strategies of rationalization are seminal artifacts for the design and implementation of information technology systems and financial markets. Numbers operate as critical materials for rationalization, but numbers are not always consumed as designers of technological systems intend. Traders who use financial technologies do not take up numbers as objective descriptions of supply and demand. In the context of both open-outcry and screen-based technologies, traders seek out nonquantitative information located within the market numbers. They find and exploit the social, where there seem to be only noninterpretive facts. Traders prosper from constructing knowledge strategies at the junction of market numbers and their material presentation.

Flexible interpretation rather than formal calculation characterizes the styles of reasoning common in financial futures markets, both in the pits and on the screen. In contemporary trading rooms, sentiments, actors, and numbers of the market are always in flux. Traders know that market numbers carry social content that cannot be computed. Searching for the hidden values and phantom figures that lurk behind the numbers is the anchoring activity in a global marketplace where the only certainty is instability.

NOTES

1 Futures contracts are standardized, binding agreements to buy or sell a commodity at a given future date and price. They are *derivatives*, contracts that gain their value from a market in an underlying product. The traders at the CBOT and Perkins Silver I discuss here trade in futures on government bonds.

2 I see both open-outcry and electronic trading as socio-technical arrangements that layer the material technologies—the architecture of the trading pits and the digital trading screens—with the specific skills for operating with them. I also draw on Claude Fischer's (1992) user-centered approach for understanding technological systems. In his book about the introduction of telephones in America, Fischer argues against technological determinist framings, showing that information technologies do not have qualities of their own that operate independently of users. Similarly, the

speed and transparency of financial technologies do not inhere in information technologies that support them. Technologies are always imbricated with the day-to-day practices of users.

3 The narrative of progressive rationalization is, of course, most familiar to us from the work of Max Weber. In *Science as a Vocation* he bluntly states, "The fate of our times is characterized by rationalization and intellectualization" (Gerth and Mills, 1946, 155). Simmel (1907/1990) also famously wrote of the rationalizing nature of money. For this essay, it is important to make a distinction between the power of rationalization as an ideal in the financial industry that parallels Weber's and Simmel's accounts and an anthropological analysis of rationalization that takes this ideal as a social fact.

4 The social context of financial interpretation is evident in the friendships and feverish affect of pit traders. Looking first at the face-to-face context of open-outcry markets, where the density of social life is overwhelming, we can observe and become attuned to the social dimensions of online calculations. This sensitivity is especially important where self-conscious rationalization has actively sought to eliminate the social as an element of economic calculations. The problem is not one of a dualistic division between face-to-face and online transactions. Rather, the problem lies in how rationalized technological systems create a specific context for financial calculation.

5 I use the masculine pronoun for gender realism. The overwhelming majority of traders at the CBOT and Perkins Silver are men. In the time that I worked at the CBOT, the largest pit held six hundred traders; two were women. At Perkins Silver, before my training group entered the dealing room, there was one woman and sixty men.

6 The difference between the bid and ask is called the "spread." Ideally, the trader can make money buying at the bid and selling the offer, pocketing the difference, but this method of making money is not always available. Bids and offers theoretically represent the totality of supply and demand for a product in a given moment. Market participants must be able to see all the bids and offers in the market to evaluate market conditions accurately.

7 The CBOT created the pit structure to solve problems that arose as the market space became overcrowded with eager speculators. Originating in the agricultural trade of the Midwest, the CBOT was established by men trading certificates of grain ownership to be delivered several months down the line from farms in Nebraska, Iowa, or Illinois to the Chicago grain elevators (Cronon, 1991). By 1869, trading at the CBOT had become so popular and crowded that the speculators couldn't see all the bids and offers available. Market reporters complained in the pages of their daily papers that traders in search of better sightlines were climbing onto their desks and obstructing the reporters' vision. After trying out several shapes for a raised structure that would provide better views of the traders in the market, the CBOT introduced the octagonal pits in 1869 (Faloon, 1998).

8 In this sense, designers of market technologies resemble Rabinow's (1989) depiction of technicians of general ideas by putting into practice normative ideas of economic action. They are self-conscious intellectuals gravitating to and instantiating ideals of rationalization and designing economic abstractions to facilitate practices more closely resembling perfect competition.

9   In *We Have Never Been Modern* (1993), Bruno Latour discusses purification, the division of the social from the natural, as a hallmark of the modern constitution. Here, the numerical representation helps to rid the financial arena of social influence. With numbers, the economic sphere is construed as a space of natural competition.

10 All quotations are from my interview with Alan Lind, January 2001. "Alan Lind" is a pseudonym.

11 In *Plans and Situated Actions*, Lucy Suchman (1987) argues that purposeful action is "fundamentally concrete and embodied." Actions are "taken in the context of particular concrete circumstances." They are "situated" and not the outcome of a process of abstract planning.

12 I use "technological frame" to indicate the way that technology shapes the content it provides to the user. Wiebe Bijker has used the concept differently. In Bijker's work, technological frame describes "the ways in which relevant social groups attribute various meanings to an artifact" (Bijker, Hughes, and Pinch, 1999, 108).

13 Frank Knight (1922/1971), in his classic work *Risk, Uncertainty and Profit*, defines uncertainty as the condition of entrepreneurial profit. He states, "With uncertainty entirely absent, every individual being in possession of perfect knowledge of the situation, there would be no occasion for anything of the nature of responsible management or control of productive activity" (267). Knight's use of uncertainty highlights problems of judgment in economic action. I prefer to use "ambiguity" rather than "uncertainty" to underscore the many possible interpretations of a present situation. Traders could be considered *informational entrepreneurs* because they create interpretations of market direction out of this ambiguity. This follows Pat O'Malley's (2000) description of the *uncertain subjects* of neoliberalism rather than appealing to older formulations of entrepreneurship that fit within a paradigm of rational modernization.

14 Differences in opinions and interpretation yield opposing views. These contrasting outlooks on the future direction of the market allow for every buyer to meet a seller and every seller to find a buyer. At the same time, anticipating and acting on the presumed interpretations of other traders in the market is a widespread profit-making strategy. This common practice can create a self-fulfilling prophecy in price action.

15 Wayne Baker (1984a) has shown how, in large pits, traders break up into trading areas within the pit, undermining the ideal of competitiveness. The noise of trading and potential errors when trading with a physically distant partner encourage traders to focus their attentions on the area closest to them.

16 This organization around ideals of pure competition and associated notions about rational calculation are not restricted to the pits at the CBOT. Ira O. Glick (1957) showed how these principles worked in the egg futures market at the Board of Trade's cross-town rival, the Chicago Mercantile Exchange. The Chicago model of pit trading spread with the financial revolution of the 1980s and formed the basis for markets in other financial centers (Kynaston, 1997).

17 See Burton Malkiel's *A Random Walk Down Wall Street* (1996) and Peter Bernstein's *Capital Ideas* (1986) for a synopsis of the "random walk" in stock and commodities pricing and its implications for traders, investors, and financial theory. According to

Malkiel, "A random walk is one in which future steps or directions cannot be predicted on the basis of past actions. In the stock market, it means that short-run changes in stock prices cannot be predicted" (24).

18 The GUI that traders use at Perkins Silver is not the only GUI available. Members of Eurex have access to the exchange's stock GUI, a screen device that is also numerically based but visually more rigid than the E-trader model. Earlier GUIS, such as those for the now defunct CBOT Project A trading system, tried to replicate the face-to-face environment of the pit by associating names and personal trade histories with each exchange. The precursor to the Eurex exchange, the DTB, never operated with a pit system. Their electronic markets have always relied strictly on numbers.

19 The term "disintermediation" came into vogue in the 1980s as a way of describing the development of new instruments, such as mortgage-backed assets, that allowed companies to borrow directly from the market rather than going through a commercial lender. The techniques of disintermediation removed institutional linkages and drew companies to the "core" processes of the market. The same rationality is operative in the logic of reducing the market representation to numbers.

20 I was practicing a technique called spreading in ten-, five-, and two-year German treasury bond futures nicknamed the Bund, Bobl, and Schatz. Spreading is a technique that, in one of its forms, takes advantage of the difference in volatility between bonds of different durations. The price of a ten-year bond is more volatile than that of a two-year bond because the longer time frame introduces more opportunities for changing economic conditions and greater uncertainties. A spreader takes opposite positions in each of two instruments, using the more stable instrument to limit the loss potential of a position in the more volatile contract.

REAL TIME: UNWINDING TECHNOCRATIC
AND ANTHROPOLOGICAL KNOWLEDGE

In his classic midcentury critique of American politics, Theodore Roszak assails the "technocracy," "that society in which those who govern justify themselves by appeal to technical experts who, in turn, justify themselves by appeal to scientific forms of knowledge. And beyond the authority of science there is no appeal" (Roszak and Weiss, 1969, 8). Like other theorists of his time (e.g., Meynaud, 1969), Roszak follows Arendt (1976), Marcuse (1964), and Weber (M. Weber and Eisenstadt, 1968) to focus on the way technocratic power is "the product of knowledge and extraordinary performance" (Winner, 1977, 139). Recent work revives this tradition to show, for example, how the assumptions and inner workings of bureaucratic knowledge impede citizen participation (Espeland, 1994; F. Fischer, 1990).

The location of the critique of technocratic power in the categories of bureaucratic knowledge has a long-standing and diverse theoretical pedigree. Michel Foucault (1991, 92), for example, has shown how the conceptualization of the knowledge practices of government as distinct from an entity known as economy is an emblem of modern governmentality. Paul Rabinow (1989) and Frank Fischer (1990) describe technocracy in terms of particular practices of reason. From a different political point of view, the defender of free markets F. A. Hayek decried bureaucratic planning as the instantiation of the engineer mentality of the technocrat, who believes he has "complete control of the particular little world with which he is concerned, a man whose supreme ambition is to turn the world round him into an enormous machine" (1975, 101–102).

For both Hayek and Foucault, the power of the knowledge-based critique of technocracy lay in the identification of the limits of technocratic knowledge. Foucault, borrowing from Adam Smith, argued that the powerful mystery of the market as an "invisible hand" was that it remained invisible to the planner as much as to the market participant (Gordon, 1991, 12). For Hayek, likewise, the repeated failure of bureaucratic planning was simply a case of the larger failure of economic theory. The mathematical abstraction of economic planning distorted the true complexity of the market, and hence such planning could not possibly make accurate predictions about the future (Bockman and Eyal, 2002). This was a fundamentally temporal problem: bureaucrats were by definition analyzing events that had already transpired, and hence economic planning was continually behind the real-time movements of the market (Hayek, 1952). In much the same way, contemporary critics have been particularly interested in the limitations of technocratic knowledge (Latour, 1996; Mitchell, 2002). Students of risk, for example, critique the efforts of scientists and planners to quantify, regulate, or plan around the unplannable (Beck, 1992; Giddens, 1991).[1] Ethnographic studies document the points at which bureaucracy's targets of intervention lose faith in, and fashion responses to, the ideals of technocratic knowledge such as "transparency" (West and Sanders, 2003).

Ethnographers of technocracy have emphasized the way these very failures become the engine of more technocracy, however—the way these failures create "gaps in the form" (Riles, 2000, 161), further "targets for intervention" (Castel, 1991, 288). James Ferguson (1990, 256) points out that failure is the norm rather than the exception in development projects, but that the failures of development, in turn, have their own productive effects: "Alongside the institutional effect of expanding bureaucratic state power is the conceptual or ideological effect of depoliticizing both poverty and the state." Science and technology studies scholars have technologically extended this last point to demonstrate how bureaucrats overcome conceptual limits by inventing devices that do the work of technocracy. Bruno Latour (1996), for example, has described Aramis, a transportation system for the city of Paris developed by French technocrats, as a continuation of bureaucratic politics by other means. Fabian Muniesa (2000b) describes a technology similar to the one at issue in this essay, an automated robot built to match trades at the Paris stock exchange, as "moral architecture" developed to do what planning could not: root out corruption in trading. Muniesa goes on to show how, in the end, the robot's algorithmic principles in many respects reproduced both the inequities in the trading system and the knowledge practices of the bureaucrats who sought to regulate them.

The bureaucrats who are the subject of this essay, officials at the Bank of

Japan, Japan's central bank, are responsible for the "payments system" by which funds move from one bank account to another in the economy. As such, they would seem to be archetypal producers of technocratic knowledge in this sense. Max Weber (1925/1966, 325) himself identified central bankers' manipulation of procedures such as the workings of the payments system as examples of bureaucratic "domination." Faith in technocracy and careful attention to its calibration are hallmarks of Japanese politics in the twentieth century (Dimock, 1968; Koschmann, 2002; Morris-Suzuki, 1994; Okimoto, 1989; Tobioka, 1993; Traweek, 1999; Tsutsui, 1998). Moreover, recent journalistic accounts of Japanese bureaucracy are full of the very critiques of technocratic knowledge practices now prevalent in the anthropology of technocracy. One recent volume, for example, asserts that "power in Japan is masked" and emphasizes that the failures of Japanese bureaucracy are the product of a culturally specific but ultimately misguided faith in bureaucracy (Mikuni and Murphy, 2002, 38).[2]

More important, in the aftermath of the Asian financial crisis of the late 1990s and the consciousness of so-called systemic risk it amplified, the failures of technocratic knowledge that anthropologists and social theorists identify were very much at the forefront of these technocrats' own minds. In the face of both the inability of sophisticated economic models to predict economic crisis or provide solutions to recent market problems (Eisenbeis, 1997) and current efforts by global banks to privatize the payment system and hence to do away with bureaucratic regulation altogether ("Is There a Private Global Central Bank in Your Future?," 1997), these central bankers were fearful of their own powerlessness vis-à-vis the market they were expected to manage. As I will describe, these technocrats resolved this crisis, in their own conception, by creating a "real-time" machine that, they imagined, would obviate the need for planning altogether.

The critical anthropological vision of technocracy as a particular knowledge practice that inherently faces its own limits elucidates much about the character of the particular technocracy I will describe. Indeed, as I suggest, this thesis replicates and amplifies a discourse about bureaucracy often heard among these technocrats themselves. The aim of this essay, therefore, is not to dispute this insight but to point to other aspects of technocratic practice that become impervious to ethnographic analysis when one begins from this point of view. Specifically, by focusing on the content or categories of bureaucratic knowledge, these critiques obscure the question of how something comes to count as "knowledge" or as "not knowledge" in the first place. This in turn has consequences for the critical project: by accepting technocrats' claims that a (conceptual or mechanical) tool is a tool, and proceeding to inquire as to what kind of tool is at issue and what its effects might be, anthropologists commit themselves to a critique of technocratic knowledge premised on showing the artificial, determinate, and situated nature of seemingly transparent and universal categories such as Economy that, as Timothy Mitchell (2002, 4) points out, "leaves the world intact. Intentionally or not, it depends upon maintaining the absolute difference between representations and the world they represent."

To address this ethnographic limitation will require more than simply filling in the gaps in the ethnographic record: as I suggest in the conclusion, to take on these matters will require attention to the points of affinity between technocratic and social scientific knowledge practices that provide the ground for shared premises about the nature of knowledge between anthropologist and technocrat. It will require unwinding the terms and practices of technocratic knowledge (anthropological and bureaucratic). And here, the efforts of the bureaucrats I describe to unwind their own technocratic practices may provide something of a model.

TECHNOCRACY IN CRISIS

By the time of my fieldwork in the late 1990s, technocracy was by all accounts a practice in crisis. After almost ten years of economic recession, the media, the academy, and the public at large were losing faith in the utopian promises of technocracy.[3] Most important, bureaucrats had their own doubts about their ability to plan. What exactly was the source of these planners' disquiet about technocracy—what had failed, from bureaucrats' point of view? A look at the perceived failures of one technocratic project, the design of the Japanese payment system, offers some insights.

Payment systems are a sociotechnical achievement of the first order (Millo et al., 2003). Administered by central bankers in each country, they are the digital, legal, and institutional apparatus by which money is actually transferred from one bank account to another. Every day, banks transfer through the Japanese payment system 300 trillion yen (approximately US$2.5 trillion) in approximately 20,000 transactions that represent the aggregate of millions of individual orders (Bank of Japan, 2003). They do this by instructing the Bank of Japan's payment systems group to debit or credit the account they hold with the central bank's electronic clearing system, known as BOJ NET.[4] At the time of my fieldwork, the BOJ's Payment Systems Division was headed by a bureaucrat in his late 40s, a graduate of the University of Tokyo and Harvard's Kennedy School of Government, whom I will call Sato.

Bureaucrats like Sato commanded considerable prestige and respect (Koh, 1989; McVeigh, 1998), although they were also the targets of jealousy and resentment of their social privilege. Almost all were graduates of the best Japanese universities' departments of law or economics and had scored high on a grueling civil service exam. The bureaucrats I knew were ardently, if paternalistically, devoted to the mission of improving welfare by carefully managing the economy. They believed in their own intellectual capacities and technical skills, and they also shared a sense of responsibility for the consequences of their mistakes. Most of the bureaucrats I knew also confessed a certain Keynesian ambivalence about the market's tendency toward self-destabilization and hence believed in the need for intervention, at the margins, through planning.[5] They also were painfully aware of the limits of their actual authority over market participants (Haley, 1987).

The Payment Systems Division staff recently had become anxiously aware of a new concern: "systemic risk." At the time of my fieldwork, BOJ NET was a "designated time net settlement system" (hereafter, Designated Time). Banks accumulated obligations to one another throughout the day and then, at a designated time each day, calculated the balance of who owed what to whom. This "netting mechanism," engineered by the Payment Systems Division, was perceived by its architects as a small technocratic triumph, an example of the contributions of planning to the smooth functioning of the market (G. C. Kaufman, 1996, 826). Planners reasoned that it made little sense for Bank A to raise the funds to pay Bank B 1 billion yen at 10:00 AM, for example, if Bank B needed to pay Bank A 2 billion yen in a separate transaction at 2:00 PM the same day. The central bankers therefore had laboriously worked out the details of a system by which banks extended each other credit throughout the day and settled all their transactions at once, at a designated time. In this sense, Designated Time was a common example of technocratic progress through conceptual and institutional systemic integration: to its engineers, Designated Time was a more conceptually sophisticated system because it was premised on the understanding that net balances were functionally equivalent to the sum total of individual transactions. In institutional terms, also, it represented bureaucrat-led coordination in the service of the common good.

As they contemplated their Designated Time system, however, these planners had recently noticed that the very interconnectedness they had so carefully engineered created a new danger of its own: if one bank was unable to meet its obligations to pay others at the designated time, this in turn could leave others without the cash to meet their own obligations, and hence create a "domino effect" (Folkerts-Landau, Garber, and Schoemaker, 1996, 1) that would lead to "systemic failure" (Bank of Japan, 1996). Although "systemic risk" indexed bureaucratic failure, its very discovery was in itself a kind of technocratic achievement, from the planners' point of view. It could be detected only through careful contemplation of the economic system as an integrated and objectified whole (Douglas and Wildavsky, 1982; Riles, 2000; Stinchcombe, 2001). They would not expect market participants, who in their view did not think about the market in systemic terms, to have an adequate appreciation of systemic risk.

I mentioned earlier that anthropologists and social theorists who point to the limits of technocracy most often locate these limits in the particular substance and character of technocratic knowledge. It is a view that the bureaucrats I knew largely shared. These bureaucrats often described themselves and their place in the market in terms of the special qualities of their knowledge. In particular, as they went about recalibrating the market, planners imagined two sides (Strathern, 1988). On one side, bureaucrats, but also academics and some prominent lawyers and executives, created and maintained systems through planning.[6] These persons were proximate outsiders, in bureaucrats' own conception. They worked at the threshold of the market they enabled and protected, looking in. On the other side, actual market participants acted within the market but did not think about it in systemic terms (Knorr Cetina and Bruegger, 2002b; Miyazaki, 2003). Who was a market participant and who was a builder of the market varied situationally. At one moment, a bank executive might epitomize the market participant; at another, he (all such executives I knew were men) might be imaged as an institution builder. In this fairly rigid and formalistic sociological view, therefore, what differentiated the two sides was the character of their knowledge.

Moreover, if for Hayek, as for Foucault, the failures of technocracy reflected the limits of economic reason, for these bureaucrats, systemic risk drew attention to the same. At the time of my fieldwork, central bankers in Japan and elsewhere were coming to view systemic risk as ultimately incalculable in economic terms. The problem was not simply computational complexity; some of the risks involved—uncertainty about what law might apply to a particular bank failure or how that law would be interpreted, for example—were altogether outside the realm of what could be quantified, in these technocrats' view. Like Hayek (1952), they struggled with the temporal incongruity between the retrospective methods of positivist science and the prospective demands of the market (see Miyazaki, 2003). As another payments systems expert, Robert Eisenbeis (1997, 50), director of research at the American Federal Reserve in Atlanta, put it, "Systems, instruments, and markets are evolving faster than the political entities can bring their various rules and regulations into harmony."

Yet, bureaucrats' own claims for or against their knowledge practices notwithstanding, this focus on the inner workings of economic knowledge does not fully capture the character of the crisis of planning these bureaucrats confronted. For the bureaucrats I knew, two other kinds of problems complemented and even superseded problems of economic calculability. The first of these was in a sense a product of the very sociological thinking about the market these bureaucrats embraced. In the past five years, bureaucrats had come under repeated attack from domestic and foreign media, politicians, and academics for failing to maintain the proper bureaucratic distance from the market—for muddying the logic of two sides. Ideological calls for "freeing the invisible hand" charged that Japanese bureaucrats were coddling the banks, stepping in to save them from bankruptcy when market logic demanded that they be left to fail (M. E. Porter and Takeuchi, 1999, 77). Hence, the banks did not "internalize the costs" of their inefficient behavior, nor did they take seriously the central bank's own threats to impose "market discipline," its threats to refuse to intervene in moments of crisis. The point here was not so much the weaknesses of economic knowledge as the personal weaknesses of the technocrat: his excessive intimacy with the market and his inability to control his own urge for benevolent intervention.

And there was another source to the crisis. As numerous observers have commented, Japanese bureaucrats maintain elaborate contacts with their classmates working in the industries they regulate (Schaede, 1995).[7] At the Bank of Japan, these relations were actively promoted through research fellowships for employees of major banks to spend a year working at the central bank, through informal study groups of bureaucrats, lawyers, and academics of roughly the same age, and through more formal committees of bureaucrats, academics, and representatives of industry (*shingikai*). Bank officials went to elaborate ends to cultivate these relationships; senior bank staff told me that one of the purposes of sending young employees to pursue advanced degrees at elite institutions overseas was to give them an opportunity to develop close friendships with other Japanese of their own age. In the late 1990s, however, a number of corruption scandals focused on bureaucrats' practice of drinking and dining with their clients. At stake were bureaucrats' personal relations. Young bureaucrats I knew roundly criticized their seniors for what they saw as an outdated style of governance, the opposite of "rationality" (see Kelly, 1986). At the end of an evening at a local restaurant, after dividing the bill down to the last yen and then requesting a receipt demonstrating that she had done so, Shimizu, a Bank of Japan employee in her early 30s, attacked what she termed the "arrogance and hegemonic behavior" of those who turned bureaucratic problems into personal relations and vice versa. Their error, she explained, was their failure to "keep things objective." Accepting entertainment from clients represented a deviation from proper bureaucratic practice, that is, the procurement and dissemination of knowledge on a rational basis.

If Shimizu's critique cast corruption in knowledge terms—as a problem of rationality and objectivity—those bureaucrats who sought to defend themselves against charges of corruption also cast their relationships with market participants as instrumental to bureaucratic knowledge. Central bankers regularly "made use" of personal friendships to "collect information," I was repeatedly told (Murakami and Rohlen, 1987). Their task depended on, indeed, principally consisted in gathering and dispersing information, on knowing the intimate details of what was happening within each institution before it happened, and coordinating a solution before problems mushroomed out of control, they lamented (Pempel and Muramatsu, 1995, 68). Often, these bureaucrats defended their actions in terms of neoclassical economic theories of market knowledge in which, because the market immediately absorbs knowledge into price, knowledge that is publicly held is by definition already worthless. If they waited to address the market's problems until everything had become publicly known and stock prices had plummeted, they would surely be blamed for failing to act quickly enough, they argued.

Yet the instrumental rubric of knowledge acquisition at work in both the critiques of corruption and the defenses of bureaucratic relations did not do justice to the character of these relationships, as I observed them. First, political scientists and legal scholars have repeatedly noted that relationships between Japanese bureaucrats and their clients serve another instrumental purpose: where the legal authority of Japanese bureaucrats to impose their policies is weak, personal obligation often substitutes for legal obligation (Haley, 1987). But what is not accounted for in this alternative instrumental explanation is the pleasure bureaucrats derived from friendship. Encounters between bureaucrats and clients proceeded according to a pattern. During the day, the two sides held formal encounters on government premises.[8] Sometimes these meetings took place in front of the division manager, who sat at his desk pretending to read the newspaper as his junior carefully executed the interview. Usually, on the night of the meeting, however, the clients would treat the junior bureaucrat to dinner (with his superior's tacit knowledge and approval), and after several rounds of drinks and conversation about a standard set of light topics, the conversation would turn back to the matter of that day (see Allison, 1994). Both sides would take pleasure in breaking through the boundaries of formality they had created for themselves earlier and "speaking in a straightforward way." Promises would be made that would serve as the basis of later action.

In response to the new discourse of accountability in the press, and among bureaucrats themselves (Gupta, 1995; Jean-Klein, 2002), the Bank of Japan instituted a new policy: henceforth, every meeting with clients would need to be cleared in advance with a manager and documented after the fact. The ironic effect of this policy was to place me, as an ethnographer, truly in the position of the participant-observer, for the difficulties I would encounter in maintaining relations with and seeking information from bureaucrats as a result of this policy were much like the difficulties they encountered every day in their relations with their clients. We shared a kind of technocratic crisis; senior staff in particular complained of paralysis. Contacting market participants was the heart of what bureaucrats do, they began to claim (Holmes and Marcus, 2005a). Yet, under the new policy, contacts with market participants were limited to office meetings that produced formulaic answers to predetermined questions and in which the parties did not feel free to make quiet requests for favors or compromises. Failure was built into technocratic practice insofar as the very technology of bureaucratic action was the subversion of formality (see Valverde, 2003), of autonomy, of the sociology of two sides. This is what one senior bureaucrat meant when he lamented, "We don't know anything about the market anymore."

It is in this context of failure, apprehended as a failure of knowledge, that at the time of my fieldwork, the Payment Systems Division staff were planning to change their system entirely. Unlike the old Designated Time system, the new system, known as Real Time Gross Settlement (hereafter, Real Time), proposed to settle each transaction individually and in full, in real time, that is, at the very moment an order to transfer funds was given (Bank of Japan, 1998).[9]

As I noted earlier, ethnographies of bureaucracy, from anthropology to science studies, would predict that the payment system staff's discovery of systemic risk in the Designated Time system, and the wider crises of bureaucratic knowledge of which it was a part, would serve as an invitation to further planning projects, to building new systems. And indeed, as a result of the discovery of systemic risk, Division staff members were busy solving technical glitches, training market participants, testing their systems, and devising policies to handle contingencies as they had so many times before. Moreover, if, as Hayek suggests, planning was conceived as inherently one step behind the movements of the market, the sheer fact of moving to real-time transactions projected an aura of technocratic progress (see Weston, 2002). Staff members were fond of reminding me that Real Time constituted progress along another axis as well. Sato had first learned about Real Time at global conferences of central bankers from around the world. The move to Real Time was a "global trend" among central bankers (O. E. G. Johnson, 1998; Kodres, 1996), he emphasized, a small but crucial step toward ever-greater international "harmonization" (see Drucker, 1998).[10]

Indeed, using terms very close to those of science studies scholars, these bureaucrats talked of Real Time as a kind of step forward born out of the discovery of failure, that is, as a machine that synthesized law and technology to solve political problems surrounding the limits of economic knowledge. Real Time was for them a hybrid artifact. It demanded complex computer networks and programs, and one team in the Division devoted itself to such issues as improving the speed of data transfer and creating backup systems. But it also demanded new laws and regulations, new policies, new norms. Sato's ultimate objective was to write into the very architecture of the machine these standards of good market practice (Muniesa, 2000a).

Yet if bureaucrats presented Real Time as just another technocratic advance, on closer examination, there was something puzzling about it from this point of view. This was most apparent in the opposition Real Time generated among economists and market participants: employees of the banks that used the payments system, who by now had come to see how Designated Time saved them money, complained loudly that it would be far more costly to clear their transactions individually, in real time, because they would have to raise funds to meet each individual payment throughout the day. Economists, likewise, insisted that Designated Time was by far the wiser system because it saved money and avoided delays (Angelini, 1998; Kahn and Roberds, 1998; VanHoose, 1991). By settling each transaction in the "now" of Real Time, in other words, Real Time replaced the very systemic knowledge that was the hallmark of economic and technocratic intervention, and to which market participants by now had learned to submit, with millions of discrete and individualized units of rights and obligations.

Real Time was not so much a new machine, therefore, as the *unwinding* of systemic knowledge, a return to how things had been prior to the technocratic interventions that had produced Designated Time in the first place. In practice, Real Time was more like a fuse box than a supercomputer; henceforth, it would not be necessary to plan for systemic crises in the payment system because Real Time would keep each transaction separate and so prevent risk from spreading like falling dominoes through the system. Like the Bank's policy on contact with outsiders, in other words, Real Time represented a defensive strategy: it responded to bureaucrats' own doubts about their ability to plan for the market by minimizing the consequences of market failure. But Real Time was also more perpetual motion machine than lever (Crook, 2004); by giving up the system, the central bank was also giving up one important means of central bank intervention in the economy (Sato, 1998). Hence, there would be neither the need for nor the tools of technocratic intervention.

Real Time therefore did not so much solve a problem of knowledge or continue politics by other means as express a particular kind of agency and respond to a particular desire, a "peculiar sort of modesty" premised on "self-invisibility" (Haraway, 1997, 32), a desire for an endpoint to knowledge itself (Miyazaki and Riles, 2005). In this respect, Sato enthusiastically encouraged market participants to develop private solutions to clearing that would decrease their reliance on the central bank altogether. "Sometimes [market participants] say these issues should not be fixed as a market practice but through guidelines from the Bank of Japan, but we refuse. We say, we're going to prepare a very flat table. And what kinds of plates and saucers you put on it is your own work," he told me.

Yet, what most clearly defined Real Time as an endpoint to technocratic knowledge was what would happen to social relations under the new system. Ultimately, it was the impact of Real Time on the character of social relations that most interested Sato. He excitedly described how Real Time would encourage "self-responsibility" among market participants by requiring each to post collateral for the full value of their transactions in advance. Sato described in vivid detail how, under Designated Time, bankers could just sit in their offices smoking away until the time of settlement each day. Under the new system, however, every second would count, and they would be forced to become far more alert, efficient, and nimble in their thinking. The initial chaos of Real Time, Sato argued, would eventually give way to a deeper level of order guided by "market practice." The difference would be that this new order would emerge on its own, from the aggregation of the actions of individuals, rather than as an artifact of his planning. Social relations would cease to be tools, in other words, and would become objects in the market, defined precisely by the way they were *not* a target of technocratic intervention. It is difficult to imagine a more powerful fantasy of the abdication of technocratic knowledge than this image of turning one's own tools into their very opposite, an object in the market, on which one chooses not to act.

So far, I have shown that, like anthropologists of technocracy, these technocrats readily asserted that failures or faults of technocratic knowledge provided the impetus for further technocratic knowledge projects. In these technocrats' ideological vision, knowledge was additive: knowledge (and its failures) begat more knowledge. Yet I have emphasized how these knowledge claims occluded a number of other dimensions of technocratic practice. First, social relations, imagined as something outside and beyond knowledge, served, in bureaucrats' own view, as the very engine of technocratic knowledge and also its demise. But second, even this notion of the social occluded something else: friendship, valued for its own sake as well as for the way personal relations generated information. Third, I have sought to draw attention to another technocratic fantasy that exists alongside the fantasy of additive knowledge, like a kind of undertow: the fantasy of the endpoint to technocracy, of abdication of authority, of unwinding. The first step in my argument, therefore, is to suggest that ethnographers of technocracy take the moment of technocratic unwinding as seriously as they take moments of technocratic building and expansion.

NEEDS

Yet, after all the anxiety, the paralysis and the fantasy of unwinding knowledge and relations I have described, Sato surprised me one day, after we had talked of the technicalities of Real Time over many weeks, when he told me that he ultimately expected the relationship between the Bank of Japan and market participants to change very little. "We decided to let the market participants go where they like," he said, "but we think they will make the right choices, they will settle in an acceptable zone." To my suggestion that once cut loose, the banks might go too far—they might, for example, develop their own private clearing system that would eliminate the need for the central bank altogether—Sato responded with skepticism. He could always create incentives for them to come back to the clearing system. And if nothing else, they would clear through the central bank some of the time because they needed bank notes.

A need for bank notes? The reference to concrete, physical money was shocking in a world of electronic transfers and numbers on balance sheets. In fact, it was the first time in the course of my fieldwork that I had been made aware of how paper money entered the system of electronic accounts. No one had ever discussed it, and I had not thought about it. Paper money had been invisible from the point of view of the technocrats' knowledge practices and my own.

Slowly I became aware of other such artifacts of the unwinding of technocratic knowledge. As planning for Real Time reached its final stages, an executive of one of Japan's largest banks worried that "the biggest problem of all is the central bank's role: to provide liquidity during the daytime." What emerged for him from the purposeful unwinding of technocracy into Real Time I have described was a *need*. In the years of Designated Time, banks had relied on the fact that they did not need funds to settle their transactions until the end of the day, and the number of transactions had increased exponentially. Yet, if every transaction henceforth would have to be settled on the spot, banks needed liquidity—cash—to meet their obligations in real time. The effect of Real Time for bankers like this executive, then, was a move from an awareness of system and systemic risk to an awareness of liquidity—a move from knowledge of systems to something of a different order, needs. The Payment Systems Division staff likewise repeatedly drew my attention to these needs. One team member emphasized needs in the form of negative balances that member banks would incur in their accounts with the Bank of Japan between the hours of 9 AM and 5 PM each day.

This conversion of risks into needs is not outside the technocratic vocabulary of planning and systems I have described. Traditional philosophical justifications for the welfare state and its planning, for example, are grounded in the provision of individual and social needs (Walzer, 1984). In fact, it is possible to understand the larger technocratic vocabulary of risk management that Real Time deployed as heir to an earlier, equally technocratic vocabulary of (social) needs (Valverde, personal communication, June 24, 2002). In the academic context, likewise, Marshall Sahlins (1996) has shown, with respect to both anthropological functionalism and neoclassical economic analysis, that the corollary to social scientists' fascination with self-perpetuating systems is a notion of needs as "pure materiality," something outside the system that renders it eternally necessary, as when society is a function of biological needs, or markets are a function of needs for liquidity. I want to suggest, therefore, that anthropologists think of systems and needs as a kind of pair. But what is important is that unlike knowledge and social relations, or bureaucracy and corruption, this particular pair is not immediately apprehensible as such by its users (technocrat or academic). Needs are not a "subject" in the anthropology of bureaucracy, for example. My ethnographic claim, in other words, is that the notion of needs works as a counterpart to technocratic knowledge that is readily available within the technocratic idiom and yet not immediately apprehensible as such.

Once needs become visible ethnographically as a technocratic resource, it will be apparent to readers that the emergence of needs at this moment of unwinding technocratic knowledge, in turn, created a new technocratic opportunity. In particular, from the point of view of needs for liquidity, Real Time represented a reassertion of technocratic authority in a different guise. The movement to Real Time was a movement from an older system of interdependence, in which the banks extended credit to one another, to a system in which each bank became individually dependent on the central bank alone to fulfill its intraday credit needs. "We are prepared to supply intraday overdraft to support RTGS [Real Time Gross Settlement]," Sato told me with a mixture of gravity and triumph, as I voiced market participants' concern about the need for liquidity. The Bank of Japan would loan funds to the users of its payment system—allow them to keep negative balances until the end of the day—so they could meet their obligations in real time. But this was easier said than done. As the bank executive quoted above told me, "[The central bank] has 3 trillion yen in all the accounts put together. But 30 trillion yen is needed to keep this system going." In other words, the banks' needs for liquidity also highlighted the Bank of Japan's own needs—and the difficulties it would have meeting the needs of its charges. The Bank of Japan emerged as a silent provider of needs that drew its strength from a kind of explicit weakness, coupled with the performance of the awesome feat of providing the impossible but acutely necessary at the moment of need.[11]

But if it is possible to see provision for needs as the continuation of technocratic politics by other means, in much the same way that science and technology studies scholars have shown bureaucratic technologies to be, it is important to take note of how this was accomplished. It was not the content of technocratic knowledge that did the work here, as critics of technocracy from Foucault to Hayek would suggest, but rather the stopping and unwinding of technocratic knowledge and its replacement by a kind of action (the provision of needs) recognizable from inside the practice of technocracy but occluded from technocrats' view by their own knowledge-based claims. This unwinding was possible because of the particular features of needs as an entity already inside the sphere of technocratic practice but also outside, utterly unrelated, irrelevant to technocratic knowledge—pure materiality, as Sahlins puts it. That is, the problem of needs obviated all earlier concerns and anxieties surrounding the logic of two sides for bureaucrats as for politicians, market participants, and journalistic and academic observers alike—it simply fell outside the scope of representational practice.[12] Unlike the technocrats' transformation of social relations into knowledge, the transformation of risk into needs did not become an object of contemplation or critique. I never heard people like Shimizu, the bank employee who critiqued her superiors' indulgence in social relations, make an issue of needs, for example. And Sato's efforts to provide liquidity did not pose a contradiction, in his own mind, with his commitment to maintaining the proper bureaucratic distance from the market. In other words, the power of needs as technocratic practice was that it was not particularly perceptible as technocratic strategy to technocrats themselves. I surmise that it is precisely because the logic of needs is so much of a piece with the logic of systems—because needs are so intimate to knowledge—that they became available as a place at which technocratic knowledge itself disappeared.

UNWINDING ANTHROPOLOGICAL KNOWLEDGE

As I have presented it here, this insight, about the work that is done by moving from what registers as knowledge to what does not count as knowledge, seems straightforward from technocrats' point of view. But it highlights a simple but intractable problem for critics who focus on the nature of technocratic knowledge: the very knowledge practice that would seek to identify the politics of technocracy in this case is incapable of doing so— because that politics works precisely by virtue of its existence beyond knowledge, for the technocrat as for technocracy's critic. To address the problem requires confronting the ways in which anthropology is of a piece with its object of critique, technocratic knowledge. The ethnographic moment when I personally could resist this insight no further came when Sato himself admonished me, as a researcher, to pay particular attention to "the location of power in the market." Another marker of this problem is the way, as mentioned at the outset, that the critiques of the power of technocracy are already anticipated and elaborated by journalists and even technocrats themselves.

In drawing attention to this problem, I build on a growing body of work that emphasizes the parallels between technocratic and anthropological or social scientific knowledge. Holmes and Marcus (2005a, 236) describe the knowledge practices of central bankers as "para-ethnographic" to emphasize that the "informants of ethnography must be rethought as counterparts rather than 'others.' " Carol Greenhouse and Marilyn Strathern point to the ways categories such as "state" (Greenhouse, 2002) and "audit" (Strathern, 2000) serve as analogs for anthropological categories such as "society" and "culture." Maurer (2002a) and I (Riles, 2000) have emphasized parallels at the level of form between anthropological and technocratic knowledge practices. Frank Fischer (1990, 16–17) and Nigel Thrift (1996, 12), in different ways, highlight the shared positivist assumptions of technocracy and its critics. Technocracy in this body of work emerges as a point at which anthropological representations and the world they represent come together in certain shared practices of knowledge.

But what interests me here is the particular problem this condition poses for ethnography and for critical work. How can anthropologists, who work within the same intellectual traditions as the technocrats I have described, apprehend precisely that which garners its power from its inaccessibility to technocratic knowledge? Here is where we need some unwinding of our own knowledge from the technocratic practices I have described: what was imperceptible to the technocrat was also imperceptible to the ethnographer.

I want to suggest that unwinding anthropological knowledge is first and foremost an *ethnographic project* rather than an analytical one. The analytical work is straightforward and after the fact; the ethnographic work discouragingly difficult. In the example I have provided, the work of seeing the politics of Real Time lay in making needs available as a subject of ethnographic description. But once this ethnographic work was accomplished, the analysis of that subject looked so entirely obvious that it engendered a further problem of *reception*; readers accustomed to straightforward presentations of data followed by baroque analytics will feel that the material is left unanalyzed. So what is required to make evident the nature of unwinding, as anthropological practice, is a kind of violation of the aesthetics of anthropological representation. I need to retrace how the ethnographic work was done, to show how the unwinding took place.

In the course of my fieldwork, I sometimes encountered a jarring statement from the executives of the private banks that the Bank of Japan was charged with regulating: "The Bank of Japan is our mother." The phrase was in no sense pejorative or cynical; it was thrown out rather as a kind of shorthand, a way of giving me, the outside observer, a means of understanding what was going on. I never heard this metaphor used by central bankers themselves, and I suspect they would experience a certain amount of embarrassment at its discovery and elaboration by a foreign observer. Their quite legitimate fear, I imagine, would be that observers would once again read into such a metaphor a critique of their technocratic practices as distinctly "Japanese" and hence as somehow less than truly modern. Their fear would be that an anthropologist would deploy such a metaphor in the service of a culturalist analysis that would seek to explain Japanese technocracy as a product of the particular features of the Japanese cultural context. This is not at all my aim.

Instead, what was productive about this metaphor, or rather the experience of encountering it, was the way it made evident to the ethnographer certain baselines in Euro-American anthropological knowledge practices.[13] It did not fit with my own assumptions about how to think about government and market. In his discussion of governmentality alluded to above, for example, Foucault (1991, 92) contrasts modern technocratic knowledge rather with "pastoralism," a notion of the state as a father figure in which economy is "the correct manner of managing individuals, goods and wealth within the family." What about central bankers' practices would be elucidated by thinking about motherhood, I wondered? Prompted by this disjuncture, I began to conduct parallel fieldwork among mothers and sons in one upper-middle-class suburb of Tokyo of the kind where many of the bankers I met in the city had grown up or currently lived.

The ground for the metaphor for my Japanese interlocutors was a taken-for-granted notion of the household. As Chie Nakane (1967) argued in her classic critique of the application of structural functionalist kinship theory to Japanese society, the Japanese household is first and last an economic unit. The association of the household with finance is so strong that in popular conversation, the word "kitchen" (*daidokoro*) serves as shorthand for a firm's financial condition (as in the question, "How are things in the kitchen?"). Since the Meiji period, official state ideology has asserted that mothers should serve as managers of the household economy, and hence motherhood is readily associated with economic productivity (Nolte and Hastings, 1991, 171–172) and financial expertise, such that men often refer to their wives as "our minister of finance" (*uchi no okura daijin*). In drawing together household and economy, therefore, my interlocutors did not relate two disparate domains. I imagine that they had no idea that what, from their point of view, was quite mundane phrasing was confusing to me.

At issue, also, was a particular understanding of the politics of motherhood. As sociologist and feminist theorist Ueno Chizuko (1994) has commented, the Japanese mother is the dominant figure in the household. Her dominance is both because of and in spite of her structurally weak position since the postwar invention of the role of full-time wife and mother (Ueno

1988).[14] As implied by the mildly derogatory phrase *kyouiku mama* (education mommy), the values at once cherished and feared in a mother are commitment, endurance, and single-mindedness about doing what it takes to see to the child's success in the competitive educational system (Allison, 1996; Lebra, 1984, 192–208).[15] Ueno observes that in the Japanese family, the mother's authority is always receding, for in encouraging her children to be different from and more successful than their father, she is also encouraging them to leave her behind. For the mothers and sons I knew, this awareness that the relationship must become attenuated over time was precisely what rendered it continually new and strong. Because a son spends most of his life pulling away, he in effect always remains close. In the popular press, mothers' inability to give up their excessive concern for the affairs of their sons results in the weak character of adult men and is singled out as a social problem, the "mother complex" (*mazakon*). Hence, in referring to the Bank of Japan as "our mother," market participants most likely flagged the intimate involvement of the Bank of Japan in the problems of Japanese banks and the willingness of its staff to share in a very personal way in the burdens of Japanese financial institutions.

Yet, for these bankers, the metaphor would also have flagged power. Ueno's description of how the Japanese mother is able to carve out from a position of structural weakness a kind of dominance within the household aptly captures the central bank's position in the Japanese market, as I have shown. Fieldwork drew my attention to the awesome power the mothers I knew derived in the household from their devotion to a managerial role imagined, as with Foucault's pastoralism, to concern economy in the widest and most intimate sense of personal and collective welfare and growth. The mother was, for these middle-aged, successful and driven sons, an icon of intervention of a conflictual, moderately repulsive, and sometimes even violent but ultimately unavoidable kind.

In the practice of thinking about one ethnographic domain by working through another, I found further metaphorical possibilities of my own. In particular, the mothers and sons I knew were intimate in a way that was impervious to articulation. In fact, they seemed to go out of their way to avoid such articulation, to the point of expressing a certain degree of frustration at my fascination with mother-son relations. Mothers and sons I knew did not verbalize affection toward one another as Euro-American mothers and children routinely feel compelled to do. Mothers seemed far more interested in the task of providing for concrete needs, such as assuring the proper combination of vegetables at dinner or a quiet place to study, than in giving explicit advice or making rules for their children (Kondo, 1990). As they grew older, sons and mothers made constant demands on one another that went unnoticed, unaccounted for, by both sides. Where most relations were carefully calibrated, always tricky to negotiate, mothers and sons of all ages tolerated a seemingly infinite amount of imposition, even hostility from one another. It would be impossible, in other words, to think of mothers and sons as two sides. Hence their puzzling assertions to me, in light of the constant demands I observed, that they had no relationship at all.

The work this metaphor did for me as ethnographic practice, in other words, is that it pushed me to think about what was not relations, and hence not knowledge. In particular, it located a new ethnographic artifact—intimacy—a condition of oneness within which it is possible honestly to insist that there is no relation, indeed to experience and assert not connection but repulsion. It made visible a form of politics imperceptible with the current tools of political critique.

It is a simple, even impressionistic account of unwinding. But I offer it here to call for more serious attention to the work of ethnographic practice, as distinct from theory and analysis, in conditions of intimacy between anthropological knowledge and the knowledge practices such as technocracy it seeks to represent. Indeed, to suggest that there are parallels between technocratic knowledge and anthropology's own knowledge practices would be far too weak a statement. I have been describing fieldwork in anthropologists' own categories: a sociological understanding of market, premised at an ideological level on the authority of science but ultimately fueled by a faith in social relations, and one that is increasingly attuned to its limits such that it entertains fantasies of its own unwinding. Here I can only account after the fact for how the jarring sensibility of a metaphor, drawn idiosyncratically from the material, served not as a means of elucidating a cultural truth but as a way of ethnographically unwinding the agreed bases of anthropological and planning knowledge that make the ethnography of technocracy so intractable in the first place.

Let me restate this another way. Materials such as those presented here are very much a part of the anthropologist's world, and yet they are also highly exotic. Unlike the exoticism that fueled earlier generations of anthropology, however, payment systems do not seem to invite anthropological reflection. Like needs for the technocrats I have described, these technocratic practices hide themselves not by their strangeness, but by denying the anthropologist the cues or hooks that engage the analytical imagination. They do not present themselves as another side to anthropology's own intellectual concerns. This is the hallmark of intimacy.

As an ethnographic subject, therefore, technocracy raises questions about how a subject engages, or remains inaccessible to, the anthropological imagination in the first place. The example I have offered of the conversion of technocratic knowledge into the unnoticed, untheorized fulfillment of needs provides an apt metaphor for how subjects become invisible, inaccessible to analysis—by bureaucrats and anthropologists alike. My contribution to this problem has been to draw attention to two dimensions of anthropological practice other than representation or analysis—the act of ethnographic unwinding and the act of the reception of the anthropological text—that serve as resources at this juncture precisely because they are *not* technocratic, they are not common to anthropologists and their technocratic subjects. Rather, like needs for the technocrats I have described, these two dimensions are part of the task and yet invisible, occluded by our own analytical practices. Perhaps the moment is ripe for further unwindings of our own.

NOTES

This article essay on eighteen months of fieldwork among financial regulators in Tokyo conducted from August to September 1997, from September to November 1998, from August 1999 to July 2000, and from August to September 2001. I am grateful to the staff of the Payment Systems Division of the Bank of Japan for so generously sharing their time and knowledge with me. I also thank Masatoshi Okawa for his support of my project and for first drawing my attention to payment systems as a research topic. Research was funded by the American Bar Foundation. Writing was conducted under the auspices of the Howard Foundation, the American Council of Learned Societies, the National Endowment for the Humanities, and the Social Science Research Council. Earlier versions of this essay were presented at the New York University Institute for Law and Society on November 13, 2000; the Society for Cultural Anthropology Invited Session, "Theorizing Failure: An Example from the Anthropology of Finance," at the American Anthropological Association annual meeting on November 18, 2000; the American Bar Foundation on November 29, 2000; the Northwestern University Center of International and Comparative Studies on January 8, 2001; the University of California at Berkeley Department of Anthropology on January 18, 2001; the Center for Transcultural Studies Working Group on Global Imaginaries, March 25, 2001; the New York Conference on Social Studies of Finance held at Columbia University on May 3–4, 2001; the Feminism and Legal Theory Conference held at the University of Buffalo on April 20–21, 2001; and the Cornell University Department of Science and Technology Studies Conference on April 12, 2003. I thank the participants in these sessions for their criticisms, and Marianne Constable, Tony Crook, Bryant Garth, Carol Greenhouse, Jane Guyer, Laura Hein, Doug Holmes, Iris Jean-Klein, George Marcus, Bill Maurer, Fabian Muniesa, Adam Reed, Marilyn Strathern, and Mariana Valverde for comments and assistance of many kinds. This essay emerges from a larger collaborative project with Hiro Miyazaki, and I owe him a special debt for his assistance at every stage.

1 In a recent book, for example, Lee Clarke (1999) has drawn attention to what he describes as "fantasy documents," institutional documents that ostensibly plan for unquantifiable risks or extraordinary disasters, but whose real purpose is to serve as "rationality badges" that assure the institution, the public, and its various constituencies that in the event of a certain disaster, the institution would know how to act.

2 Marilyn Ivy (1995, 3) warns that anthropologists should be particularly suspicious of these ubiquitous critiques of Japanese culture, and suggests that anthropologists understand these anxieties rather as statements about "the dialectically entwined status of the United States (as the paradigm of the West) and Japan as national-cultural imaginaries."

3 The U.S. bond rating agency, Moody's, had even downgraded Japanese government bonds (JGB) in what bureaucrats took as a humiliating suggestion that the government itself was not entirely on sound financial footing (Dore, 1999).

4 BOJ NET handles transfers of cash from the accounts of 916 member banks. It handles "wholesale" fund transfers (between banks on behalf of their individual clients, or between participants in a special foreign exchange clearing system). In addition to cash, BOJ NET also handles transfers of Japanese government bonds (JGB).

5 Laura Hein (2003) has shown how, in the postwar period, Japanese intellectuals and bureaucrats have understood the technocratic manipulation of capitalist economic models as a progressive project associated with anti-imperialism (see Harootunian, 2000, 101). Tessa Morris-Suzuki (1994, 163) describes how the ideology of a technocratic project in the service of militarism in prewar Japan was effortlessly converted into an ideology of technocracy in the service of democracy and economic growth in the postwar period, and how the technocratic dimension of U.S. politics held particular appeal for Japanese elites. Likewise, in his exposition of debates among bureaucrats and their intellectual advisors in the prewar period, Vic Koschmann (2002) demonstrates that technocrats shared a concern with the "crisis of capitalism"—the disunities and imbalances it creates, and the need to offset those imbalances through bureaucratic intervention.

6 Bank executives often serve as semipublic figures in Japan; they represent their industry on government committees and devote a considerable amount of their time to drafting regulations and working with bureaucrats on policy issues. In this role they are expected to speak for their industry as a whole rather than to represent the interests of their own institution (although in practice their efforts often favor their own institution's interests in subtle ways).

7 Until recently, Japanese bureaucrats usually retired to positions as titular heads of private corporations, from which they continued to serve as conduits between government and industry (Calder, 1989).

8 Each bank and securities firm assigned particular employees the full-time responsibility of meeting regularly with bureaucrats in each ministry that regulated their activities (see Schwartz, 1998, 187).

9 Real Time ultimately went into operation on January 4, 2001.

10 Real Time was first implemented by the U.S. Federal Reserve in the aftermath of the bank failures of the 1980s.

11 How the Payment Systems Division staff solved this problem is a fascinating but highly technical story beyond the scope of this essay.

12 In this respect, it is ethnographically significant, in my view, that the Real Time system received no academic attention and practically no journalistic attention and was also ignored by the politicians who routinely critique the Japanese bureaucracy.

13 I use the awkward phrase "Euro-American anthropological knowledge practices" to distinguish the work of Japanese anthropologists, which, in my opinion, does not always replicate the particular assumptions about knowledge and markets at issue here.

14 Unlike in the ideology of the middle-class Euro-American family defined by "horizontal intimacy founded on the romantic sexual intimacy of one man and one woman" (Fineman, 1995, 145), as Nakane (1970, 132) puts it, "The structure of the family is based on a central core, mother and children, to which husband (father) attaches."

15 As Kathleen Uno (1999) has pointed out, this ideology of motherhood as complete devotion to the education of children obscures the variety of actual practices of motherhood in Japan, including, in particular, those of rural and working-class women (see also Allison, 1996, xiv). On the expectations of midcentury employers of "salary men" about the full-time devotion of their employees' wives to motherhood, see Rohlen (1974).

Greg Downey

THE INFORMATION ECONOMY IN NO-HOLDS-BARRED FIGHTING

The proliferation of media channels, including cable television and limited access, pay-per-view narrowcasts, has transformed professional sports. "Extreme" sports, events more spectacular, violent, or dramatic than those traditionally broadcast on television, arose, in part, from the insatiable demand of these new outlets for programming. Driven by the content-craving technologies of the New Economy, a group of entrepreneurs founded the *Ultimate Fighting Championship* (UFC), a "no-holds-barred" fighting sport, for cable broadcast. Critics decried the events as the most violent of spectacles, a return to barbarous blood sports on a par with gladiators battling in the Roman Colosseum or "human cockfighting." Some of the most dedicated fans of the sport, however, approached these competitions as information, reconverting athletic spectacle that was broadcast through satellites and fiber-optic cable into embodied knowledge. For critics, the UFC might represent a limit case of the media industry's willingness to transgress social taboos in pursuit of market share. This essay instead explores how market and technological developments led to the emergence, development, and diffusion of this sport, as well as how forms of bodily knowledge entered the athletic information economy through the UFC.

The UFC, a deregulated combat sport, started in 1993. Rules were minimal: no eye gouging, no biting, and no "fish-hooking," that is, reaching a finger into the cheek, nose, or ears and tearing at the flesh. Practitioners of different martial arts such as jujitsu, tae kwon do, and Muay Thai (Thai kickboxing), combat sports such as boxing and wrestling, and even street fighters squared off in a single elimination tournament. Contestants fought without rounds or time limits until they were knocked out, the referee stopped the fight, a fighter "tapped out" or signaled surrender, or—according to hyperbolic publicity—one of the fighters was dead. Early tournament winners had to defeat multiple opponents on a single night.

The sport attracted enormous attention. Viewership soared, politicians raged against the promoters, and journalists fed the scandal with sensationalist reporting. A decade-long running battle ensued between promoters of no-holds-barred events and various national politicians, states' sports governing bodies, local governments, and citizens groups. The sport was nearly squashed by legislation and cable provider boycotts as promoters wrote and rewrote regulation to appease critics. Then, when it looked like the sport was doomed in the United States, it witnessed a startling resurgence.[1]

The early tournaments shocked the martial arts world. Assumptions about the relative efficacy of different fighting techniques were shattered. Fighters in the chain-link Octagon distinctive of the UFC events developed increasing knowledge of the human body, its capacities, relative strengths, and weaknesses. Fighters rapidly absorbed this information, changed their tactics, and hybridized their styles. Fans looked to the UFC not merely for vicarious thrills or spectacular violence, but also for information about fighting techniques and examples of successful tactics. What emerged was an athletic laboratory producing knowledge about pain, resistance, and submission.

Critics of the UFC decry what they perceive as the event's excessive violence and alleged corrosive effects on public morality. They claim that the sport's primary appeal is prurient bloodlust. Journalist Edward Ericson (2001), for example, distinguished between the "small core of connoisseurs" interested in technical dimensions of fighting and the much larger audience of "violence junkies with little or no martial arts training." Likewise, academic accounts of violent entertainment often assume that it appeals to a sordid scopophilia, a lowbrow love of watching injury (see Goldstein, 1998). This assumption no doubt draws strength from some of the more egregious forms of broadcast violence: theatrical pandemonium in professional wrestling, gruesome accident footage in "reality" shows, and a never-ending series of man-hit-in-the-crotch home videos alleged to be "America's funniest."[2]

In the case of the *Ultimate Fighting Championship*, however, producers, participants, and spectators suggest that the appeal of the event is its ability to produce accurate information about the body and fighting. The violence is not consumed passively as spectacle, but sought as a proving ground for fighting efficiency. As in market rhetoric, deregulation is seen as a critical step in producing both genuine competition and unequivocal progress in athletic knowledge.

Transformations in the television industry and sports broadcasting paved the way for no-holds-barred fighting, the development of the UFC, and the way the sport's broadcasts became, for some fans, a source of embodied knowledge. The incorporation of bodily techniques through electronic media suggests that some models of passive, superficial media consumption, even of the media as primarily a generator of images for the "imaginary," must also take account of the possibility that intimate information, even skills, might be acquired through these channels.

THE IMPORTANCE OF SPORTS ON TELEVISION

Since World War II, television has become the most powerful technological force for the globalization of mass culture. Although New Economy discussions tend to focus on the Internet, the spread of television and the multiplication of broadcast channels have made it the archetypal mass medium.[3] In some developed countries, televisions are now in over 95 percent of all households. Children in the United States, on average, will spend more hours watching television than in school by the time they reach adulthood. UNESCO estimates that 23 percent of the world's populace owns a set and 80 percent of families have regular access to television. In rural China, more people have access to television than to fixed telephone lines (Balnaves, Donald, and Donald, 2001, 46). In scarcely more than a half-century, what was once a clunky experiment with a tiny audience has become a seductive purveyor of dense imagery, an almost universal presence, and a highly concentrated industry in the hands of a shrinking number of corporate colossi.

The development of cable television, especially in the United States and Western Europe, broke the television audience into smaller fragments and decreased the major networks' share of the total. "Between 1996 and 1999 broadcast television's share of total media consumption in the USA fell from 59% to 45%. Over the same period, cable and satellite television's share rose from 35% to 45%" (Balnaves, Donald, and Donald, 2001, 45). Cable and satellite media multiplied the number of channels available in different areas, in extreme cases a hundredfold. Broadcast television is in no danger of disappearing, but competition for audience has become "more complex and fierce" (54; see Klatell and Marcus, 1988, 45–69).

Programming strategies for cable channels and free-to-air networks in the postcable market differ significantly from those of early terrestrial networks. Network economics are a kind of triangle trade: programmers try to herd together a large public that they can then sell for short bursts of advertising time to corporations. Whereas a network like NBC or CBS traditionally struggled to gain a large audience—so large that it was necessarily diverse—a homogeneous niche of the public may prove an adequate audience share to justify a program on a cable channel or a network startup. Instead of *broad*-casting to reach the largest market and most diverse demographic possible, *narrow*-casting can target much more clearly defined publics with entertainment offerings that may not be palatable to a wider audience.

Although sports journalism is considered to be, according to an industry cliché, the "toy department of news media," sport is a powerful sector of the television industry (Rowe, 1999, 36). Exclusive coverage of marquee events has proven to be one of the most effective weapons in cable programming; sport gets consumers to invest in cable systems and can inspire consumers to demand a particular station from their providers. For example, only twenty-one days after launching BSkyB (British Sky Broadcasting) in the United Kingdom, Rupert Murdoch transmitted Mike Tyson's thrashing of Frank Bruno, the British hope for the world heavyweight boxing title (Barnett, 1990, 190). High-profile boxing matches were the ideal incentive to entice consumers to invest in Murdoch's new cable system: big-name athletes, high audience draws, world titles at stake, no long-term, costly commitments to a season-long sport, few parties with which to negotiate, and relatively slight technical challenges. Even an inexperienced production team could broadcast a match from a confined, indoor space. Balnaves, Douglas, and Douglas (2001, 66) contend that Murdoch's "canniest instinct" "was to grasp the value of exclusive live coverage of sporting events. In the UK, BSkyB prospered only after winning the rights to the cream of the English football in 1993. In the same year, Fox snared the rights to NFC American football from CBS. By 1998, Fox's top ten programs were all sporting events, six of them featuring in the national chart."

Because sporting events attract new viewers to a network, expensive rights to high-profile events may serve as a kind of loss leader. William MacPhail, former vice president of CBS Sports, admitted, "We do great if we break even. Sports is a bad investment, generally speaking. The network needs it for prestige, for image, to satisfy the demands, the desires of our affiliated stations. The rights have gotten so costly that we do sports as a public service rather than a profit maker" (quoted in Diez, 1980, 162). Altruistic motives aside, networks are also willing to spend more on sports broadcasting rights than they might recover in advertising revenue in order to get potential viewers to see promotions for the station's other shows and because new advertisers often buy airtime for the first time during a sporting event.

Sports not only heighten public recognition of recent entries into the crowded television marketplace; they also consistently attract one of the demographic niches most desired by advertisers: "The business of television sports has been built on the unique ability of sports programs to deliver male viewers to advertisers" (Blumenthal and Goodenough, 1998, 228). Sports programming traditionally draws young men from 18 to 36, coveted by advertisers for a number of reasons: they will eventually earn more than their female peers, they have not yet developed brand loyalties, and they are notoriously difficult to reach through other media. Widespread masculine interest in sports has prompted both radio and television news to dedicate from 25 to 33 percent of broadcast time to the subject, according to some studies (Diez 1980, 161).[4] Nevertheless, at the launch of ESPN, currently the highest-rated all-sports cable network, "skeptics wondered if there were enough sports addicts to keep the network afloat" (Rader, 1984, 136). The founders of the station were confident: "We believe that the appetite for sports in this country is insatiable" (ibid.).[5]

CABLE TELEVISION AND EXTREME SPORTS

The exploding New Economy of television meant that it was cable providers, not the public, that first had an insatiable demand for programming. As Steven Barnett (1990, 198) points out, the proliferation of channels was not driven by market demand: "In most areas of economic activity, theory suggests that demand and supply will eventually achieve some kind of equilibrium. Television's technical revolution has certainly provided a remarkable abundance of supply which has, almost overnight, more than doubled the volume of available airtime in the UK and throughout Europe. This particular economic equation, however, has been driven almost entirely by technological availability rather than consumer demand." All these new media channels craved content, raising the stakes in a mergers and acquisition wave. The challenges posed by new conduits meant that producers of proven television content could suddenly demand a higher percentage of the proceeds (Todreas, 1999, 7). Technological innovation and large-scale capital investment drove a supply-side transformation of negotiating dynamics within the production chain, shifting radically the actors' bargaining positions and destabilizing social relations of media production. Producers would have to manipulate demand or find niches of unmet "need"; otherwise, they faced a grim future of heightened competition among retailers of airtime.

With contenders for broadcast rights to major sporting events springing up like a dragon's teeth in fertile soil, the "distribution bottleneck" discussed by Timothy Todreas (1999) was broken, and the outcome was a wholly predictable bidding war by distributors. Sports were once a relatively inexpensive way to fill airtime, costing far less per hour to produce than original programs, such as situation comedies or made-for-TV movies (MacClancy, 1996, 13); this would rapidly change (Eastman and Meyer, 1989, 114–116). The NFL's deals for rights in the mid-1990s with Fox, NBC, ABC, TNT, and ESPN cost these stations a total of $4.4 billion, and the costs kept mounting. By 1998, CBS had to pay over $500 million for American Football Conference broadcast rights from the NFL, more than twice what NBC had paid several years earlier (Blumenthal and Goodenough, 1998, 230). Between 1986 and 1996, broadcast rights to the four major sports leagues in the United States—football, baseball, basketball, and hockey—had increased 142 percent. The price of Olympic broadcasting rights likewise soared. By the mid-1990s, spending on sports accounted for 15 percent of all television spending (Todreas, 1999, 157).

Sports programming expanded and became more diverse in the 1990s, both in response to these rising price tags and as a result of the raw increase in airtime to fill. As media outlets proliferated and established networks scrambled for programming to plug holes left by the rights bidding war, all sorts of athletic events reached television sets in the United States: European soccer leagues, sumo wrestling, Australian rules football, beach volleyball, even a resuscitated roller derby. New sports, including the Eco-Challenge and *The eXtreme Games*, and nouveau sports schlock like *American Gladiators*, *Battle Dome*, and Fox's *Celebrity Boxing*, joined more traditional offerings.

This was not the first time that a crisis in broadcasting led to innovations in sport. According to Benjamin Rader (1984), one of the most recent waves of what George Sage (1998) termed "synthetic" or "trash" sports was tipped off in the 1960s and 1970s by ABC's *Wide World of Sports*, which brought such athletic fare as a national wrist-wrestling championship and a rattlesnake hunt to sports fans. Even the recent *Celebrity Boxing*, which presented to the world disgraced former Olympian Tonya Harding chasing tabloid celebrity Paula Jones around the ring to pummel her, had many predecessors in the period; *Celebrity Billiards* and *Celebrity Challenge of the Sexes* were among them.

In the 1990s, some innovative sports managed to cross the legitimacy divide, establishing themselves not merely as short-term marketing phenomena, but as longer-term changes in the topography of sport. In the early 1990s, the all-sports network ESPN—owned by ABC, the loser in a bidding war for Olympic broadcast rights—sought new products for its young second station, ESPN2. Ron Semiao, ESPN2's programming director, put together *The eXtreme Games* (now usually referred to simply as the "X Games") from obscure thrill sports in 1995: skateboarding, bungee jumping, street luge, mountain biking, skysurfing, snowboarding, and motocross.[6] According to David Ferrell (1997) of the *Los Angeles Times*, the X Games were an extraordinary commercial success that captured the imagination of young fans and advertisers alike. "Alternative sports," once celebrated for their refusal to adhere to the Olympic paradigm, were some of the most-watched events in the 2002 Winter Olympics in Utah. Skateboarder Tony Hawk has become a subcultural icon, more widely recognized among young boys than Michael Jordan, with concomitant endorsement deals.

The standard in the world of alternative sports, however, is World Wrestling Entertainment, Inc., or "the WWE," a media and marketing behemoth. The WWE is the openly scripted "sports entertainment" franchise that founder Vince McMahon has grown from a small-time, seedy regional operation into a mammoth entertainment empire. WWE programming is a pervasive global peddler of hyperviolence.[7] WWE programs are broadcast in 135 countries and twelve languages, and the company grossed $456 million is 2001.[8] The WWE (recently changed from the WWF to end a long-running trademark dispute with the World Wildlife Fund) produces the highest-rated regularly scheduled program on cable television—even among young women—and is the leading producer of pay-per-view television with 7.5 million buyers in 2002.

Professional wrestling has been "worked," with predetermined outcomes and collaboration between the participants to produce a spectacular performance, since matches were a staple of vaudeville. In the late 1990s, to overcome upstart World Championship Wrestling, the Ted Turner–sponsored rival that McMahon's organization eventually acquired in 2001, the WWE ramped up the violence and sexuality in its broadcasts to the consternation of parents' groups.[9] The organization's writers decreased the amount of "wrestling" in their broadcasts to leave more screen time for the development of "subplots" that found the wrestlers' fictitious personas, including McMahon family members, involved in complicated rivalries, convoluted intrigues, and vicious betrayals.[10] In contrast, the *Ultimate Fighting Championship* adopted the opposite tactic, rejecting elaborate story lines and choreographed fighting as they developed what has been called "reality fighting."

The *Ultimate Fighting Championship* started as a partnership between Robert Meyrowitz of Semaphore Entertainment Group (SEG), former advertising executive Arthur Davie, and martial artist Rorian Gracie, founder of the Gracie Jiu-Jitsu Academy in California.[11] Rorian was one of the many heirs to the Gracie family's tradition of no-holds-barred fighting in Brazil. The Gracie clan had learned jujitsu through Mitsuyo Maeda, a Japanese champion who settled in Brazil in the early twentieth century. In gratitude to Gastão Gracie for his help settling in Brazil, Maeda taught the Japanese art to Gastão's oldest son, Carlos. Carlos eventually taught his brothers, most notably his frail youngest brother, Helio, and opened a school in Rio de Janeiro. Many sons, brothers, nephews, and cousins took up the family business. Various family members, especially Helio and Carlos, refined the art, deemphasizing throws and developing grappling techniques in *vale tudo* ("anything goes") challenge matches. Since the 1930s, the Gracies distinguished themselves with their willingness to accept nearly any challenge. The 140-pound Helio, for example, fought matches with adversaries as much as eighty pounds heavier. These fights, some held in soccer stadiums and broadcast on television, established the family as a Brazilian national legend.

Helio's son Rorian permanently settled in the United States in 1978. He opened a martial arts academy in Southern California and earned a national, albeit niche, reputation after a 1989 *Playboy* article described a $100,000 challenge offered by Gracie. The author of the article made the wager sound like a standing challenge, and the martial arts community took notice (see Gentry, 2001, 23–24). Advertising executive Arthur Davie read the article and began pitching the idea of a no-holds-barred tournament to cable production companies. He and Gracie finally sent the *Playboy* article and a videotape of some matches, including grainy footage of Helio's old fights in Brazil, to the Semaphore Entertainment Group, a small but innovative television production company, in 1993. The people in the front office, especially programmer Campbell McLaren, were mesmerized, and SEG, Davie, and Gracie became partners (26–27).[12]

Robert Meyrowitz, the creator of the *King Biscuit Flour Hour*, the first syndicated rock radio show, had started SEG in 1988 to produce pay-per-view programming. His early projects were almost entirely concerts: Ozzy Osbourne, Barbra Streisand, and The Who. When his office received Davie's proposal, SEG's production of a New Kids on the Block concert had just been the highest-grossing pay-per-view event to date but had earned little profit for the company. According to David Isaacs, SEG's vice president of marketing and planning, the move from producing concerts to original programming like the UFC was attractive because it might remedy the company's lack of control over key stages in the television supply chain: "We had been doing lots of music shows where there were a lot of difficult and legal aspects to doing those deals—working with artists, recording labels, licensing content from third parties. From a business side, [the UFC] was very appealing. Instead of being a content licensor, we would be a content creator" (quoted in Gentry, 2001, 27).

SEG's first no-holds-barred tournament, the *Ultimate Fighting Championship*, was held November 12, 1993, in Colorado. The partners chose Colorado because the state was without a boxing commission and thus could not regulate bare-knuckle fighting. The event drew a packed house as well as eighty thousand viewers who paid $14.95 each to watch from home.

The economic dynamics of pay-per-view, in contrast to network television, are relatively straightforward. The revenue stream in the case of the *Ultimate Fighting Championship* is composed of direct payments from viewers, ticket sales, video sales, and potential tie-in purchases like T-shirts and souvenir programs. Because they do not have to deliver large audiences or an atmosphere amenable to advertisers, pay-per-view programmers need not respect either marketers' scruples or the broader audience's squeamishness. Producers may appeal directly to the most dedicated viewers. To do so, they must offer a product sufficiently compelling or unique to get the consumer to pay for viewing. Pay-per-view products, for this reason, tend to be movies not yet released to other outlets, adult programming, and "special events." As Blumenthal and Goodenough (1998, 89) detail, special events are disproportionately violent sports: "Fighting accounts for nearly all PPV special-event revenue. In 1996, here's how the numbers played: boxing (56.7 percent), wrestling (35.2 percent) and combat sports (6.4 percent)." These numbers can be volatile, especially depending on the fortunes of the most profitable boxers.[13]

By 1996, the thirteenth UFC tournament was seen by more than 350,000 households that paid $24.95 for the privilege. Ratings for individual programs rivaled boxing and professional wrestling. Prizes climbed to $150,000 for tournament winners, and the event drew top-quality athletes. Former Olympic wrestlers, European martial arts champions, Brazilian vale tudo fighters, and veteran Japanese martial artists all entered the UFC's Octagon.

Success inspired competition: *Extreme Fighting, Extreme Challenge, International Fighting Championship, World Combat Championship, World Extreme Fighting, World Fighting Federation, Martial Arts Reality Superfights, King of the Cage, Rage in the Cage, Hook 'N' Shoot, Superbrawl, Bushido, Shooto, Pancrasse, Rings, Pride, World Vale Tudo Championship,* and *International Vale Tudo Championship* are just a few of the more widely known. Competitors sought to lure away UFC stars with bigger contracts and, sometimes, with less evenly matched opponents or worked matches (one of the persistent criticisms of some other organizations).

"Lots of money has been lost on developing programs for pay-per-view television," Randall Lane (1995, 48) of *Forbes* magazine proclaimed in 1995. "Robert Meyrowitz has finally beaten the jinx." The UFC was "pay-per-view's first successful series," a dependable franchise that produced steadily climbing revenue. "With the exception of one-time events like boxing and wrestling matches, pay-per-view has been a miserable disappointment . . . producers have lost about $200 million trying to produce pay-per-view programs, led by NBC's $50-million-plus bath on its 1992 Summer Olympics 'Triplecast.'"

UFC events not only brought in substantial revenues, they were also inexpensive to produce. Total production costs for UFC V in 1995, for example, ran about $600,000, including prize money. SEG's share of the cable proceeds came to about $2 million. Ticket sales for live attendance added significantly to that sum, as did international rights and videocassette sales. Vidmark Entertainment purchased the rights to sell taped versions of the tournaments in 1994. As a marketing vice president from another video production company asserted, capturing the ambivalence and excitement that seemed to pervade the industry: "On one hand it was sick and I was horrified because it was so brutal. It was new, unique, and like nothing I had ever seen before" (quoted in Fitzpatrick, 1994, 57). By the following year, video sales had quadrupled (Fitzpatrick, 1995). Scandal, however, shadowed the UFC during every step of its amazing growth.

SCANDAL ENGULFS NO-HOLDS-BARRED FIGHTING

Early response in the mainstream media to the UFC liberally mixed horror at what popular culture had wrought, indignation about the dangers posed to the fighters, and lurid sensationalism that paradoxically fed interest in the events that so outraged reporters: "Ultimate Fighting's fans, who watch the sport on pay-per-view television and fill arenas from Tulsa, Okla., to Wilmington, N.C., crave the sight of ungloved fist against bare flesh. They delight in head butts. They go wild for scarlet. And they have little use for rules: Like headgear, rules just get in the way" (Marks, 1997, 46).

Local governments sought to prohibit the fights, or at least get them to move elsewhere. New York proved to be a decisive and costly legal battleground for the UFC. After approximately $1 million in lobbying, New York State appeared to have sanctioned no-holds-barred fighting at the beginning of 1997, but then the state Boxing Commission handed down 114 pages of regulations that, in practice, made UFC-style competition impossible (Ferrell, 1997, A1). UFC XII, scheduled for February 11, 1997, in New York State, had to move in twenty-four hours. Ticket holders arrived in Niagara Falls to find that three chartered planes, at a cost of a half-million dollars, had moved 150 fighters, crew, television equipment, lights, and gear to Dothan, Alabama. Surprised folks in Dothan received free tickets that SEG handed out to fill the hastily assembled location (Gentry, 2001, 148–150; Ferrell, 1997, A1).

A truly heavyweight nemesis for the UFC weighed in from the U.S. Senate; John McCain, life-long boxing fan and Arizona Republican, saw a videotape of a UFC tournament and found the fights "barbaric." McCain began a crusade in 1995 against mixed martial arts tournaments, sending letters to all fifty governors calling for a ban on "human cockfighting." "We don't allow Americans to put two cocks in a ring or two pitbulls. Why should we allow people?" (quoted in Brooke, 1995, 22).

Individual state bans on tournaments did not profoundly damage the UFC; events could be filmed anywhere for broadcast, as the last-minute Niagara-to-Dothan relocation demonstrated. Senator McCain's crusade created enormous pressure on cable companies, however, especially after he became the chairman of the Senate Commerce Committee, the body that oversees the industry. When cable companies declined to make the pay-per-view program available to their subscribers, SEG was devastated. On his arrival at TCI, after he purchased the cable conglomerate serving 14 million viewers, Leo Hindery describes in his own words, "I came here, found out where the bathrooms are, and I canceled Ultimate Fighting" (quoted in Ferrell, 1997). Almost overnight, the number of households that could receive the events, its addressable audience, contracted from 35 million to 7.5 million; TCI, Time Warner, and Viewers' Choice all discontinued carrying the program. Pay-per-view buys plunged from a peak of around 350,000 to 15,000 as only those with satellite systems could receive the program.

Although the UFC continued to wheeze along, the days of no-holds-barred fighting in the United States appeared to be numbered. SEG lost its contract with a video distributor for the new events. Many fighters joined Japanese promotions that provided steady paychecks and larger stadium audiences.[14] By 2000, SEG was losing money and patience with the constant legal problems and shrinking attendance figures (Gentry, 2001, 228). Meyrowitz sold the entire franchise on January 10, 2001, to Zuffa Entertainment, a Nevada-based corporation owned by brothers Lorenzo and Frank Fertitta, whose other properties include Station Casinos and a brewery. (Lorenzo is also a former vice chairman of the Nevada Athletic Commission, experience that proved invaluable in the UFC's subsequent renaissance.)

When media attention passed to other scandals, a dedicated band of supporters and promoters continued the fight to have mixed martial arts sanctioned, eventually getting the sport legalized in Texas, California, New Jersey, and, in 2001, Nevada, the premier venue of fight sports in North America. The executive director of the Nevada State Athletic Competition, Marc Ratner, argued in 2001 that increased regulation made the sport more palatable: "I've been a proponent for the last four to five years. They changed their rules, which made it easier to regulate. I think the rules are very safe now" (quoted in Gross, 2001).

Under new management, the UFC made remarkable gains. They have secured approval by the most influential states' sanctioning bodies (Nevada and New Jersey). Zuffa has parlayed the widely recognized UFC trademark into other opportunities, including popular video games and a line of clothing. Recent UFC events have sold out the Trump Taj Mahal and the Meadowlands Arena in New Jersey, the Mandalay Bay Hotel and Casino and MGM Grand Garden Arena in Las Vegas, and the Royal Albert Hall in London. An event held in 2002 drew the largest live audience for a fight in Las Vegas that year.

Starting in 2001, the events returned to cable television, boosting the addressable audience to 52 million households, and the UFC established distribution contracts with broadcasters in Japan, the United Kingdom, Brazil, and several other European countries ("UFC and LMNO," 2002). Public relations officials at Zuffa report that the events are seen in fifty countries. The company has produced a successful weekly series through British Sky Broadcasting and has marked high ratings with broadcasts on Fox Sports. Much of this success can be chalked up to savvy management by the new owners, but to fully understand the sport's resilience, one has to recognize the relationship that devoted fans have to the Octagon, not simply as violent spectacle, but as a source of information about corporeal techniques.

When the UFC began in 1993, the partners who created it felt that one draw for an audience was that the UFC was poised to end debates heard myriad times in martial arts *dojos*, boxing gyms, locker rooms, and bars among sports fans and martial artists. For many of the most fervent fans, the UFC was not merely a spectacle, it was a revelation of an important truth, one that was long in coming: "Politics and business aside, the Ultimate Fighting Championship opened the eyes of a world blinded by a centuries-old mystique shadowing martial arts. This was a devastating revelation for those who had bought into that false sense of security taught by their so-called masters. With over 10 million people studying martial arts around the world, it is time for the truth to be told" (Gentry, 2001, 201). What would happen if a karate practitioner squared off against a wrestler, or a boxer against a jujitsu champion, or a sumo wrestler, or a Thai kickboxer? Would board-breaking chops and nerve strikes actually work in a fight? What would really happen if athletes training in fighting techniques put them to the test?

The early pairings were, for this reason, intentional mismatches, some of them shockingly unequal. Fight consultants who chose contestants sought to sort out the claims of different martial arts and to provide compelling realizations of imagined scenarios of unarmed combat. Long-legged women, like those who carry cards announcing the round in boxing matches, displayed signs with each fighter's discipline before a match: boxing, wrestling, ninjitsu, tae kwon do, karate, submission wrestling, pit fighting. The inaugural fight of the UFC in Denver was between a sumo wrestler (allegedly 620 pounds but actually closer to 400 pounds) and a much smaller European champion of *savate*, a French kickboxing style. In less than a minute, the sumo wrestler lost the fight as well as a few teeth, and the tone was set for the early events.

Some of the fighters, although excellent practitioners of their respective arts, were utterly unprepared for what they faced. Much smaller men sometimes forced heavyweights to submit through superior technique (there were no weight divisions). Rorian Gracie's tall, wiry younger brother Royce won the first tournament and two more of the first four UFC events. He made opponents "tap out," or signal surrender, using chokeholds and tendon-stretching submission locks. The result was no surprise to Rorian. He originally promoted a UFC-style tournament in the United States to demonstrate the efficacy of Brazilian jujitsu, a fighting style refined in over a half-century of similar matches, to attract students to his California academy.

Black belts in other martial arts and long-time veterans in such sports as wrestling and boxing, however, were stunned by the results. Kirik Jenness, cofounder of one of the most popular Internet sites on mixed martial arts, admitted, "I took martial arts for twenty years before watching the UFC and after that, I came to the realization that I don't know anything" (quoted in Gentry, 2001, 221). Commentator Rodney King (n.d.) wrote about the "evolution" of no-holds-barred fighting after the UFC: "Up until then many people who were practicing the martial arts did not view grappling as a viable option in fighting. This is probably due in part to martial arts movies that have always portrayed fighting in a stand-up environment." King, like many "stand-up" martial artists classified as "strikers," was "shocked" by the victories of fighters using grappling "floor techniques."

In a postfight interview after his first UFC championship, Royce Gracie pointed out the importance of technical knowledge rather than just raw strength: "[This victory] will open everybody's eyes, especially the weaker guys, that you don't have to be a monster to be the champ. You don't have to be the biggest guy or the one who hits the hardest. And you don't have to get hurt in a fight" (quoted in "Hall of Fame," 1994). More than just cheerleading, Gracie's message about the significance of corporeal knowledge for fighting resonated throughout the martial arts community. Over and over again, martial artists I interviewed described Gracie's victories in the first UFC events as revolutionary events in their lives. Joe Silva, a fan who went on to become a UFC fight consultant helping to set matches, was impressed from the start: "At the end of that first show, I was so happy that I was practically in tears. This is the reality I've been trying to tell people about what would happen in a real fight. This is not just people running their mouths; this is people putting it on the line" (quoted in Gentry, 2001, 221).

But the UFC did not simply demonstrate an eternal truth, it created a hothouse for the developing knowledge about fighting. Athletes observed and learned rapidly, integrated successful techniques, developed tools to neutralize early advantages, and revolutionized fighting technology in the Octagon. If, according to Keith Vargo (1999), "after his easy victories in the first two Ultimate Fighting Championship events, Gracie really did seem invincible," this pattern of dominance did not hold for long. Developments in the sport accumulated quickly and, in the opinion of many insiders, made pre-UFC techniques obsolete. According to Frank Shamrock, one of the most successful fighters in mixed martial arts, "In modern combat, in this arena in the UFC, the Gracies are dead . . . the technique, the approach, the style, the discipline, everything has moved to the next level. It just has evolved" (quoted in Sloan, 2002).

Without going into great detail—detail that dedicated viewers of the UFC know well and discuss frequently—rival fighters developed ways to counteract the strengths of Brazilian jujitsu and to exploit weaknesses in the fighting style. Fighters began to borrow liberally and learn from each other. Kevin Jakub, a fighter from Atlanta trained in Muay Thai, told Jim Nesbitt (1997), "It's gone beyond discipline. Really, now in no-rules, you don't go discipline against discipline any more. Every fighter has kicks, every fighter has strikes, every fighter has holds. You have to be able to do it all." According to Stephen Quadros (1999), editor of *Black Belt Magazine*'s offshoot *FightSport*, "It's safe to say that it has been proved there is no clear-cut dominant style of fighting." A "hybrid style" had emerged "as a result of crosstraining . . . making the claim of a winner being a practitioner of any one style almost technically obsolete."

Whereas other North American sports can be resolutely parochial—one need only reflect on the hubris that Major League Baseball's season-ending contest is called the World Series—no-holds-barred fighting is expressly international. The UFC has already held major events in Japan, Brazil, and England. Fighters hail from a host of different countries. Japan, Brazil, Russia, and the United States are, in some ways, the superpowers of the Octagon, but a number of other countries have been consistently represented. At UFC events, among fewer than twenty fighters on a night's card, typically four or five countries will be represented.

Moreover, the hybrid fighting style that emerged is a transcultural one. Most fighters liberally borrow from different national martial arts traditions. They envision the global "fighting-scape" (borrowing from Appadurai, 1990) as having pockets of specialized technical knowledge about bodily punishment. Fighters combine many traditions, among them, international Olympic-style wrestling, Thai kickboxing expertise (now internationalized so that Europe and the United States are strongholds of talent), American boxing styles (an English transplant with heavy African American and Cuban technical influence), Brazilian jujitsu techniques (a modified Japanese import), Russian sambo wrestling (itself a hybrid of diverse regional styles), and Japanese excellence in martial arts and fight sports, including *shooto* and *pancrasse* (which takes its name from a classical Greek Olympic contest), predecessors to the UFC's deregulated fighting.

If kung-fu films have long been a beachhead for awareness of Asian culture in the United States, the UFC has expanded this opening to allow the entry of other national traditions into popular consciousness about fight sports. Brian Piepenbrink (2002), for example, nonchalantly writes about an American instructor with a background in Brazilian fighting styles winning two national championships in a Russian sport (sambo) and teaching at a school of Korean martial arts (tae kwon do), with no comment on this mixture. Fighters I have interviewed in northern Indiana frequently bring similar awareness of and competence in different national fighting systems. Columnist Robert Ferguson (1998) suggests in his "prescription for curing Brazilian Jujitsu's biggest ailments" that "if Brazilian jujitsu representatives ignore the facts and remain true to their system, learning to take advantage of their stubbornness will give you the edge in competition against them." National loyalty may be a fighter's Achilles' heel in this environment of globalized fighting skills. Successful fighters have become cross-training "cosmopolitans," in Ulf Hannerz's terms (1990), attuned to a global stream of information and able to blend diverse national traditions into their own fighting abilities.

In a sense, the motivation for globalizing and deregulating prize fighting in the first UFC tournaments mirrors the rationale for deregulating industries and removing tariffs more broadly: proponents suggested that lowering barriers to innovative combat techniques would allow the "most efficient" fighting form to emerge. Other sports—Olympic judo, boxing, freestyle wrestling, kickboxing—were distorted tests of fighting ability, according to this view, like sheltered markets protecting those who might not prevail under free competition. As Dan Rose (2002) writes, no-holds-barred fighting is what "amateur wrestling, karate as well as kick boxing . . . evolve into"; with artificial barriers dissolved, the techniques mix.

The lack of rules may have been scandalous to critics, but proponents believed that minimal regulation produced the most straightforward, conclusive competitive format for discerning what fighting skills would prevail in a "real" fight. Clyde Gentry (2001), like many commentators, argues that the marketing demands placed on the martial arts but external to physical confrontation originally led to this chronic obfuscation of the truth. To gain an advantage in the *Yellow Pages* and kung-fu magazines, teachers pandered to students' egos and aesthetic reservations. Instructors promoted spectacular techniques like board breaking and high kicks, techniques that looked good in photos and demonstrations, rather than teaching students effective strategies that might require uncomfortable close grappling. With deregulation and competition, superior arts might emerge and false claims be de-bunked. "The cold, honest truth" could be found "in the unscripted contests between experienced martial artists who dared to step in the octagon," the unprotected market for martial arts knowledge (205).

Stripped away along with the illusions and outright fraud were all non-essential features of the martial arts. Insiders argued that what was left under the harsh light of the Octagon and deregulated competition were only bodily techniques that really worked. As fighter Ken Shamrock writes in his auto-biography, "We do not do *kata* in the Lion's Den [his training facility]. We do not bow to one another. We fight" (Shamrock and Hanner, 1997, 127). Super-fluous rituals such as bowing were gone.[15] Insiders like Shamrock insist that the driving necessity of combat dispelled ineffective training techniques such as kata, an Asian martial arts tradition of using choreographed sequences of shadow-boxed attacks and defenses, many highly ritualized, to train. I can-not help but be reminded of Marx and Engels's (1848/1978, 476, 477) por-trayal of bourgeois market competition sweeping away "all fixed, fast-frozen relationships, with their train of ancient and venerable prejudices and opin-ion" and battering down "all Chinese walls." Unfettered competition—no-holds-barred competition—would separate the champions from the poseurs.

TELEVISION TRANSMITS FIGHTING TECHNIQUE

The *Ultimate Fighting Championship* emerged out of opportunities created by new television technologies and media distribution networks. But the relationship between no-holds-barred fighting and electronic media is not merely macroeconomic. On the technical level, television facilitated an ex-plosion in athletic expertise. This relationship is not unique to mixed mar-tial arts:

> It is a fascinating but unanswerable question: is it simply a gradual process of evolution that athletes are fitter and races run faster than fifty years ago? And that this evolution happens to coincide with the widespread avail-ability of athletic and sporting spectacles via the broadcast media? . . . It is a sobering, and certainly not implausible, thought that television has been indirectly responsible for creating these very pinnacles of sporting achievement which it then conveys to its armchair spectators. (Barnett, 1990, 176)

Steven Barnett goes on to suggest that the relationship between superior athletic performance and broadcast media is primarily a financial one: endorsements and soaring salaries freed athletes to devote themselves wholly to perfecting their abilities. The development of mixed martial arts techniques in the wake of the UFC, however, suggests that gains may not simply be driven by new market opportunities in television. New flows of athletic information sprang up around no-holds-barred fighting in mass-mediated form.

At first, UFC competition created widespread confusion, even among announcers. They puzzled aloud during the broadcast of the first tournament, for example, when Ken Shamrock tapped out, signaling that he could not continue his first fight against Royce Gracie. Only after several replays of action at the end of the match could announcers discern that Gracie had grabbed the lapel of his own heavy fabric *gi*, the jujitsu uniform, and used it like a garrote across Shamrock's throat.[16]

Viewers did not understand the spectacle they were seeing. In early events —and still, on occasion—fans became impatient as fights dragged on, sometimes booing loudly when the fighters tangled for prolonged periods on the floor of the Octagon. Promoters and announcers struggled to educate the public about the "science" of fighting, the subtleties of joint locks, chokes, and jockeying for leverage on the floor, so that the audience might appreciate their athletic product.[17] The effort was hardly unprecedented; television had been the key to educating the public about another peripheral, violent sport: American football. In the case of football, as Barnett (1990, 35) describes, "television converted a fringe pastime into a national obsession," in large part by educating viewers to the strategic subtleties and tactical intricacies of a sport that, "to the uninitiated, appeared violent and virtually incomprehensible."

When the cable boycott led to a tremendous drop in the number of viewers, educated aficionados of mixed martial arts disproportionately remained loyal to the sport. Gentry (2001, 221) describes them in almost religious terms: "The casual fans moved on. . . . But a renegade group of believers never stopped fighting for the sport, and the Internet became their salvation." With television sources of information disappearing, multiple Web sites and e-mail lists, some distributed to thousands of in-boxes daily, carried news, offers of bootlegged videos of overseas events, and inquiries about schools and training partners. A small minority of the sport's spectators, it should be noted, participated directly in the technical aspects of fighting. According to SEG founding partner Art Davie, a focus group study revealed that "only 27% of the audience were martial artists" (quoted in Gentry, 2001, 59). Nevertheless, I daresay that percentage exceeds rates of participation among fans of boxing, American football, and auto racing.[18]

For these participant-fans, the barrier between athlete and spectator that is characteristic of spectacle did not seem so high. Sportscaster Lisa Guerrero suggests that this is part of the appeal of no-holds-barred fighting:

> It's a fairly new phenomenon here in the U.S., but I am aware that more and more people are watching it, interested in it and participating in it. Joe Smith next door cannot participate in [the majority of sports that I cover]. You can't put on a Cincinnati Reds uniform and go out and play [in a major-league game] the next day. Martial arts are something everyone can participate in, if they put the energy into training . . . and that, to me, is really interesting (quoted in Quadros 2002, 62; additions to text made by Quadros)

The UFC and other mixed martial arts competitions became a form of distance learning. Each installment produced a set of televised experiments in physical confrontation, training techniques, and the body's athletic potential. UFC fans defy Umberto Eco's (1986, 165) description of "sports chatter" as "the glorification of Waste" and "the maximum point of Consumption." Martin Stokes (1996, 21) captures the tone and content of Eco's analysis: "Umberto Eco sees in sport the epitome of passive consumption: the feats of athleticism on the screen positively demand an admiration from the television viewer which is powerless and inert, and its battery of facts, figures and statistics fill proletarian minds with a knowledge which is both diversionary and deceitful." In contrast, chatter about mixed martial arts is often intended to become working, embodied knowledge. The voluminous flow of online discussion among fans is premised on both admiration for competitors' accomplishments and the assumption that spectators themselves actively participate and want to refine their skills.[19] Specialty publications such as *Full Contact Fighter* and *FightSport*, unlike those that cover World Wrestling Entertainment, for example, contain not only the de rigueur profiles of dominant fighters, they also feature numerous columns on training tips and fighting techniques, with photographic guides to executing more esoteric moves.

The UFC's management encourages this educational relationship; the Fertitta brothers, the new owners of the UFC, are often reported as having "rolled on the mats," grappling and learning from the fighters in their employ. Both were initially skeptical, according to their own accounts, but became more convinced of the sport's merit through their own apprenticeship in Brazilian jujitsu, eventually resolving to buy the UFC. Zuffa is even rumored to have an in-house ring where top company executives grapple and get private instruction.[20] Fans respond enthusiastically to this approach; about UFC president

Dana White, the Submission Fighting UK site organizers write approvingly: "This man is no mere suit brought in to run the show, he's one of us" ("UFC President," 2002).

Although successful fighters often parlay their winning records into careers or sidelines as coaches and instructors, the nature of the events as televised spectacle makes direct personal instruction unnecessary. Fighters often learn a tremendous amount from videotapes, some merely films of competitions but others that are explicitly made as instructional materials. Former UFC lightweight champion Pat Miletich, founder of one of the most prominent schools for no-holds-barred fighters in Iowa, told author Clyde Gentry (2001, 169–170) that, after seeing a demonstration of Brazilian jujitsu, he bought an eleven-videotape instructional series and studied it for over a year. Jason Walls, a four-time champion of *Hook 'N' Shoot*, a respected southern Indiana tournament, described in an interview how he learned submission techniques by watching videos and experimenting: "Basically we [he and his brother] went out in the backyard, rolled around and would try different things that they were doing [in UFC videos], until we were able to come up with enough money to get the Gracie Jiu-Jitsu beginning training videos" (quoted in Onzuka, 2001, 19). Practitioners with whom I talked often pursued similar learning strategies, mixing firsthand instruction with videos and experimentation. As one fan told me at UFC 39, when I described the subject of this essay and my hypothesis that fans were learning bodily techniques from the videos: "You just described my life."

That television is the mediating technology for the sport facilitates the transition from passive consumption as spectacle to active engagement as instruction.[21] Videotapes of fights including close-ups and slow-motion replays become virtual instructional manuals in the technical dimensions of the sport, especially holds and chokes and their defense. Interested spectators replay tapes repeatedly to dissect body movements. A number of aficionados with whom I spoke collected video recordings of the UFC and other no-holds-barred events; some had libraries of scores, even hundreds, of videos and DVDs. Specialty publications advertise a range of instructional tapes, some of them quite specialized. As Steven Best and Douglas Kellner (1991, 20) point out, the boundary between information and entertainment in modern media often seems to collapse into "infotainment." Some of the most dedicated spectators of ultimate fighting are able to extract bodily knowledge from this mix.

The translation of visual spectacle into embodied knowledge may seem to be a difficult leap, but in fact, television enhances this possibility. For a spectator in the stadium, far from the Octagon's fence, translating distant action seen for a moment into intimate knowledge is impossible. For a pair of aficionados with a videotape, using pause and replay buttons in their living room with the furniture stacked in a corner, as one informant described to me, the task is much simpler: "When 'the slo-motion replay became the super slo-motion replay, magnificently re-capturing a part of the present we may have missed' . . . the ability of the spectator to interrogate, appraise, regard, reflect on, and evaluate that which was viewed, formerly confined to things artistic, was now possible within sporting endeavors" (Rinehart, 1998, 30; quoted passages are from an HBO program on the history of sport). Technology not only permits contemplation, it also allows distant knowledge to become second nature, and mixed martial artists are a kind of knowledge worker. Television and video in the New Economy of no-holds-barred fighting act as what Susan Buck-Morss (1994) calls a "prosthesis of perception." With a sense of sight enhanced by video, fighters can incorporate skills from remote sources: fighters in Iowa learn to grapple like a legendary Brazilian family, competitors in Indiana adopt instincts developed by Thai kickboxers.

CONCLUSION: TURNING VIOLENT SPECTACLE INTO PAINFUL TRUTH

When Lorenzo Fertitta, co-owner of Zuffa, insisted about the UFC, "This is not a spectacle; this is a sport" (quoted in Gold, 2001), I believe he meant only that the event had become well-regulated, safe, respectable, and sophisticated. He was suggesting that the UFC had put its earlier sensationalist marketing, mismatched thrashings, public relations debacles, and gory circus atmosphere behind it. But his statement that the UFC had matured from spectacle to sport also characterizes a change in how a significant group of very dedicated fans understand the events. Although many viewers no doubt consume no-holds-barred fighting as spectacle, a sprawling network of athletes, far larger and more widespread than we might initially imagine, does not. Instead of treating the UFC as a distant spectacle, divided from everyday life by an unbridgeable gap, this segment of the viewing population turns to these competitions for information about superior fighting techniques. They attempt to incorporate embodied knowledge and skills into their own physical repertoire, often by translating digitally transmitted imagery of athletic achievement back into corporeal practice. Although, as Ingrid Richardson and Carly Harper (2002) explore, some cyber enthusiasts suggest that new media make imaginable a disembodied existence, unencumbered by corporeality, the practitioner-aficionados of no-holds-barred fighting suggest that not all avid users of these new technologies seek a disembodied utopia.

The transmission of bodily techniques through mass media has precedents. Marcel Mauss (1935/1973, 72) discussed in the 1930s how "American walking fashions had begun to arrive" in France, "thanks to the cinema." *American Bandstand* introduced urban modes of dance into communities across the United States. Anyone possessing the slightest familiarity with the bodily hexis of hip-hop videos no doubt will recognize characteristic confrontational poses—arms crossed, hands flashing gang signs, heads tilted—in photographs of youth from across the globe (see Comaroff and Comaroff, this volume).

This mimetic transmission of comportment, gestures, skills, and bodily techniques is an important palpable dimension of what we refer to abstractly as "globalization." Through a market of pay-per-view television, bootlegged videos, and instructional tapes, aspiring athletes incorporate the kinesthetics of mass-mediated worlds into the most intimate realm of their lived worlds: their own bodies. The mimetic capabilities of the human body suggest that video transmission of physical techniques may be the rule rather than a curious exception, the almost inevitable outcome of circulating images of styles of moving and being. Resources coursing through the capillaries of the global mediascape and the New Economy of television are not merely food for the imaginary, they are raw meat for the corporeal.

NOTES

This research was supported by the Institute for Scholarship in the Liberal Arts of the University of Notre Dame. Thanks to Melissa Fisher and Paul Silverstein for their comments on earlier drafts of this piece and to Marita Eibl and Melissa Gomez for assistance in conducting the research. A very special thanks to all those in the mixed martial arts community who have helped me out, especially Jack Taylor and Josh Hedges at Zuffa, Rick Morrison of Intensecombat.com, Terry Gruel, co-organizer of Cage Rage in Indiana, and all the fighters who took the time to talk to me, particularly Allen Cook, John Hanlon, and Richard Bentley.

1 Part of this public relations campaign is a general move in the community to call the sport "mixed martial arts" rather than "no-holds-barred fighting." I use both terms in this chapter. "Ultimate fighting" is not used widely because *Ultimate Fighting Championship* is a registered trademark.

2 In my research, the most outrageous examples I came across of violent sport as snuff video included compilations of amateur "backyard wrestlers," teenagers leaping off garage roofs and smashing objects over each other's heads. Perhaps the most disturb-

ing was *Bumfights: Cause for Concern, Volume 1,* a collection of stunts by and fights among homeless men in Las Vegas sold online (Squires, 2002). According to some accounts, the video sold 250,000 copies between its mid-April debut and early June (Friess, 2002).

3 Timothy Todreas (1999, 202) argues that television companies will continue to be the dominant economic entities in the "Digital Era" because of "the primacy of video and the durability of brands." Even such media players as Bill Gates are of the opinion that terrestrial broadcasting, cable television, and digital satellite broadcasting will remain the standard means of transmitting imagery for some time. The substantial and continual investment by major media conglomerates in these systems suggests that Internet transmission is not yet viewed as a viable competitor and is not expected to become one in the near future, due to various technical limitations (McChesney, 1998, 21).

4 The national newspaper *USA Today* included a substantial sports section as part of its formula for achieving success; approximately a quarter of its column inches are dedicated to sports. The cooperation of various media in producing the sense that sporting events are "news," the gravitas that helps generate excitement around live events, may explain some of the synergies created by massive horizontal mergers among different media (Rowe, 1999, 148).

5 Astoundingly, in 1998, ESPN reported a net profit of $600 million; this was more than the profit of ABC, NBC, and CBS *combined* (Sherry et al., 2001, 473).

6 See Rinehart (1998) for a more thorough discussion of *The eXtreme Games* as well as other contemporary sports phenomena such as the WWE and *American Gladiators.*

7 Peter Metcalf (2001), for example, in a fascinating critical reflection on Arjun Appadurai's (1990) theoretical framework for grappling with the "global cultural economy," discusses the pervasive media presence of Hulk Hogan in upriver communities in Malaysian Borneo. The term "hyperviolence," borrowed from Manning and Singh (1997), signifies a presentation of violence without causes or consequences.

8 Since 2001, WWE revenues have slipped, and the company's stock price has fallen to its lowest level since it went public in 1999 (Beech, 2002).

9 For discussions of research on the relationship between media violence and violent crime, see Jonathan Freedman's (2002) critical survey of relevant studies or the volume edited by William Dudley (1999) in the *Opposing Viewpoints* series.

10 There is an extensive literature on professional wresting. See, for example, Atkinson (2002), Barthes (1957/1972), De Garis (1999), Henricks (1974), Lincoln (1989, 148–159), and Webley (1986).

11 The Gracies follow the Brazilian spelling of jujitsu's name as "jiu-jitsu," even in their American schools. The Japanese word is also sometimes rendered as "jujutsu."

12 Just before the fifth event, Art Davie and Rorian Gracie sold their shares of the UFC to SEG and Bob Meyrowitz. Changes in the rules intended to prevent long grappling matches (grappling favored jujitsu practitioners) and increasing pressure from states allegedly caused friction among the partners. For a more complete history of no-holds-barred fighting, Clyde Gentry's (2001) book on the subject is an invaluable resource.

13 According to ESPN, Mike Tyson is the undisputed pay-per-view champion; four of

his fights provoked more than 1.5 million pay-per-view buys, one almost reaching 2 million. In comparison, the extraordinarily popular fight between Oscar De La Hoya and Felix Trinidad in 1999, the best-selling nonheavyweight match in history, garnered 1.25 million buys.

14 U.S. professional leagues are the top of the global economic pyramid in many sports, such as baseball and basketball. Ironically, in the world of fight sports, the United States is a "semiperiphery" country, to borrow Immanuel Wallerstein's term. A "brawn drain" exists in no-holds-barred fighting, with Japanese promoters siphoning off much of the top talent (on global "brawn drain" in sports, see Rowe et al., 1994, and Bale and Maguire, 1994). Zuffa, the current owners of the UFC, attempted to staunch the flight of top talent by raising prizes and promising fame in the home market of American fighters.

15 Of course, other rituals were substituted. For example, in matches I have seen, fighters often touch one outstretched glove before fighting, help each other up at the end of rounds, embrace after fighting, and stand with the referee for the victor's hand to be raised after the fight. Insiders firmly believe, however, that extraneous ritual has been reduced. Nevertheless, strong standards for "sportsmanship" are a part of many of these competitions; proponents worry that those promoters who do not defend these standards endanger all events with being banned by state governments.

16 In fact, gis were later prohibited due to the fact that they gave "unfair advantage" to some fighters (other fighters found them cumbersome and stopped wearing them), and fighters' clothing has become standardized.

17 Their effort has achieved limited success. While watching one of the Fox Sports broadcasts of the UFC in a northern Indiana sports bar, I was impressed that the crowd not only responded favorably to hard strikes to the head but also to a very subtle escape from a chokehold by one of the fighters. Among a group paying close attention to the fight (other televisions showed golf, baseball, and auto racing highlights), almost all that I surveyed informally had previously seen broadcasts of no-holds-barred fighting.

18 Allen Guttmann (1986, 150–153) surveyed research on sports participation and spectatorship and discovered that participation rates are actually very high among avid fans, even of Olympic sports.

19 Not all aficionados participate in competitions. Many have modified their own hobbyist martial arts training based on what they have seen in the UFC, taking grappling classes or participating in more vigorous sparring, for example. There are a host of local competitions; some of them follow UFC-style rules, others are more restricted, for instance, not allowing participants to strike each other. Until I began this research, I was unaware of the number of competitions occurring in the region where I lived. Even if practitioners do not participate in no-holds-barred fighting, the UFC has reoriented large portions of the martial arts community.

20 According to Peter Kafka (2002) of *Forbes Magazine*, "The brothers say their limited liability company contract calls for any dispute between them to be resolved by a fight [between the two partners] judged by Zuffa's president."

21 An online poster pointed out that video also makes turnover at the top of the mixed martial arts field higher and championship belts hard to hold. Frequently be-

fore fights, competitors watch compilation videos of their adversary's fights, choose training partners with similar styles, and retool their strategies to take advantage of any perceived weaknesses. As fighters become renowned, videos of their fights circulate widely, and less well-known contenders study their every move and technique in exhaustive detail. In this way, television facilitates innovation and increasing physical proficiency in the sport, but also makes expertise less stable.

AbdouMaliq Simone

INTERSECTING GEOGRAPHIES? ICTS AND OTHER VIRTUALITIES IN URBAN AFRICA

A substantial effort on the part of the "development community" is under way to expand and expedite information and communication technology (ICT) infrastructure and programming in Africa. A plethora of new initiatives in teleconferencing, knowledge dissemination, entrepreneurial networking, and the configuration of other spaces of virtual exchange and transaction are seemingly launched every few days. Although these initiatives have been undertaken with great fanfare, and a substantially increasing proportion of development assistance is being deployed for them, it remains unclear how Africans from various walks of life and in various national contexts are engaging with these particular aspects of the New Economy.

Cities everywhere have become the critical locus of technological developments, embedding residents across diverse geographical spaces and scales into complex networks of exchange and interdependency. Here cities embody virtual or immanent forces provisionally concretized in diverse associational networks of varying duration, reach, and function, open-ended sites of circulation that mediate, redirect, and translate flows of information and matrices of connectivity. A conceptual language based on metaphors of territoriality and place, capable of privileging the actions of discrete urban citizens—whose behaviors are accountable through their placement in specific local dynamics—is increasingly less applicable to urban life. The interweaving of individuals with technology and virtual knowledge systems produces a very different kind of urban social subject from those of autonomous, self-contained human agents.

On the other hand, many cities embody a very different kind of virtuality. Their progressive impoverishment and deindustrialization, coupled with the enormous demands made on urban space, engenders a reliance on the sheer density of inhabitants, actions, and possibilities for association to produce an urban life falling largely outside of any available conceptual language to understand it or governance frameworks to regulate it. Although these cities are in reality no less connected to a larger urban world, they convey the sense of being off the map, marginalized from the "real" global urban world. Yet, they are increasingly becoming the locus of their own versions of immaterial economies, where the focus of the "secondhand," on piracy, repair, improvisational reassemblage of cannibalized objects and information creates a specific sensate urban experience (Larkin, 2002). Additionally, these cities give rise to capacities to participate in specific networks specializing in their own forms of translocal flows and exchanges, for example, the vast trade in illicit goods and the extensive spread of religious economies.

The key issue for deliberation here concerns how to conceptualize actual or possible interrelationships between these apparently disparate forms of urban virtuality. Whereas one seemingly represents the future frontier of urban life, the other embodies the persistence of the archaic, or a retrogressive frontier. Obviously, this framing is of limited value in terms of understanding the interrelationships among diverse urban areas. More important, it elides critical sources of urban knowledge, not only in the relegation of many cities of the South to a version of premodernity, but in keeping apart what may be highly interrelated forms of urban change.

In this essay, I attempt to make more visible the differences and possible convergences among these superficially distinct notions of virtuality. I am particularly concerned with how urban Africa's increased dependence on the city as a locus of imagination, performance, dissimulation, and "the making of something out of nothing" correspond with the effort being made to socialize Africans as proficient navigators of the virtualities inherent in ICT and the New Economy. ICT is and will continue to have a significant impact on African urban life. But beyond the statistics that demonstrate huge increases in the volumes of cell phone and Internet use, beyond the proliferation of programs on e-governance, translocal marketing networks, knowledge management systems, and capacity building, just what this impact will be is unclear. It is unclear in most respects because the processes of subject and livelihood formation, of the spatialization of social collaboration and social power themselves are increasingly recalibrated and dispersed in urban Africa. ICTs are as likely, then, to elaborate local instability as they are to promote democracy or urban productivity.

Larger numbers of urban Africans are disconnected from both the post-independence narratives of national development and the collective social memories that had established an interweaving of individual life histories with the prospective and "eternal" return of ancestral knowledge (Bayart, 2000; De Boeck, 1998a; Devisch, 1996; Laakso and Olukoshi, 1996). The possibilities of social reproduction are foreclosed for increasing numbers of youth (Al-Kenz, 1995; Diouf, 1996; Monga, 1996; Moser and Holland, 1997). The incessant provisionality of the actions, identities, and social composition through which individuals attempt to eke out daily survival positions them in a proliferation of seemingly diffuse and discordant times. Without structured responsibilities and certainties, the places they inhabit and the movements they undertake become instances of disjointed histories, that is, where places are transformed into mystical, subterranean, or sorceral orders, prophetic or eschatological universes, highly localized myths that "capture" the allegiances of large social bodies, or daily reinvented routines that have little link to anything. The places of daily routine—the market, the street, the compound, the public square—all become potential sites for the emergence of the uncanny, the spectral, or the archaic. For the complexities of multiple engagement with exterior worlds, engagements long sought as the valorized modality of internal cohesion and problem solving (Bayart, 2000), are inscribed in the very spaces that we otherwise would see as excluded or impoverished.

At the same time, the complexity and burgeoning creativity of African urban life is revealed in these moments of rupture, redistributing what has come before and opening up to what is yet to come. New, uncharted directions that are a city's capacity for life are formed in the interstices of the apparently "dysfunctional," underserviced city and those spaces of livelihood formation that fall outside conventional notions of urban economic development (D. M. Anderson and Rathbone, 2000; Becker, Hamer, and Morrison, 1994; Chabal and Daloz, 1999; Halfani, 1996).

Accordingly, this essay attempts to situate the incorporation of new economies within the African context. It attempts to raise critical issues related to the capacity of such new economies to develop productive interfaces with prevalent understandings and deployments of African-produced virtualities.

EVACUATION, EXPULSION, EXTENSION, AND THE OLD (STILL NEW) ECONOMIES

At times, it seems especially difficult to deal with the implications of a new economy in Africa, when much of the region seems so ensconced in the "old." But if we dispense with conventional narratives of development and progress, it is possible to discern certain inversions taking place.

The latest United Nations Conference on Trade and Development report indicates that the share of primary products in global trade fell below 20 percent for the first time in fifty years. Accordingly, many African governments are narrowing attention to those aspects of primary production that, regardless of volatile price fluctuations, seem to have assured long-term demand. This usually means a concentration on gold, diamonds, and oil. There is an estimated US$308 billion worth of identified mineral reserves in the Democratic Republic of Congo, Gabon, Angola, Cameroon, Guinea, Congo, Equatorial Guinea, and Sierra Leone (*African Research Bulletin: Economic Series*, 1998). Large-scale gold reserves have recently been identified in Tanzania, Niger, Guinea, Ethiopia, Burkina Faso, Mali, and (off and on) Senegal. Uganda, Rwanda, and Zimbabwe have little gold and few diamonds in their own territories, but they are heavily engaged in the mineral business via their participation in the conflict in the Democratic Republic of Congo. Sudan, Chad, Mozambique, and Cameroon are making efforts to widely expand oil production. Competition to acquire fields off the Atlantic coast has become exceedingly intense, with the Elf Girassol field off Angola alone worth an estimated US$15–20 billion. Angola, however, has over three years of future production tied up to serve high-interest credit lines.

In a hurry to earn what they can, states often offer concessions at a discount, even in spite of bidding wars between multinationals. Throughout their history, African states have usually had to accept unfavorable economic, financial, and political conditions to maintain their positions. Canada and Australia operate the bulk of the major mining companies: Barrick, Sutton Resources, BHP, Caledonian Mining, BKS Hatch, Auridiam, Redaurum, and Canyon Resources, to name a few. But the overall process of opening new "frontiers," of making new deals, of goldrushes and overnight cities, of "shoot 'em ups" and sudden gains and losses of riches gives the whole thing a flavor reminiscent of the U.S. Wild West. Whether this is necessarily a good or bad thing perhaps remains to be seen. But this economy does emphasize the extent to which wealth arises through the intervention of magical processes. With tens of thousands of young men working as itinerant prospectors across vast expanses of mud from Tanzania to Sierra Leone to Congo, who manages to strike it rich or, increasingly, even to survive entails the relative skill in navigating various mystical realms. As urban Africa experiences even more inexplicable rhythms of sudden accumulation and loss, the mechanics through which wealth is produced appear to residents as something increasingly occluded, and thus accountable only in terms of ephemeral events and forces (Apter, 1999; Bastian, 1993; Bernault, 2000; Geschiere, 1997; Shaw, 1996).

In the process of decentralization that has intensified during the past decade, states are in many ways simply conceding territory to be managed precariously on its own. In other words, operating under the auspices of subsidiarity, of reducing management to the local level, where it supposedly is most efficient and democratic, states are basically abnegating responsibility for providing livelihood and services to their populations.[1]

As official economies of scale become more informal and more narrowly based, much of the population finds itself outside of official economies of any kind (P. Collier and Gunning, 1998; Economic Commission for Africa, 1999; Mkandawire, 1999; Sethuraman, 1997). Whereas unemployment has long been a persistent reality, compensations available today require more drastic action (Guillaumont, Guillaumont-Jeanneney, and Varoudakis, 1995; Van Arkadie, 1995). Despite the rhetoric of local initiative and small enterprise, states continue to accord recognition primarily to large-scale, extractive enterprises capable of earning foreign exchange. Floods of cheap imports made possible through trade liberalization end up shrinking local production systems (Aryeety and Nissanke, 1998). At the same time, various components of economic rationalization have opened up possibilities for the appropriation of formerly public assets—land, enterprises, services—by private interests, particularly for emerging elite well-positioned in the apparatuses managing structural adjustment (Hashim and Meagher, 2000; Hibou, 1999; Lemarchand, 1997; Mahieu, 1995; Reno, 1998). These trends further amplify the need to identify vehicles through which force, influence, and claims can be deployed without clear mediation, without having to go through channels. There is a need to identify vehicles of enactment capable of upending conventional scalar composition—that is, a narrative that runs from the household to the local to the metropolitan to the region, and so forth—just as the immediate contexts in which urban actors operate themselves are interpenetrated by and penetrating various scalar arrangements (Bach, 1999; Bangura, 1994; F. Cooper, 1994; Niang et al., 1997; Rogerson, 1997; Watts, 1993).

In the limited institutionalization of modernizing urban economies, the familial domain has remained the crux of social security. Networks of connections based on extended family systems or "invented" out of a patchwork of conventions, memories, and contacts must be maintained as the real locus of economic survival. The most common form of these networks remains the actual extended family, with its kinship ties, rights, and obligations.

In the past, extended families have enabled urban residents to survive precarious economic conditions, which, in the absence of these relations, would have been unlivable (Berry, 1997; Hopkins, 1973; Jamal and Weeks, 1993; Tripp, 1997). These same conditions, however, make the ability to tend to kinship obligations nearly impossible (Carter and May, 1999; Kelsall, 2000; Levin et al., 1999; McCulloch, Cherel-Robson, and Baulch, 2000). The display of solidarity remains an important value and social performance, even if the limitations of such solidarity are increasingly apparent. Cooperation is then priced higher, and no one wants to be left out of the possibility of exacting various concessions.

Meanwhile, the number and complexity of obligations and ties are increasing. Although this increase may differentiate and extend available safety nets, taking care of one's participation in them now requires more work. The size of primary household and residential units also seems to be growing in many urban areas.[2] This increase is not because nuclear families are themselves getting larger, but because increasing numbers of extended family members, affiliates, and boarders are consolidated within a single compound or unit and, more important, enacting their ties with one another on a kinship basis. In this setting, the political intricacies of extended family relations become more difficult to navigate and more easily conflicted.

It is for these reasons that Geschiere (1997), in his discussion of contemporary sorceral practices and discourses in Cameroon, amplifies the popular conviction that the most dangerous forces come from inside the house, from the very heart of the possibility for survival. This conviction, according to Geschiere, expresses the desperate need for, and the lengths people will go to in order to maintain, good familial relations, even though no matter what is done, one remains vulnerable. Sorcery is deployed both as a way to level apparent inequities in the distribution of resources and as a strategy for gaining wealth. Illness and misfortune, then, are largely attributed to the failure of individuals to share resources with kin. By implication, the failure to do so invites misfortune and even death. There is a preoccupation on the part of many residents in African cities with the extent to which they are tied to the fates of others whom they witness "sinking" all around them. At the same time, they hope that the ties around them are sufficiently strong to rescue them if need be.

In inner-city Johannesburg, for example, where jobs are scarce and everyday life precarious and there is an acute need to maintain strong social support systems, the very act of counting on those close to oneself leaves an individual vulnerable to further difficulties. In many public appearances and in presentations before the Johannesburg Metropolitan Council, a critical problem for local governance has been the instability of household composition in the inner city. Families who reside in an apartment unit for several months frequently disperse, with new household arrangements being established in other parts of the inner city or elsewhere. In part, this instability is directly related to the intensifying uncertainty permeating everyday kinship relations. A person cannot interweave the details of his or her daily life too closely with those of family members. If something goes wrong, if one member discovers that he or she is HIV positive, or if a growing divide in economic capacity becomes apparent, one is left vulnerable to witchcraft accusations and thus vulnerable to being ostracized, or even killed. As a result, the very process of mobilizing social capital that is needed to elaborate a viable sense of belonging is precisely that process which becomes the most difficult to perform.

Across the region, households are simply expelling children by late childhood in order to resolve these dilemmas (World Bank, 2001a). It is estimated that one quarter of children under the age of 12 in Douala has experienced such expulsions, and that similarly, one quarter of all households in the city keep many of these children in an involuntary state of servitude.[3] On the other hand, the preadolescent, the *kadongo* (child soldier), the *kumuke sukali* (the "little sugar," the dangerous little girl siren), the *schengeni* (the street kids) are widely celebrated as embodiments of a social order that is not what it appears to be, that exists in some state of virtuality in the very heart of the city in demise.

The tactical navigation of the intricacies of connectivity—of the extent to which individuals are able to insinuate themselves into the lives and, thus, opportunities of others without implicating themselves unknowingly in whatever goes wrong—configures new geographies of collaboration, transmission, and exchange. The dissipation of family ties sometimes makes independent action easier, sometimes makes it easier to move. But as the capacity to move has often been predicated on resources mobilized through family ties, any extensive weakening of them can limit these opportunities. On the other hand, a long-standing strategy, especially in West Africa, is to disperse family members across various countries and regions so as to play on the differences in customs regulations, currency valuation, market strengths, and so forth. The possibilities of coordinating these family networks are strengthened through heightened access to ICT.

It is well-known that the degree of informatization in African societies lags significantly behind the rest of the world. The common way of indicating this has been to point out that five countries, South Africa, Morocco, Zimbabwe, Egypt, and Botswana, account for 98 percent of the total number of Internet hosts. The same figures basically hold for PC density, and main and mobile line density, with approximately one Internet user for every 1,500 people (Molla, 2000). Nevertheless, the telecommunications sector is being substantially reorganized, and with this reorganization comes substantial growth in the use of cellular phones, computers, and other information technologies. All fifty-four countries in Africa now have direct Internet access, an increase of forty-three countries during the past five years. During the 1990s, US$20 billion was invested in the telecommunications sector, with 65 percent of this total coming from the private sector (Economic Development Institute/ World Bank, 1998). Only 14 million lines—fewer than the number of phones in Manhattan—are presently installed, and, as of 1999, there were fewer than 100,000 dial-up Internet accounts (Jensen, 1999). With the exception of the marine optic link connecting South Africa to a cross-Atlantic hub in the Canary Islands, the use of fiber-optic cable for international traffic is just beginning. With the exception of South Africa, the region has only 2 percent of the world's telecom circuits (Jensen, 1999). Over US$50 billion will be required to achieve a minimum teledensity of five lines per 1,000 inhabitants. There has also been a rapid spread of community telecenters and public access points, particularly in Senegal (which now has over 10,000; Sagna, 1999), Ghana, Nigeria, and Mali. Regional institutions, particularly the United Nations Commission for Africa through its African Information Society Initiative, have devoted substantial attention to helping states develop national information and communication infrastructure plans to deal with the political, organizational, legal, regulatory, and technical issues in the application and use of ICT.

Much effort has been expended on the development of subregional and regional approaches, institutions, and cooperation. This requires (1) the necessary infrastructure, that is, submarine cables, gateways to satellite systems, international accounting settlements, and the elimination of tariff barriers; (2) common technologies and standardization to create a local manufacturing base, economies of scale, and streamlined licensing and type approval; (3) spectrum management and frequency bands for radio-based connectivity, as well as the sharing of bandwidth and pipes;[4] and (4) greater levels of articulation in telecommunication systems among African countries, particularly the establishment of direct connections within the region (Economic Development Institute/World Bank, 1998). Most African states are party to WTO agreements on liberalization of the telecom industry, and further negotiations are under way. Regional collaboration is drastically needed given the radically different profiles that often exist in contiguous countries, for example, Rwanda's sophisticated digital system and neighboring Uganda's anachronistic analog one. Substantial variation exists between countries in telecommunication costs, with ISP rates ranging from US$10 to US$100 a month. With the exception of the South African hub, which links Lesotho, Namibia, and Swaziland, and a link between Madagascar and Mauritius, there are few other regional backbones or links between neighboring countries. As telecom operators tend to charge high rates for international service, ISP providers are not inclined to establish multiple international links (Jensen, 1999).

In this line, a wide range of developments is under way. For example, the Pan African Telecommunications Union is seeking to develop 50 million new lines over the next five years; RAMSCON, a satellite consortium owned by African public telecom operators, has launched its own telecommunications satellite; the donor community has established Partnerships for ICTs in Africa to collaborate on technology and infrastructure inputs; the USAID Leland Initiative delivers connectivity infrastructure and programs in return for the liberalization of the telecommunications market to third-party ISPs; and the Institute of Development Research (Canada) Acacia Project has committed $60 million over five years to promote ICT use by local organizations.

The Advisory Network on African Information Strategies (AINSI) has begun to establish and assess pilot projects in various countries to explore development applications of ICTs and then exchange assessments among a wide network of partners. The Bamako 2000 Plan of Action, initiated by AINSI, brought together a broad range of sectoral actors to establish an operational basis for infrastructure development, access, contents, information rights, information quality, cost and funding policies, capacity building, ethics, and the role of state regulation and private sector participation (http://www.bamako2000.org and http://www.anais.org). The Observatory on Information Systems, Networks and Information Highways in Dakar has established a cooperative venture across West Africa to develop appropriate software technologies in accordance with tracking the particularities of local uses of ICTs. Credit and funding cooperatives are monitoring prices of raw materials through the Internet for farmers to negotiate better prices with exporters; emerging medium-scale industries are better able to manage compliance with varying quality standards.[5]

African newspapers and journals from almost every country on the continent are readily available on the Web, with many having the capacity to be delivered via e-mail on a daily basis. Thus, there is the potential for more immediate and wide-ranging comparative work and an opportunity to discern interrelationships among discrete political and cultural situations in the region. Interconnected observation posts and rapid dissemination enable the broad publicity of human rights violations. Treatment plans and a wide range of epidemiological information regarding various health concerns, particularly HIV/AIDS, are shared widely via electronic channels. ICTs are broadening basic literacy programs and improving the quality of education service provision. Weekly newsletters, such as from the Kabissa/Fahmu partnership, provide an important framework for articulating discrete African NGO initiatives, projects, and alerts. Country-focused list-serves provide an important forum for deliberating and exchanging information for nationals residing throughout the world. SITA, the airline cooperative, now provides roaming dial-up service in forty African countries.

Despite these advances, connectivity costs to international Internet backbones remain high, as do the cost of supporting and maintaining Internet nodes and systems and the tariffs on information technology products, putting the cost of regular use well beyond the reach of most potential users. The current average cost of using a local dial-up Internet account for five hours a month in Africa is about US$60 per month (not including line rental; Jensen, 1999). In Tanzania and Ghana, respectively, per annum Internet costs are US$5,425 and US$1,270, but expenditure on communications in these countries is only US$1.20 and US$3.20 per capita.[6]

End-user awareness remains limited, and uncertain electricity supplies act as a deterrent to incorporating ICT in regular routines. There is widespread concern over the extent that new ICTs may increase the already wide disparities in the directions of information flow, where North to South flows are 100 times the volume of their reverse (Kole, 2000). Major problems remain for those who have Internet access and capacity to configure viable ways of disseminating and applying information within communities that have limited access (McConnell, 1999). Little attention has been paid to lateral linkages across the region and to how local knowledge can be consolidated and applied elsewhere, although the World Bank's Indigenous Knowledge Initiative is experimenting with various possible vehicles. Given the fact that ICT infrastructure investment has constituted a major part of donor assistance during the past ten years, attention to the sustainability of ICT systems remains important (Nath, 2000).

The desperation of urban living, coupled with a wearing away of the former conventions of solidarity, orient increasing numbers of youth to varying notions of virtuality. On the one hand, the young girls who make up 80 percent of Cameroon's Internet café consumer base spend the bulk of their time online trying to cultivate a wide range of potential amorous connections in Europe and North America. The particularly beautiful and literary among them seek to foster "bidding wars" among potential suitors.[7] There are constant discussions over which turns of phrase and which kind of look (as they send online photos as well) might render specific categories of recipients "helpless" in the face of their communiqués.

Youth organizations, increasingly the object of intervention for international NGOs, construct intricate Web pages and portfolios—that is, online performances—as a means to attract attention and projects. In many communities, such organizations have become recipients of significant funding, a process that can upend local authority relationships. In Thiaoroye sur Mer, a periurban area of Dakar where I have worked, a youth organization, GIS Goorgoorlu, managed to get French funding to open a telecenter with Internet capacity. It has used this center to mobilize a large constituency of children who otherwise would remain out of school, as well as a group of more mystically inclined *marabout* (religious authorities), whom the organization has convinced that the Internet has substantive spiritual powers. By mobilizing support at both the top and the bottom of the age gradation hierarchy, these youth have been able to constitute themselves as an important political force. This has led the internationally known musician Youssou N'dour to establish the Youth Network for Development, whose centerpiece is the establishment of *Joko* (Wolof for "connection") clubs across Senegal to provide training and low-cost access to the Internet to Senegalese youth across the world (http://www.jokoclub.org).

A MOVEMENT MACHINE?

In fact, with 50 million international migrants (McKinley, 2000) Africa has become a "movement machine" of individuals, groups, and communities in various stages of voluntary and involuntary motion. The movements have often been characterized by an oscillating rhythm of incursion, exodus, and expulsion. Many national economies would simply collapse without the remittances of citizens who have migrated elsewhere—from countryside to city, from African city to African city, from African city to the North.[8] Yet, the capacity to migrate, with its concomitant institutional underpinnings and preliminary planning, is also used to support a carefully cultivated political orientation to place. For example, in some instances, migration embodies a willingness to up the ante, so to speak, in struggles for access to and control over resources and power (C. McDowell and Haan, 1998). Prospective or actual movements can serve as bargaining chips to win greater concessions or opportunities from the state, as cross-border movements can affect interstate relations. Ethnic and regional groupings have also been known to configure themselves transnationally to exert control over specific flows of cross-border commerce. These groups can draw on migrations outside of these immediate contexts, such as work in Europe, to promote greater control over such trade (Braathen, Bøås, and Sæther, 2000; Egg and Herera, 1998).

Roitman (1998) documents growing "frontier" economies at the confluence of Cameroon, Chad, and Nigeria. Borders, military bases, crossborder flows, and fluidly configured social conflicts become critical elements in the elaboration of new economies that operate outside, yet in tandem with, national regulatory frameworks. These parallel economies intersect with national regulatory frameworks by reinventing economic and cultural practices that once predominated in this region, that is, raiding and smuggling. A sense of continuity or relinking is constructed, but one that entails a rupture with prevailing formal power relations. Here, as Roitman indicates, the *real* fiscal subject exceeds the fiscal subject of the state because it has moved into more diverse and unpredictable relations with emergent figures of regulatory authority. These newly reinvented (and largely familiar) modalities of accumulation—through smuggling, raiding, and parallel taxation —undermine the regulatory logic of development, national progress, social welfare, and their concomitant institutions. Accordingly, local populations invest in new forms of security and welfare.

In some contexts, migration has long been a normative means of articulating places and exchanges, of the mutual interpenetration of discrete activities and domains, and as such, an integral part of multiplying livelihood opportunities as well as ensuring their flexibility (C. McDowell and Haan, 1998). For example, in Jens Andersson's (2001) work examining Buhera migrants in Harare, rural investment as a sociocultural disposition—that is, as a means of elaborating particular frameworks and practices of belonging— becomes a basis for different ways of working in the city. Access to work, shelter, and sociality in urban areas is contingent on how Buhera urban residents relate to particular rural resources, such as land, rural livelihoods, and local politics. In other words, what urban residents are able to do in the city—how they can acquire urban shelter, how they can work collaboratively with others to elaborate urban livelihoods—remains in large part a function of how they position themselves in relationship to their rural historical ties.

In Lilongwe, Malawi, Harri Englund (2002) found rural and urban areas linked in complex moral economies that, at the same time, required clear differentiation between the two domains but also thick interlinkages that made clear distinctions between domains difficult. Residents frequently tolerated poor urban living conditions as a means of maintaining relatively prosperous rural positions, whereas many rural residents were clearly dependent on a range of inputs derived from urban social networks. As the price of food and shelter increased substantially in the city as a result of structural adjustment policies that eliminate price subsidies and permit a liberalization of trade, attachment to rural areas was reiterated as a means of access to food production. Given an overarching context of economic hardship, such complementarities require both the reiteration of reciprocal obligations between rural and economic households and a means of modulating the degrees of mutual demand. Such a task requires moral economies that both efface the "distance" between the urban and the rural and amplify it. A translocal topography predominates which incorporates urban and rural, not as clearly defined and opposed domains, but as fractured ones, with different connotations, expectations, practices, and strategic orientations (Chukwuezi, 2001; J. Ferguson, 1999).

Across Africa, individuals have known since childhood that emigration was probably inevitable and that one should prepare for it years in advance. Even if emigration is not possible, as is often the case for many of the poor, it is still often necessary to become accustomed to and seek opportunities from continuous internal migration within a limited radius of movement. Such is the case, for example, in Greater Nairobi, where limited security of tenure combines with land grabs and land speculation to force large portions of the population to move from one informal settlement to another (Werna, 1998). In Brazzaville, the political cum ethnic balkanization of the city has in the past forced residents to relocate into homogeneous ethnic enclaves, which then serve as platforms for invasion to claim "external" territories, forcing relocation for others yet again (Bernault, 2000). Disparities in land and housing costs between central cities and the periphery combine with diminishing formal employment to motivate homeowners to rent out their properties and relocate to self-built informal housing at the periphery. So intricate interconnections continue to evolve among discrepant urban spaces. They do so in such a way that collective action can no longer afford to simply focus on trying to consolidate so-called local economies, rooted in a specific territory or sense of home. Urban actors must be prepared to rethink their life chances in terms of how to use their local setting as a way of reaching a larger world of operations, and how that larger world can be more effectively brought to bear on changing their own experience of that local setting.

The undoing of conventional modalities of social cohesion and the pro-liferation of uncertainty that is, in part, both its trigger and consequence lead to a promiscuity of sociality. This is manifested and institutionalized in an increasing number of forms, from nightly prayer services to neigh-borhood cults and ghostly reinvention of traditional hunting armies (such as the Leonian *Kajamors* or the Ivoirian *Dozos*). In all of these contexts, the talk is often about how to navigate the purported secret highways that run across the city and along which pass large volumes of cash and essential bodily forces.

The visible and invisible are constantly toyed with. A common belief in many urban quarters is that development will become visible only to those who invest in invisible forces. Additionally, visible corruption is explained through a devotion to invisible bodies, whether *Mami Wata* (the key figure in an animist belief system prevalent along the coastal regions of West Africa) or other "spirit-creatures," that satisfy highly visible desires for money, love, or success. As both individuals and money often disappear in highly visible ways from public view and use, stories, as forms of speculation, circulate as to who these individuals—uncles, neighbors, local shopkeepers, community leaders—were really working for. Disappearance through extrajudicial kill-ing, extreme economic marginalization, HIV/AIDS, or sudden emigration is a powerful feature of everyday life in many urban quarters. Additionally, city life, especially at the economic margins, propels an incessant opportunism to make use of all kinds of knowledge, relationships, and positions in multiple social networks to access some kind of opportunity to consolidate one's position. Here, a practice of being what one needs to be at any given moment enters into an ongoing tension with needing to be someone specific in the city. Different social arrangements and temporalities are mutually reinforced and undermined.

If events and actions are to be coordinated, then new forms of linkage have to occur. This is especially the case in cities that have been hard hit by various forms of disintegration, and where the modernist vision of a better life through hard work, education, and virtuous citizenship is the object of widespread mockery. For youth, particularly, there is the growing conviction that everything familiar—the quarters in which they grew up, their family ties, their values and beliefs—is a kind of curse. Rather than confidence in local institutions being able to domesticate a dangerous, diffuse global world, one's only chance is to take a chance in the undomesticated wildness of a larger unknown world.

In Freetown, Monrovia, Brazzaville, and Kinshasa, I have on occasion met with participants in shadowy youth clubs that purposely mobilize themselves as consorts of strangers. By appearing to belong to no clearly identified quarter, political faction, or religious group, they also pretend to make themselves available for almost any unspoken task to various competing elites in an effort to become beholden to no one. These are people with no prior connections to each other but who cement some kind of tie to each other by staging operations at public events. For example, diffuse gangs of young adolescents have used musical events in Kinshasa to strip naked and attack police, who, having come to believe the popular mythologies about the power of young virgins, are uncertain whether to flee or to kill. In Brazzaville, similar gangs have been known to make elaborate plans to sneak into fancy hotel ballrooms, where they shout down speeches and disrupt various social functions. In Freetown, one group arranged for a late entrant into the Ms. Sierra Leone contest. This young woman eventually won, only to be discovered two weeks later as a feared operative of the East End ghettos (abandoned buildings where youth have established their own drug-laden parliaments) and burned to death shortly afterward.

In many of these clubs, rules are established obligating young men and women to constantly exchange sexual partners. This practice is believed not only to be a form of protection against HIV, but ensures a more general protection. In highly divided cities, this sexual practice symbolically means that no quarter of the city can penetrate or disrupt the activities of the group, because all parts of the city have slept with each other. Each known neighborhood must be represented in the club before its activities can be set in motion. There can be only one representative from each quarter involved, as each member must embody the entirety of a specific territory.

Again, these clubs are one embodiment of a practice whereby urban residents throughout much of Africa invest time and energy pursuing collaborations among people often very different from themselves operating in diverse parts of the city. Together, they work out highly particularized ways of dealing with each other without having to make irrevocable commitments to those relations. It is a means of getting accustomed to both expected and unforeseen future developments.

The overwhelming visibility of urban poverty and collapsing physical and social infrastructures occludes the elaboration of circuits through which Africans are extending themselves into the world. In part, much of this extension is Africans taking their chances to reach better economic climates; others go back and forth, increasingly to cities such as Dubai, Mumbai, and Karachi, substantiating a more South-South chain of commodity transactions that have been building up over the years. At larger scales, valuable primary commodities, such as minerals, timber, oil, and agricultural products in particular, are diverted from official national export structures into intricate networks where large volumes of underpriced electronics, weapons, counterfeit currencies, bonds, narcotics, laundered money, and real estate circulate through various hands (Ben Hammouda, 1999; Duffield, 1998; Mac-Gaffey and Bazenguissa-Ganga, 2000; Misser and Vallée, 1997; Organisation Geopolitique des Drogues, 1999). In economies of great fragmentation and acute competition for control of the state as well as for survival, highly elaborated complicities exist among politicians, technocrats, soldiers, customs officials, lorry drivers, maritime workers, religious authorities, NGO personnel on the move, and even employees of multinational corporations to enlarge the volume of smuggled goods and smuggling opportunities.

The elaboration of a new translocal urban domain is more than a matter of migrants seeking economic opportunity in the expanding service economies of the North and Southeast Asia, or the purchase of cheap goods from urban markets in these regions. It is being created through individual travel, the cultivation of permeable boundaries through which goods and money can pass with minimal regulation, the incorporation of formal financial and political institutions within informal mechanisms of disposing goods and accessing markets, practices of dissimulation, and a willingness to take substantial risks.

Religious brotherhoods and fraternities, ethnically based trading regimes, syndicates, and even community-based associations are functioning with increasing scope (De Boeck, 1998b; Diouf, 2000). Urban quarters not only serve as platforms for popular initiatives—waste management, microenterprise development, and shelter provision—but readapt local modalities of cohesion and sociality to more regional and global frameworks.[9] In many cities, religious associations, fraternal brotherhoods, associations of people sharing a common village of origin, women's groups, and so forth become important in configuring new divisions of labor. They help coordinate the cross-border, small- and medium-scale trade of individual entrepreneurs and work ways of pooling and reinvesting the proceeds of this trade to access larger quantities of tradable goods, diversify collective holdings, and reach new markets.

It is true that operations at this translocal level are limited to a small section of Africa's urban population. Nevertheless, the attempts on the part of various associations, syndicates, and networks to articulate themselves and to access possibilities to act within this "worlded" domain are not insignificant in the everyday social life of many African quarters.

THE LOGICS OF THE NEW AFRICAN URBAN ECONOMIES

The prevailing rationale for expediting the development of ICT infrastructures and capacities in African cities is to enable urban economies to move away from relying on low-cost factors of production and, instead, to consider new models of development. These models focus primarily on socioeconomic organizations based on networks of small- and medium-scale enterprises clustered according to flexible specialization and subcontracting, and the upscaling and agglomeration of informal sector activities (Humphrey, 1995).

Whereas developed countries have built up their stock of physical and social capital to the point of being able to attain significant value through technology investments, this has not yet been the case for most developing countries. There, informalization of much of the labor force, the reliance on primary production, and substantial problems with the capitalization of most productive activities do not allow these contexts to take advantage of the redesign of production, work, and management practices offered by technological advances (KPMG Consulting, 2000).

Sub-Saharan African entrepreneurs tend to consolidate around "solidarity" networks to reduce information asymmetries and share risks (Fafchamps, 1996). Such networks are labor-intensive. They require the sharing of information and experiences as the basis for establishing trust and reciprocity. In local systems, economic practices that differentiate actors outside of agreed upon or customary hierarchies and patrimonial relations are usually avoided.

The heavily relied upon informal sector is a domain of particular articulations and reciprocity between social identity and economic activity. Economic activity is particularized and secured through the mobilization or reformation of specific social identities. At the same time, economic activities reproduce or change the status and development of specific identities. Such interactions between economic activity and identity take place at the level of households, communities, and ethnic and national collectives. For example, small-scale entrepreneurial activities in Nairobi have largely been differentiated on the basis of gendered access to land. Women urban traders must generate savings through selling their own produce or that of women with some form of access to agricultural production. In a survey conducted by C. C. Robertson (1998) in Nairobi markets, only 2.5 percent of the 1,018 traders surveyed owned land, and 63.6 percent of them, including a large number of unmarried women, had no access to land.

The consolidation of female labor into a proletarian, low-wage sector in the formal economy is often blocked by the ability of male heads of nonfarm households to keep women out of such labor (Sender and Smith, 1990). Low-level informal sector activities can then become a means through which women conduct household struggles to acquire an independent income that can be used as a basis to access wage labor (Rogerson, 1997). Although women may find themselves in the lower end of the informal sector, it is important not to underestimate the substantial economic capacity they have attained in most African cities. Without the varying initiatives and projects of women, cities would have been unable to get through the past twenty-five years of economic crisis. Tripp's (1997) documentation of female entrepreneurship in Dar es Salaam holds true for nearly every African city where the majority of women are involved in some form of self-employment or farming.

These entrepreneurial activities are heavily embedded in the multiple dimensions of everyday domestic life. In other words, they emanate from, respond to, and incorporate child and family care, fetching fuel and water, house building, health care, community and family celebrations, assisting with childbirth and funerals, and tending animals. Domestic, commercial, and social relations are intertwined, each becoming a resource for the other. In the process, intricate networks of collaboration are formed around various trade-offs, the shared use of equipment, shared markets, side-by-side selling, and the bulk purchase of supplies. A form of regulation also emerges, as does an overarching, but highly flexible, social umbrella that ties together distinct households and social identities.

But the emphasis in a broad range of capacity-building endeavors in urban Africa on information- and knowledge-based production models and performance criteria is viewed as enabling the consolidation of a transparent and accountable entrepreneurial culture regardless of its efficacy or legitimacy in specific local contexts (Platteau, 2000). ICT is viewed as encouraging the development of new, modern regulatory institutions. But so-called modern regulatory institutions and practices in urban Africa simply don't address a wide range of uncertainties affecting the social relations of work in the informal sector. Traditional local practices are then revalorized as a way of ensuring trust and predictability. However, the degree to which such local practices of trust formation and social solidarity are based on coherent and consistent social attributions or customary moral institutions varies greatly in different settings (Hart, 1988).

Shrinking public sector employment, overcrowding in informal sectors (Mhone, 1995), increased competition for resources and services, and a growing survivalist orientation on the part of many urban residents also can narrow the ways everyday work relationships are structured. Firms deal with those most familiar to them. Transactions are conducted with those with whom one is in regular contact. For all of its problems—mutual resentments, obligations, and loss of autonomy—family relations largely are reaffirmed as the basis of business relations. This is especially the case when particular sectors are unable to effectively absorb any new entrants (Kanji, 1995).

There are also large elements of trickery or dissimulation involved in this process. What appears to be parochial, narrowly drawn identities and practices may actually operate as markers in a complex social economy. Here, actors attempt to participate in many different identities at the same time. This is a game where individuals become different kinds of actors for different communities and activities. Thus, heterogeneous yet highly localized residential domains of African cities are used by individuals to do two things at once. On the one hand, a largely kinship, neighborhood-based solidarity is reiterated at home. At the same time, individuals are involved in very different ways of associating, doing business, gaining support, sharing information, and performing their identities in other neighborhoods across the city.

Additionally, there is often a proliferation of officially clandestine (but in actuality, highly visible) economic arrangements. Here, actors from different religious, ethnic, regional, or political affiliations collaborate on the basis that no one expects such collaborations either to take place or to work. As a result, resources can often be put together and deployed with great speed and effectiveness. This is because the process is not excessively deliberated, scrutinized, or subject to the demands and obligations usually inherent in kin- and neighborhood-based solidarity systems.

Instead of the rapidly expanding increase in the volume of cell phone and Internet use being put to work as instruments for tracking transactions with greater scope, rapidity, and accountability, these tools are being engaged as a means to intensify dissimulation. For example, cell phone and Internet use is a crucial element of being a *thiof* in Dakar. The concept appropriates the word for the fish that is a staple of the daily diet; in its contemporary rendition, thiof means the diet of unwritten rules that need to be adhered to for an individual to appear to be successful. Most of these rules specify the contents of one's lifestyle, that is, the kinds of products one must own, the places one must go. They also deal with how one is supposed to behave and talk. Most important, thiof concerns how a person circumvents the constrictions imposed by local cultural norms, social organizations, and politics by constantly communicating to an ever expanding network of people that one is in communication with an ever expanding network of people. In other words, there is no defined activity, product, or project that is being conveyed other than the very act of using these instruments themselves. Again, a nearly magical process of making something out of nothing is valorized. As such, the invocation of "thiofness" as a measure of success in Dakar is not only a practice increasingly incorporated into various aspects of the public realm. It also implicitly reinforces the salience and reinvigoration of traditional family and religious ties for those who fail in their "thiofness."

NEW FRAGMENTATION AND CONJUNCTION

African cities are subject to the same polarizing tendencies taking place elsewhere. The gap widens between the economic capabilities of those few who have been able to manage connecting local economies to more globalized transactions and the growing numbers of urban residents who must scramble to make ends meet. This polarization affects how economic opportunities and chances are calculated. It results in greater market segmentation. For example, increases in crime mean that the welding business is expanding, whereas tailoring and other garment production tends to decline in the face of the booming secondhand clothes market. Between 1976 and 1991, one third of all tailors disappeared in Ouagadougou, Burkina Faso (Van Djik, 1998). The cost of petrol and declines in public transportation have opened up new markets for bicycles and bicycle repair. Carpentry and furniture production compete fiercely to capture the market opened up by a small nouveau riche, while small-scale vulcanizing suffers from the glut of plastic imported products.

The desperate constriction of urban livelihoods connects an expanding number of locations (different towns, subregions, regions) that households must operate in to piece together some kind of livelihood. At the same time, the urban poor also become more ghettoized and less mobile. Disillusionment with urban modernity also reinforces a retreat into what might be

viewed as highly "rural" patterns of subsistence: the return to primary agricultural production, the pooling of available assets, and the reorganization of
households into interweavings of extended kin and associates all involved in
discrete yet complementary economic activities that provide a hedge against
seasonal and sectoral declines in any one specific kind of activity. As was
mentioned earlier, different household members seek entrance into very
different economic activities in the event that any particular activity is too
competitive, too seasonal, or no longer lucrative (Harts-Broekhuis, 1997).

Even in these arrangements, it is often necessary for one member of the
household to have a consistent income that can be used to support more
informal activities. In a similar fashion, when entrepreneurs diversify their
economic activities, they tend to do it in different sectors within a given city,
rather than expanding a business into nonlocal markets. This way of diver-
sifying acts as a means of spreading risk, maintaining personalized business
connections, and dealing with the fear that growth means that the owner
must relinquish direct control over the enterprise (Billetoft, 1996).

Despite these limitations, there are strong internal and external moves
toward engendering new forms of association among discrete economic activities and enterprises, including clustering diverse industrial or petty commodity activities and similar activities that divide subcontracting opportunities (Pedersen, 1997). This has been attempted in the formation of small
production zones where tools, orders, infrastructure, and resources can be
shared among groups of small enterprises.

Clustering aims at attaining collective efficiency, in terms of the exchange
of information, the shared use of equipment and orders, enhanced access to
suppliers and markets, and the improvement of knowledge stock (Schmitz,
1997). Despite depressions in demand and the limited absorption capacity of
African markets, most African firms operate at excessively small scales that
limit rates of return. By deploying information technologies to promote new
forms of association, it is believed that subsequent developments in levels of
specialization and complementarity will lead to increased efficiency and output. Additionally, it is anticipated that clustering of small enterprises, such as,
for example tailors or vulcaneers, will enlarge the scope of production systems operating in small markets with limited capital. It is assumed that
producing multiple products from the same materials and with the same
machinery or using the same labor and machinery to produce different
products at different times and cycles means greater flexibility (McCormick,
1998).

More important, it is anticipated that innovation will be fostered by sharing information, engaging in activities that enhance the skills and knowledge of everyone involved, sharing techniques and technology, and joining together to diversify sources of inputs and markets (Swyngedouw, 1998). Yet, in precarious African urban environments, small entrepreneurs tend to oscillate between dealing with a lot of different actors and with a great deal of provisionality and turnover or, conversely, playing their cards close to their chest. This constant hedging of bets fixes these actors to either a narrow series of relationships or a continuous ad hoc process of dealing wherever and with whomever they can.

Most African entrepreneurial clusters and commercial districts have a makeshift quality, given their exposure to political and economic uncertainties and lack of access to a wide variety of resources. As a result, much informal sector activity is marked with a debilitating sense of the temporary. When things are temporary, trust is usually something that can be accomplished only within a small circle of kin or other associates. On the other hand, a proliferation of institutions and social membership acts as a hedge against intensifying instability in livelihood. This plurality of institutions represents an effort to diversify channels through which resources can be accessed. By maintaining multiple memberships in various associations, religious groups, clubs, and community organizations, the channels through which resources can be accessed are diversified. Investments are made in broadening the kinds of social networks individuals and households have access to, as well as the positions they assume within them. Given the labor intensity of this task and the limited number of hours available in a day, participation often cannot exceed being sporadic and intermittent. This intermittent participation limits how effective or consistent any one institution can be in managing the collective effort necessary to attain long-term objectives (Berry, 1993; Kenny, 1998).

Because individuals find that their participation in any one network produces only limited gains, their participation moves elsewhere. A rippling effect takes hold that extends the reach of actors into a broader circuit of potential exchanges. At the same time, it dissipates any concentrated mobilization of collective force. These practices become the conventional way of operating in the city and, thus, shape the spatiotemporal parameters of everyday urban life. As such, it becomes difficult to solidify long-term and sustained collective action in forms that we would usually associate with social movements or institution or enterprise building.

Still, effective instances and mechanisms of collaborative action often do take place. The question becomes, then, who can socialize various actors to think and deal with each other in different ways? How can collaboration be sustained across a sufficient number of different actors, neither too small nor too large?[10]

CONCLUSION

There has been a great deal of understandable excitement concerning the application of ICTs to restructuring relationships among actors and contexts within Africa and between Africa and the rest of the world. What has largely been experienced as a distant, sometimes impenetrable continent can now be rendered more accessible and engaging. Time lags in the give and take of various transactions, the direct application of African sentiment to decision making and deliberation, and a more direct, unmediated representation of African realities—all seem promised by the current capacities of ICTs. Implicit in these prospects is a sensibility that the intricate political and economic problems confronted by African societies might be found to be largely attributable to past limitations in the means through which these societies communicated with the larger world. In other words, by more comprehensively incorporating African actors within heterogeneous and growing networks of more global interaction, what are conventionally viewed as intractable problems of development may be viewed instead as the byproducts of societies being out of the loop.

Herein lie the problems in much of the excitement about the applications of ICTs. Instead of viewing ICTs as supplements to the restructuring of internal and external political and economic relationships, enthusiasts often act as if they believe that these technologies are both the content and means of the restructuring itself. Although these enthusiasts would quickly downplay such an assumption, the amount of attention and money being invested in ICTs for Africa seems to suggest that this assumption is not far-fetched. After all, there is a nearly universal exasperation with the paucity of effective development interventions, the persistence of various forms of "bad" behavior—corruption, authoritarianism, civil conflict—and the indifference of the "developed" world to the intensity of African marginalization. For each of these problems, ICTs are being claimed to offer prospects for sweeping change.

But African societies have long histories of using the practices of communication as a means of producing opportunities for livelihood in contexts where political and economic resources were limited. In other words, investments were made in cultivating the capacity of specific persons to embody particular skills and knowledge. This investment was supplemented with a larger framework that ensured that individuals possessed of singular capacities would collaborate with and complement each other. For the trajectories of communication—who communicates with whom—constituted important vehicles to ensure that Africans from different walks of life not only paid attention to each other, but also sought to establish some basis to operate in each other's lives. Highly intricate communicational webs ensued. These webs proved to be important circuits of economic accumulation and distribution capable of making up for some of the substantial deficiencies in the way both states and private sectors ran economies.

Again, the critical question is what kind of comparative advantage emerges through expanded use of ICTs. Nigeria, long seen as a sleeping giant, particularly in the area of ICT development, has been taking giant-like steps in terms of e-readiness. But they have often displayed themselves in the resuscitation and expansion of a wide variety of confidence games and, perhaps more important, in the elaboration of parallel circuits of exchange, evacuation, dumping, the transshipment of illicit goods and bodies—in sum, a parallel economy of expanding reach and scope. Such connections are increasingly configured across South-South domains: significant movements of Pakistani entrepreneurs into Cameroon during the past five years (Amin and Dubois, 1999), large-scale acquisitions of marginalized mining operations and timber concessions by Malaysian interests, and the substantial expansion of Nigerian syndicate operations in textiles, auto parts, and electronics in Dubai, Mumbai, Bangkok, Taipei, Karachi, Bahrain, and the Caribbean (Opara, 2000)—all indicate the possibilities of an expanding parallel South-South economy that could be significantly capacitated by increased access to ICTs.

Urban Africans have continuously been involved in remaking their cities in ways that enable them to use the shifting agglomeration of different bodies, stories, and spaces as a means of livelihood. In this way, urban life has a sense of home-grown virtuality. This virtuality is being combined with the virtual environments opened up by ICTs and the New Economy to enable a still small but increasingly wider range of actors to participate in an emerging, albeit limited, configuration of world-level transactions that emerge from the initiatives of Africans themselves. These initiatives include increasingly elaborated migratory and remittance circuits, the establishment of trade platforms in, for example, Southeast Asia and Dubai, and expanded transactions among African subregions. These initiatives are, of course, enjoined to and shaped by the circuits of economic transaction elaborated by more powerful economic institutions and monopolies.

At the same time, these activities can significantly loosen the moral coordinates through which urban quarters might maintain a semblance of coherence and social cohesion. The dissolution of cohesion in turn can precipitate and extend urban-based conflicts about who belongs where to rural areas that now often constitute the most direct links to the global economy through extraction activities. Thus, the greater reach and rescaling of local initiative possible through participation in gradually emerging translocal urban domains must be balanced by efforts to reinvent at least provisional modalities of social cohesion. Otherwise, the fight over resources may keep actors within highly parochial and localized spaces of operation or throw them out into an increasingly diffuse existence in the lengthening shadows of the world's cities.

We know that the city is the locus for many different kinds of networks spread out over diffuse and extended regions (Soja, 1997). The experience of cities, however, remains highly localized for the majority of African urban residents. Accordingly, the objective must be to better use the array of local urban practices, logics, capacities, and aspirations to develop new approaches for navigating and incorporating a larger, more intricate urban world.

NOTES

1 Decentralization has encumbered municipalities with increased burdens of tax collection that are not compensated by an increased share of national revenue. This is particularly the case in Francophone countries. Composite figures for West Africa show that local government budgets represent less than 1 percent of GDP and 3–5 percent of state budgets in economies where public revenues are only 15 percent of the GDP (Farvacque-Vitkovic and Godin, 1998). Whereas US$20 per annum is spent for residents in the somewhat better-off cities of Abidjan and Dakar, only US$4–6 is spent on average for other African capital cities (ibid.). West African local authorities spend 1/100th the amount per capita of their European equivalents (Municipal Development Program, 1998). If medium-size West African cities were to set aside 3 percent of their budgets for routine maintenance and 2 percent for larger operations and renewal projects, they would spend twice the amount of their overall budget and more than twenty times what they actually do spend in these areas (ibid.).

In most African urban contexts, a variety of revenue burdens predominate:

Rate-of-return targets are too high.
Loan repayments tend to exceed local government capacity.
Municipal governments are often bogged down with time-consuming cadastral projects that will increase revenue generation only in the long-term.
Indirect taxes are the only real source of cost recovery for non-revenue-generating services such as road maintenance, waste management, and drainage.

Whereas municipalities in "normal" conditions would be expected to rely heavily on revenue generation through property taxes, such a practice proves difficult in most African cities. Reliance on property as the locus of taxation is often constrained by inadequate cadastration, lack of formal property titles, excessive exemptions available to those who develop land, and a lack of compliance due to poor delivery of services.

There has been a significant devolution of responsibility to the local level. Yet, there has not been an equivalent devolution of political and fiscal power. States may now have more options to access development and operational financing for municipalities, but they are not generally providing a fair share of the national treasury for cities. In most Francophone countries, the state has first claim on whatever resources are available. The state is supposed to raise money for municipalities and inform them well in advance of the budgeted allocation. But this is seldom the case. The system becomes distorted with too many tax exemptions and too much wrong information. As a result, cities find it difficult to generate realistic plans, leading almost always to excessive amounts of deficit spending (Farvacque and Godin, 1998).

In Guinea, 40 percent of business taxes and 60 percent of property taxes go to the state, with the rest shared between Conakry and its constituent districts. Central government transfers account for only 10 percent of the capital city's budget (Africa Regional Office, 1999). As large urban centers are also decentralized into multiple municipalities, a skewing of capacities within the urban centers is taking place. In Côte D'Ivoire, the ten municipalities that make up Greater Abidjan can borrow from a local authorities' fund to complete district servicing projects. These projects are aimed at bringing in rapid returns through the construction, for example, of markets and bus stations. This fund was established with 71 percent World Bank and 29 percent national government funding. Yet, there are increasing disparities among districts. For example, the per capita capital budget of the former European district of Plateau was sixty times higher in 1987 than that of the peripheral district of Attécoubé, but in 1990, it was ninety-nine times higher (Dubresson, 1997).

2 Based on household interviews conducted in eight cities on a project comparing local governance strategies conducted by the African NGO Habitat Caucus.

3 *Le Messager* (Doula), February 27, 2001. See also "Modernized Slavery," a report of the Constitutional Rights Project, Lagos, 1996.

4 On average, seven dial-up users must share each 1 kbps of international bandwidth, making connections to remote sites quite slow.

5 Africa Technology, Information and Development, 2000.

6 World Bank, 2001b.

7 *Le Messager*, March 3, 2001.

8 Based on percentage of GNP constituted by remittances; see World Bank, *Series: Workers' Remittances, Receipts*, World Development Indicators, 2000.

9 This is the conclusion of a broad range of initial field study reports under the auspices of the MacArthur Foundation/Council for the Development of Social Science Research in Africa Programme on Africa's Real Economies.

10 In one of the most detailed studies of clustering in Africa, Dorothy McCormick (1998) concludes that there is a long way to go before existing entrepreneurial asso-

ciations can even approximate the dynamism and reach of industrial districts elsewhere. Surveying distinct garment, metalworking, and car repair clusters in Kenya and Ghana, she found that operations were hampered by sporadic power, cramped facilities, negative impacts of trade liberalization, and a continued reliance on basic technology. Horizontal linkages were often limited to the lending and borrowing of tools. Such linkages are more developed in the vehicle repair sector, where subcontracting relationships are often well-elaborated according to various specializations (i.e., among mechanics, welders, straighteners, upholsterers, electricians, and sprayers). Fabricated metal shops may be extending their production lines, but the available market may actually be shrinking, forcing lower wages and product quality (K. King, 1996). Although trade liberalization has opened up opportunities in the trade of secondhand cars, and thus expanded the car repair business, this sector has become intensely competitive with, for example, at least 3,000 vehicle repair workshops in Kumasi already established by the late 1980s (Dawson, 1992).

Associations are formed for most clusters to protect the interests of enterprises. They often focus primarily on providing welfare and mediating disputes, rather than on quality control, price setting, or securing improved infrastructure. These latter functions, however, have taken place in some sectors. Often, associations face difficulties from more powerful interests, especially when they try to make direct bulk purchases from large companies. The position of intermediate retailers is thus threatened. In many instances, associations are umbrella organizations made up of enterprises from various sectors and thus find it difficult to represent the interests of a specific grouping of enterprises (Haan, 1995). Clusters have often developed as a product of government spatial policies, but they usually emerged from preexisting clusters that were relocated to different sites and which new enterprises joined. As such, the internal dynamics of the re-formed clusters are often shaped and constrained by prior allegiances.

In the few examples where clustering has facilitated access to international markets and has introduced technological upgrading—for example, fishing clusters on Lake Victoria—growing income inequality has ensued. Here, there are increasing divisions in the gains available to large-scale processors and traders in relation to the marginal gains of artisan fishermen and small traders (Mitullah, 1996).

PART II

NEW SUBJECTS, NOVEL SOCIALITIES

Aihwa Ong

CORPORATE PLAYERS, NEW COSMOPOLITANS, AND GUANXI IN SHANGHAI

TECHNIQUES AND ANTHROPOS IN THE NEW ECONOMY

The Asian financial crisis (1997–1998) stimulated a war of words about the relations between emerging powers such as China and the New Economy. Hong Kong and Malaysian officials have responded to the crisis by erecting capital controls and by attacking a "naked" or "Anglo-Saxon-style capitalism" that pays no heed to the social and political costs of market speculation. In response, the CEOs of global corporations have complained that such moves to protect society amount to the "theft" of corporate assets.[1] Such media images of globalization have framed academic research in terms of binary opposites such as the New Economy and nationalism, market rationality and local culture, the bottom line and moral values. Although these categories aim at broad questions of changing relations between the market and society, they are not an appropriate analytical lens through which to view the changing connections and forms that are emerging. Thus, this essay seeks to gain a different entry into the question of social change, focusing on specific rationality and practices that are responses to identified corporate needs operating in transnational contexts. Drawing on research in Hong Kong and Shanghai, I explored the new international labor market being shaped by the arrival of hundreds of the world's biggest corporations. But what is the current wisdom on China's "transitional economy"?

Scholars of China's transition have argued the merits of its gradualist approach, in contrast to the "shock therapy" approach to market liberalization embraced by Western socialist regimes. In particular, they note that the Chinese have kept their state sector enterprises dominant, while allowing a foreign investment sector to grow. An evolutionary-teleological perspective suggests that the forward march of market rationality will gradually wear down preexisting modes of social relations and cultural forms. Andrew Walder (1995, 964), for example, argues that "the steady introduction of competition and market mechanisms" alters the incentives and behavior of actors. Thus, a rational-choice model, focusing on "shifting opportunities and constraints" or revenues and taxes as critical incentives (976), is used to account for the changes in social behavior that have led to expanded economic activity. There is one study of the rationalizing effects of market reforms in Chinese cities. Drawing on research in Shanghai, Doug Guthrie (1998, 32) argues that managers in large industries are paying "more and more attention to the laws, rules, and regulations." As a result, *guanxi* (personal connections and social relationships) is steadily on the decline and even considered "unnecessary and dangerous in the light of new regulations" (32). This is a tantalizing observation, and a challenge to anthropologists to explore how managerial concerns about rules and regulations in new markets have effects beyond the domain of the corporation.

The links between historically specific forms of technology and the making of *anthropos* is fundamental to anthropological inquiry (Stiegler, 1998). The study of *homo faber* ("tool maker") focuses on the specific rationalities and techniques (which include reflection) through which individuals and institutions make possible particular kinds of social life. Earlier generations of anthropologists inspired by Max Weber (1930/1998) have studied how specific economic logic and action come to shape values in other spheres of rural society (Geertz, 1960). But more recently, anthropologists have shifted their attention away from the study of practical behavior to the "softer" moral values of culture (Marcus, 1998b). A reflexive anthropology, I argue, need not abandon the study of human techniques and their objects, which are the fundamental things that make us human. To understand the forms associated with the New Economy, for instance, an anthropologist would consider a range of corporate technologies responding to specific problems, such as shaping new international markets, determining investment projects, and defining corporate subjects. This focus on the techniques of corporations and associated institutions gives us access to the rationalities and practices responding to specific problems and their varied outcomes within as well as outside the corporation.

My approach heeds Nigel Thrift's (1999, 59) recent call for the study of "the practicalities of business"—the mobilizations of business knowledge and practices that are directed toward solving a host of problems in different locations. Because global business practices are concerned with "the promotion of intelligence about competence within specific problem spaces," the spread of management techniques, business schools, manuals, and media to the Asian Pacific is central to the process of reflective management. Reflexivity in business refers to the thinking on business and is fed back into business practice through self-management. What Thrift does not stress is how such business information affects people's sense of who they are and who they want to become, nor how their assessments and choices shape corporate practice and social relations. Here, I consider how reflexive management problematizes human conduct and what the consequences may be for shaping subject formation and sociality. The study of global management requires us to be highly attentive to this existentialist doubling of modern knowledge (as a product and as a shaper of social forms), as well as of individuals who are socially engineered and self-fashioning within the technologies of modern life.[2]

Fieldwork in a city such as Shanghai reveals that the archetypal New Economy figure of the Internet entrepreneur fails to capture the diverse kinds of actors who have emerged in this latest encounter with Western capitalism.[3] David Stark (2001) has noted that figuring out the cultural logics of exchange and accounting is part of the learning that firms and individuals alike must take up in an environment of risk and uncertainty: "Flexibility requires an ability to redefine and recombine assets: in short, a pragmatic reflexivity" (8). In Shanghai, one can identify at least three emergent categories of professionals who display this kind of pragmatic agility that traverses knowledge domains, social fields, and value spheres: foreign management trainers, midrange Chinese employees in global firms, and returnee Chinese professionals who are cultural entrepreneurs. These actors—differently located in relation to knowledge domains, social fields, and the logics of self-fashioning— represent two potent streams of social, cultural, and economic innovation. Their talents include bridging the global business and urban sociocultural milieus, converting cultural knowledge into economic projects, and folding Western rationality into Chinese social mores. Knowledge and technical workers employed by foreign companies appear to be most concerned about reassessing guanxi and forging a new ethics of sociality for the global Chinese marketplace. Thus, a study of the global circulation of business culture is approached via the exploration of how a particular assemblage of corporate, educational, and consumption forces puts into play different actors, networks, and logics.[4]

My analytical angle also challenges the structural approach to the global economy that homogenizes corporate rational and social forms across transnational contexts. For Manuel Castells (1996, 199), the network enterprise is able to operate in diverse settings because of a "common cultural code" that "informs the strategies of the various participants in networks, changing at the same pace as the network members, and following the organizational and cultural transformation of the units of the network." However, as will become clear later in the essay, this desired uniformity in corporate practices and values is something still unevenly distributed and yet to be achieved in the global milieus of transnational companies. For instance, "rationality" is a vexed term in the transnational corporate world; American managers use it to mean something close to a form of corporate governmentality, whereas rationality as a notion of means-to-an-end technology (M. Weber, 1978) more closely describes the systematic pursuit of individual and social interests displayed by their Chinese employees. Other slippery and ambiguous terms—such as "localization," "flexibility," "guanxi"—have various meanings depending on specific actors, social logics, and domains of action. The flexibility of actors and the heterogeneity of values and practices are elements that help us understand the intriguing problem of American managers: that a new knowledge class in China with the appropriate skills and training is found not to have the right habitus (Bourdieu, 1977) or "character." I argue that the knowledge elite and cosmopolitan professionals in Shanghai call into question our assumptions about the kind of rational action and New Economy heroes that managerial technologies seek to shape at home and abroad.

THE NEW SHANGHAI

In the new century, China is to be the site of an interesting experiment of corporate power, a kind of grounding of globalizing forces in a startlingly different sociocultural landscape. The influx of global corporations is accompanied by the new reflexive management that is fine-tuning their global strategies to the particular conditions of the local context.

In the early 1980s, Shanghai was chosen by the Chinese state to be the "snakehead" for leading development in the country. For the past decade, Shanghai has been in the midst of the most rapid urban reconstruction in history. A Manhattan of shining towers is arising across the river in Pudong, as Shanghai, with its growing concentration of service industries, prepares itself to be the chief financial and business center in East Asia. The metropolitan economy is dominated by state-owned enterprises on the one hand, and by foreign companies (often in joint partnership with state enterprises) on the other.[5] This meeting of state and capital comes together in two sites: the foreign corporation and the social world of locals and expatriates. Thus, in the space of a decade, Shanghai has become once again (as it was into the 1930s) a key node in global corporate networks, linking China, Asia, and the West. Foreign firms eager to cash in on China's economy shift their Asian base from Hong Kong to Shanghai. Coca-Cola, Price-Waterhouse, General Motors, McDonald's, Unilever, Ogilvy & Mather, Citibank, and others have based themselves here to penetrate China's vast interior markets. Shanghai's rise as a globalizing city is different from its earlier status as "Paris in the East." If one considers contemporary global cities in terms of the high concentration of global capital and corporate, banking, and other specialized services (Sassen, 2001), then Shanghai is poised to eventually take over from Tokyo its position as the Asia-Pacific global city.[6]

Shanghai's emerging status is reflected in its grand hotels, shopping malls, restaurants, exclusive neighborhoods, and major arts institutions. It is home to an international business class, drawn from Western countries, Japan, and other Asian countries, that lives in brand-new gated communities. Many residential compounds are near the airport, each equipped with its own hotels, shops, swimming pools, tennis courts, and golf courses. Japanese, American, and European managers and their families live in the villas and pursue a luxurious lifestyle apart from local Shanghainese, very few of whom can afford living on such a scale. Asian expatriates, employed by most foreign companies, also live in these corporate villages. English is the common language for various business communities. Shanghai, like New York, draws the best talent from across the country, but Western and American companies find that, to do business, they must also transform the children of the Red Guard generation into global corporate workers.

Many Western managers find that their experience and training have not prepared them fully for the challenge of taking on the city. Besides the shock of having to operate in a socialist Chinese context where political guanxi is de rigueur, they are perplexed by qualified Chinese employees who nevertheless differ in attitude and practices from corporate norms. The misunderstandings surrounding rationality and guanxi merely highlight substantial differences in social logic and styles of subjectivity in play in Shanghai's corporate world. American managers consider the reengineering of Chinese knowledge workers and the production of new business ethics the most challenging part of their work in Shanghai. A new kind of Chinese managerial subject is still being formed and has to be produced through encounters with global business knowledge and technology.

Reading Anglo-American business school texts, Susan Roberts (1998, 1–2) has identified a "global strategic vision" spelled out in discourses of global management. This vision constructs a "hegemonic set of imperatives" that are often portrayed as "extra-territorial and extra-social," in origin, "leaving places and populations no choice but to 'compete' on its terms." This global vision discursively and materially produces space in which "the global is demarcated as the domain of capital" and the global corporation and the global manager are the strategic actors, shaping world spaces that are differentiated by race, gender, and nationality. How does the global vision get translated into on-the-ground policy and practice? Roberts cites the chief executive officer of a major firm who argues for the need to "think about the world in total *and* about its parts in particular" (8; italics in the original). Nevertheless, the global city as a spatial scale (Sassen, 2001) is too broad for marking out the modality of analytical spaces within which corporate strategists must make decisions about investments, products, and people in a highly fragmented and stratified regional economy. In particular, global firms entering global markets require a heightened reflexivity in business management and must be strategic about a series of problems that pertain to labor conditions and social relations at a number of scales.

In Shanghai, foreign managers have to deal with different levels of political power and technical expertise. On the one hand, corporations must navigate the bewildering welter of rules and regulations as well as the socio-political networks that can cut through them to get a business on its feet. On the other hand, managers must shape new thinking and practices about business space, the diverse labor markets, and the quality of corporate employees. Business manuals claim that at its most general level, the global manager's concept of localization means flexibility, that is, "know[ing] the particularities of local markets" and having the ability to "act like an insider" and to "face a host of risks and volatilities" (Roberts, 1998, 8). In Shanghai, American firms refer to this totality of strategic problems as "global-localization."

American managers told me that the main goal of the global localization strategy in Shanghai was to "indigenize" global companies as soon as possible.[7] Corporate policies focus on the practical, day-to-day task of adjusting foreign expatriates to the local scene. Expatriate managers in Shanghai are encouraged to take business seminars on the challenges of working in urban China. Ironically, to help foreign managers understand local cultural and social conditions, companies turn to the China Europe International Business School (CEIBS), China's foremost business school, which is run by professors from top business schools from Europe and the United States (e.g., the London Business School and the University of Michigan Business School). Although the main goal of CEIBS is to train Chinese Masters of Business Administration (MBAS) for employment in global companies, the school also runs four-day seminars for foreign expatriates on how to navigate Chinese society. The business school portrays China as "a difficult and uncertain environment." Business courses introduce expatriate managers to "the 'ecology' of this environment through intensive sessions on China-specific topics taught by prominent experts" (CEIBS, 1998). These experts, of course, are all Western business professors, though some are drawn from Hong Kong and Singapore, where they have acquired some local experience. Courses offered include "Impact of Culture on Business" and "Managing People in China." A theme that runs throughout the courses is a stress on the need for foreign managers to be "flexible," as expectations of rational market behavior may be disappointed in a "business environment that can be startlingly different from the one they are used to" (CEIBS, 1998). There is no guarantee that rationality will gradually win the upper hand over Chinese cultural practices. I interviewed a secretary employed at the business school who remarked, "If Americans are not flexible, they will lose control." Flexibility, a term we associate with flexible capital accumulation (Harvey, 1989), is applied to flexibility in encountering various cultural milieus where insistence on a single rational way of doing business will be unrealistic and self-defeating.

Global localization for foreign enterprises in Shanghai is dominated by the goal of producing a local managerial class who possess various technical and social skills and who can replace expatriate managers. The term "indigenization" embraces programs that seek at once to cut labor costs and to improve the morale of local staff by gradually replacing expatriates with mainland professionals. Indigenization is the counterpart of the global vision in that the overriding goal is to make the foreign corporation appear and become in practice a local one. Top officers of foreign firms are anxious about the image of "corporate imperialism," but localizing managerial staff has very practical considerations. A chief officer at IBM in Shanghai told me that within a decade, he wanted the public to view IBM China as a Chinese corporation, not an American one. Indigenization is not merely an ideological move, it is a strategic practice for embedding capitalist norms and practices within the local milieu and transforming it from within.

In the initial stages of moving into the Chinese urban markets, global corporations relied heavily on Asian expatriates from Hong Kong, Taiwan, and Southeast Asia. Up until ten years ago, Hong Kong and Taiwanese middle managers positioned themselves as ideal mediators between their Japanese or Western bosses and the local Shanghainese. Over time, global companies have questioned their claims to an intimate knowledge of local language and culture, and they have been judged less effective than expected. American managers complain that Asian expatriates do not speak Shanghainese, or their Mandarin is not good enough to work effectively with locals. Besides, many do not have local contacts and have not been effective in negotiations and in translating company policy into compliant behavior from the locals. Shanghainese workers have complained about the arrogance of foreign Asian supervisors. Another major problem is that ethnic Chinese, especially from Hong Kong and Taiwan, use the opportunity of working with foreign firms to build up contacts and knowledge in order to set up their own businesses on the side. Furthermore, overseas Chinese managers often do not understand American rules and in effect create a triangular rather than a bilateral relationship between managers and staff. A Chinese American lawyer in Shanghai observed that Asian expatriates tend to resist paying income taxes and are more ready to accept "irregularities," practices that would be construed as illegal under U.S. laws. She complained that overseas Chinese in fact encourage local workers to "circumvent the rules in their everyday focus to get fast results." Although many Asian expatriates have been highly effective as middle managers, they have not proven to be uniformly ideal for training locals to be corporate team players.

Given the uncertain benefits of Asian expatriates, the "Asian crisis" has spurred corporations to cut costs by gradually phasing out foreign Asians and replacing them with local Chinese. Furthermore, top company positions, held by Westerners or Japanese, and even middle managerial positions usually occupied by foreign Asians command high salaries. A separate salary structure pays locals at a lower rate. In 1998, a typical expatriate package for a foreign middle manager with family cost US$200,000 to US$300,000 per year, whereas a highly qualified local counterpart will cost only around US$60,000 (Harding, 1998). Unsurprisingly, Chinese professionals are disheartened by such disparity in earnings. Foreign companies routinely claim that they have yet to make profits in China, and the mismatch between high executive requirements and the short supply of local management talent has limited conditions for localization. Company strategies of localization must be careful about timing, because too much localization without proper training of Shanghainese may result in the firm's losing control over quality, efficiency, profits, and corporate identity. But an expatriate-heavy management discourages locals from applying and is demoralizing to local executives. And, we may add, to the foreign company as well.

What should have become apparent is that strategies of localization and indigenization—to make American firms look and be received as Chinese companies—are a process that simultaneously enforces the internalization of foreign business techniques. Here, the challenge to global corporations is daunting, and I was told repeatedly that for the foreign firm, more than political guanxi and infrastructure breakdowns, "human resources" and cross-cultural differences were the most important and intractable "problems" to solve.

ENGINEERING CORPORATE PLAYERS

Many foreign managers readily agree that the training of Chinese science and engineering graduates is "world-class." Furthermore, the best university graduates and most talented people from all over China stream into Shanghai to seek employment with foreign companies.

However, as the modules of global business schools have shown, becoming good corporate subjects entails much more than accumulating technical knowledge. To their dismay, foreign firms find these bright Chinese university graduates lacking in what managers call a "modern, rational, and fair-minded" attitude that is desired in corporate employees. Management experts point to problems identified with Chinese professionals such as not following company rules, guidelines, and goals (nonefficiency); non-responsiveness to feedback behavior (authority and learning); and difficulty with teamwork (social relations). Managers mention a high degree of self-interested behavior in pursuing individual agendas (often at odds with the interest of the company) and a lack of social knowledge and norms to operate comfortably in the corporate setting. For the global company, the most immediate problem is to transform Chinese employees into the kind of corporate subjects who will think and behave in accordance with global business norms.

This is an especially interesting challenge in a society where, until recently, the socialist state controlled every aspect of subject formation. In the first forty years of the People's Republic of China, technocrats and professionals were entirely trained by the state (as well as in Soviet institutions), and often overriding political substance and style took precedence over technical expertise (as in the slogan "Red and Expert"). In today's China, a new knowledge class that possesses technical education and knowledge finds itself lacking in the kinds of social attitudes and skills that are expected in capitalist institutions. The corporate mantra "We need to find and train the right talent" points to a demographic shortfall as well as to the lack of social training in otherwise technically qualified workers. Despite the increasing numbers of Chinese enrolling in Western-style business schools such as CEIBS, the shortage of qualified managers continues to be severe. Foreign firms are plagued by a high turnover of English-speaking Chinese MBAS, thus forcing companies to recruit among Asian expatriates.

Hong Kong provides a vantage point for seeing how transnational firms produce information about Chinese workers and identify where they need to measure up. To foreign managers, mainland workers usually compare poorly with their Hong Kong counterparts. At the American Chamber of Commerce, an American manager in charge of human resources issues noted that Chinese professionals were generally well educated, and the science-trained ones were among the best in the world. But "the number one problem is personal development and performance rewarding." Chinese professionals did not normally play by the rules of global business, doing things their own way despite specific orders and assignments. She attributed the lack of a normative structure in business to "the high level of corruption, and the need to build in regulation—like the U.S. in the nineteenth century." Business contracts required approval from different levels of government, thus making guanxi with officials more important than law. Like many before her, she declared that China was still operating under "the rule of man, not the rule of law." In addition, "The rules are constantly changing, and applied unequally, in hiring, in pay levels, and so on," across firms and industries. This irrational market situation contributed to dissatisfaction among employees. As a result, the majority frequently changed companies in search of better salaries elsewhere. Thus, American managers found themselves wrestling with the day-to-day performance of their Chinese employees in order to regularize their work habits, as well as seek ways to increase their satisfaction so that they would stay and grow with the company. A Hong Kong trade official said that for the Shanghainese, "international standards and practices are not considered important in everyday life, but self-interest is." This view is widely shared by American managers, who consider Chinese employees "overly individualistic," "undisciplined," and "disloyal" to their companies. Foreign companies want efficient and reliable employees who are team players, not entrepreneurial go-getters looking out exclusively for their own interests.

Corporate discourse frames the problem of a mismatch between Chinese knowledge workers and company goals in terms of a clash between Western rationality and Chinese culture. Two Western business professors identify the problem in terms of "the pitfall of cultural misunderstanding" (Goodall and Burgers, 1998). They argue that Westerners operate according to the norms of a "specific" culture, and the Chinese adhere to the practices of a "diffuse" culture. By this they mean that Western managers have a technological approach focusing on rational performance that leads directly to overall company gain, especially in the form of profits. In contrast, Chinese workers seem to be driven by excessive self-interest on the one hand, and by "diffuse" social gains (guanxi interests) outside the corporate domain on the other. These different modes of work habits, the professors argue, "collide" in the corporate setting. Another cultural clash is the variation in "power distance" dynamics exhibited by Western and Chinese managers. Driven by rational thinking, Western bosses tend to maintain a high status but expect automatic compliance from subordinates kept at arm's length. In contrast, Chinese managers try to minimize social distance and adopt a low posture to cultivate guanxi as a way to elicit the desired outcome. In other words, the focused, direct, and hierarchical behavior of Western bosses collides with the diffuse, indirect, and personal approach of Chinese employees. Corporate chains of command seem to violate worker preference for indirect and face-saving techniques for making requests or assessments or getting feedback. Following this line of reasoning, business courses for expatriates claim that firms need "a holistic approach to retention," as Chinese MBAs look for job satisfaction beyond a competitive salary, seeking especially "quality interpersonal relations at work" and a "clear promotion path" (CEIBS, 1998). In short, "business speak" presents corporate technologies of disciplining as rational, whereas the relentless self-interested behavior of Chinese employees to take advantage of the firm is considered irrational and cultural. Such corporate discourse is in keeping with the technologies of managerial governmentality to reengineer Chinese subjects as disciplined workers and team players dedicated to the good of the firm.

NOT COMPANY MEN

To make company men out of intransigent Chinese, American managers tend to take a strong ideological position on their own "practical" approach as manifested in teamwork, meritocracy, and quick action. They thus paint an idealized picture of business practices that are resolutely rational and unbiased by social or self-interest in order to draw a distinction between American rational business ethics and those of "others." This contrast is highlighted by the practical challenges presented by China's revolutionary generation for the forging of a new international knowledge class. It is remarkable that American managers and lawyers agree that the generation that came of age during the Great Proletarian Cultural Revolution (GPCR) is largely irrelevant for the creation of an international knowledge class. People in their late 30s, 40s, and 50s are unanimously written off as too "scarred and spirit-deadened to learn new things," as an American lawyer remarked. Besides the suffering inflicted by the turmoil of the GPCR, most have had their education interrupted and attained only mid–high school qualifications. Some may have since gone back to school and become computer literate, but they are said to have the "mind-set of survivors who have difficulty with long-term planning, since their attitude is that 'the government determines everything.'"

Hong Kong professionals stationed in Shanghai have a slightly different view from that of American managers. They argue that the GPCR upheavals produced endemic self-interested behavior among survivors, for whom foreign business was just one major arena where individuals could make up for the lost years. Hong Kong expatriates note that the GPCR generation tended to be driven by strategies for accumulating personal wealth and was not overly concerned about the overall benefit to their company. A trade officer claims that it is very common for local employees to ask for a commission: "This is a general practice—in hospitals, schools, and so on—to ask for a direct payment for services rendered." He considers this an effect of an overall collapse of moral authority, as there is "loose control" and corruption at the top: "Everyone does this. Shanghai is a little better than other cities, but it is not separable from the rest of China." Hong Kong managers thus stress not the lack of initiative among mainland workers, but rather their lack of accountability to their employers. Furthermore, many working people seek to benefit from employment both in the business sector and in the government. This familial strategy, called "one family, two systems," allows usually the husband to make money quickly in the entrepreneurial or corporate realm, while his wife gets a less lucrative job in the state sector but gains access to state subsidies and contacts (see Hoffman, 2000). This straddling strategy reinforces the tendency of white-collar workers to pursue their own ends and to be cavalier about corporate rules and norms.

Hong Kong managers in an advertising company observe that it is necessary to teach Chinese workers "professional and ethical standards: the importance of transparency, honesty, and fairness." They argue that the locals need "self-discipline" and a sense of "self-requirement like punctuality and devotion to work," values that are "not so important even to college-educated people." Comparing mainland workers to the taken-for-granted business attitude of their Hong Kong peers, they argue that Chinese workers need to be "made aware" of the relation to the company's headquarters and of "global client expectations." In their view, the self-propelling urban worker, coming out of decades of political uncertainty and economic poverty, has to be resocialized to identify with the ethics of modern corporate teamwork. They list the kinds of disciplinary norms that mainland workers must be taught:

Quality-expectation: the need to pay attention to the organization of data, quality control, time control, budget control, and the filing system. "Do not internalize procedures and insist own practice is more efficient."

Time schedule: the importance of keeping to schedule, of deadlines, and of maintaining progress. "Mainland workers often miss deadlines because of family affairs."

Attitude: there is "not enough of the [company as] family" and there is "a tendency to disobey." "Mainland people do not follow orders and instructions . . . nowadays they are more challenging and demanding."

Overall, the GPCR generation is considered pretty hopeless as potential employees for global corporations; in the words of the American lawyer, most of them are "some distance from thinking that it's all up to you what you do" (one might add, only within the company). The workers appear to view foreign companies as a means to self-advancement and have little patience with norms, procedures, and rules. The irony is that American managers see what they consider the "rigidity, hierarchy, and collectivism" of their white-collar workers to be in fact the expressions of highly rational strategies of exploiting conditions in different employment contexts for self-advancement and wealth making. They can neither be easily disciplined nor induced to become new kinds of corporate subjects desired by global companies.

Why do we need consultants on human resources?

Management trainer: "People are the greatest controllable element in China; not market, not politics!"

Over the past two decades, as Asian economies catapulted into the fastest-growing economies in the world, a less well-known fact was the army of management training consultants who descended on Asian cities to retool Asian bosses and workers according to Harvard Business School manuals. While international business schools have sprouted like mushrooms after the rain (Olds and Thrift, forthcoming), global managers now turn to management trainers to transform subjects not yet fully divested of precapitalist sensibility. A Hong Kong management trainer, founder of the Core Transformation Center, argues that Chinese workers need to have their values, their personalities, and even their souls "reengineered, like computers, for the global age."[8] His company offers small workshops during which participants are asked to focus on "life values" that will promote their careers and are taught techniques to build team spirit and signals to keep communication channels open. Hong Kong workers, known primarily for their technical expertise but not for their cross-cultural networking and communication skills, are considered prime candidates for these new reflexive, communicative skills.

Business management is thus concerned not only with disciplining white-collar workers, but also with producing reflexive corporate subjects.[9] Whereas in Hong Kong, companies consider such management training desirable but not essential for their cosmopolitan workforce, in Shanghai, the need to instill international norms of flexibility and reflexivity is urgent. A CEIBS professor notes that "the lack of local talent in China" is a tremendous constraint on the growth of international business: "The pool of locals who possess the requisite business skills and mindsets is in acute shortage."[10] A Chinese worker bearing a technical or business degree is "an unfinished product" and has to be subjected to training programs to be turned into a "manager of the future." Consultancy firms based in Hong Kong have been streaming into Shanghai to "coach management and coach workers" so that they will acquire the necessary "intellectual management skills" and "social skills" to work in a global firm. Let us meet two culture experts devoted to reengineering "Chinese personalities."

Dr. Heyman (pseudonym) is in his early 50s, a British subject who became a naturalized American. He used to be a professor of cognitive psychology in Texas. After his marriage to a Taiwanese woman, he stumbled on the big problem for global firms in China: how to transform the new generation of white-collar workers. In 1993, Heyman gave up his academic job and set up the first management consultancy in China. His goal was to "bring American corporate culture to make a hybrid culture." In 1997, his firm joined a multinational consultancy firm with 8,000 employees in thirty-one countries. In 1998, Heyman's parent company had 150 transnational clients in China, half of them American.[11]

Heyman does not speak Chinese and, prior to his marriage, had no experience in China. Nevertheless, he now sees himself as an expert on intercultural communication and training. He told me that when he saw the confrontation between students and Li Peng, in the prelude to the Tiananmen crackdown, he was appalled at the way the student leader, unwashed and clad in rumpled pajamas (because of his hunger strike), spoke to the premier in a scene that was broadcast on world television. Heyman declared that if "those kids" knew anything about teamwork, communication, and problem solving to deal with political dealers, the subsequent slaughter could have been averted.

The sad state of social communications in China, Heyman continues, is "created by culture and China's unique history." More specifically, the management problem is "not dissimilar from other emerging economies like Malaysia, but raised to the power of ten, or [the situation] that used to be in the U.S. in the 1950s. But in China, the management evolution is from that of a command economy to a more market-responsive one, plus political control. . . . And the GPCR is still part of the culture." His evolutionary model claims that the growth of a rational management style is hampered by the political culture that grew out of Maoism. The high level of technical training, which is a legacy of socialist constructionism, is not matched by equivalent management skills. He cited an assessment of over-40 technocrats who displayed "a built-in hierarchical model" that leads to "bad management." White-collar workers, especially those from state-owned enterprises and joint ventures, tend to take a punitive approach to rule breaking and yet are not comfortable criticizing a subordinate's performance. At the same time, there is, in the view of Western business consultants, a lack of communication skills, self-presentation, and politeness in their interactions with subordinates that is said to reinforce the latter's lack of initiative and sense of responsibility to the company. Heyman claims that this mix of political and cultural styles has led to demands for business consultants like himself. Many transnational firms partly blame their slow progress toward making profits on the lack of a rational managerial force in China. The problem is so widely recognized that companies now have special budgets for training and translation.

Heyman's company has trained about a thousand managers in Shanghai. In advising global firms about hiring, development, marketing and retailing, compensation and wages, he identifies these problematic areas:

Face: a kind of defensiveness that often results in not telling the truth, in not taking responsibility for action, in taking offense at being given direction, and in a lack of initiative.

Teamwork: "The Chinese are excellent only in physical projects, like building roads. But intelligent management skills are lacking, because they have never had role models."

A *"silo model" of control:* "The top-down government control has induced a 'wait to be told what to do' attitude. Locals are good at guanxi to get things done, rather than show leadership."

Heyman wrote the first foreign-based training manuals for sale in China. In contrast to the knowledge-based and case study method in the United States, he uses an action-oriented approach based on small steps. Trainees are gradually introduced to incremental bits of changes in organization, attitude, and behavior over the course of a few days. Applying a modeling survey, he found a positive correlation between desired behavior and education, and a negative correlation with age. He expects that over time, there will be more internalization of rational procedures. Heyman sums up his approach this way: "We train people on how to bring about change: intelligent problem solving in a creative context." Clearly, Heyman sees himself as doing great social good in training Chinese workers in "leadership" skills, the acquisition of which he believes were blocked by Chinese values concerning "face," guanxi, and authority. Chinese flexibility and initiative in interpersonal relations are not considered the kind of social skills that can facilitate corporate problem solving.

Another kind of management training focuses less on the need to adopt rules of corporate behavior and more on gently inducing the Chinese employee to become a reflexive subject, capable of self-management. Ethnic Chinese trainers are popular for helping workers manage the social interface between Chinese social norms and American managerial expectations. I interviewed a Taiwanese woman I call Flora Kang, who works for a major Boston-based firm. Kang visits the United States regularly to collect ideas about human resource management that she can apply in China. Her company mainly advises foreign finance companies operating in China, where the stress on "achieving customer service" is primary. When I met with her, Kang was dressed in a brocade Chinese dress (*qibao*) with slits down the side and a matching set of jade jewelry. Her face was immaculately made up, and she gestured elegantly. Her main role in the company is to localize successful American concepts and stories in China, but she regrets that many people are skeptical they will work. She sees herself as a cultural translator, converting American messages into Mandarin, and also tailoring them to the local power settings. Kang's "knowledge-based" approach first works on the attitude of Chinese clients, before proceeding to their behavior. She tries to stress the usefulness of knowledge and self-reflection to her clients as a way to break with the problems usually identified by foreign companies (defensiveness, lack of initiative, awkwardness at social relations). Her workshops define the directions and norms for clients to attain desired performance; participants are first motivated and then tested to see if they reach the goal. She identifies three kinds of changes that are especially important in helping Chinese individuals adjust to American work environments:

Resistance to feedback: Chinese workers are uncomfortable about reviewing the performance of subordinates and about being evaluated themselves. What management considers objective assessment is often viewed as threatening, being put in a "hostage" situation. For Chinese clients, "constructive feedback" is considered a tendency of foreigners to focus on conflict. Kang believes her first step is to reassure Chinese employees that suggestions made by management are not a punishment, nor a sign of breaking relations. She stresses the need for Chinese employees to understand that management corrections are not viewed as a black-and-white final assessment but an ongoing, dynamic process of continual adjustments to feedback. Only when the workers understand the reflexive process involved in management, she claims, can they develop a sense of accountability and interest in improving future performance.

Need for "soft skills": "Because locals are used to taking orders, they are not so good at social relations." There is also what she delicately calls the "hygiene problem," which is a major complaint of the foreign hotel industry. Her coaching includes personal cleanliness, greeting customers with a smile, making light conversation, presenting one's name card, and learning to circulate at parties with a drink in hand. Her manuals draw on Harvard Business School texts, but they simplify the case studies and practice sessions. She spends much time getting her clients to engage in role-playing and demonstration as a way to think through their interactions in uncomfortable situations.

Planning priorities: Kang criticizes other management consultants who measure Chinese subjects in terms such as "motivation," "discipline," and "quality" in order to judge them as lacking a "rational" approach to the organization of time, data, and responsibility. Instead of focusing on their purported "irrationality," Kang's technique is to get workers to think about how to spend time at work and to distinguish between business and private interests. Human resource managers are of course aware that Chinese workers are "de-motivated" by global practices such as the stark differences in salary structure for expatriates and for locals. Thus, when managers accuse Chinese employees of not understanding the importance of keeping schedules and for ignoring company deadlines in favor of family matters, Kang understands that workers are signaling their lack of investment in their companies. Managers complain about such "failures to internalize procedures," but their Chinese staff often feel justified in believing that their "own practice is more efficient."

Kang's job is to bring the thinking of Chinese employees closer to management norms and expectations and to consider the possible effects of their noncompliance with company rules on their own career interests. She makes them more aware of the need to be responsive to client expectations and to think globally. She retranslates "acting locally," not as adhering to Chinese preferences and norms, but in terms of making more cross-cultural connections with foreigners and developing a greater awareness of how non-Chinese, nonlocal matters can affect employment chances.

Heyman and Kang represent two management modalities, one aimed at changing behavior to conform to corporate governance, the other at producing a self-conscious, reflexive corporate subject. These business consultants see themselves as vital for the "transfer of learning" necessary for China's new knowledge class. International management firms, not the Communist Party, are the new legislators of Chinese humanity, working not through political browbeating and a crude reward and punishment system, but through the micropolitics of corporate training sessions that both cajole and induce workers to make themselves over into reflexive corporate subjects suitable for global markets. Clearly, corporate techniques for transforming subjectivity have turned on the most elite employees of foreign firms, perhaps even more than on the rank and file. The demands of globalized economic systems act very strongly on the elites, the executives, and those who wield power at the intermediate level. The disciplinary mechanisms are intended also to get them to think of themselves as part of the company's "global family." But our glimpse of the relentless "self-interested" maneuvers of Chinese professionals suggests that they are operating according to another set of social logics, making connections across local and foreign domains in the self-fashioning of new, agile, and reflexive subjects.

SELF-FASHIONING BY THE KNOWLEDGE ELITE

Shanghai, like other coastal cities but on a larger scale, is a center not only of luxury and cosmopolitan people, but of devastated neighborhoods, the new homeless, and thousands of migrant workers piling up around railway stations. In the chaotic traffic, alongside imported cars and trucks, old men push bicycles loaded down with pieces of cardboard retrieved from construction sites. In less than ten years of rapid growth, Shanghai now represents in microcosm the yawning disparities between the rich and the poor.

In 1997, journalist He Qinglian wrote a bestseller entitled *China's Pitfall*, a book that documents the ways market reforms have opened up great opportunities for a robber-baron class in alliance with the Communist Party to plunder state property, run rip-off schemes, engage in smuggling, and manage whorehouses. Unexpectedly, the book has become popular with leaders of the Communist Party. Although Chinese dissidents in the United States have interpreted this book as an all-out attack on market reforms (B. Liu and Link, 1998), the author maintains that China cannot do without market reforms, but that things have gotten out of control: "We have to look at what has happened, to take stock and to see what kind of society we have created" (He, 2000, 84). She argues that the collapse of ethics was the most dramatic change during the Deng Xiaoping era, when market reforms compromised politics, giving rise to a government-mafia alliance. She labels as the "marketization of power" the kinds of corrupt practices that have enabled officials to "rip off" (*zai*) the multitudes. A new robber-baron elite has been produced.

Market reforms have also led to a kind of knowledge elite, among them the 7 million technical experts, engineers, and managers who are connected to foreign capital, technology, and training (He, 2000, 84). Whereas the robber-barons, according to He, have abandoned society, it remains to be seen how the new professionals and managers are disruptive of older patterns of social reproduction and what kinds of new sociality are being imagined and configured. Mayfair Yang (1994, 6) has viewed guanxi *practice* as "the manufacture of obligation and indebtedness" that flourishes in conditions of market reform, as people turn more and more to personal connections to get what they want—from everyday items to jobs and apartments. Other scholars such as Doug Guthrie (1998) challenge the assumption that guanxi-based decision making and expectations will continue to be relevant in the corporate sector. It is interesting to see how the reflexive cosmopolitan and knowledge subjects are dealing with guanxi in ways that both cross-cut social divides and contribute to the overall class polarization.

THE NEW COSMOPOLITANS

There are now many Chinese expatriates educated in Europe and the United States who have internalized some of the values sought by Western companies. All consider themselves Chinese patriots, owing their loyalty not so much to the government as to their vision of the Chinese nation, its cultural integrity, and its making of a modernity different from those found in Western societies. They have different ways of expressing their roles as cross-cultural mediators whose work also contributes to the fashioning of a Chinese modern subjectivity that is tied to the conversion of new knowledge into capital and social status. One meets these people by hanging out with the well-educated and well-traveled, many of whom spend their evenings in Xintiandi ("New Heaven and Earth"), the refabricated neighborhoods, restaurants, and nightclubs in Shanghai's former French Quarter.

I met Lin, a chain-smoking, thoughtful, and lean man in his 30s, educated in cultural studies in Paris; he prefers Bourdieu to Foucault. His interest is really in French literature. Lin has been back in Shanghai for a couple of years, but still dresses in tight black turtleneck and jeans. He is still single, an unusual status for elite men of his age. Lin is fluent in French but non-English-speaking and mildly scornful of the United States. At first glance, one may think that Lin is a Francophile misfit back in China, but he was recently hired as the head of the Shanghai TV station, a position in charge of cultural affairs. Lin intends to use his position to shape the cultural forms that he thinks should be part of a distinctive Chinese modernity, rooted in its history and literary sensibility, but he is not likely to easily bend to some state-dictated version of what Chinese culture is all about. He seemed offended at such a suggestion, confident that his specific blend of cultural capital and political connections will provide the means to shape public culture without the direct interference of the Chinese Communist Party.

Television is one site for the production of modernity; the other is restaurants and bars, where global managers, their clients, professionals, capitalists, and hangers-on congregate and live it up.[12] I was given a list of bars and restaurants in Xintiandi, where the new professionals gather with foreigners in their leisure hours. There, in the most au courant restaurant in Shanghai, I met the owner, Tang, a savvy, professional-turned-entrepreneur in his early 30s. Born in the city soon after the GPCR, Tang emigrated as a teenager and later studied mechanical engineering at the University of Southern California. He gained experience working for American companies and then decided to return home and help shape the new urban scene. With financial backing from a Hong Kong restaurant group operated by Australian and British expatriates, Tang wanted a high-end eatery that will cater to the expatriate-cosmopolitan crowd in Shanghai.

His nightspot is the first to be located in a park in Shanghai, "like the Tavern on the Green" in New York City. Decorated in a knowing fashion, the restaurant is filled with art deco icons—furniture, light fixtures, and design motifs—taken from the Shanghai nightlife of the 1930s. Outside, a billboard with the image of early modern Chinese ladies beckons. Inside, we are served Asian-Californian fusion cuisine. The customer is immediately greeted by a wall-to-wall mural of a naked, buxom young woman supine against a drapery backdrop, her image doubled on the other side of the room by a mirror above the long, gleaming bar. The features of this figure are Asian without being Chinese, her body Western but odalisque in pose. The effect is an updated art deco Orientalism inspired by Ingres. To Tang, the mural captures the image and the attitude he wants to introduce to the new technocorporate elite: hybridity, California consumer culture, affluence with a touch of decadence, rather like the Asian and Western elements intermixed in the Singapore Sling from the bar. He told me the full-bodied image "represents freedom, East-West cross-currents, and some sexiness." The nightly crowds are international, mostly white expatriates with young Chinese women dressed in daring outfits, who come to mix, drink, and dance.

Tang has been featured in newspapers as one of the leading lights of the new Shanghai trying to recapture the glamour of the city when it was "the Paris of the East." He is quoted in a newsmagazine as saying, "The rest of Asia is so dead. I'm convinced that I came back to the right place at the right time."[13] In person, Tang is modest, and he seems effective in the local scene. He managed to wrangle permission from local authorities to build his restaurant in the park, something totally unprecedented. He sees his patriotism not in terms of a devotion to a pure Chinese past, or to the recent socialist transformation, but rather to reviving the cosmopolitanism that flourished in colonial Shanghai. His passion is directed toward creating the kind of elegant international culture that will position Shanghai in the new century. Tang confesses that he is so busy he has no time for marriage. He has started a new magazine, which will be free, about "what's in and what's out in Shanghai," a version of *The Village Voice* but without the urban politics. New York City, the current financial capital of the world, is clearly a model for this new financial city of Asia.[14] Returning Chinese expatriates such as Tang are producing the urban milieu for an emerging transnational class linked to global commerce and overseas education.

At the end of the evening, I walked through the wooded park (a miniature, dusty Trocadero) and exited at the other end, where I stumbled on a statue of Marx and Engels, fused and looming in the dark. An earlier cosmopolitanism seems to be in eclipse. Today, returnee Chinese professionals are enacting a kind of global localization different from that sought by management trainers. They have picked up the habits and practices of self-fashioning in their sojourns abroad, from domains of academic specialization and cultural consumption rather than corporate employment. As fully realized self-making individuals, they selectively assimilate and refashion global cultural forms for the urban cultural market in China. They are also comfortable with one-party rule in China, which they view as crucial for sustaining economic stability so that business can flourish and China can grow powerful.[15]

REFASHIONING GUANXI

There is some evidence that less well-heeled professionals, even as they are being daily subjected to the bombardment of corporate management and consumer culture, have trouble freeing themselves from the guanxi expectations of their relatives and friends. The lucky few working for global companies are thus ambivalent about internalizing corporate practices that purport to use totally objective, impersonal criteria in hiring. Below the Chinese MBAS—managers, engineers, and accountants—is a second tier of technical workers who daily interact directly with shopfloor workers. As employees of foreign companies, they are the ones who daily translate Western corporate policies and meaning to their Chinese compatriots. I received a tantalizing glimpse of how the technical workers recast corporate practices by giving equal or unavoidable attention to guanxi claims of relatives and friends.

Ms. Bao is a research assistant at CEIBS who both promotes and yet disagrees with the goals of the international business school in changing Chinese society. She is critical of the program because in her view the management ethics taught, with its focus on cross-cultural understanding, is "contradictory." The training of MBAS puts all the emphasis on Western methods, while Chinese culture is treated as an obstacle course to wade through. She points out that in Chinese society, Confucian ethics, especially as expressed in guanxi, are very important. It is ironic that foreign professors (Americans and British) teach business ethics, without any method to deal with guanxi. Foreign managers think of guanxi as corruption (backdoor/ *houmen* stratagems), but they themselves rely on guanxi to establish and consolidate links with state-owned enterprises (for joint ventures) or with officials to access business contracts.

As Bao sees it, guanxi has deep roots in China and cannot be eradicated. What is significant is that its moral worth has changed in recent conditions of market opening. In her view, guanxi had a bad connotation under Mao because it referred to the system of clientelism linked to the system of political classes. Members of the CCP were power brokers who monopolized guanxi, or the relationships that provided a conduit for the exchange of patronage from above to the supply of goods and services from below. In the era of market reforms, the market has opened up a new domain of worth to challenge the political sphere of value. There is now a diversity of decision makers and power wielders, and guanxi bubbles up from below. "This new horizontal form of guanxi is more diluted," Bao claims. She seems to differentiate between the older guanxi of instrumental patronage and clientelism and what she sees as the new, diffuse links arising from multiple sources that are involved in the transfer and conversion of values across various domains. As Bao asks, "The question now is, how much is guanxi worth?"

David Stark (2001) has argued that the problematization of worth requires us to pay attention to the practical system of accounting. How do we, in our own words and actions, make practical and ethical judgments, size up the situation according to different measures of worth, and how may we be "called to account for our actions"? Indeed, the rethinking of guanxi—after all, is there a more self-conscious, quotidian weighing of exchange and accountability—and the redeploying of guanxi reflect new strategies to interweave fragments of the social world rent by employment in global companies.

Bao notes that the question foreigners should ask is "how to mix guanxi with the Western system of doing business." This is a practical problem that foreign firms doing joint ventures with state-owned enterprises (SOES) have been grappling with for years. The overall responsibility toward workers in SOES means that Western practices of quality control must often take a back seat to guanxi considerations, such as taking care of workers who have become unproductive. An American manager at the General Motors joint venture outside Shanghai told me that thousands of Chinese workers should have been retired, but they remain on the books because GM wanted to accommodate Chinese demands for state workers. While the American manager bemoaned the irrationality of the Chinese public sector, his statement shows that GM was involved in a trade-off, whereby unproductive Chinese workers were a social value in exchange for setting up an automobile joint venture in the lucrative Chinese market. The Chinese state enterprises also gained as fewer workers would be rendered unemployed because of joint ventures.

Bao's friend Liu, who is a quality control supervisor at General Motors, notes that "everyone's in a big pot; we are responsible for each other. Individual responsibility is very new." In the hierarchical system of the state enterprises, there are no rewards for people's involvement in the broader aspects of their tasks, so that "workers develop the attitude of 'don't sweep the snow beyond your gate.'" This attitude has carried over to the GM joint venture, so that quality control is not well maintained, and defective goods are often made and shipped. He has had to continually remind the workers that they are responsible for defects and will be punished after they are caught the third time. Liu sees fundamental differences between Western and Chinese culture: "In the West, everybody's equal, and talent and performance are the only judge of a person. But in China, the confidence and trust of a friend, that is, social obligation and responsibility, are just as important."

In his everyday life, Liu deals with the conflict between objective Western norms and Chinese guanxi practices; he feels that Western managers err by focusing only on technical skills, while ignoring the importance of social values. He thinks that punishing people for their mistakes, for example, will cause them to hide their future errors. GM does a number of things to eradicate guanxi, but ultimately has failed. The firm will test the technical skills of applicants and see if they can work with bosses before hiring them. GM pays higher salaries than local firms in order to discourage workers from engaging in "guanxi," here meaning using their personal connections to engage in shady deals with outsiders. For instance, at Liu's workshop, "guanxi sometimes leads to purchases of low-quality equipment, at the same or at a different price." In his estimation, only about 20 percent of such actions are ever caught. But Liu thinks that firing workers for getting kickbacks, even if legal, is "not reasonable." In his view, GM managers simply think that "money talks." He mimics American talk: "Let's get him, he's the best!" American managers will make the first assessment of applicants, testing them for their technical skills. But their Hong Kong employees will say, "You don't know

Chinese culture. If there is not consideration of guanxi, you cannot get people!" There are usually many applicants for any one job, and the problem is how to select the few. Here guanxi steps in and makes the final cut, choosing applicants on the basis of friendship or payback for past favors to coworkers. Liu puts it this way: "In the final analysis, everything being equal, you have guanxi, you're in!" When I indicated my surprise, Liu told me he got into GM himself through guanxi. He was a CEIBS translator when a friend who worked at GM told him to apply. Out of twenty tested by GM, he got the job, was given further training, and got to travel to the States. In Liu's view, a method that combines Western rational-technical standards and Chinese guanxi is "a reasonable system. The most important issue is that if the most qualified person can get the job, guanxi is still important. A clever manager will not employ a stupid employee, but only one who can make profits for them. But he will still prefer those who 'have guanxi with me.'"

In other words, you hire someone with different kinds of worth (production and social), and the benefits will accrue to both the technical performance and to social relations in the workplace, and beyond. A narrow Western view of production worth blinds managers to the kind of benefits gained from also paying attention to the social values of workers.. Although some kinds of guanxi practice have been used for kickbacks and other corrupt behavior, the corporate system cannot ignore the importance of how Chinese people define social worth based on Confucian ethics: specifically, being accountable to coworkers and to relatives and friends outside the workplace. Just as the foreign corporation participates in a trade-off with Chinese authorities, exchanging the right to joint ventures for the political requirement to keep defunct workers on the job, so Chinese employees view the economic power gained from working in foreign firms as a resource for accruing social value in the public sphere. In these ways, guanxi practices—as relations for the transfer of worth across different domains and as a diffused sense of social responsibility emanating from the market sphere—continue to construct a sociality that interweaves ties between the new middle class with people in lower socioeconomic groups. The midrange employees of foreign firms display sophistication in reassessing different regimes of worth and how they can be recombined in a kind of practical flexibility that reconnects the privatized market world with society at large.

Global business knowledge is involved in shaping new corporate subjects through management programs that stress rationality, initiative, and soft skills. This new technoknowledge class is very different in structural location and consciousness from its predecessors, the bureaucratic intelligentsia produced by the CCP during the first decades of communist rule. The post-Mao knowledge class is not disciplined by state mechanisms, but increasingly is shaped by the reasoning, techniques, and consumer habits associated with the reflexive subject of global markets. They dominate not in the name of technical political knowledge (e.g., "Red and Expert" during the GPCR), but in the name of technical and cultural knowledge (of global business and consumer culture). The new knowledge class is itself dominated by the big entrepreneurs (robber-barons), whose power is drawn from their alliances with state bureaucrats. Instead of drawing on state resources for their wealth, the new technocrats, managers, and engineers draw power from their credentials and corporate links that orient them toward urban capitalist forms and interests. Because the majority are technocrats and office knowledge workers like Bao and Liu, they can be distinguished from cosmopolitan subjects like Lin and Tang, who are more integrated into the international scene. Nevertheless, their intermediate position between the robber-barons and the multitudes indicates that these middling figures have a crucial role to play in bridging and converting values across market, corporate, and social spheres. They appear to be the ones who most directly mediate the management techniques of foreign companies and the demands for solidarity with less fortunate others in the city. Global management techniques will have to contend with these knowledge workers who are in an interstitial position to redefine economic techniques and their moral worth in relation to other domains of values, shaping a practical reflexive subjectivity that is responsive to a sociality they call Confucian ethics.

The issue of subject formation and the "suitability" of various subjectivities for global capitalism explored here shows that a particular assemblage of diverse relations, actors, and social logics is a more useful conceptual framing than a structural theory of a homogenizing new economy and heroes. This discussion of business schools, management trainers, midlevel managers, and cosmopolitan cultural entrepreneurs in Shanghai challenges the notion that there is a uniform Chinese subjectivity that global capitalism must reform, or that there is a single universal hero figure in the new economy. Instead, we see that diverse subjects become part of the economic project itself, and that there is a variety of social engineering and self-fashioning logics at work in the new markets.

There are tensions between business consultants and Chinese knowledge workers, differences between survivors of the Great Chinese Cultural Revolution and returnee Chinese professionals and twentysomethings employed by foreign companies. The frictions and interconnections between Chinese urbanites and global business have engendered an explosion of different subject positions that diverse actors have taken up in relation to the New Economy, showing us how contingent and unpredictable the process can be.

NOTES

1 "Led by Increase in Asia, Stocks Abroad Rise Sharply," *New York Times*, September 9, 1998, p. C6.

2 Elsewhere, I discuss such an approach as a central concern in the anthropology of modernity (Ong, 2001).

3 Clearly, translational and bicultural actors—merchants, gangsters, and intellectuals—were also key figures in Shanghai when it was a Treaty port (1842–1949) dominated by colonial European powers (see, e.g., Elvin and Skinner, 1972). But arguably, the crucial actors in Shanghai's business world today are knowledgeable and flexible in a different constellation of knowledge, networks, and ethics.

4 For a preliminary discussion of the assemblage concept for studying globalizing social forms, see S. Collier and Ong (2003). For a different view of new figures in "Chinese capitalism," see X. Liu (2002).

5 The fifty major companies in Shanghai are state-owned, representative across industries such as silk production, electricity, and railways. The other key players are foreign companies, who are given more leeway and power than private Chinese entrepreneurs (Burstein and de Keijzer, 1998, 256–257).

6 See Olds (2000) for a discussion of how international architectural firms are playing a major role in designing Shanghai as an international finance center, and the state limits to their internationalist norms.

7 I interviewed American, Hong Kong, and mainland Chinese managers employed in American companies (IBM, Citibank, Proctor & Gamble, subsidiaries of American consulting firms, etc.). The business meaning of strategic localization or indigenization is different from the use of the term localization by academics to describe the effects of global forces at the local level (Burawoy, 2000; R. Robertson, 1995).

8 Quoted in "Embracing a New Culture," *South China Morning Post*, June 14, 1998.

9 In Singapore, state practices promote risk-taking, reflexive behavior as values for who counts as a worthy citizen-subject (see Ong, forthcoming).

10 Quoted in "Bigger Campus for Managers of Future," *South China Morning Post*, May 9, 1998.

11 He has had no Japanese clients; they do not seem to use consultancy firms. Japanese companies do not appear to have a need to micromanage Chinese workers, as Japanese managers tend to assume broad cultural sameness with, rather than difference from, the Chinese.

12 For an anthropological view of the impact of mass media on urban Chinese culture and gender, see Yang (2000).

13 "City on the Make," *Time* (international edition, Hong Kong), September 18, 1998, pp. 20–25.

14 Since 1990, more than 1,000 skyscrapers have been built in Shanghai, a city of 13 million people (ibid.).

15 A recent book argues that the rise of China's "business elite" has produced a new kind of state clientelism that is unlikely to promote "civil society," meaning democratization (Pearson, 1997, 4–5).

Neil Smith

GENTRIFICATION GENERALIZED:
FROM LOCAL ANOMALY TO URBAN
"REGENERATION" AS GLOBAL
URBAN STRATEGY

From the 1970s to the early years of the twenty-first century, a new urbanism has taken hold, and gentrification is a central dimension of that new urbanism. Consider the founding statement that revealed gentrification as a discrete process:

> One by one, many of the working-class quarters of London have been invaded by the middle classes—upper and lower. Shabby, modest mews and cottages—two rooms up and two down—have been taken over, when their leases have expired, and have become elegant, expensive residences. Larger Victorian houses, downgraded in an earlier or recent period—which were used as lodging houses or were otherwise in multiple occupation—have been upgraded once again. . . . Once this process of "gentrification" starts in a district it goes on rapidly until all or most of the original working class occupiers are displaced and the whole social character of the district is changed. (Glass, 1964, xviii)

Almost poetically, Ruth Glass captured the novelty of this new process whereby a new urban "gentry" transformed working-class quarters. A third of a century later, a very different vision of urban centers was being promulgated, again in London. The following is an excerpt from the 1999 decree for an "Urban Renaissance" released by a special Urban Task Force appointed by the UK Department of the Environment, Transport and the Regions (1999):

> The Urban Task Force will identify causes of urban decline . . . and practical solutions to bring people back into our cities, towns and urban

neighborhoods. It will establish a new vision for urban regeneration. . . . [Over the next twenty-five years] 60% of new dwellings should be built on previously developed land. . . . We have lost control of our towns and cities, allowing them to become spoilt by poor design, economic dispersal and social polarization. The beginning of the 21st century is a moment of change [offering] the opportunity for an urban renaissance.

The language of urban renaissance is not new, of course, and was liberally applied in the United States even before Ruth Glass coined the term "gentrification," but its significance is wholly transformed. There has been an iterative expansion in the scale of ambitions for urban rebuilding: whereas state-sponsored postwar urban renewal in Western cities helped to encourage private market gentrification, that gentrification and the intensified privatization of inner-city land and housing markets since the 1980s has in turn provided the platform on which large-scale multifaceted urban regeneration plans, far outstripping 1960s urban renewal, are established. The current language of urban regeneration bespeaks a generalization of gentrification in the urban landscape.

Consider some key differences in the visions presented by Glass and the British Department of the Environment. Whereas 1960s gentrification for Glass was a marginal oddity in the Islington housing market, a quaint urban sport of the hipper professional classes unafraid to rub shoulders with the unwashed masses, by the end of the century it has become a central goal of British urban policy. Whereas the key actors in Glass's story were implicitly assumed to be middle- and upper-middle-class immigrants, thirty-five years later the agents of urban regeneration are governmental, corporate, or corporate-governmental partnerships. A seemingly serendipitous, unplanned process that popped up in the postwar housing market is now ambitiously and scrupulously planned. That which was utterly haphazard is increasingly systematized. In scale and diversity, the process of gentrification has evolved rapidly to the point where the narrowly residential rehabilitation projects that were so paradigmatic of the process in the 1960s and 1970s themselves now seem quaint, not just in the urban landscape but in the urban theory literature.

Most important, perhaps, a highly local reality, first identified in major advanced capitalist cities such as London, New York, Paris, and Sydney, is now virtually global. Its evolution has been both vertical and lateral. On the one hand, gentrification as a process has rapidly descended the urban hierarchy and is evident not only in the largest cities but in more unlikely centers such as the previously industrial cities of Cleveland and Glasgow, smaller cities such as Malmö and Grenada, and even small market towns such as Lancaster, Pennsylvania, and České Krumlov in the Czech Republic. On the other hand, the process has diffused geographically as well, with reports of gentrification from Tokyo to Tenerife (Garcia Herera, 2001), São Paulo to Puebla, Mexico (G. A. Jones and Varley, 1999), Cape Town (Garside, 1993) to the Caribbean (Thomas, 1991), Shanghai to Seoul.

Of course, these experiences of gentrification are highly varied and unevenly distributed, much more diverse than early European or North American instances of gentrification. They spring from quite assorted local economies and cultural ensembles and connect in many complicated ways to wider national and global political economies. The important point here, however, is the rapidity of the evolution of a highly marginal yet distinct urban process, first identified in the 1960s, and its ongoing transformation into a significant dimension of contemporary urbanism. Whether in its quaint form, represented by Glass's mews, or in its socially organized form in the twenty-first century, gentrification portends a displacement of working-class residents from urban centers. Indeed, the class nature of the process, which is transparent in Glass's version of gentrification, is assiduously hidden in the verbiage of the British Labour government. That symptomatic silence says as much about the city's changing social and cultural geography, twinned with a changing economic geography, as does its more visible and voluble signs. As a means of tracing transformation that has taken place in the experience of gentrification, I begin with the case of New York City, where the process has now taken hold as a central determinant of urban form and where three phases of gentrification can be identified. My purpose is not in any way to present New York City as a core model for gentrification. Rather, my intent is to fill in the historical argument about the development of gentrification as a discrete process before moving toward Europe, where its evolution may have proceeded furthest.

DIMENSIONS OF CHANGE: NEW YORK CITY

The history of gentrification in New York City can be divided into three waves. The first wave occurred prior to the recession and fiscal crisis that unfolded after 1973, and the second wave followed in the late 1970s, lasting through most of the 1980s. The third wave of gentrification in New York City followed the rather late recovery of the city's economy between 1994 and 1996. As Jason Hackworth (2000) has argued in his historical analysis of gentrification in the city, each of these waves has a distinct character. The first might be called "sporadic gentrification," the second an "anchoring" process, according to Hackworth, and the third we might think of as "gentrification generalized."[1]

Sporadic Gentrification (1950s–mid-1970s)

In the first wave, much as in London, early gentrification was incidental and isolated; in other words, sporadic. The rehabilitation of dilapidated housing had occurred periodically in earlier centuries, and when a rash of rehabilitations began in places like Greenwich Village in southern Manhattan in the 1950s, accompanied by the influx of middle- and upper-middle-class residents, there was little immediate sign that this represented a new process justifying the moniker "gentrification." This, after all, was a neighborhood that had experienced various surges of Bohemian immigration since the nineteenth century, and although the folk/art and countercultural scene that emerged in the 1950s and 1960s represented a radical cultural departure, in real estate terms it could easily be incorporated as a revisitation of past cycles of change rather than the beginning of anything new. Incipient gentrification was thoroughly overshadowed by continued white migration to the suburbs and the closure or migration of obsolete manufacturing concerns clustered round the central business district.

As new experiences of gentrification began to emerge in other New York neighborhoods in the 1960s—in SoHo, the Upper West Side, Brooklyn Heights—and appeared in other cities from Philadelphia and Washington, D.C., to San Francisco, indeed from London to Vancouver, the commonality of these different experiences was increasingly recognized. But it was not until the 1970s that the London-born label gentrification began to circulate in New York as the descriptor of a new process. Urban boosters welcomed it as a potential sign of cultural and economic reversal after decades of apparent urban decline, whereas tenants, housing activists, and many working-class residents greeted with suspicion a process that threatened to displace them from their neighborhoods.

To a significant degree, gentrification remained sporadic and small-scale because financial institutions remained unwilling to invest significant amounts of capital in areas they still saw as "blighted."[2] Nor had the state developed any serious plans, in the wake of the failures of urban renewal, for a more comprehensive urban rebuilding. The new urban plan proposed in 1977 by President Jimmy Carter failed to materialize, and this marked the last time in the twentieth century that there was any serious attempt to link the economic fate of cities to the fate of the U.S. economy.

Anchoring Gentrification (late 1970s–1989)

The fiscal crisis of New York City (1973–1977) precipitated a profound structural shift in the geography, economy, politics, and culture of New York City that is still being played out in the twenty-first century. There were local causes, including the inordinate dependence of many large banks on the stable interest rates that flowed from high interest rate municipal bonds and other forms of public lending, and the extraordinary indebtedness of successive city governments. But the fiscal crisis was also a response to the contradictory historical geography of suburban expansion and urban economic disinvestment and decline at the center, as well as to the national and international economies in severe depression after 1973 (Tabb, 1982).

According to the rent gap theory, the root causes of gentrification lie in the geographic mobility of capital and the historical patterns of investment and disinvestment in the urban landscape: suburban investment through much of the twentieth century and consequent disinvestment in urban centers establishes the economic and geographic conditions for a major place-specific reinvestment in the center, taking the form of gentrification (N. Smith, 1979, 1996). Accordingly, the restructuring of the city's political economy in the wake of the fiscal crisis had a major effect on gentrification. In the first place, it deepened and intensified the levels of disinvestment in the central and inner city, cheapening land and housing prices in older, deteriorating neighborhoods. Smaller, local landlords who were unable to survive the recession sold out to larger real estate investors. As reinvestment picked up in the late 1970s, an unprecedented amount of capital flowed into land and property in Manhattan and surrounding boroughs and municipalities to take advantage of the devalorized market there.

The gentrification process that took root in the late 1970s, lasting through the 1980s boom, was therefore quite distinct from the earlier, more sporadic process. In the first place, whatever agentic role individual home buyers had with sporadic gentrification in the earlier round was increasingly eclipsed. The local state became centrally involved, with new public programs providing generous subsidies for building rehabilitation. The extraordinary centralization of political and economic power in the wake of the fiscal crisis—the city government was initially run by a small Municipal Assistance Corporation, then the Emergency Financial Control Board, both dominated by bankers—led to the provision of other public incentives to developers, ranging from tax abatements to zoning waivers to cross-subsidy plans in which developers were permitted to build luxury housing on publicly owned land if they also set aside a percentage (often 20 percent) of the total units for moderate- or lower-income tenants. (The subsidized units were often not in the same location as the luxury units: typically, the latter were located in central gentrifying neighborhoods, and subsidized units were in the outer boroughs.) As public subsidies helped grease an already rising supply of private capital into gentrification projects, the character of gentrification evolved significantly. Sharon Zukin (1982, 126–148) documented this transition in SoHo in the late 1970s, where the initial investors in previously loft manufacturing space—individuals, often artists or architects—were increasingly surpassed by professional developers whose interest in gentrifying properties was their resale and/or rental value. Bigger money in turn meant bigger projects.

The increased involvement of corporate developers in the process was matched by a greater willingness of established financial institutions to invest in areas they had previously avoided. This was in part prompted by state regulations against redlining policies, according to which banks would draw red lines on a map around "blighted" neighborhoods and refuse to make any mortgage loans in the area. But the new greenlining policies applied to the same neighborhoods: green lines replaced red lines and loan officers were encouraged to make as many loans as possible. These policies were also motivated by a realization that central and inner-city property markets, where significant rent gaps existed, now represented a gold mine for capital investment. During this period, the locus of gentrification also began to expand as neighborhoods that were unaffected by the process in its sporadic origins became more systematic targets. The Lower East Side, a very diverse neighborhood that mixed East European Jews and Puerto Ricans with Chinese immigrants to the south, saw the first sustained gentrification following the fiscal crisis. More distant neighborhoods, such as Park Slope in Brooklyn, Hoboken, and parts of Jersey City, became new real estate hot spots. Even such an unlikely place as Harlem became the object of gentrification in the late 1980s (N. Smith, 1996).

Meanwhile, the federal government under Ronald Reagan began a broad withdrawal of support for the systems of social service provision established during the New Deal. The city's poor and working class were targeted as already diminished programs to build new public housing were curtailed and existing subsidy programs cut. Laissez-faire became the motto: when the state becomes lazy, activists retorted, the result is assumed to be fair. But the state was anything but lazy. Although some federal subsidies available for larger-scale urban development and gentrification were also affected, the process was sufficiently established and private market sources of funding sufficiently forthcoming that a real estate scramble nonetheless ensued in the 1980s; gentrification was taking on a life of its own. For want of alternatives, by the end of the 1980s in New York City, gentrification was the housing policy.

None of this happened without opposition. As the language and reality of gentrification flooded the media in the roaring 1980s, and the new young urban middle class earned the name Yuppie, the effects of gentrification were increasingly obvious. The number of people evicted from their homes soared, as did the number of homeless people, estimated by homeless advocates to number almost 100,000, or 1.5 percent of the city's population. In neighborhoods all around the city, tenants' organizations mobilized in defense of tenants' rights, connected via a loosely organized citywide network of housing. Gentrification was one of their main targets. The struggles against gentrification culminated between 1988 and 1991 with the takeover of Tompkins Square Park in the Lower East Side by homeless people, squatters, activists, and neighborhood residents responding to a riotous police attempt to enforce a curfew. Not until 1991 was the park reconquered by the New York City Police Department (N. Smith, 1991, 1996).

In contrast to the sporadic gentrification that occurred prior to the fiscal crisis, this second-wave gentrification was much more systematic. It anchored gentrification, as Hackworth (2000) puts it, as an ingredient of a broader urban restructuring. No longer a local anomaly of big city housing markets, gentrification was developing into a recognizable residential component of a wider economic, social, and political remaking of urban space (N. Smith and Williams, 1986). As New York City consolidated its grasp on many of the command functions that became associated with "global cities," gentrification increasingly supplied the housing for *new generations of young, upwardly mobile professionals operating the city's financial, corporate, and myriad related enterprises*. At the same time as the Lower East Side faced an onslaught of gentrification, the art emanating from this neighborhood in the 1980s earned a significant reputation on the international art scene, suggesting the imbrication of economic and cultural globalizations, of which local gentrification was simultaneously a stimulant and an expression.

Gentrification Generalized (1994–?)

Despite the recession of the mid-1970s and the consequent fiscal crisis, which seriously affected the city's housing market, gentrification proceeded apace in the 1970s. Likewise, the shallower recession of 1980–1982 had a minimal effect on gentrification (for parallel evidence from Adelaide and Vancouver, see Badcock, 1992; Ley, 1992). Until the 1980s, then, gentrification seems to have remained sufficiently marginal to the larger housing market and the city's political economy that it survived recession largely unaffected. By contrast, the economic depression that began in 1989 following the 1987 stock market crash short-circuited gentrification in neighborhoods throughout the city. Now sufficiently integrated into the circuits of capital mobility, gentrification was severely curtailed, along with much of the rest of the housing market. Rents fell, vacancy rates rose, and residential rehabilitation and new construction were reduced to a minimum; a new wave of bankruptcies affected small landlords. Also new in this economic depression was the prediction from real estate pundits and some academics that gentrification had been a momentary phenomenon that went the way of the 1980s stock market boom. The new reality, they suggested, was "degentrification" (Bagli, 1991; Bourne, 1993).

Certainly in more marginal neighborhoods, where the first significant transformation came during the second wave—Williamsburg and Fort Greene in Brooklyn, Long Island City in Queens, Hell's Kitchen in Manhattan, and many others—gentrification dried up along with most investment in residential real estate. In Harlem, too, the late 1980s surge of brownstone rehabilitations effectively ended. But in more central neighborhoods, from SoHo to the Upper West Side, the process was never entirely halted in the early 1990s but continued at more of a trickle. In the Lower East Side, the reopening of a refurbished and tightly policed Tompkins Square Park in 1993 kindled a new, if still localized, wave of gentrification. But the prediction that degentrification was the new norm was historically short-lived and theoretically short-sighted (Lees and Bondi, 1995), and although it was a long and deep recession for the city, and the recovery was uneven geographically, gentrification began to rebound in 1994 and was in full sway by 1996.

In both geographical and sectoral terms, this third wave has generalized gentrification throughout the landscape of the inner city. Geographically, it has taken root in neighborhoods further and further out from the center, where the housing stock is younger than the nineteenth-century neighborhoods first affected by gentrification. By the late 1990s, for the first time, the hottest gentrifying neighborhoods tended not to be in Manhattan but in

Brooklyn, Queens, and New Jersey. At the same time, the more central districts affected by second waves began to fill in the interstices, block by block, neighborhood by neighborhood. In the Lower East Side, many of the initial gentrifiers connected with the art world were evicted by soaring rents as the logics of economic rather than cultural circulation reasserted themselves, and this previously edgy neighborhood was increasingly tamed into a high-rent playground for young white professionals (N. Smith and DiFilippis, 1999). In Harlem, whereas 1980s gentrification had colonized the edges, 1990s gentrification began to fill in the central blocks (Brash, 2000), much as the city's 1982 "redevelopment strategy" had planned.

Even more important is the sectoral generalization of gentrification. Whereas sporadic gentrification was limited to narrow niches in the housing market, and the anchoring of the process during the second wave implanted residential class transformations in a broader web of urban restructuring, third-wave gentrification since the mid-1990s has transformed gentrification from the inside out. More than rehabilitated mews and refurbished flats, gentrification increasingly implies new restaurants and shopping malls in the central city, waterfront parks and movie theaters, brand-name office towers alongside brand-name museums, tourist destinations of all sorts, cultural complexes—in short, a range of megadevelopments in the central and inner urban landscape. New York gentrification in the 1950s and 1960s represented a middle-class rejection of the commercial modernity of a place like Times Square. By the 1990s, the comprehensive reconstruction of Times Square and the Atlantic Terminal in Brooklyn, each with its distinctive mix of brand-name shops and malls, tourist arcades, offices, theaters, and restaurants, does more than create a new integument of work, play, and living in the city; it re-presents the gentrification of the city as a highly integrated conquest of urban space in which the residential component cannot reasonably be dissociated from the transformed landscapes of employment, recreation, and consumption.

Gentrification is no longer simply a housing strategy; it represents the leading edge of metropolitan change at the urban center. Now, as before, gentrification is a class conquest of the city, but it no longer expresses the narrow class interests found in Ruth Glass's Islington, the aristocratic nostalgia of Philadelphia's Society Hill, or the Bohemian Greenwich Village of the 1950s and 1960s. This generalization of gentrification is in part its democratization. Gentrification now produces urban landscapes that can be consumed by the middle and upper-middle classes—homeless people are quickly moved on—and that contribute to the formation of class identities across a significant class spectrum, albeit in highly differentiated ways. Anyone can walk through the new Times Square, but only a few people get the jobs at the new Reuters and Condé Nast office buildings. Anyone not intimidated by its highly defensible space, nor interdicted by the visible and vigilant security force, can gape at the garish commercial opulence of the Trump Tower on Fifth Avenue, a building devoted to amalgamating residential with commercial consumption, but very few can afford the $10,000 per month for a modest two-bedroom apartment. Much as popular television gives the masses a sense that the lives of the rich and famous represent the social norm to which all can aspire, gentrification now produces an urban landscape that conveys the same aspirations. Within this apparently democratized landscape, the extraordinary inequality of consumption expresses the redoubled power of class that gave rise to the language of gentrification in the first place.

GENTRIFICATION AS GLOBAL URBAN STRATEGY

The argument so far has focused on New York because that city lends itself to one version of the evolution of gentrification, in barely four decades, from a local anomaly to a concerted urban strategy. In reality, of course, this evolution of gentrification has occurred in markedly different ways in different cities and neighborhoods and according to different temporal rhythms. In some cities, for example, Mexico City, the process is nowhere as highly capitalized or widespread as the New York example would suggest; there the process remains more confined to the central district, in addition to Coyoacán, and the demarcation of three identifiable waves of gentrification has little if any empirical validity. In Seoul and São Paulo, the process is geographically isolated and in its infancy. In the Caribbean, the increasing connections between gentrification and global capital generally filter through the tourist industry, giving it its own distinct flavor. By the same token, the transformation of mile after mile of old wharf and warehouse properties along both banks of the Thames suggests that gentrification in London is, if anything, more expansive than in New York. It would be a mistake, therefore, to posit the "New York model" as some kind of paradigm and to gauge the progress of gentrification in other cities according to the stages of gentrification identified there. This is very explicitly not what I am suggesting here. Insofar as it is an expression of larger social, economic, and political relations, gentrification in any particular city will express the particularities of the place in the making of its urban space.

Having said this, however, the trajectory of gentrification highlighted by the case of New York does have a broader validity. This is the larger argument I want to make: to differing degrees, gentrification by the 1990s evolved into a crucial urban strategy for city governments in consort with private capital in cities around the world. Liberal urban policy, which in Europe dated back in some places to the end of the nineteenth century and in North America to the Progressive Era and was cemented with Roosevelt's New Deal, was systematically defeated beginning with the political economic crises of the 1970s and the conservative national administrations that followed in the 1980s. From Reagan to Thatcher and later Kohl, the provisions of that liberal urban policy were systematically disempowered or dismantled at the national scale, a task completed by the coterie of neoliberal leaders that followed: Clinton, Blair, Schröder. These political shifts removed public policy constraints on gentrification and encouraged subsidized private market transformation of the urban built environment. The new phase of gentrification therefore dovetails with larger class conquests not only of national power but of urban policy, and by the end of the twentieth century, gentrification, marking a concerted and systematic partnership of public planning with public and private capital, has moved into the vacuum left by the end of liberal urban policy. Elsewhere, where cities were not governed by liberal urban policy during much of the twentieth century, the trajectory of change has been very different, yet the embrace of a broadly conceived gentrification of old centers as a competitive urban strategy in the global market leads in a similar direction. In this respect at least, turn-of-the-century neoliberalism hints at a thread of convergence between urban experiences in the larger cities of what used to be called the First and the Third Worlds. This argument should not be pushed too far, however. The old First World countries remain the predominant location of gentrification in the early years of the twenty-first century, and it is less than clear how the process will develop in Asia, Latin America, and parts of Africa.

The generalization of gentrification has various dimensions, and these can be understood in terms of five interrelated characteristics: the new role of the state, penetration by global finance, changing levels of political opposition, geographic dispersal, and the sectoral generalization of gentrification already alluded to. Let us examine each of these in turn. First, between the second and third waves of gentrification, the role of the state has changed dramatically (Hackworth and Smith, 2001). The absence or significant withdrawal of the national state from subsidies to gentrification in the 1980s has in the 1990s been replaced by the intensification of partnerships between private capital and the local state. Early versions of the entrepreneurial city have blossomed as a central vehicle for capital investment in the urban landscape; private-public partnerships, a relative novelty in the late 1970s, have become the norm, yet in the process, the valence of power binding the private and public sectors has changed. Thus, in 1998, the City of New York announced that along with the state, it would provide almost $1 billion of subsidies for the New York Stock Exchange to keep that institution from moving a mile across the Hudson River to New Jersey. Unlike in the past, there was never any threat that the NYSE, awash with capital sloshing in from around the world, actually needed the subsidy. The city justified it instead as good business practice. Whereas two decades ago, city governments became involved in similar, if much more modest "partnerships"—"geobribes," we might call them—largely as a means of greasing the wheels of local economic development, today the local state's involvement adheres more explicitly to the rules of the market. Instead of the political rationale helping to steer the economic, the political rationale is now entirely folded into the economic. Urban policy no longer aspires to guide or regulate the direction of economic growth so much as fit itself to the grooves already established by the market in search of the highest returns (either directly or in terms of tax receipts).

The new role played by global capital is also definitive of the generalization of gentrification. From London's Canary Wharf to Battery Park City—developed by the same Canadian-based firm (Fainstein and Gladstone, 1994)—it is easy to point to the new influx of global capital into megadevelopments in urban centers. Just as remarkable, however, is the extent to which global capital has percolated into much more modest neighborhood developments. Emblematic in this regard is a new sixty-one-unit condominium building in New York's Lower East Side, two miles from Wall Street, where every apartment is wired with the latest high-speed Internet connections. This is a small development by global city standards, but it was built by nonunion labor, the developer is Israeli, and the major source of financing comes from the European American Bank. The reach of global capital to the local neighborhood scale is a hallmark of the latest phase of gentrification.

Third, there is the question of opposition to gentrification. From Amsterdam to Sydney, Berlin to Vancouver, San Francisco to Paris, gentrification's second wave was matched by the rise of myriad homeless, squatting, housing, and other antigentrification movements and organizations that were often loosely linked around overlapping issues. These rarely came together as citywide movements, but they challenged gentrification sufficiently that in each case, they were targeted by city politicians and police forces. Apart from anything else, the heightened levels of repression aimed at antigentrification movements in the 1980s and 1990s testified to the increasing centrality of real estate development in the new urban economy. Cities' political regimes were changing in unison with their economic profile, and the dismantling of liberal urban policy provided a political as much as an economic opportunity for new regimes of urban power. The emergence of what can be called "the revanchist city" (N. Smith, 1996) was not just a New York phenomenon but can be seen in the antisquatter campaigns in Amsterdam in the 1980s, attacks by Parisian police on homeless (largely immigrant) encampments, and the importation of New York's zero-tolerance techniques by the Berlin police in the mid-1990s. In all of these cases, the new revanchism was explicitly justified in terms of making the city safe for gentrification. In São Paulo, highly repressive tactics applied to the city's street people are rationalized in terms of the "scientific" doctrine of zero tolerance emanating from New York.

The fourth characteristic of this third generalizing phase is the outward diffusion of gentrification from the urban center. This is far from a smooth or regular process, but as gentrification near the center results in higher land and housing prices, even for old, untransformed properties, districts further out begin to be caught up in the momentum of gentrification. The pattern of diffusion is highly variable and is influenced by everything from architecture to parks and the presence of water, but above all, it is geared to the historical patterns of capital investment and disinvestment in the landscape. The less even the initial outward growth of capital investment and the less even the disinvestment in these newer landscapes, the less even will be the diffusion of gentrification. By the same token, in cities where the majority of spatial expansion has occurred in recent years and where the opportunities for sustained disinvestment have been circumscribed, the diffusion of gentrification may be similarly limited.

Finally, the sectoral generalization that typifies this most recent phase goes to the heart of what distinguishes the new gentrification. Whereas urban renewal in the 1950s through 1970s sought a full-scale remaking of the centers of many cities, and galvanized many sectors of the urban economy in the process, it was highly regulated and economically limited by the fact that it was wholly dependent on public financing and therefore had to address issues of broad social necessity, such as social housing. On the other hand, whereas the early waves of gentrification that followed urban renewal proceeded, by contrast, with considerable independence from the public sector, for all that they received hefty public subsidy in the early stages, the full weight of private market finance was not applied until the third wave. What marks the latest phase of gentrification in many cities, therefore, is that a new amalgam of powers and practices has been forged in a much more ambitious effort to gentrify the city. Retaking the city for the middle classes involves a lot more than simply providing gentrified housing, and a new institutional "gentrification complex" now pioneers a comprehensive class-inflected urban remake. This gentrification complex weaves global financial markets together with large and medium-size real estate developers, local merchants, and property agents with brand-name retailers, all lubricated by city and local governments for whom beneficent social outcomes are now assumed to derive from the market rather than from its regulation; the logic of the market, not the provision of social services, is the new state modus operandi. Real estate development becomes a centerpiece of the city's productive economy, an end in itself, justified by appeals to jobs and taxes, tourism, and the construction of large-scale cultural complexes (see Vine, 2001), in addition to the multisectoral megadevelopments and consumption palaces of the new downtown. In ways that could hardly have been envisaged in the 1960s, the construction of new gentrification complexes in central cities across the world has become an increasingly unassailable capital accumulation strategy for competing urban economies.

Understood in this broader framework, the post-1990s generalization of gentrification as a global urban strategy came as heir to the abandonment of twentieth-century liberal urban policy on one hand and, on the other, although its first appearance came much earlier, as a consummate urban expression of an emerging neoliberalism. That which began as a coincidental occurrence in the housing market has evolved into a systemic expression of global social and economic change. This was neither inevitable nor accidental. Much as cities became global, or so we are told, so did some of their defining features. The emerging globalization of gentrification, like that of cities themselves, represented the victory of certain economic and social interests, generally along class and sometimes race lines, over others.

THE NEW EUPHEMISM: URBAN REGENERATION

The strategic appropriation and generalization of gentrification as a means of global interurban competition finds its most developed expression in the language of "urban regeneration." Consonant with the importance of the state in the new wave of urban change, it is not in the United States that this process has proceeded furthest, but in Europe. Tony Blair's Labour administration may be the most outspoken advocate of reinventing gentrification as urban regeneration, but it is a Europe-wide movement. Denmark, for example, made regeneration official policy in 1997, with a separate National Secretariat for Urban Regeneration, and Berlin bureaucrats have come to view the entire period of rebuilding after 1991 as one of urban regeneration. A major conference was held in Paris in December 2000 on the theme "Convergence in Urban Regeneration and Housing Policy in Europe." Attended by senior policy directors and advisors representing all governments of the European Union, together with some neighboring states aspiring to EU membership, the conference, according to its publicity announcement, tried to push the "debate on housing and regeneration . . . beyond the narrow span of physical development to examine the institutional arrangements which have to be put into place" to make urban regeneration a reality. Their mission was practical and comprehensive: large-scale urban transformation will require solid links between "the providers of social housing, private investors, [and] those responsible for training or policing" as well as between "local regeneration agencies, local authorities and national governments." It makes sense to see these initiatives—the British urban regeneration manifesto, different European state policies, and the efforts to establish a Europe-wide urban regeneration strategy—as the furthest attempts yet to establish gentrification at the heart of transnational urban policies.

There are a number of striking aspects to these new urban regeneration agendas. First is a question of scale. The coordination of urban regeneration strategies across national boundaries is unprecedented. Various international sources certainly contributed to the rebuilding of European cities after World War II, but the subsequent urban renewal programs were resolutely national in origin, funding, and scope. Today, by contrast, Europe-wide initiatives on urban regeneration are pioneering cross-national gentrification strategies at a scale never before seen. A central concern lies with efforts to integrate housing initiatives with "other regenerative activities," and so, as the title of the Paris conference conveys, this transition from housing-centered gentrification policy to a broad-based multisectoral regeneration is still in process. And unlike in the United States, the question of social housing cannot be entirely excluded from the vision of regeneration. Although a Europe-wide, state-centered strategy of urban regeneration is by no means yet in place, for Eureaucrats, developers, and financiers throughout the continent, it is very much in sight.

Second is the question of geographic focus. The 1999 British regeneration manifesto, apparently watchful of the environmental consequences of continued suburban sprawl, declares that over the next twenty-five years, 60 percent of new housing provision should occur on brownfield sites, that is, on urban land that has already gone through one or more cycles of development. Clearly, this initiative will be aimed at older urban areas that have undergone sustained disinvestment, and although these can be scattered throughout metropolitan areas, it is reasonable to expect that they would be concentrated in or near urban centers. Thus, gentrification is recast as a positive and necessary environmental strategy. Connected, therefore, is the question of "social balance" and the need, as the British document puts it, to "bring people back into our cities." Social balance sounds like a good thing—who could be against social balance?—until one examines the neighborhoods targeted for regeneration, whereupon it becomes clear that the strategy involves a major colonization by the middle and upper-middle classes. To the politician, planner, and economist, social balance in London's Brixton means bringing "back" more of the white middle classes. Advocates of social balance rarely if ever advocate that white neighborhoods should be balanced by equal numbers of people of African, Caribbean, or Asian descent. Thus, it is not people in general who are to be brought "back into our cities"—certainly not Welsh coal miners, Bavarian farm workers, or Bretton fisher folk; rather, the appeal to bring people back into the city is always a self-interested appeal that the white middle and upper-middle classes retake control of the political and cultural economies as well as the geography of the largest cities. Probing the symptomatic silence of who is to be invited back into the city begins to reveal the class politics involved.

Then there is the question of the anodyne language of regeneration. In the first place, where does this language come from? A biomedical term, regeneration applies to individual plants, species, or groups of species—a liver or a forest might regenerate—and its metaphorical application to cities is highly revealing. Although the language of regeneration has always been present to describe gentrification, it seriously took off in the neoliberal 1990s. The implication is that the strategic gentrification of the city is actually a natural process: the advocacy of regeneration strategies disguises the quintessentially social origins and goals of urban change, erases the politics of winners and losers out of which such policies emerge. Thus, a second symptomatic silence concerns the losers. Historically and not at all accidentally, gentrification has been associated with considerable levels of displacement and homelessness, yet this central result of regeneration is loudly unconsidered. Missing in the entire script of urban regeneration—from the British manifesto and from the concerns of the Paris conference—is any recognition of what happens to those people displaced or made homeless by such a large-scale reconquest of the city.

The language of regeneration is deliberately substituted for the more direct and honest language of gentrification. Precisely because the language of gentrification tells the truth about the class shift involved in regeneration of the city, it has become a dirty word to developers, politicians, and financiers, and we find ourselves in the ironic position that in the United States, where the ideology of classlessness is so prevalent, the language of gentrification is quite generalized, whereas in Europe it is suppressed. Also symptomatic, therefore, the whole language of gentrification is conspicuously absent from European regeneration agendas. Thus, even seemingly progressive planners and local councilors from Bochum to Brixton, who still think of themselves as socialists and who may be keenly aware of the dangers of displacement, have become captured by the bureaucratic promise of regeneration to such an extent that the underlying agenda of widespread gentrification of urban centers is largely invisible. Not only does urban regeneration represent the next wave of gentrification, planned and financed on an unprecedented scale, but the victory of this language to anaesthetize our critical understanding of gentrification in Europe represents a considerable ideological victory for neoliberal visions of the city.

CONCLUSION

In 1970, Henri Lefebvre argued that urbanism had supplanted industrialization as the motive force of capitalist expansion: industrialization may have bred systemic urbanization, but urbanization now engendered industrialization. That claim has not withstood the test of time, especially in light of the globalization of industrial production and the expansion of East Asia that was well in tow as Lefebvre wrote, and yet Lefebvre seems to have anticipated something very real. In a global sense, urbanization has not, of course, supplanted industrialization; all of the products that fuel urbanization are made somewhere in the global economy. Still, urban real estate development—gentrification writ large—has now become a central motive force of urban economic expansion, a central sector of urban economies. Urban regeneration is a central strategy in the global competition among different urban agglomerations in the context of a newly globalized world. The generalization of gentrification comes with extraordinary social costs. Much as with globalization, it is anything but an anonymous economic logic, and opposition to such global and urban change will play a crucial role in the direction taken by the new geographies.

NOTES

1 My historical account here draws substantially on Hackworth's (2000) analysis.
2 Planners and urban scholars used this epidemiological term, "blight," when talking about poor, often black or Latino neighborhoods. It is a social euphemism for the results of economic disinvestment by property owners and the state.

Melissa S. Fisher

NAVIGATING WALL STREET WOMEN'S GENDERED NETWORKS IN THE NEW ECONOMY

In 1954, the Eisenhower bull market ushered in a new period of economic prosperity for the United States and an unprecedented growth spurt on Wall Street. Corporate expansion, aggressive stock selling, and increased consumer activity contributed to the financial climate. In 1957, in the wake of these changes, the *New Yorker* ran an article entitled "Growth Situation" about a group of female security analysts. The writers began their piece with the following introduction:

> We had long looked upon Wall Street, above the secretarial level, as one of the last almost-exclusively male preserves, but now, having spent a lively hour with the Young Women's Investment Association, we know better. Miss Jones Williams, chairman of the program committee, called one morning last week to invite us to a y.w.i.a. luncheon at the City Midday Club where three noted male security analysts were to speak—on drugs, steel, and of all things aluminum. Drugs, steel, and aluminum be damned, we replied; we'd come anyhow. Good said Miss Williams, adding that we would be able to spot her by her plaid dress. On arriving, we found this recognition device effective, and Miss Williams looked fine in it, too. ("Talk of the Town," 1957)[1]

According to the article, the group, a year old, was composed of twenty-seven members. Miss Williams explained that "membership is open to any woman under thirty-five who works in a professional capacity in an investment bank or brokerage house, but in fact we're mostly security analysts. Most of our members are from Ivy League colleges—you know, Radcliffe, Smith, Vassar,

Wellesley, Bryn Mawr, Barnard, and so on." Miss Susan Zuger, the group's president and founder, told the reporters the story of the creation of the Young Women's Investment Association (YWIA). She and her female friends wanted to join the Investment Association of New York, an organization of young financial men, to help them make "Street contacts" to find better jobs. Barred from entry because of their gender, they chose to form their own organization. These female entrepreneurs were convinced that "the Association is definitely a growth situation." Indeed, by 2004, the YWIA, now known as the Financial Women's Association of New York (FWA), had developed into "a leading executive organization of 1,100 members committed to shaping leaders in business and finance with a special emphasis on the role and development of women" (http://www.fwa.org).

Forty-plus years after the creation of the FWA, the nation was again flush with enthusiasm, this time about the "New Economy." "Flatter hierarchies," "global networks," and "start-ups," were part of the vocabulary of business. In October 1999, the *New York Times* ran an article entitled "A Network of Their Own: From an Exclusive Address, a Group for Women Only" (Abelson, 1999). According to the piece, two years earlier, Janet Hanson, president and CEO of Milestone Capital, the country's first women-owned firm to specialize in managing institutional money market funds, had invited a group of Goldman Sachs female alumnae to meet at the Water Club in New York City. The women discussed their lives since leaving the firm. Some, like Hanson, a veteran of Goldman Sachs, had launched their own businesses. Others were full-time mothers living in the suburbs. Yet, in spite of the intervening years and geographic distances between them, the women all, Hanson told the reporter, still "spoke the language of Wall Street."

In 1999, Hanson decided to recreate the reunion atmosphere online. From her firm's headquarters in Westchester, New York, this New Economy female entrepreneur called the first Wall Street women's network in cyberspace "85 Broads," a play on the physical address of Goldman Sachs, 85 Broad Street in Manhattan and the colloquial term "broads" used for women. The group is composed of women currently working at Goldman Sachs and female corporate refugees from the firm. According to an 85 Broads observer, "The power of technology connects women in one space, like they are in the same room. Geographical barriers dissolve and become invisible. Technology provides the ability for women to communicate across oceans" (from field notes).

I highlight these two stories about networks because I am interested in locating transformations in Wall Street women's organizational identity in relation to shifts in post–World War II financial markets, corporate structures, and feminist politics. The FWA emerged during the heyday of the Eisenhower bull market (1954–1969). The period of the extended postwar economic expansion witnessed a shift from the partnership to the corporation as the predominant organizational form on Wall Street. The hierarchical authority structure, the linchpin of modern bureaucracies, dominated the ways managers thought about the world and about themselves (Jackall, 1988, 17). Striving for success in corporations entailed moving up or getting ahead in a single organization.

Buoyed by the feminist movement's struggle to open up formerly male professions, women in finance began their careers in the area of research during the late 1950s and 1960s (Fisher, 2004, 299–302). The primary goal of the FWA, however, from its inception in 1956, was occupational mobility, ensuring that women move up the corporate ranks on Wall Street. FWA women viewed the network as an elite female, financially focused entity defined by business principles, rather than a pro-feminist organization oriented toward fighting gendered discrimination and sexual harassment in the workplace.[2]

But by the 1990s, the vision of a Manhattan-based female corporate network, void of a gendered political agenda, began to appear difficult to sustain. Legal battles over sexual discrimination on Wall Street, emerging in the 1970s, gathered momentum in the last decades of the twentieth century as increasing numbers of women entered the workforce. Hence, in contrast to the group's formative years, a financial women's community, without any feminist perspective, became a source of struggle among the FWA's leadership. This complaint was common, especially among women who came of age in the 1970s and 1980s and eventually became FWA participants in the 1990s. Lenore Diamond, a board member, witnessed and participated in this process. She describes the political shift in the FWA in the following manner:[3]

> The FWA, when I first started working on Wall Street, was like a downtown Junior League, sort of Republican conservative group. My first experience with the FWA was when the Equal Rights Amendment was up for passage in New York, and they banned us from putting up flyers. They got a court order that we had to stand more than 200 feet from the organization's meeting place to give the women going to the FWA meeting a petition. . . .

So I was one of the first members to be a liberal of the new guard. . . . I was a peripheral person—until more women joined the FWA who had sort of my political and sensitivity issues. . . . Even in the early 1990s the FWA was still very cautious about women's issues—publicly saying something. There was still this tremendous feeling, in the majority of the members, "We can't talk about that we're discriminated [against] or we are not going to get the corporate money for our dinner."

At the same time, rigid work structures that provided life-long career stability gave way to a more fluid New Economy, driven by technology and the globalization of markets. Corporate bureaucracies became more flexible and less secure institutions (Sennett, 2000, 1). The assumptions of successfully building a life-long career in a single firm, or even a set of firms, on Wall Street—working hard, making a lot of money, and becoming a managing director—began to disappear. Indeed, one out of every ten employees in the securities industry has been relieved of responsibility since April 2001 (Kolker, 2003, 24). The number of women working in New York City's financial industry dropped by more than 20 percent in the first two years of the new century, to an estimated 60,000 from more than 70,000 (Gandel 2002, 1). This is a significant reversal in Wall Street women's fortunes after two decades of advancement in the industry. Layoffs, however, are not the only factor responsible for the decline. In the wake of September 11, more and more women have decided to walk away from Wall Street of their own accord, in search of alternative career paths (2).

Reflecting these cultural, political, and economic shifts, contemporary Wall Street women's networks consist of a series of disparate projects, agendas, and practices. Some focus on occupational mobility, others on life outside of work; some address diversity in the workplace, and still others center on philanthropic endeavors. In recent years, for example, the FWA has added a diversity committee advocating and recruiting African American, Asian American, and other "minority" women for FWA membership, programs, committees, and speakers. As of 2003, 85 Broads, now a global online Wall Street women's network, consisted of two interrelated organizations: 85 Broads provides a cyber forum for former and current Goldman Sachs women to make contacts as they make career transitions in the new information-based business environment; Miles to Go, a nonprofit organization established by 85 Broads, raises, manages, and distributes charitable funds in support of primarily gendered humanitarian, philanthropic, and educational causes around the world.

The cornerstone of the FWA was (and still is) pushing women's occupational mobility. A key mission of 85 Broads is also helping women advance in their careers. However, by the turn of the millennium, these women's networks were dealing with new issues and obstacles: calls for diversity in business, a loss of permanent work, and a search for the meaning of success in an increasingly postcorporate world. Although a multiplicity of logics have always operated in Wall Street women's networks from their inception, there was an initial ordering, "a 'hegemony' in the sense of a relative dominance of some meaning and practices over others" (Ortner, 1996, 147).[4] This hegemony has gradually been destabilized. Specifically, dominant, older definitions and practices associated with professional business success circulating among the early generation of FWA women dated from a period in which work was "valued as a means to the end of professional or community status and career advancement, as defined by the organization" (Heelas, 2002, 80). However, as the expectation of lifetime tenure in a single corporation has begun to dissolve, other success ideologies have gained importance, especially among the younger generation of women participating in both the FWA and 85 Broads. Notably, contemporary women's success narratives and associated activities, including their increased focus on gendered corporate social responsibility and diversity, are increasingly concerned with finding "one's destiny" beyond the parameters of the workplace.

A series of challenges from both within and outside of the financial women's community—the feminist movement, the globalization of markets, and the virtualization of and sometimes disappearance of work—have destabilized the ordering principles of women's networks. This does not mean, for example, that the older ideologies of success have disappeared, but rather that alternative ones are emerging alongside the old ones, which can sometimes trump the latter. Moreover, the dominant medium in which women discuss career success is being partially transformed. Network practices are increasingly taking place within the intersections of city-spaces and cyberspace.

In the following, then, I explain transformations in Wall Street women's organizational practices and why they occurred, in some detail. What does Wall Street women's talk about themselves and their networks reveal about the ways shifts in success ideology register and respond to historically engendered cultural tensions? What does their discourse disclose about reformations in the ways women relate to the market, workplace, technology, and feminism over time? What does it tell us about metamorphoses in women's corporate subjectivity during the transition from the old to the New

Economy? And what might all of these changes tell us about the political trajectory of financial women's networks?

THE CATEGORIES OF MEMBERSHIP, GOALS, AND SUBJECTS

Addressing these questions requires taking a look at internal discussions over network objectives and membership. Although the FWA's official mission was never completely static, it did have a hegemonic project. Its goals, from early on, were, according to the board, "to encourage women to seek professional careers within the financial community; provide a strong network of professional contacts; promote cooperation and understanding among its members; [and] provide further education" (FWA 1977–1978 board memo). The FWA attempted to forge a stable collective identity around the category of the professional financial female subject and to construct an institutional structure that would undergird that identity. Stabilizing the terms of "finance," however, proved to be a source of contention in the rapidly changing world of Wall Street.

Forty FWA board and regular members met in New York City in August 1978. The purpose of the meeting was to debate the future directions of the organization. However, the event was overcome by disagreements over the definition and significance of "financial" and, by extension, arguments over who would be admitted. One woman, according to board meeting minutes, "defined 'financial' as dealing in financial services, with a background in finance: current job responsibilities key: example, marketing and corporate planning are financial, buying is not." A board member responded that she "believed that the FWA is not any better by being financial." A fellow leader "questioned what the FWA would be if not financial; we represent the financial area of business that has been historically difficult for women." A member replied that "while we must not dilute our purpose, we should not eliminate lawyers who want to know more about finance" (FWA board meeting minutes, August 30, 1978). Lacking a consensus on the meaning of finance, and its relative importance to the group's identity, made it increasingly difficult to construct a unified network.

Debates about which occupations belonged to the financial services industry became commonplace at FWA board meetings. The difficulty of defining the category "financial" was rooted in transformations in both the women and the industry at large. Specifically, during the earlier years, defining membership criteria along occupational lines was a straightforward task.

In the 1960s there were only about sixty professional women on Wall Street, the majority of whom worked in research. The only other women in finance occupied "nonprofessional" clerical and secretarial positions (Brooks, 1973, 108). Membership criteria for the YWIA were based on the self-description of the FWA's founding members, a group of eight security analysts. Accordingly, "anyone could join the group as long as they were under thirty-five and worked in a *professional* capacity in an investment bank or brokerage house" ("Talk of the Town," 1957; emphasis added).

The group was first forced to broaden its base by loosening the age requirements, as its potential membership base grew older with the initial influx of women into the professional workforce. Initially, FWA participation was open to Wall Street women under the age of 35. In 1965, amid calls to disband the group, FWA president Marguerite Beer Plant sought to expand the membership to include women under the age of 40. By 1966, the group's name was changed legally to the Young Financial Women's Association. In 1968, they formed a constitution committee, transforming the organization into the Financial Women's Association, officially launched in 1971, with no age limits (FWA Newsletter, 1996).

The women initially constructed the categories along the definitions of "professional" financial careers. However, these definitions were continually being reformulated as some women moved up the executive ladder on Wall Street while others entered into previously male-dominated areas such as banking and trading. Hence, in creating membership categories, the FWA of the 1970s struggled to take into account that the career subject positions women occupied were not static, but mobile. The shift in women's career paths was discussed in 1976 during the FWA's twentieth anniversary held at Windows on the World, the restaurant on the top of the World Trade Center. Reporters from *The New Yorker* interviewed FWA members during the celebration. Specifically, the writers asked the women if their "organization had changed much" since 1957. FWA president Elaine Rees, a security analyst for the Dreyfus Corporation, provided the following answer:

> We took our present name in 1971. We've dropped the cut-off age of thirty-five since many of our members move into the really important jobs after forty. And we've increased our membership from twenty-seven to a hundred and eighty. The original group was mostly security analysts—the first professional job open to women on Wall Street—but now we have bankers, stockbrokers, traders, management consultants, financial analysts, portfolio managers, economists, and even several lawyers. In the last

few years, banks and brokerage houses have been aggressively recruiting women for a wide variety of professional jobs. ("Financial Women," 1976)

If early membership criteria emphasized the occupational category of holding a professional position in an investment bank or brokerage house, with time, this definition, like that of age, broadened as well. FWA debates about the meaning of "financial" intensified in relation to transformations within the industry, especially Wall Street's new emphasis on the value of financial knowledge. This change occurred in the wake of the deregulation of finance in the mid- to late 1970s, allowing institutions to compete more intensely with one another. Specifically, in the new competitive atmosphere, firms' research capacities and the art of financial forecasting were on the rise as banks diversified into national and international business areas (H. Kaufman, 2000). The growing stress on financial expertise produced a shift in the logic used by the FWA to determine its membership and goals. Rather than define members exclusively along the lines of specific occupations, FWA members were now women who shared a specialized knowledge.

Thus, on March 23, 1979, two co-chairs of the FWA's Long Range Committee drafted a document entitled "Some Proposed Guidelines for the Financial Women's Association—A Professional, Not-For-Profit, Volunteer Organization." The statement opened with the following proclamation: "The FWA is, and should remain, a financially oriented organization. The focus should be the core of its membership and program policies. The financial knowledge of the membership is the cornerstone on which all aims of the organization revolve." Using financial knowledge to define the center of the association made sense in a late capitalist economy. In such an economy, as many, including feminist theorist Linda Singer (1993, 35), argue, "profit is generated less from the primary production of material goods and far more from the production of services—a move from an economy generated toward production to a knowledge and service based economy." Already in the late 1970s and 1980s, a shift in identity from being based on one's role in an organization to one's expertise, a transformation that would later be identified as fundamental to the emergence of New Economy forms of occupational subjectivity, was on the rise.

Debates over defining the category "financial" marked a growing preoccupation among FWA leaders with maintaining network boundaries, making membership more exclusive, and publicly portraying the image of the FWA as a group of senior-level successful women. Leaders were intent on setting network boundaries to ensure commitment and guard against divisions within its ranks, particularly in view of senior members' increasing desires to create their own elite group. By the late 1970s, qualifying for membership required not only holding a clearly defined professional financial position, it also necessitated member sponsorship. Hence, in the 1979 document on guidelines, the co-chairs drafted sponsorship guidelines:

> After attending a minimum of three meetings, a qualified candidate should be sponsored in writing to the Membership Committee by three members. The proposer and the other must have been actively *contributing* members for at least one full year. We believe the role of the sponsor should be considered seriously by the proposer. It is expected that he or she would introduce the candidate to as many members of the FWA as possible during the admission process and for the first year of membership. In addition, all three sponsors must be employed by different organizations in order to avoid concentration of sponsorship by any one company. (The rationale behind these requirements is to *encourage the membership of the FWA to consider* membership *as a commitment, to encourage stability, and to discourage membership aspirations from the unqualified.*) ("Some Proposed Guidelines for the FWA," March 23, 1979; emphasis in the original)

The rules of sponsorship reveal the ways FWA women attempted to carefully police the boundaries of the organization. The bylaws, effectively prohibiting any one Wall Street firm from being overly represented in the group's membership, ensured that the network would be composed of subjects who would not dominate and push the association in a direction that would serve their own institutional or career needs. Moreover, although as women they might be experiencing forms of exclusion from male-dominated financial institutions and networks, they nevertheless created their own exclusionary practices, allowing only the "right" women to become members of the FWA. Indeed, they created a range of "exceptional membership procedures" to permit well-known senior women, such as Muriel Siebert, the first woman to own a seat on the New York Stock Exchange, into its ranks ("Some Proposed Guidelines," March 23, 1979). The FWA coined the term "shepherding" to refer to a "strategy of pinpointing especially desirable potential members . . . and carefully leading them through the introductory and membership process" (FWA board minutes, June 10, 1981, 2–3).

Throughout the years, the FWA created "fire-side chats" and "elite luncheons" for senior members only (FWA board minutes, February 10, 1981). These affairs emulated the types of events traditionally held by elite men's organizations in business and government (Domhoff, 1974; C. W. Mills, 1956). Moreover, beginning in the mid-1980s, the group began to pay homage to famous female figures within the Wall Street community, a practice that they continue to engage in to this day. The board initially focused their attention on women who had attained at least the senior vice presidential level and were well-known throughout the industry. They created a list of eight criteria for selecting award recipients. Below is a partial list of their guidelines:

> Activities, particularly social or philanthropic, are not particularly important. However, a long-standing commitment to helping women succeed in business is a vital element to her ultimate selection. *She should be someone we would all want to have as a mentor or that we could point to and say "this is my idea of a successful woman!"* . . .

> While not a requirement, *evidence that she has risen above strife and "against all odds" might be another part of her background which would make her a viable candidate.* . . .

> *There should be evidence of some "balance" and "multifacetedness" to this woman's life, i.e. Work should not be the only activity upon which her world revolves.* (FWA Award Recipient Guidelines; emphasis added)

By attempting to select a woman who had "risen above strife" and "against all the odds," the FWA was wedding the American Dream narrative—the belief that anyone with talent can make it regardless of their gender, race or class—to the biographies of Wall Street women. Moreover, they were constructing particular, iconic types of female executives to register with the historical moment in capitalism. In effect, the women drew on traditional ideas of the American self-made man, written about by Horatio Alger, and turned that figure into a contemporary corporate woman. Success heroes are radical individuals. They transform themselves and their situation through personal initiative (Traube, 1992, 72). By celebrating these types of figures, the FWA subtly valued the challenges of individual achievement over forging a collective movement to advance women's causes.

What is especially interesting is that the discourse of the FWA was rooted in American notions of inclusion. However, their practices ran counter to it. At their best, FWA practices provided women with "successful" female business role models. But, at their worst, they hardened the boundaries of its network, effacing differences of class and race among women. In this sense, the FWA built a gendered network of distinction, a network based not only on a member's economic capital, but her symbolic or cultural capital as well (Bourdieu, 1979/1984). A woman's participation in philanthropic endeavors was not especially valued. This lack of emphasis on women's charitable practices would shift during the next several decades. However, already by the 1980s, a corporate woman's identity beyond the world of work, a notion that would become central to Wall Street women's subject formation in the New Economy, was beginning to emerge.

The FWA constructed female business icons and gendered mobility narratives. Equally important, they created female financial subjects. Specifically, the network provided a space for women to slowly take on a corporate habitus. Through participating in FWA events, women gradually developed a system of bodily movements, gestures, expressions, eating habits, and ways of dressing that helped distinguish them as professional-managerial-class women (Bourdieu, 1979/1984, 192). For example, in March 1996, I attended an event entitled "Celebrating Women's History: Defining Moments in the Lives of Five Leaders." Organized for the fortieth anniversary of the FWA, the affair's invitation opened with the following questions:

At what point in your career did you first know you were successful? When did you realize that you had power and influence? What, so far, has been your greatest moment? Has it all been worth it? You've probably been asked these kinds of questions from time to time. If you're curious about how other women would answer, then join us for a panel discussion featuring five, prominent, accomplished, history-shaping women. Each will candidly recount "herstory": The pitfalls and pinnacles, roadblocks and opportunities, choices made, challenges undertaken, resulting risks and rewards. (FWA Newsletter, March 1996)

During the panelists' discussions of career success, they alluded to a historical process of habitus making in the FWA. An audience member asked the panelists—women who had been active FWA members in the late 1970s and throughout the 1980s—if they had any female role models during these early days. Linda Super, a former high-ranking financial professional in New York State government, provided the following response to the question:

There were no women role models for the corporate paradigm. There was no one around to tell you if it was okay to wear nail polish to the office, what office dress meant, if black tie meant your dress could be cocktail length or if it had to be an evening gown. There were no women to show you how to stand, to watch what they did, to explain and define all of the cues. There were no women to tell you how much to drink, to order white or red wine, or if you should laugh at a bad joke. You did not have someone to talk to about these things. But the FWA is great because you have women to talk to, to be around. You can find out where something fits in, what is corporate behavior, and things that are not easy to define. Subtle cues make a difference. The glass ceiling revolves around these issues. (From field notes)

Within the ranks of the professional-managerial class, bureaucratization throughout most of the twentieth century has traditionally affected criteria for advancement (Traube, 1992, 73). Hard work is a necessary but not sufficient means for successfully climbing the corporate hierarchy. Mastery of the techniques of self-presentation, particularly in the top echelons of institutions, is equally essential. Properly managing one's external appearance—face, dress, and speech—provide crucial signals to one's peers and superiors that one is willing to undertake other forms of self-adaptation required in the business world (Jackall, 1988, 46–47). Indeed, body image and maintenance is increasingly an essential part of performance in financial work (L. McDowell, 1997). Normally, one learns the managerial codes in the course of repeated, long-term social interaction with other managers and one's superiors, especially a mentor (Jackall, 1988, 61). However, historically women have encountered difficulty in securing a mentor to show them the corporate ropes (Kanter, 1977). Participating in FWA events therefore provided an alternative means for women to attempt becoming proficient in the rules of survival and success required to move up the executive ladder. The FWA's stringent membership criteria ensured that their subjects had begun their retraining of the self in business school and on the job.

REMAKING SUCCESS AND THE CORPORATE SELF IN THE NEW ECONOMY

Entry into 85 Broads is even more policed than that of the FWA. Membership is restricted to former and current Goldman Sachs women. It is a password-protected site, allowing only Goldman Sachs female employees and alumnae to post a profile and search the Web site's database for contacts. According to an 85 Broads member, "A password probe net is so valuable because it allows the women to create bonds with each other, not just anyone. They can compare themselves to their peers: 'Here's a gal who got ahead: Let me see how she did it!' The net can provide women with a timetable. They can see that they were successful before, and they are able to believe that they will be again."

85 Broads women are constructing a new script for success in the New Economy moment marked by the precariousness of work. Indeed, the network is a response to the ways flexible, short-term work and downsizing are destroying the signposts that people traditionally use to define success in the workplace (Sennett, 2000, 2). Loyalty and sacrifice to a collective entity, the firm, are vanishing in the wake of these developments. The old narrative of steadily moving up the business and social ladder in a single institution or even industry is no longer viable. The traditional model of having a hierarchical superior act as a mentor to help one get ahead is also disappearing. The new paradigm operating within 85 Broads is co-mentoring, mentoring between and among women at all stages of their careers and across occupational disciplines. In a more virtual and less hierarchical work environment, the face-to-face vertical organizational pipeline is being replaced with a co-mentoring women's community in cyberspace (85 Broads Best Practices). Indeed, the goals of 85 Broads are driven by the women's structures of anxiety over their next move in a world void of clear-cut career paths. Hanson elaborates on these concerns in the description of her motives for building the network:

> The driving passion for me [in creating 85 Broads] was in realizing what can happen to people after they leave Goldman Sachs because the Goldman Sachs bond is so strong it might just as well be woven into the DNA. When people leave the firm, it's a similar experience to leaving graduate school or any major institutional experience in your life. You have a shared identity with the people you work with in close quarters under intense circumstances. So, I think of 85 Broads as a giant Outward Bound adventure. It can be grim to be out there on your own after being in such a team-oriented culture like Goldman Sachs. My original objective was to make the women that left Goldman Sachs not feel like they had fallen off a cliff—at any age. After you leave the workplace and also when you decide to reenter the workforce after time away, your confidence in yourself can diminish. (From fieldwork interview, January 2003)

In an article entitled "The New Political Economy and Its Culture," Richard Sennett (2000) writes about the new "dispensable self." When labor becomes dispensable, workers feel that they "can simply disappear from view" (5). Individuals must struggle for security and a coherent sense of self (10). 85 Broads not only provides a site for the reconstitution of a "diasporic community" for Wall Street female refugees in the New Economy. It also provides a site for identity reconstruction. Some of the women have quit, left, or been laid off by Goldman Sachs. However, the fact that some are no longer official employees of Goldman Sachs does not matter because the women now carry the firm in their DNA! Financial knowledge, something that one acquired by working on Wall Street, once defined membership in the FWA. Surface appearance once sufficed to signal one's membership in the corporate order. Now a contemporary biological metaphor, DNA deep within the molecular structures of the self, defines the category of the female financial subject.

Moreover, 85 Broads women appear to cling to their Wall Street identity even when many are no longer necessarily part of the actual occupational scheme. They name themselves—their group identity—after a building that, presumably, many no longer have security access to enter. They literally try to remake their work life on the Internet by bringing together disaffected (and current) members of Goldman Sachs to form an autonomous cyber organization that attempts to redefine the meaning of success.

Yet, once again, the women's talk about their network is embedded in American discourse. Hanson equates the network to a "giant Outward Bound adventure." Outward Bound programs "emphasize personal growth through experience and challenge in the wilderness" (www.outwardbound.com/aboutob.html). In the spirit of independence and self-reliance, 85 Broads women exhibit their kinship with the American frontiersman, whose self-transformation takes the form of mastering the savage in the name of civilization (Slotkin, 1986, 86–87, cited in Traube, 1992, 72). However, in the contemporary moment, the frontier is no longer located in nature: it is rooted directly in mastering the new global economy of technology, the unknown, and self-realization.

In contrast to the FWA's weekly events held in New York City, 85 Broads tends to stage all-day conferences every few months for its members in various global cities: New York City, San Francisco, Frankfurt, Tokyo, and London. Unlike many FWA meetings that historically examine being successful in finance, 85 Broads events center on key questions, echoing the focus of Oprah Winfrey's self-styled television program, such as "What's Your Destiny?" and "What's Your Gift?" Indeed, it is not altogether surprising that in an interview with a younger member of 85 Broads, the woman called Janet Hanson "Oprah-esque." Janet, "like Oprah," she told me, "is all about asking what's your life about—what our destiny means to us."

The notion of the self articulated in these events is not about mastering surface appearances; it is an essence to develop and cultivate. This version of success as self-fulfillment and empowerment, embodied in new age thought, promises compensation for the degradation of or loss of work. Its roots are in the 1950s American definition of success as the product of a partial retreat from work into a familial world of leisure (Traube, 1992, 74). In the New Economy, one in part trades traditional career advancement for the emotional fulfillment of finding one's inner gift and destiny.

Former Goldman Sachs managing director Jacki Hoffman-Zehner drew on the idea of destiny throughout the speech she gave during the event "What's Your Destiny?" held on May 16, 2001. She wove together American gendered notions of destiny, survival, and power into a single narrative to contextualize her decision to leave Goldman Sachs. She plans to pursue her "personal destiny" to make a movie about "women who are going to change the world." According to Hoffman-Zehner (2001, 3), "I never thought I was *destined* to be a mortgage bond trader, but I do feel that I *am* destined to help empower women."

> So when I was thinking about today's theme—"What's Your Destiny?"—I thought back to my research on Destiny's Child, the coolest girl group out there right now, and I thought an appropriate song would be "Survivor." . . . At the beginning of the song one of these three young women obviously just broke up with a dude, and he's essentially thinking you poor thing, you're a chick, you're sort of lost without me, without your man. But as the song continues, these women basically come out and say—I don't think I'm lost, in fact "I'm better, stronger, richer, wiser, and smarter" because I no longer have you in my life. What this youngest, coolest group is really saying is—*know your power*. You don't need anyone but yourself to exercise your power and take control of your life. (2)

The new economic rhetoric in play today—"informational competence," "flexible labor," and the like—"shifts the focus from impersonal conditions like the possession of capital to more personal matters of competence" (Sennett, 2000, 5). When the successful fall from grace, it places the responsibility for failure on the individual. However, Hoffman-Zehner turns the business discourse of self-empowerment on its head to regain a sense of personal control in a volatile and uncertain work environment. Women no longer need a man or a (male-dominated) corporation for their sense of self-worth. All they need to do is exercise their own power and free will to survive in the New Economy. What is especially interesting about Hoffman-Zehner's talk is the way she subtly equates a song about African American women's loss of men to the loss of a stable work life and identity among (predominantly white) professional-managerial-class women such as herself.

Notably, much of the discourse articulated by 85 Broads speakers—primarily American financial, government, and managerial elites—centers on self-management. Let us now focus on one speech giver who participated in the "What's Your Gift?" event, held at the University Club in New York City in November 2001. Mark Schwartz, the former chairman of Goldman Sachs Asia, spoke about "Visionary Leadership in Today's Complex World." He recently retired from the firm after twenty-two years. Today he spends his time "as a chauffeur, housekeeper, and homework helper—as well as soccer and field hockey-coach" (M. Schwartz, 2001, 1). After discussing the ways Goldman Sachs "promoted concepts such as globalization, privatization, free trade, and free flows of capital," Schwartz identified eight rules for self-conduct in light of his personal transition and the world economy's transformations (3). Below is the eighth:

> Finally, realize that many of you are now setting the standards and setting the examples in your organization to follow. You're the role models and the mentors. Many of you are running important businesses, so your actions and behavior will have significant consequences for your company. You can distinguish and differentiate yourselves in your level of preparation and in the passion that you bring to the business. When you're down, pick yourself up. Most people don't. That is the reason why many people fail. A lot of people get knocked down, but they lack the energy and willpower to get back up. And when you get back on your feet, pick up someone next to you. Boost those around you and show them you've got strength, character, and the determination to succeed. That's called leadership. (3–4)

Clearly, Schwartz views himself as relaying important information he has garnered through his experiences. However, his talk further reveals the ways the rules for survival and success in business are transforming in the new era. Building a career, as discussed earlier, is no longer exclusively about determining the criteria required to advance in a single bureaucratic hierarchy. In the New Economy, each individual must direct his or her career trajectory. Such a process entails managing the entrepreneurial self for the current challenge, including accumulating skills as best one can in order to prepare for the next moment. Success depends on inner willpower and the discipline to dust oneself off when one falls down. The possibility and, indeed, reality of failure is now written into the new formula for the contemporary successful corporate self. The purpose of Wall Street women's networks—moving women up the career ladder—has, indeed, been partially destabilized in the new postcorporate world of work.[5]

FINANCE AND FEMINISM: QUANDARIES OF IDENTITY AND ALLIANCE MAKING

Both the FWA and 85 Broads are built around their members' shared identity as *women* in finance. As discussed earlier, the women not only want to unite on the basis of who they are as women, but also want to assert a certain social status and to insist on the particularity of their industry, and, in the case of 85 Broads, their firm. Historically, they do not add issues of race or ethnicity to the mix; their self-definition is extremely narrow. As women, they could not have entered the workforce without the feminist movement's insistence on the opening up of formerly male professions, such as law, medicine, and management. Indeed, as professional-managerial-class women, they have incorporated mainstream feminism's strategy for assimilation. As a result, they have focused on how to "make it" in the business world (Ehrenreich, 1989, 216). However, the more radical agendas of the movement—revolution, overthrowing the corporate order, and improving the plight of poor and African American women—have proved far more problematic for financial women and their networks to incorporate into their identity and mission. Accordingly, in the mid-1990s, Deidre Parliament, a senior-level woman on Wall Street and former FWA board member, articulated her shifting thoughts on transforming corporate life:

> [During] the 1960s I had the philosophy that business was at the heart of social change and that somehow if people with the right liberal ideas would be part of corporate structures that the world would somehow be a better place. So I figured I would be a force for social change—going into business. . . . [My ideas] have changed in that I am more modest in what I think people can actually do. . . . I think that I bring with me a certain kind of fairness and support of individual growth that in a modest way affects the people that I work with. But I don't have visions of social change—as somehow hiring vast numbers of different classes and changing the structure of Wall Street on my own. (From fieldwork interview, 1994)

Parliament's philosophy reflects the ways Wall Street women traditionally prefer to be faced with the challenges of individual achievement and growth, rather than with forging a social movement. Given women's uneasy relationship to the more radical dimensions of feminism, we need to closely look at the process by which the women's movement has influenced the politics of financial women's networks over time. Accordingly, I want to reexamine the histories of the FWA and 85 Broads as a series of steps in identity reformation and political alliance making. Notably, FWA leaders attempted to strategically incorporate parts of the women's movement agenda into their mission without taking a public stance on their point of view.

The first FWA board meeting of the 1981–1982 calendar year started off with debates over the public and private relationship of the organization to women's politics. Officially, the association took the standpoint that the FWA was a professional, not a political or feminist, group. Dealing with women's issues, however, became increasingly complicated in the wake of the feminist movement and antidiscrimination suits on Wall Street in the 1970s and 1980s. During the meeting on September 2, 1981, FWA women confronted decisions regarding their public support, or lack thereof, for the ERA:

> Mindy Shapiro relayed to the board the fact that Linda Brown from [a city organization for business and professional women] had contacted her to ask if the FWA would help to sponsor a November march on Washington in support of the ERA. A brief discussion ensued during which it was pointed out that in 1978 the Board decided not to take a stand on that issue. It was concluded that this activity was too political and had the potential of a disastrous outcome. However, although the FWA would not become involved as a sponsor, mention could still be made in the newsletter that the [city organization] has announced that it is undertaking this activity. (FWA board minutes, September 2, 1981, 1, 3)

The women's talk about the FWA's relationship to the ERA reveals their anxieties about deciding which facets of their multiple identities they were going to continue to build their network around. Having initially chosen to construct it around women, they were then pulled toward the ERA and feminist politics by the unfolding logic of their identity's implication in the network. Yet, by electing not to take a public stand on women's political issues, they attempted to control the ramifications of drawing on "femaleness" as a foundation for solidarity. Making sense of their decision requires examining the conservative national and political forces of the 1980s shaping Wall Street women. Anthropologist Elizabeth Traube (1992, 20), in her book *Dreaming Identities: Class, Gender, and Generation in 1980s Hollywood Movies*, writes that during this era, "Hollywood joined New Right Leaders in directing socially rooted discontents against independent upwardly mobile women. Movies as well as political discourse attacked uncontrolled, ambitious women in the cause of a moral crisis that, given its definition, called for a stronger authoritarian patriarchy."

The FWA "solved" the problem of becoming aligned with women's politics and issues by creating indirect and less overt ways to lend support. For example, they decided to publicize the ERA march in the Newsletter, but to ensure that it was clear that the city organization for business and professional women, not the FWA, were the sponsors. Hiding behind the political cloak of other women's organizations became a common FWA strategy. This was especially true of the FWA's early relationship with other national associations of professional women. In October 1981, FWA president Jill Hoffman, along with several other FWA members, went to an East Coast city to participate in a National Women Executives meeting. Hoffman reported to the FWA board in November that the national group "is still substantially less sophisticated and professional than the FWA. Therefore the FWA is placed in the position of sharing its resources with them without the likelihood, at this time, of receiving reciprocal benefits of equal value" (FWA board minutes, November 4, 1981, 2). Notably, Hoffman did not suggest that the FWA withdraw its support or involvement with the group. Rather, she concluded that the network's "potential does seem to be in the area of Washington representation and of being able to take a political stance on certain issues on the national level and thereby reduce the pressure the FWA experiences to take political positions on the local level" (2).

The women's frustration regarding the lack of power, leadership, and resources available in other executive women's networks in the nation had some serious consequences for their political alliance-building strategies. In the end, they used their affiliations with women's national networks to avoid taking official political stances on women's issues. Furthermore, they chose to focus on making international rather than national connections to cement their identification with other financial women and to bypass dealing with feminist issues at home. Indeed, during the same meeting in November 1981, the value of international networking over the national became a major source of interest. Mindy Hamilton, FWA board member, drew the board's attention to their "sister organization," the Hong Kong FWA, an alliance of the FWA composed of 100 members, many of whom held financial positions and were associated with the FWA of New York.[6] She "suggested that the existence of such an organization provides the potential for an international scope, which may prove a more fertile direction than the national organization efforts of the National Women Executives Group" (FWA board minutes, November 4, 1981, 2). The board immediately pursued a tighter bond with the Hong Kong FWA. By the following month, President Hoffman invited Laurie Butler of Banker's Trust Hong Kong and founder of the sister FWA organization to meet the board. After the board meeting, the women went to dinner, where the "whole issue of national and international affiliation would be explored" (FWA board minutes, December 2, 1981, 3).

During the 1980s, the FWA continued to privilege international networking over national alliance building. They also maintained their strategy of creating links with women who shared their financial identity. Groups of about thirty FWA women traveled to visit the (women's) financial community in London in 1985, followed by a trip to Tokyo, Peking, and Hong Kong a year later. They returned to London in 1987 to celebrate the "Big Bang," the deregulation and restructuring of finance in the City of London (see Leyshon and Thrift, 1997, 134–135). These expeditions were filled with activities devoted to learning about global finance: management seminars, panels on markets, and tours of stock exchanges (FWA London symposium schedule: February 16–19, 1985).

The FWA during the same period also sought to make ties with financial women in corporate America. This was a striking and historic move. As discussed earlier, the FWA had drawn almost exclusively from women working in brokerage houses, investment banks, and other affiliated Wall Street occupations. In 1981, Rachel Wagner, FWA member and treasurer of the International Paper Company, drafted a letter asking for women's "help in our efforts to expand FWA membership among women financial executives in industrial corporations, in and around New York City" (Wagner letter, December 2, 1981): "Our first step is to identify these women; our second step is to be sure that they know about the FWA, and about the opportunities for professional growth and for rewarding contacts among talented successful women actively engaged in a wide range of financial professions. We realize that most of you are yourselves at financial institutions, but your professional activities may well bring you into contact with corporate financial women."

During this period, the globalization of the economy created particular organizational requirements. Corporations began developing top-level financial, legal, accounting, and other functions required to manage the complexities of operating in multiple countries (Sassen, 2002, 9). As a result, the FWA sought to include women working in these areas as the boundaries of financial work expanded beyond Wall Street.

The cultural logic of women's network formation must first be understood in relation to the logic of financial capitalism. Beginning in the 1980s, Wall Street began to witness major changes. There was a huge expansion of employment in the financial services industry in the United States, as well as Britain and Japan (Sassen, 2001). The globalization of markets, the introduction of new risk-management technologies to deal with increasing volatility and uncertainty, and securitization (the conversion of nonmarketable into marketable assets), all radically reshaped the landscape of Wall Street (H. Kaufman, 2000). In response to these changes, firms dramatically expanded their research, trading, and banking departments and capabilities (Geisst, 1997). The growth and internationalization of the industry forced institutions to enlarge their managerial structures and emphasize partnership and leadership (Eccles and Crane, 1988). Indeed, as markets and firms went global, a new global power structure in finance emerged. High-status and well-paid jobs in the higher echelons of management became increasingly concentrated in global cities such as New York, London, and Tokyo (Sassen, 2001).

The FWA women's decision to privilege the local and international must therefore be analyzed in reference to the shifting geography of power operating within New York City and globally. In her book *The Global City*, Saskia Sassen (2001) argues that New York, Tokyo, and London have become central nodes in the new financial economy, strategic sites for the concentration of top-level control and management of spatially dispersed global market activity. One effect has been that such cities have gained in importance and power relative to nation-states. Flows of capital, people, and information have bound global cities in networks, creating a global city web whose constituent cities and city-actors become "global" through the networks in which they participate. Sassen's emphasis on cities allows us to identify concrete local effects and instantiations of globalization. Her analysis also provides the basic scheme to explain why FWA women made decisions to privilege, at least partly, incorporating themselves into circuits of financial women that were operating on an international scale.

Given that the overarching goal of the FWA was moving women into positions of power in finance, the women's networking decisions were generated by and made in relation to the male-dominated geography of global city managerial power. It therefore is no coincidence that the women found themselves frustrated with the lack of power, leadership, and resources available in the national networks of executive women. Indeed, it is not surprising that they turned their entrepreneurial attention toward making links with New York City corporate women engaged in finance and women's groups in Hong Kong and London. The women working in these financial areas were, after all, also participating in the new circuit of transnational financial power embedded in their global cities.

The FWA's networking strategies must also, however, be understood in terms of the women's relationship to feminism. Privileging alliances with financial women in global cities produces a network that separates wealthy transnational female professionals (those in the "group") from underpaid and poor women to whom they have some responsibility in the public space of the nation. Through this separation, the FWA builds a constituency for the global mobility of women in finance. In this light, the organization's move to international over national connections provides a way to bypass feminist issues at home that could be divisive among members or place the group in a position where they might not benefit as much from networking. The FWA does not, for example, build alliances with other American women's groups that might potentially force them to deal with problems facing "other" women, such as poverty. Forming these kinds of connections might pull the association away from focusing on their agenda to push women up the career ladder in finance. As a result, the FWA in the 1980s created new arenas of financial all-female sociality that drew on but extended local forms in transnational directions and produced global female financial subjects.

Although the FWA leveraged their place in New York City to give the group a global reach, they retained their name. They did not reconstitute themselves into the "FWA of the World." In the mid-1990s, however, they began creating sister satellites in major U.S. cities, including Washington, Chicago, and Boston; more recently, in 2002, they helped to launch the FWA's first "connected" international chapter in Quebec. These affiliated organizations mimic the mission of the original association: pushing women's mobility in global finance. According to one FWA Quebec member, "Most of our members work in financial services and our mandate is heavily oriented to education and training and career development" (quoted in Gibbens, 2002). Notably, the chapter is receiving help from IFC Montreal, a provincial agency promoting the city as an international financial center (ibid.).

DIVERSITY AND PHILANTHROPY IN NEW
MILLENNIAL WALL STREET WOMEN'S NETWORKS

In the new millennium, calls for diversity on Wall Street are further trans-forming the relationship between the FWA and feminism. Indeed, FWA leaders have responded by beginning to shift their organization's mission away from an exclusive focus on gender to one that incorporates the language of diversity and multiculturalism. Specifically, in 2002, FWA president Joan Green named diversity as a key priority for the organization. Accordingly, the FWA, in a historic move, created a Diversity Committee. The Committee focuses on "increasing [their] visibility with diverse groups such as the Urban Bankers and Asian Women in Business; ensuring that women of color are represented as speakers, members, and FWA leaders; and partnering with corporate sponsors to support their internal diversity efforts" (FWA Newsletter, March 2003).[7]

The emerging multicultural logic of Wall Street women's networking practices must be understood in relation to contemporary institutional logics in global finance. It is tempting to suggest that the recent incorporation of diversity efforts by Wall Street women's networks implies that (predominantly white) executive women are finally building alliances with professional women of color that acknowledge that women are caught up in hierarchies of gender as well as race/ethnicity and class. Here, a more utopian reading of these developments might argue that although corporate women have historically focused on individual achievement, the time may have come for them to join forces in a collective movement. I have no doubt that there are individual managers, organizational communities, and firms on Wall Street devoted to improving equality in the workplace, yet I believe that their practices must be viewed in relation to the business of finance, including especially the management and development of a "diverse" workforce. In that light, I turn to the rapid growth and proliferation of employee networking groups.

During the 1990s, Wall Street began to implement worldwide diversity efforts. Firms such as Heritage J. P. Morgan developed policies to define and deal with forms of difference. Today, part of that effort includes the participation of more than 18,000 employees worldwide in approximately ninety affinity groups at the now named J. P. Morgan Chase.[8] Although the women's network boasts one of the largest memberships (around 5,000), a wide range of networks based on race, cultural heritage, gender, sexual orientation, disability and other defining criteria are sprouting up. For example, network groups now include African Americans, Asian Pacific Americans, generational-over 40, and lesbian, gay, bisexual, and transgender employees. Thus, if we are to make sense of the new multicultural approach taken by female financial organizations, such as the FWA, we cannot ignore the ways such practices are directly tied to the recent history of the business of identity politics in financial corporations.

Philanthropic activities are also serving as an avenue for Wall Street women's networks for dealing with issues of race/ethnicity, gender, and civic participation. Miles to Go, a nonprofit organization established by 85 Broads, supports humanitarian, philanthropic, and educational causes around the world. Projects supported include Room to Read, an organization devoted to educating children in poverty; StreetSquash, a youth enrichment program in Harlem; Junior Achievement of Nigeria, an organization devoted to children's welfare; and the National Council for Research on Women, an alliance of ninety-five leading women's research and policy centers involved in scholarship, advocacy, and programming on behalf of women and girls worldwide (Miles to Go, 2002). Notably, the twenty-first FWA International Conference took place in the Dominican Republic in March 2005. Part of the agenda focused "on the economic prospects for this country, with special emphasis on the role of microfinance for women seeking to lead their families out of poverty" (FWA News, September 2004).

Wall Street women's giving operates in a fashion that is consistent with traditional gendered forms of philanthropy practiced among American elites. Historically, women of the upper class have dedicated major gifts to causes related to their life, concerns, and priorities as women (Ostrower, 1995, 73). There is a continuity in financial women's current support for social services. Like elite women before them, members of 85 Broads focus on providing funds for youth and women. In this sense, the network continues to build their identity around the category of women. However, philanthropy is also a mark of class status that contributes to defining the women as part of the New Economy elite (6). Thus, even as Wall Street women integrate feminism and diversity into their organizational practices, they construct themselves as elite female subjects.

CONCLUSIONS

In this essay I have drawn attention to the way transformations in Wall Street women's networked organizational identities and politics are grounded in larger historical frameworks of various sorts. These include epochal shifts (the globalization of financial capitalism), the virtualization and sometimes disappearance of permanent corporate work, social movements (feminism), and women's "own imaginings and practices in relation to [changing] cultural conceptions of 'success' " and self (Ortner, 2003, 1).

First, I have tried to show how the two narratives about women's success on Wall Street draw on and refashion two competing American styles and notions of the work ethic. Specifically, I have illuminated the ways Wall Street women's talk about themselves, and their network, reveal how shifts in success ideology register and respond to historically engendered cultural tensions. On the one hand, dominant success narratives produced in the FWA (during the 1980s) represent a traditional "old economy" emphasis on the organizational work ethic. Here, "work is valued as a means to the end of professional or community status and career advancement, as defined by the organization" (Heelas, 2002, 80). On the other hand, 85 Broads women's articulation about finding their "destiny" reveals the ways a new generational network of financial women are elaborating a more New Economy exploratory type of self-work ethic (80). Here, in an increasingly postcorporate era, work becomes more broadly defined and is "taken to provide the opportunity to 'work' on oneself; to grow; to learn ('the learning organization'); to become more effective *as* a person" (du Gay, 1996, cited in Heelas, 2002, 83).

Notably, although my analysis points to the ways these different notions of success and work ethics articulate with different stages of the economy, I want to make sure to emphasize that these are ideal-type differentiations. In contemporary everyday life, these distinctions may collapse, collide, and/or contradict one another (Heelas, 2002, 81). For example, in the fall of 2002, I attended a political women's group event held in the penthouse of a New York City department store. The evening event, composed of many of the earlier generation of FWA women, focused on how to "rewire" your life. Some of these former high-ranking executive women spoke about their recent experience leaving Wall Street and trying to create a new career that was more connected to their true sense of self. Hence, I suspect we are in the midst of witnessing attempts by Wall Street women to reach some kind of cultural consensus of the meaning of success in a work world fraught with economic change and uncertainty.

Second, I have shown how a closer look at the different narrative constructions of success helps us to sort out the shifting gendered politics of Wall Street women and to illuminate the cultural backdrops to debates over the relationship between financial women's networks, Wall Street firms, feminism, and society at large. On the one hand, historically the FWA has taken a rather conservative approach to corporate feminist politics. Building on the older organizational work ethic, FWA women have traditionally viewed their network as an elite organizational entity defined by business principles, rather than a pro-feminist institution oriented toward overtly fighting gendered and/or racial forms of discrimination. Hence, the network, until relatively recently, has focused most of its energy on moving women (who have been, by and large, white) up the corporate ladder. It is only recently that they have begun to address diversity issues, in light of the current emphasis on diversity in the securities industry as a whole.

On the other hand, 85 Broads has infused the more contemporary exploratory self-work ethic with what we might call an emergent professional-managerial-class new age feminism. Here, 85 Broads women espouse an ideology in which, if they are to ever achieve their real potential (as women), they must effectively search for the meaning of life and success in themselves beyond the borders of the corporation. This belief takes form, for example, in their turn to charitably raising money for the benefit of "other" women both at home and across the globe. Thus, we seem to be observing how, in the New Economy, a significant number of professional-managerial-class women are becoming somewhat disillusioned with "what the 'primary' institutions" (particularly the workplace) "have to offer with the regard to the meaning of life" (Heelas, 2002, 92). Indeed, this shift may, in part, help illuminate some of the reasons underlying the *New York Times* writer Lisa Belkin's (2003) much disputed article identifying the recent phenomenon of highly educated, successful women in the United States giving up or curtailing their careers. Such a discussion is beyond the scope of this essay; however, it is clear that changes in the nature of the corporation as well as feminism are producing shifts in the ways women (and presumably men) relate to the workplace, and consequently construct their sense of personhood, success, and political practice (Guthey, 2004, 325).

NOTES

This research was supported in part by a grant from the Alfred P. Sloan Foundation's Program on Workplace, Workforce and Working Families.

A version of this essay was presented at the American Anthropology Association meetings in Chicago (November 2003). Diane Perrons, Mary Yeager, Christina Garsten, and Barbara Czarniawska all invited me to present drafts of this work at, respectively, the Gender Institute, London School of Economics; the Business History Conference in Le Creusot, France; the Stockholm Center for Organization Research, Stockholm University; and the Göteborg Research Institute, Göteborg University, Göteborg, Sweden. I benefited from the helpful comments of the participants in all these venues.

I am also grateful to Melissa Cefkin, Greg Downey, Rachel Esner, Laurel George, Pam Laird, and Paul Silverstein for their insights. Janet Hanson and my anonymous informants generously contributed their time to this research. Wall Street women may disagree with some of the interpretations of their experiences suggested here, but I have tried to capture the complexities, ambiguities, and anxieties of their world. I am also grateful to Roberto Luis Reyes-Gaskin for his help with research tasks.

A note on style: quotations that are reconstructed from my field notes are not verbatim transcriptions; these passages are cited as "From fieldwork interview" or "From field notes."

1 See the list of archival sources at the end of this chapter.
2 Notably, as Helen McCarthy (2004, 42) points out in her study of professional women's groups in the United Kingdom, "Despite the history of networks being intertwined with that of the women's movement, few networks explicitly espouse feminist or equality goals." For a further discussion of the FWA's primary mission as focused on moving women up in finance rather than addressing feminist concerns, see Sastry and Lee (2000). For works on gender in international finance, see L. McDowell (1997), Fisher (2003), Czarniawska (2004), and de Goede (2005).
3 I have disguised the names of Wall Street women as well as some of the professional women's organizations cited in the FWA archives, fieldwork interviews, and field notes.
4 For an important discussion on gender hegemonies and counterhegemonies, see Ortner (1996).
5 Notably, Wall Street women's use of gendered networks as forms of support during periods of economic uncertainty is not entirely new. The FWA, for example, soon after the 1987 Crash on Wall Street, created seminars for female members who had been laid off and were actively seeking jobs. However, these women's understanding of their loss was articulated in narratives that linked the post-Crash recession to the increased presence of glass ceilings blocking women from moving up the corporate ladder. They did not, in general, draw on the idea of failure to explain their circumstances. For a more detailed history of shifts in FWA practices and narratives, see Fisher (2003).
6 Currently, FWA Alliances share the FWA name but are fully independent (www.fwa .org/committee/fwa—network.htm, accessed January 17, 2006).
7 The Urban Bankers is an organization devoted to serving the needs of minorities in the financial services industry.
8 J. P. Morgan Chase, "Diversity: Workplace Initiatives," http://www.jpmorganchase.com/ cm/cs?pagename=Chase/Href&urlname=jpmc/community/diversity/workplace (accessed January 17, 2006).

ARCHIVAL SOURCES CONSULTED

Financial Women's Association Archives, FWA, New York City
1957. "Talk of the Town." *The New Yorker* (FWA clipping).
1976. "Financial Women." *The New Yorker.* September 6 (FWA clipping).
1977–1978. FWA fiscal year, memo.
1978. FWA board minutes meeting, August 30.
1979. "Some Proposed Guidelines for the FWA," March 23.
1981. FWA board minutes, February 10.
1981. FWA board minutes, June 10.
1981. FWA board minutes, September 2.
1981. FWA board minutes, November 4.
1981. FWA board minutes, December 2.
1980s. FWA award recipient guidelines.
1985. FWA London symposium schedule: February 16–19.
1996. FWA Newsletters.
2003. FWA Newsletter. March.
2004. FWA News. September.

85 Broads Archives, Yonkers, New York
2001. "85 Broads Best Practices: Principles of Success."
Hoffman-Zehner, Jacki. 2001. "Happenings at 85 Broads." Speech presented at May 16 event, "What's Your Destiny?"
Schwartz, Mark. 2001. "Seize the Day: Visionary Leadership in Today's Complex World." Speech presented at November 10 global event, "What's Your Gift?"
2002. 85 Broads Global and Regional Event. Public relations statement.
2002. 85 Broads: Miles to Go. Public relations statement.

Siobhán O'Mahony

DEVELOPING COMMUNITY SOFTWARE
IN A COMMODITY WORLD

I think the best way to explain Debian's position in the commercial environment that Linux [has become] is that Debian has been around for a long time, and it has carried forward a lot of the feel of the community that existed when it got started [1993]. Over time it has become more and more deliberate, I think. In the beginning to say that Debian is a free software system was stating the obvious.
—Debian project founder, February 16, 2001

During a time of unprecedented economic prosperity and heightened interest in how the Internet might change the organization of work and the world of business in general (1996–2000), a group of programmers distributed around the world worked on the Debian project. Debian is a free operating system that uses the Linux kernel developed by Linus Torvalds.[1] While new firms were founded to profit from the emerging market for Linux products and services, the Debian project created a nonprofit organization to protect their work from being commercialized. As new versions of the Linux distribution were created and sold for commercial purposes, the Debian project renewed their vow to create a noncommercial variant of the Linux distribution. Amid the hyperexploitation and surge in expectations over the Internet's promise, these programmers renewed their social contract to develop code for the public good. Over the course of nine years, this project grew from 60 to more than 1,000 volunteer contributors who improved the performance of their operating system to the stage where it became adopted as an internal standard for research and development at one of the largest computing firms in the United States, Hewlett Packard (Weiss, 2001).

This phenomenon raises several questions that traditional behavioral theories may be hard-pressed to explain: Why didn't this group of programmers form a firm so they could more easily profit from their work? How did this community manage their collective development efforts in a business environment that increasingly valued their work as a commodity? Economic theory would predict that even those programmers developing software as a hobby would, in pursuit of their own self-interest, try to collect revenues if a commercial market for their work emerged. Sociological theories would predict that programmers pursuing a collective hobby and relying on normative controls would gravitate toward more bureaucratic and formal structures as their project scaled and became more commercially valued. Neither of these outcomes fully captures the evolution of the social structure of Debian. This essay examines how the values embraced by project members affected the new social order they created. It also provides empirical grounding of an alternative form of organizing that may expand our understanding of the possibilities for postindustrial work.

In the past ten years, there has been much speculation as to the types of new organizational forms that might emerge in a "New Economy." With the benefits of distributed computing, we are told that new organizational forms should become flatter, less hierarchical, more team-based, and independent of geographic terrain (O'Mahony and Barley, 1999). Ten-plus years of positive economic growth contributed to the illusion that everyone could be a "free agent" and work from a laptop at a mountain-top resort. Knowledge workers would actively and equally collaborate. These utopian images rarely discussed the challenges inherent in operationalizing these types of work arrangements. And, as anyone who has ever worked remotely will quickly tell you, there are some significant challenges. Research has shown that distributed work arrangements can affect patterns of information sharing, productivity, and career outcomes. In depictions of work in the New Economy, the very features of an organization that are most resistant to change (governance, power, politics, resources, rewards) are abstracted or left out of the picture. In these scenarios, a firm's greatest challenge is to design a physical and technical environment that can facilitate appropriate intellectual exchange. Why, then, would programmers choose to do their most challenging work outside of firms?

The Debian project is a community-managed software project.[2] An individual or group of individuals initiates a project by posting a proposal on a public mailing list. Project founders set up a new mailing list, claim a private or nonprofit Internet domain, create a technical architecture and code tree for the project, recruit others to participate, and grow the project as it attracts more interest. New contributors (most likely, users of the software attracted by word of mouth) may identify bugs or submit improvements to the software by sending patches or responding to inquiries on project mailing lists. As experience with the project builds, a core team emerges, most often based on responsiveness and talent. Membership in the core team usually is distinguished by "commit access" (ability to commit changes directly to the code base; Behlendorf, 1999) or by being recognized as a "maintainer." The code base or repository is hosted on privately donated servers, and core members of the group manage access to it. Maintainers of specific packets or modules of code review code contributions submitted by a wider body of contributors and, based on their usefulness and their effect on other components, may accept or reject them (Behlendorf, 1999; Raymond, 1999). Although periphery contributors are volunteers whose primary qualification may be their interest in the project, the group selects and manages the rights of core contributors more carefully.

There are on the order of 87,500 community-managed software projects hosted on http://sourceforge.net and 2,097 projects hosted on http://savannah.gnu.org, the two largest hosts for such projects. These sites offer software management tools such as hosting, version control, and access right management[3] that allow developers from all over the world to collaborate in a distributed fashion. There is a smaller subset of about fifty large, well-established, mature projects that have provided major contributions to the evolution of the Internet and to the development of a free operating system.[4] I knew about only a few of these large projects when I started this research. What I wanted to understand was how programmers who valued egalitarian norms and produced commercial-grade software managed themselves when even firms armed with far more resources and support have trouble doing this. Would the project be forced to adapt formalized structures to support its scale and popularity? How would growing commercial interest in Linux affect the egalitarian norms typical of community-managed projects and the hacker culture in general?

To assess which projects would be ripe for study, I spent several months going to Linux user group meetings in Silicon Valley. These meetings are held once a month after work and run late into the night, when the venue changes from a donated corporate conference room to a restaurant or bar. As of September 2004, there were 885 Linux user groups in 109 countries; even Iraq and Rwanda have at least one Linux user group.[5] These groups form the foot soldiers of what my informants call "the Linux Revolution." Community projects exist independent of any geographic place, but loyalists attending or presenting at Linux user groups help make the global local. User groups invite project leaders to come and give technical talks that explain how their projects work. Meeting attendees listen raptly to technical talks about the architecture of the code, programming protocols, the project's mission, and operation.

The user groups that I visited in Silicon Valley also put on what they called "Installfests," informational sessions advertised to the technical community at large and staffed by user group volunteers. User group members would gather once a month or so at a donated site and "free" participant's computers from the Microsoft Windows operating system by installing Linux. The Computer Literacy bookstore in San Jose was a frequent gathering place. Installfests were viewed as a public education effort. Even those most devoted to Linux recognized that Linux was still too difficult for the average computer user to install. Installfests were a way to help disseminate information about the benefits of Linux.

User group meetings are probably one of the few venues that provide programmers the opportunity to learn about new community-managed projects and meet other contributors in person. These meetings are also essential to marketing a project and recruiting volunteer contributors. At my first meeting, I was amazed at the camaraderie people shared. Although they had not always lived in the same area, many had interacted with each other online for years. Founders and leaders of key projects were spoken of with great reverence. Several programmers told me about the Debian project, but they just called it Debian, as if it were a personified entity. Debian was known within the programming world as the "hacker's operating system"; it was not for "newbies." Debian was also known for its unusually well-developed organizational structure and for its commitment to the principles of free software. When I joined some of the hackers after the meetings, people would nod their head solemnly and say "You should study Debian" with some emphasis. It was special and distinct even among the hackers who knew it best. I selected Debian and three other projects for further study and examined how these four projects developed formalized structures to manage their growth amid a developing commercial market (O'Mahony, 2002). Debian, however, remains somewhat distinct from the other projects, and although this essay examines the project's evolution, many mysteries remain.

In the field of organizational studies, scholars such as Van Maanen (1998), Strauss (1987), and Whyte (1982) have advocated an inductive ethnographic approach to understanding social orders that challenge existing theoretical frames, but this approach is still not as popular as it is in other fields, such as anthropology. William Foote Whyte, author of one of the most well-known ethnographies among organizational scholars, *Street Corner Society*, suggested that scholars, "having discovered a social invention, move in to observe, interview, and gather documentary material so that you will eventually be able to provide a systematic description of that invention" (1982, 11). Because Debian is much like a naturally occurring social experiment, this is precisely what I did.

I attended and observed twenty-three Linux user group and project meetings, conducted seventy-five interviews of informants who were part of the open source community, and reviewed project data archived on the Internet that detailed the project's interactions and structural developments. Informants were assured of anonymity, and they granted me permission to record the interviews.[6] Each interview was different depending on the person's role on a particular project. Gaining an understanding of the informant's introduction to the project and subsequent role was a common starting point. The history of the project was followed by discussions of how things were done and how practices had changed or been affected by commercial interest in their work. Membership, sponsorship, decision making, and the governance of projects were important foci. Project data, such as mission statements, charters, bylaws, meeting minutes, and mailing list archives, helped triangulation and validation of theoretical constructs that could withstand analysis from varying perspectives. I analyzed these data and used them to pull together the story of how Debian evolved from a single mailing list posting to the structure it is today.

DEVELOPMENT OF DEBIAN:
VALUES AND INFRASTRUCTURE

The Debian project is composed of more than 1,000 volunteer programmers distributed around the world who collectively produce a freely available operating system: the Debian GNU/Linux software distribution.[7] This system includes the Linux kernel, or core of the operating system, as well as other prepackaged applications.[8] Developers who contribute to the community consider themselves to be part of "an association or a club, much like your local LUG (Linux User Group) or Rotary, with the principle exception being that we hardy ever meet face to face."[9] Over the past ten years, this community has developed several mechanisms to support the technical and ideological goals of the project. Table 1 summarizes selected project events over time, and Table 2 provides descriptive data about the project.

Table 1. Debian Timeline of Selected Events: 1993–2002

Date		Number of pkgs.	Number of people
Building Support and Infrastructure			
8/16/93	Project proposal e-mail and separate mailing list created		1
8/93–12/93	**Release 0.01–0.90**/Package system/file format designed		
1/94	**Release .91**/Debian Manifesto drafted by founder		30
11/94–11/95	Project sponsored by Free Software Foundation (FSF)		
Strain and Structure: Rearticulating Values			
3/96	Founder resigns from active leadership		
4/96	Second project leader appointed (called president)		
6/96	**Release 1.1**		474
7/21/96	Resume use of GNU/Linux, agree to partner with FSF		
12/96	**Release 1.2**	848	120
2/1/97	First Board of Directors elected		
3/7/97	Announcement of intent to incorporate		
6/10/97	Certificate of Incorporation filed		
6/97	Drafted and adopted Social Contract		
7/97	**Release 1.3**	974	200
11/7/97	Trademark filed with U.S. PTO		
11/25/97	Recruitment notice/mentoring mail list established		
12/10/97	Bylaws for foundation created		
Institution Building: Stabilizing and Scaling			
1/98	Third project leader, de facto election		
7/98	**Release 2.0**	1,500	400+

Table 1. *Continued*

Date		Number of pkgs.	Number of people
8/98	Board turnover (3/4 members leave)		
8/13/98	5th birthday celebrated with IRC party		
9/98	Constitution proposed, with project leader role outlined		
9/24/98	First board meeting and resolutions		
10/29/98	Foundation Web site launched		
12/12/98	Constitution ratified with first project vote (86 votes)		
2/3/99	1999 election: fourth project leader/second elected leader (208 votes)		347
3/9/99	**Release 2.1**		2,250
5/3/99	New project logo chosen		
6/2/99	Nonprofit (501(c)(3)) status awarded by IRS		
12/21/99	Foundation successfully registers trademark in U.S.		
3/16/00	2000 election: fourth project leader serves second term (216 votes)		347
8/15/00	**Release 2.2**	6,500	450+
2000	New Maintainer Committee develops membership process		
7/11/00	"0th" Debian Conference— Projects increase of 1,600 developers maintaining 40,000 packages by 2005		
11/10/00	100 new maintainers admitted through new process		
5/10/01	HP Adopts Debian for internal R&D		
3/28/01	2001 election: fifth project leader elected (311 unique votes)		
4/16/02	2002 election: sixth project leader elected (475 unique votes)		939
7/19/02	**Release 3.0**	8,710	1,084

Table 2. Project Descriptive Data

Project Founding and Leadership
    Project duration: 9 years
    Number of leader elections: 4
    Number of leaders throughout project history: 6
    Mean leader tenure: 20.2 months

Contributor Demographics
    Number of developers: 1,084
    Countries represented by developers: 40+
    Percentage of developers outside the U.S.: 66
    Languages supported: 20
    Number of applicant developers in process/on hold: 235

Technical Environment
    Active mailing lists: 186
    Machine hosts: 26

Donors, Sponsors, and Corporate Relations
    Equipment donors: 17
    Sponsors of official mirrored sites: 41
    Corporate partners: 8
    Fortune 500 corporate partners: 2

Distribution and Sale of Project's Work
    Vendors selling/distributing project software: 143
    Countries represented by vendors: 39
    Percentage of vendors that collect funds for Debian: 57

The Debian project was founded on August 16, 1993, with an announcement to a Usenet newsgroup by an individual who sought help in developing a noncommercial, easily installable packaged version of the GNU/Linux operating system: something that was not available at the time. The initiator of the announcement had technical and social goals in mind. Technically, he recognized that existing Linux systems lacked the management tools necessary to easily install the software.

> The thing that was really lacking, as far as I was concerned, was a complete system that you could take and incorporate all this interesting open source software. . . . What we did have at the time was very primitive. Basically, at that point, you downloaded twenty or thirty floppy disks of data and there

was a file that contained all the commands that you had to type to set everything up. You did not go out to the store and buy a CD Rom and boot up into a nice graphical program that steps you through the process. (Debian project founder, February 16, 2001)

The founder also had a social goal: to create a noncommercial version of Linux that could be managed by more than one person. In his founding manifesto, the initiator of the project stated: "Rather than being developed by one isolated individual or group, as other distributions of Linux have been in the past,[10] Debian is being developed openly in the spirit of Linux and GNU. The primary purpose of the Debian project is to finally create a distribution that lives up to the Linux name.... It is also an attempt to create a non-commercial distribution that will be able to effectively compete in the commercial market" (Murdock, 1994). This project was intended to be a collective effort explicitly organized around noncommercial goals. From an outsider's perspective, a noncommercial distribution that could compete in commercial markets might seem incongruous, if not irrational. If a product had the capability to compete in commercial markets, why wouldn't one want to profit from it?

Informants did not, however, view this goal as contradictory. They wanted their software to be commercial-grade, but they did not want to sell it. One way to explain this is by drawing on Weber's concept of *wertrational* or value rational.[11] Weber defines value-rational action as "determined by a conscious belief in the value for its own sake of some ethical, aesthetic, religious, or other form of behavior, *independently of its prospects of success*" (M. Weber, Roth, and Wittich, 1978, 24; emphasis added). Weber described value-rational action as the result of a conscious formation of values: action based on thoughtful conviction.

> Examples of pure value-rational orientation would be the actions of persons who, regardless of possible cost to themselves, act to put into practice their convictions of what seems to them to be required by duty, honor, the pursuit of beauty, a religious call, personal loyalty, or the importance of some "cause" no matter in what it consists. In our terminology, value-rational action always involves "commands" or demands that, in the actor's opinion, are binding on him. It is only in cases where human action is motivated by the fulfillment of such unconditional demands that it will be called value-rational. (25–26)

A value-rational orientation is "evidenced by actions that put into practice people's convictions" (Rothschild-Whitt, 1979, 509).

By stating that this project would be run in the spirit of GNU, the Debian founder aligned the project with principles of the free software movement founded by Richard Stallman in 1985. This movement protests proprietary restrictions of software and is organized to preserve the freedoms to run, copy, distribute, change, and improve software (Stallman, 1999). The movement's first goal was to develop an operating system that would be freely available, the GNU system, which Linus Torvalds (1999) later integrated with the Linux operating system.[12] In recounting his decision to found the movement, Stallman (1999, 55) viewed leaving the profession as his only other alternative to developing proprietary software: "Another choice, straightforward but unpleasant, was to leave the computer field. That way my skills would not be misused." According to Stallman, creating proprietary code constituted misuse. His commitment to the goal of free software is held without regard for its commercial success.

About two dozen people responded to the initial posting in the Usenet newsgroup, and the founder created a new mailing list specific for this project that he named Debian.[13] Aware that the Linux kernel's modular architecture helped it to grow in complexity of code and participants, the project initiator, with the help of the original Usenet respondents, collectively designed a package management system. A modular package system would enable many people who were not physically colocated to contribute to the project by permitting different development activities to be conducted in parallel: "So we developed a package [system] in order to divide this big job into manageable pieces that we could give out to people that were potentially living with oceans between them and that possibly did not speak the same language [and yet] could still work on these little pieces of the distribution, and then take all of those pieces and put them together" (Debian project founder, February 16, 2001). A package is a discrete unit of code that can be maintained independently from the rest of the operating system but that has a standardized interface that allows integration with other packages. To maintain a package is to manage the receipt and review of code contributions from other contributors and to "package" these smaller contributions into a discrete module.

The group worked together over the new newsgroup to define file names, format conventions, and common interfaces that would allow them to disaggregate the system into packages and reintegrate the packages into one system build. With shared conventions for project components, potential developers could more easily identify areas of the project to which they might be able to contribute and direct their efforts toward particular packages. These conventions became the basis of a policy manual that outlines the precise format for code contributions. In Tuomi's (2000, 20) analysis of the architecture of the Linux kernel, defining interfaces between modules narrows the learning curve for contributing to a specific module: "As long as the protocol for using the resources and the service associated with it are not changed, the users of the interface don't have to know the internal details of the technological artifact or the organization of its production network." As Tuomi suggests, and informants confirmed, well-defined file protocols saved developers from needing to understand the entire system. This helped to make the founder's vision for the project more accessible to developers eager to work on the new system and helped recruit new developers.

The Debian project's alignment with the goals of the free software movement was formalized when the group adopted the GNU General Public License (GPL) and the Free Software Foundation's (FSF) support of the project for a year.[14] This helped grant the project legitimacy in the free software community. First, the GNU GPL allows others to use, modify, and redistribute software, but requires enhancements (derivative works) to be licensed under the same terms. This prevents software that the group develops from being distributed under proprietary terms (O'Mahony, 2002). Second, the movement's financial support for the project allowed the founder to devote more time to refining a technical infrastructure that could support distributed collaborative work. Adoption of the GNU GPL license and affiliation with the FSF signaled the project's commitment to being noncommercial to other potential contributors. "Before [the project initiator] founded Debian, all the other Linux distributions were proprietary.[15] And I thought, 'Well, Linux has made this great kernel and there is all this free GNU software and everybody is putting it together with big dollar signs on the front.' So [he] decided, 'No, I am going to do a free one.' And I liked that, and I liked that people could participate just because they wanted to" (sponsored contributor, former volunteer contributor, March 20, 2001). By the time the project became independent from the FSF, in late 1995, there were about sixty developers active on the mailing list.

Creating a modular technical design, obtaining institutional and financial support, and using legal mechanisms to protect the group's work were resource-mobilizing mechanisms. Mobilizing supporters and drawing resources from the social and economic infrastructure in which challengers to a social order are situated is necessary for achieving change (J. D. McCarthy and Zald, 1977). The development of packages and standards was critical to outlining a framework that participants could learn and to which they could contribute. The backing of the FSF helped provide resources, institutional recognition, and legitimacy for the project in the free software community. The GNU GPL assured the community that the project's code would remain under the control of members. These three mobilizing tactics helped attract more volunteer contributors and sustain the goals of the community. The number of developers increased from one in 1993 to more than 1,000 by mid 2002.[16] This growth was also very dispersed around the world, as almost two-thirds of contributors live outside of the United States.

THE ONLINE INTERACTION ORDER

The interaction order (Goffman, 1983) of the community exists primarily in two electronic mediums: mailing lists and the Debian IRC (Internet Relay Chat) channel. Goffman viewed the interaction order as "that which uniquely transpires in social situations, that is, environments in which two or more individuals are physically in one another's response presence" (2).[17] The Debian interaction order is not physical, but core project members interact with each other through these mediums as part of an ongoing ritual in their daily lives. Core Debian developers may participate on the IRC channel sporadically during the course of their wage-earning employment as well as after work and on weekends.[18] Most members belong to several mailing lists directly related to the specific area of Debian they are working on, as well as to lists that discuss project organization and announcements.

Mailing lists are the primary way contributors coordinate project activity.[19] Issues central to the project are discussed on the main list for core developers, those currently maintaining packages that make up the Debian distribution. This list grew from 1,000 subscribers in August 1998 to 1,925 in 2002. New subprojects, activities, and issues are often raised on this list. As this informant explains, when new topics are raised that are not central to development, contributors construct an additional list in the hope that a new community will grow around it: "The Debian devel[opers] list: That is where all of the, most of the active developers hang out. That is where new ideas get hashed out. And then from there, they go in to subject specific list. Everything sort of starts on Debian devel, that is the core list for Debian. That is one of the things that I do, [I] keep an eye on that list and see if there is one thread or one big subject that keeps coming up, that could use a separate list and take some traffic off there" (Debian volunteer contributor, February 19, 2001). In Yates, Orlikowski, and Okamura's (1995) study of the use of electronic media to structure activities, two strategies were observed: explicit shaping and emergent norms. Debian list maintainers engage in explicit shaping in response to changes or challenges to existing norms. Designing new lists is an example of an explicit way project members sanction activity. Topics that do not belong on the primary development list are diverted elsewhere, but new ideas are encouraged to grow in other places. Orlikowski et al.'s (1995) research suggests that the active and ongoing structuring of activities through online media can be a powerful way to help organizations adapt to changing conditions and contexts.

The founding project mailing list fostered 186 different project-related mailing lists by mid-2002. Each list is its own subcommunity and maintains its own set of norms that guide activities on the list. There are lists for specific languages (Chinese, Russian, Spanish, Portuguese, French, Dutch, Catalan, among others); topic-specific technical lists that focus on bugs, security, and testing; and project lists for events, news, vendors, books, and announcements. The largest mailing list, the project announcement list, has more than 26,000 subscribers. Different mailing lists enable project subcommunities to identify each other and help newcomers locate areas of interest. They are actively maintained: if a new community grows around this list, then the list remains. If not, the list may be pruned. Like those in Orlikowski et al.'s (1995) study, a few key people take an active role in managing the lists. "I pointed out some mailing lists that weren't being used any more and the list administrators chop off lists and I just keep track of how traffic is going and then [whether] we do something to the lists or not" (Debian volunteer contributor, February 19, 2001). This informant, who is an active maintainer of such lists, enjoys this task as it allows him to contribute to the project on his own time but relieves him of the need to stay current with day-to-day development efforts. He is a volunteer with a busy day job, and these structuring tasks allow him to participate in a more periodic fashion.

Managing list activity is more than just an administrative function: it is the primary way the project's activities are structured. Because the lists constitute the entire interaction order of the community, maintaining old lists and creating new lists is an act of structuration (Giddens, 1984). Orlikowski and Yates (1994, 542) argue that communication through mailing lists is "an essential element in the ongoing organizing process through which social structures are produced, reproduced, and changed." Mailing lists are templates for social action: using and structuring the lists reinforces the social order (Orlikowski and Yates, 1994; Yates and Orlikowski, 1992).

Most mailing lists are open to the public. Membership rights and access to the code base are more carefully guarded. Status as a developer member entails four specific privileges outlined in the Debian constitution: the right to (1) make technical or nontechnical decisions with regard to one's own work, (2) propose or sponsor draft resolutions, (3) run as a project leader candidate in elections, and (4) vote for resolutions and leadership elections. Project membership was unproblematic when Debian was relatively small. Individuals who heard of the project and expressed interest in a particular packet were welcomed if Debian old-timers sensed that they were skilled enough to know how to contribute: "When I applied, I told [the Debian project leader], 'Here are the packages I want to work on.' Back then it was pretty easy to assume that if you knew about Debian back then, you were fairly competent and probably understood the basics of what free software was about. It was a new thing back then—free software particularly" (Debian contributor). Technical competence was assessed according to the nature and format of the request. In other words, if a potential contributor was articulate enough to define a packet to work on, he or she was likely to be technically competent enough to contribute to it.

Over time, the process developed more structure, partly because more people became interested in the project and partly because, with growing commercial interest, new potential contributors were less likely to share the founding values of the group (the next section provides more detail on these challenges). In 2000, project members who were interested in these issues formed the "new maintainers committee" to design a process to verify, indoctrinate, and certify new members. The process they designed has five steps: (1) sponsorship by an existing member, (2) identity verification, (3) demonstration of an understanding of the community's philosophy and procedures, (4) demonstration of technical ability, and (5) final evaluation and recommendation. A person who wishes to join the project can apply through the Debian Web page. Only after an advocate (an existing Debian development team member) has authorized the applicant will the committee begin processing the application. Once an applicant is sponsored, the community must then verify the existence of that person. In the eyes of Debian members, verification of identity "closes the loop between hand and eye" (http://www .debian.org/devel/join/nm-step2). This is a measure designed to remove anonymity from a potential member and certify that an individual represents only himself or herself.

Identity verification typically takes place at a "key-signing party" or may become a part of other hacker events such as project meetings and conferences. A potential member must first generate a GnuPG (GPG) key. The GPG key is the open source version of PGP (Pretty Good Privacy), a cryptography protocol that provides a unique digital signature that makes it possible to verify the identity of the sender. To authenticate each other's keys, developers meet face to face, exchange government-issued identification, and sign each other's keys. This way, project members can be sure that the person behind the e-mail address is the person he or she claims to be. Project inductees must have at least one person sign their key in order to become a member. However, all members are encouraged to get their keys signed by as many people as possible to enhance the security of the system. Key signatures are maintained in a file called the "keyring" or the "web of trust."

At a key-signing party, project members sign each other's GnuPG key, but the primary purpose is socializing. However, members are fairly strict about following the procedures for key signing and encourage other people not to violate the web of trust. "It is nice to get more signatures on one's key, and it is tempting to cut a few corners along the way. But having trustworthy signatures is more important than having many signatures, so it's very important that we keep the keysigning process as pure as we can. Signing someone else's key is an endorsement that you have first-hand evidence of the keyholder's identity. If you sign it when you don't really mean it, the Web of Trust can no longer be trusted" (www.debian.org/events/keysigning). These instructions on the project Web sites encourage vigilance in verifying the identity of others, while also recognizing that having many people sign your key can be interpreted as a sign of status: those who have had more people sign their keys have actually met more project members in person.

Identity verification can be seen as a measure of technical security, but it also helps support normative control. Anonymity in computing environments is often associated with greater risk taking, less uninhibited behavior, and less conformity to social norms (Kiesler, Siegel, and McGuire, 1984; Sproull and Kiesler, 1995). People who enter anonymous computing environments may also play with multiple identities (Turkle, 1995, 1999). Identity verification helps prevent the creation of multiple identities. And, with confirmed identities, project members can more accurately learn of each other's skills and competencies and make assessments of trust that are critical in a development environment.

ADAPTING TO SUCCESS AND CHALLENGES OF SCALE

Project members faced three critical challenges in 1997: growth in size and complexity of the project, the emergence of commercial interest in Linux, and leadership turnover.[20] Each of these strained the informal organizing mechanisms on which the group had relied. Under the first two leaders, there was no formal resolution-making process for the project other than discussion through the mailing lists. List discussions could help build consensus on key issues or exacerbate disagreements. Decisions were made at the leader's discretion, and there was no guarantee that decisions would reflect a democratic process: "Well the project leader was essentially a dictator. Because there was no formal structure whatsoever at that time. And you had to lead where people would follow, otherwise they would just walk off" (second Debian project leader, March 14, 2001).

This model is very similar to the "benevolent dictatorship" model Raymond (1999) describes in his analysis of the development of the Linux kernel. One key leader retains final decision-making authority over technical matters but depends on the input and advice of many "lieutenants." As the informant above suggests, this model was not well suited for a rapidly growing membership of active developers all directly contributing to the development of an operating system.[21] Contributing members to the project doubled in 1997 and then again in 1998. It became difficult and time-consuming to come to consensus or make any decisions at all. "I mean the Debian project was growing really big and at that point we had grown from 100 people to 200 people and then to 500 and then fallen off a little bit. Things were getting really hard . . . and it was getting really hard to get a consensus with 500 people, 100 is hard enough, you know. With 500, it's basically impossible [laughs]" (Debian volunteer contributor, November 9, 2000).

Growth in the number of packages and members made release coordination increasingly difficult. Newcomers did not know where to direct their efforts. "As Debian gets bigger, you start having a need for those structures. You can't just say, 'Hey, I am going to go work on this.' You need a little bit more organization. You have to say, 'Well, the ftp people have to coordinate, and the release people have to do this, and the packages have to work with it this way.' You have to formalize everything, because everybody can't know everybody else anymore" (Debian volunteer contributor, February 19, 2001).

As the group grew beyond a size where this informant felt that "everyone was familiar with everyone else," decision making stalled, coordination grew more difficult, and the time between releases grew. The adoption of a new package manager helped to resolve some of the problems associated with package integration. Even so, when Debian doubled in size from 200 developers in 1997 to 400 developers in 1998, the time between release cycles extended to more than a year. This is unusual as, Raymond (1999) characterizes open source projects as releasing their software "early and often."

Research on collectivist organizations formed during the 1970s countercultural movement (Rothschild and Russell, 1986; Rothschild and Whitt, 1986; Rothschild-Whitt, 1979; Swidler, 1979) suggests that this problem is typical of collectivist organizations: they often take a long time to come to decisions or may avoid making any decisions at all. Collectivist organizations are marked by an ideological commitment to autonomy and a rejection of hierarchy and the inequality that often accompanies it (Rothschild and Russell, 1986). Size is a critical issue for collectivist organizations, for without discernible divisions of labor, the number of relevant parties to any decision is not reduced in any simple way. The propensity of collectivist organizations to fail is more likely as they grow (Michels, 1949; Webb and Webb, 1920). Cooperatives such as those in Mondragon, Spain, spin off into smaller units when their size grows larger than 200 members (Whyte and Whyte, 1988), but large-scale participatory democracy remained a struggle for them (A. G. Johnson and Whyte, 1977), as it has for many collectivist organizations (Rothschild and Whitt, 1986).

The inability to come to consensual agreement with this number of people strained the second project leader: he felt uncomfortable representing a large group of people without any process for democratic decision making. This, coupled with the growth in complexity and concomitant responsibilities of the project, led to the idea of creating a board of directors that would be elected directly by members. "This election [the first board election] relieves me of the (often quite awkward) position of being the only person with any real authority over Debian. . . . It's critical that we establish a leadership team for Debian that can survive the departure of any team member" (second project leader, announcement, February 1, 1997). Creating a structure that would endure beyond an individual was considered a way to help preserve the stability of the group, but it did not completely eradicate leadership challenges.

The second strain the project faced was from firms selling Linux distributions, hardware, and professional services and from the media's attention to Linux and open source in general. Although the Debian community had every opportunity to sell their work, and could well have done so, they were not interested in selling copies of their software. Instead, they released an authorized CD master of the distribution on their Web site available for others to download. "That is where Debian stops. That is sort of the last, the last step of Debian . . . *the Debian project doesn't sell*. The Debian project's objective is reached once that [CD] image [master copy] sits there. At that point, we are providing a Linux distribution that will work. Right? And that is as far as, that is the objective of the project right there" (Debian volunteer contributor, February 19, 2001; emphasis added). This, coupled with the creation of a logo and trademark, allowed them some degree of control over how their work was represented to the public. Some members still worried about what Jenkins (1977) would refer to as goal transformation or drift: losing the common cause that first drew the group together: "I think the main concern was not [the fact] that [Linux] was becoming commercial. It was, you know, let's make sure that as it becomes commercial, the reason that it happened in the first place doesn't get lost. . . . To say that Debian is a free software system in 1993, you know there wasn't really any need to do that" (Debian founder, February 16, 2001).

In the early stages of the community's formation, the GNU GPL and association with the FSF provided some sense of an implicit value-rational foundation from which project members could make sense of their efforts. However, the founding principles held by project members had never been clearly articulated since the founder had left: it was assumed that those who joined the community shared a collective goal. With commercial interest in their work, some project members felt the need to distinguish their efforts from start-ups jumping on the Linux bandwagon. Greater public attention was also beginning to attract project contributors who were more heterogeneous in their attitudes toward commercial work and toward the project's founding mission.

Prior research has shown that the emergence of new public referents can create a crisis of meaning that inspires challenging groups to clarify their goals or frame (Snow and Benford, 1992) or to create a spin-off organization (McAdam, 1995). The second project leader recalls a moment when the project encountered a challenge that he felt required rearticulation of the group's values:

> A guy who is now with [an open source firm] had suggested putting a particular package in [the Debian distribution]. And I felt that the package was not free software. And I objected to it, and I, *I needed more than "I don't like it" to be my objection.* . . . I got this idea that there should be a social contract between Debian and the free software community that says how that Linux distribution should behave. So I decided that I could justify the choice of what goes in Debian and what does not, that we could have a Debian Social Contract. (Second Debian project leader, March 14, 2001; emphasis added)

This experience led the second project leader to articulate a basis of authority from which decisions could be evaluated, one that would be independent of any leader but that preserved and justified the group's mission. This led to the collective drafting of two documents, the Debian Social Contract and the Free Software Guidelines, which were discussed and revised over the mailing lists during the summer of 1997.

The Social Contract stipulates the community's intent to remain noncommercial and specifies how the community will treat contributors. It promises that the product of the group's efforts will always remain free and that all future development will be licensed as free software. It explicitly states that the group's first priority will be to the community and the user base. Three years later, project members still spoke of the Contract as having a guiding influence over the project and viewed it as important in defining an identity that both insiders and outsiders could understand.

> The Social Contract says what we are here for and what we will do and it is important to us. (Debian volunteer contributor, November 9, 2000)

> The Social Contract is I think a good example of the, of the evolutionary process in action. Because that was, I think, the year after I left and when the Red Hats and the Calderas of the world were starting to gain traction.[22] Debian decided it needed to take a particular stance and tell everybody what they were and [what they] were not. . . . So in that document they basically said, Debian is a free software system and you know even though it looks like Linux is becoming more and more commercialized, Debian will always be free software. (Debian founder, February 16, 2001)

The Free Software Guidelines state explicit behaviors that are acceptable to the Debian community. For example, in keeping with the GNU GPL, it permits redistribution of source code and derived works, but it also prohibits discrimination against persons or groups or fields of endeavor.

The second project leader spoke earlier of lacking a basis of authority by which to prevent commercial code from being integrated into the group's operating system. The process of creating these two documents formalized the previously unarticulated values on which the group was founded. It also helped ensure that a growing body of contributors new to the group's history and norms could share them. Sources both internal and external to the project suggest that gaining internal consensus of the group's mission and articulating a basis of authority was critical in preserving the project from commercial interests.

Developers also feared that, as their work was adopted for commercial purposes, they withstood a greater chance of being found liable for damages related to their software in some unforeseen context. The second project leader thus began raising funds to found a nonprofit foundation. However, to gain the benefits that corporations enjoy (namely, protection from individual liability), individuals must forfeit some of their rights (J. S. Coleman, 1974). The second project leader understood that a transfer of rights to a corporation would be perceived as a reduction in individual control and autonomy: "I had intended for the corporation to be a liability shield for the developers. To act as a liability shield, the developers needed to be acting on behalf of the corporation. Which meant at the direction of the corporation" (second project leader, March 14, 2001). Many project members were wary of incorporation primarily because they feared losing their individual autonomy to make technical decisions. Some were not sure they wanted a foundation and were suspicious of the project leader's motives. They feared that the creation of a foundation would enhance the leader's power.

Those who supported the idea wanted a minimal structure that could hold their assets and protect them from liability without forming an organization that had jurisdiction over their work: "We need this kind of organization behind us, but we don't want them telling us, 'No, you are not going to release right now, you are going to release in two months.' ... You have to let the projects develop how they want to develop, and [the foundation] is just there to just do what the projects themselves can't do. Which is [to] be a legal entity and handle the kinds of things a legal entity can handle that Debian, since it doesn't exist [legally], can't handle" (Debian volunteer contributor, February 19, 2001). Conflict within the group over the role the foundation would play in relation to the project contributed to dissension over the role of a project leader.

When the founder of the project stepped down at the end of 1996, he simply appointed a new leader who had become very involved in the project. The group largely accepted this appointment, as the appointee had a long tenure and had de facto assumed many project responsibilities prior to the appointment. Some, however, felt that the second leader's guidance in coming to an earlier decision to adopt a new package manager had been heavy-handed. They questioned the heretofore previously undelimited authority of a project leader: "It was clear that it wasn't going to happen the way [the second project leader] wanted it to happen. He wasn't really pushing it through as the Debian project leader, and there are some things that a Debian project leader can't push through" (sponsored contributor, former volunteer contributor, November 9, 2000).

During 1997, the second project leader had been active in establishing an elected board of directors and organizing the collective drafting and approval of the Social Contract and the Free Software Guidelines. He also played an important role in filing for a trademark to represent the project and in incorporating the group through a nonprofit foundation. These changes may have been too many too fast, as they led other developers to grow wary of the leader's apparent growth in power. The influx of organization-building projects was viewed by some to be a necessary evil, but others feared that these changes were too formal, invited hierarchy, and deviated from the group's democratic spirit. Most important, volunteer contributors did not want any one person to have authority over their work. Members began actively raising concerns about the management of the project. The leader, consistent with the norms of the project, first attempted to channel this dissension by creating a new mailing list: "There is a small but vocal group who feel that the Debian project is undemocratic and needs to be re-organized. As project leader, it would be incorrect of me to suppress dissent. Thus I've decided to announce their mailing list to the world and invite people to participate in it" (second project leader, announcement, October, 27, 1997). This turned out to be an ineffective solution, as project members effectively recalled the second leader's authority and he stepped down at the end of the year. "A number of developers convinced me that it was time for a leadership change, and I thus withdrew from the project leader election" (announcement, December 1, 1997).

One attribute of value-rational authority is the ability of a group to recall the authority of a leader (Rothschild-Whitt, 1979; Satow, 1975; Willer, 1967). For authority rooted in collective ideals to rationalize social action, the leader must subjugate himself or herself to the same norms as the collective (Rothschild and Russell, 1986; Rothschild and Whitt, 1986; Rothschild-Whitt, 1979). Only if those in authority obey the same ideological norms as those under their leadership can they preserve their ability to lead (Satow, 1975; Willer, 1967, 236). Unlike Weber's definition of charismatic authority, obedience is not owed to anyone personally, but to the ends of the ideology. The collective grants authority to a leader only in pursuit of shared ideals. The perceived overextension of the second project leader's authority and his subsequent recall motivated project members to reevaluate their approach to governance of the project.

The Social Contract and Free Software Guidelines gave project members assurance that their collective efforts would remain in their control and provided a frame to which individuals could link their own motivations for participating in this group. Incorporating as a nonprofit foundation allowed the project to retain minimal assets and protect individuals from personal liability. Neither of these mechanisms fully resolved the problems of leadership and scaling consensus-based decision making. Maintainers still had difficulty with projectwide decisions, although many technical issues that occurred in primary packages could be resolved at the maintainer level.

The third project leader decided that one way to ease the strain on future project leaders was to craft formal rules to govern decision making in the form of a constitution:

> He [the third project leader] said we should formalize things and come up with a structure that could address the problems faced by a Debian project leader. He did address a lot of problems as a [Debian project leader] and drew a lot of flak for some of the things he did, but as a Debian project leader he had to do them and make some tough decisions. So that did centralize a lot of pain on one person. [The project leader] was looking at the way the project was going and extrapolating out things and saying, "No way is this going to work," and "We have to do something, and, you know, here is what I think we should do." (Volunteer contributor, November 9, 2000)

The constitution was drafted and revised over the mailing list throughout 1998 and ratified in September 1998 with a unanimous vote from 357 developers.[23] The constitution outlines the rights and limitations for developer-members and the project leader. It also creates a committee to resolve technical disputes, establishes procedures for submitting amendments and propositions, and outlines a voting process for general elections and propositions.

The articles of the constitution are consistent with characteristics of value-rational authority (Rothschild-Witt, 1979; Satow, 1975; Willer, 1967). Members have a means to recall the project leader or override his or her decisions. Project leaders must follow the same formalized process as members to propose projectwide resolutions. Leaders are directed by the constitution to "make decisions which are consistent with the consensus of the opinions of the developers" (Article V). When crafting the constitution, project members took special pains to research how to sustain democracy in their selection of a leader. Thus, leaders are directly elected for one-year terms using a variant of the Condorcet voting method.

This method of voting, commonly known as approval voting, allows people to rank all of the candidates they approve. Candidates are then compared pair-wise with each other. In effect, this simulates a two-party run-off election among many parties. Any number of people can run for an election without fear that a winner will emerge without the approval of the majority. Political scientists have found this method to increase the likelihood of a majority winner in plurality contests (Brams and Fishburn, 1978, 831). Brams and Fishburn's theorem indicates that, for elections with more than two parties, this method is most likely to reveal voters' true preferences. It is not clear whether Debian members were aware of this empirical research, but informants indicated that this voting method was chosen to enhance the chance that election winners will have the approval of most project members. This method has been used successfully in four elections, despite the fact that some informants claim not to understand exactly how it works.

To avoid future stalemates, project members crafted a Technical Committee, authorized to "decide any technical matter where Developers' jurisdictions overlap." The Technical Committee has the authority to resolve disputes but is not authorized to engage in design work. A supermajority (3:1) is required to overrule a developer. The committee is restricted to choosing from decisions proposed and discussed elsewhere or adopting compromises: they are a last-resort solution. In addition to delimiting the authority of the Debian project leader and the Technical Committee, the constitution also bounds the group's authority over each other by stating explicitly that the project poses no obligations on anyone to do work for the project: all are volunteer.

NEW ORGANIZATIONS, OLD CHALLENGES

The Debian project is now incorporated, owns intellectual property, has formalized rules, a policy manual, a Social Contract, a constitution, a defined division of labor, and a directly elected leader, but little hierarchy. Does the adoption of these mechanisms signal a collectivist organization's transformation into a formalized bureaucracy? Informants referred to the project's social order as a "meritocracy" or an "organized anarchy" and spoke candidly about the strains they had endured and the mechanisms they created: "We have just ratified the constitution and it will be interesting to see how it works out. It introduces a bit of official rules and politics, but I think it will allow us to work as the sort of organized anarchy that we have always used while adding some much needed safety nets" (candidate platform, 1999 leadership elections). The safety nets that this informant refers to help maintain minimal order without threatening individual autonomy. Informants viewed a successful organization as one that allows individual freedom, constrained only by the wishes of the collective: "What people don't see is really how unorganized it is behind the scenes. Unorganized, not in the sense that everyone does what they want. But everybody works toward a central goal, and *that is what provides the organization.* It is not that there is a real hierarchy or somebody who really makes a decision. The decision process [is], somebody decides what [he or she] want[s] to work on and they work on it and it will get accepted or not" (volunteer contributor, February 19, 2001; emphasis added).

Individuals have the right to pursue their own path and process while working toward the same goal, subject to the shared understandings of other members. The accepted minimal order also helps to sustain a common appreciation of the project's mission and functioning among a group that is globally distributed: "If we didn't have a constitution or a way to publicly chastise people, right? If we did not have a way to say, 'Look, you are not following our rules,' then anybody could do what they want. And with 500 people who are spread all over the world, not all of them speak English as well as other people do. I mean we have people in India, in Europe, in South America, Japan, everywhere" (sponsored contributor, former volunteer, March 20, 2001). Informants' own satisfaction with their organizing mechanisms is important because the form the project takes is an end in itself. Most of these programmers volunteer their time outside of work. If the form becomes untenable, the project's sustenance would be in danger. For organizations focused on ideological goals, the form of organizing must not just solve problems of scale, but represent the very values the movement hopes to promulgate, such as direct democracy and lack of hierarchy (Calhoun, 1995, 192).

The very fact that this project has been able to maintain its organization over a ten-year period during which several hundred Internet start-up firms were founded and disbanded is suggestive of the project's resilience. Yet, to what degree could such a project continue to scale? Research on collectivist organizations suggests that growth in size can shorten their life span. Managing the degree to which all members can equally participate will be paramount to their survival: "Decisions become authoritative in collectivist organizations to the extent that they derive from a process in which all members have the right to full and equal participation" (Rothschild-Whitt, 1979, 512). If all members exercised this right all the time, the project would suffer under its collective weight. What may matter more is that all members maintain that right, but exercise it with discretion.

Because the project's entire interaction order is online, it may be inoculated from the types of dangers that befell many collectivist organizations in the 1970s. First, all activities of the community are visible to all members. This helps create social awareness of what others are doing, enhances the development of a transactive memory of the group's activities, and can help build trust. Very few of the project activities are private or not available to all online. Second, collectivist organizations can be undermined if skills and knowledge are unevenly distributed within the group, for the diffusion of knowledge is a precursor to the diffusion of influence (Rothschild and Whitt, 1986). The visibility of the Debian project's activities enhances individual learning and the diffusion of shared knowledge.[24] Thus, the very public nature of the interaction order could reduce the likelihood of individuals gaining undue influence based on specialized domains of knowledge.

Third, in collectivist organizations such as the "free schools" studied by Swidler (1979) and the communes studied by Kanter (1972), participants can suffer from stress and burnout associated with the demands of extreme loyalty from their group (Rothschild and Russell, 1986; Rothschild and Whitt, 1986). Members of a collectivist online organization may suffer from overuse of the medium, but the degree to which demands of the organization itself create stress and burnout may be limited. Unlike collectivist organizations that are total institutions and try to assert control over all dimensions of members' lives (Goffman, 1961), Debian has a very limited domain: programming and the politics of information distribution. The project, although oriented by strong ideological principles, has very little to say about other aspects of members' lives.

The primary advantage of bureaucratic structures is their efficiency: their ability to reduce transaction costs internal to an organization and to enable domain-specific decision making. A capitalist market economy "demands that the official business of administration be discharged precisely, unambiguously, continuously, and with as much speed as possible" (Max Weber, 1946, 214, cited in Rothschild and Whitt 1986, 113). To the degree that this project is insulated from the time dictates of a market economy, slow and inefficient decision making may not affect the project's health. To the degree that corporate actors become more interested in Debian, time pressures may become paramount. The project's largest challenge may thus be managing the growing technical complexity of the project and decision making with a large direct democracy.

Bureaucratic structures are also more easily recognized by other economic actors. For example, *Infoworld*, a popular computing magazine, awarded the Best Technical Support Award to the Linux user community in 1997 (Foster, 1997). Readers in the December issue of the magazine reported that they got more technical support from mailing lists, postings, Linux Web pages, and e-mailing developers directly than they did from commercial vendors who sold support. Perplexed as to how to make such an award, *Infoworld* stated that "this year marks the first time we're going to have to figure out just what our winner's name is" (Foster, 1997). Maintaining a form that a market economy is unaccustomed to can unearth new challenges, especially if firms view community-managed software projects as direct competitors.

DISCUSSION

This case differs from prior studies of open source projects, such as the Linux kernel (Lee and Cole, 2003; Moon and Sproull, 2002; Tuomi, 2002), which operates with a centralized decision-making model. Six different leaders played important roles in organizing project members to design new social structures, but they did not successfully lead the group beyond a point the collective authorized. Project leaders often initiated the need for formalizing an emergent social order, but the design of such structures was a collective effort: members maintained and exercised the ability to recall their leader's authority.

This research examined how members of a community-managed software project organized their development efforts in a business environment that came to increasingly value their work as a commodity. The values embraced by project members influenced their construction of organizing mechanisms that have contributed to the project's sustenance. Articulating the group's philosophy and creating a technical architecture, governance structure, and legal mechanism to hold assets and represent the project in a commercial environment enabled the project to continue to produce community software in a commodity world. This case provides empirical grounding for several propositions.

First, it shows that commercial-grade software can be created and continuously managed over time without formal sponsorship from any one corporate or government entity.[25] This is an example of the type of productivity gains that can be recouped through information-communication technology without capital investment. Second, it suggests that organizing mechanisms that might otherwise appear to be bureaucratic and purposively rational can be applied to support egalitarian norms. Even when norms are unsettled or shaken by environmental factors, those on the forefront of creating new social orders are selective in recombining organizational elements from traditional bureaucratic organizations with nontraditional elements.

Third, online communities can form new organizational forms that have implications for the offline world. Organizations such as Debian can affect supply chain dynamics in the software industry. For example, more than 143 vendors in thirty-nine countries sell the Debian operating system,[26] but these firms do not have ownership rights to Debian's work. Many of the counter-cultural organizations studied in the 1970s were in specialized niches, "such as custom and craft production and services, where they [were] not in direct competition with capitalist enterprises" (Rothschild and Russell, 1986, 310).[27] Whether a collectivist form of organizing can be sustained in areas of the economy where they directly compete with capitalistic enterprise is an interesting theoretical and practical problem to consider.

There are thousands of community-managed projects on the Internet. Few have structures as well developed as this one, but it is likely that others may emerge. Daft and Lewin (1993, 11) encourage organizational researchers to take on grounded theoretical work of those experimenting with developing new forms. They ask "scholars to . . . break with the tradition of deriving and testing normal science research hypotheses" and recommend a "grounded study of some part of a new organizational form [that] would enable a scholar to learn firsthand about it and provide new theory" (11). This research is an initial attempt to do just that and to inspire others to do so as well, for few have responded to their challenge.

Many of the ways the New Economy was purported to change organizational life made deterministic assumptions about what the Internet would change. The flaws inherent in predicting how the Internet will change the organization of work are too vast to critique here. One example of this type of thinking will suffice: "The Internet will link individuals and groups among themselves and to the shared multimedia hypertext. This hypertext constitutes the backbone of a new culture, the culture of real virtuality, in which virtuality becomes a fundamental component of our symbolic environment" (Castells, 2000, 694). Such predictions do little to shed light on problems of collective action that the Internet does not "solve." Hypertext and an electronic architecture do not create new forms; they provide new resources to help resolve problems of governance and control that are endemic to most social groups.

The mechanisms adopted by the Debian project show how the Internet can change the solutions applied to problems of trust, order, and coordination in a distributed environment. People facing a real, but not a virtual, challenge designed a means to preserve the integrity of an autonomous distributed group as it scaled. This research shows that the problems of governance, control, and autonomy that firms wrestle with when managing distributed work do not disappear in a community-managed software project. The lens of ethnography offers rich insight as to how technical and social change is mutually constitutive, but as the editors of this volume suggest, the result is a picture with a finer resolution, but less clarity as to unifying trends.

Child and McGrath (2001) predict that although a theory explaining the emergence of new forms may be beyond the bounds of the empirical work available, managing the paradoxes involved in balancing participation, scale, and reach with accountability, governance, and control will continue to be paramount. This research provides one example of an organization trying to manage paradoxes of participation and scale with democracy and control. It provides a glimpse of the types of organizational outcomes that the Internet makes possible. I have deliberately avoided discussions of the "virtuality"[28] of this group to highlight the source and structure of messiness that occurs when groups try to manage such paradoxes.

Instead, a very grounded understanding of a group struggling to devise a different way of working and creating value that is not inconsistent with their values is revealed. The social structures this project designed are not predicated on any particular attribute associated with the Internet. What is different and most interesting about collectives supported by electronic mediums is not their virtuality, but the wider range of solutions from which human actors can draw and apply to problems of organizing. Technology is likely to be at the fulcrum of these types of decisions, but its use is in our hands. Our imagination of the types of organizations the Internet makes possible does not need stroking. More fieldwork is needed to understand changes in the organization of postindustrial work. Our attention should instead turn to ways in which collectives supported by new mediums devise ways to resolve age-old problems.

NOTES

This research was supported by a grant from the Social Science Research Council with funds provided by the Alfred P. Sloan Foundation as well as by funds from Stanford University's Center for Work, Technology and Organization and the Stanford Technology Ventures Program.

This essay has benefited from the helpful comments of editor Greg Downey as well as Steve Barley, Bob Sutton, Mark Granovetter, Jason Owen-Smith, Woody Powell, Michael Schrage, Neil Fligstein, Doug Guthrie, Fabrizio Ferraro, Victor Seidel, Mark Mortensen, and Keith Rollag. All errors are mine. Thanks also to Deepak Malhotra for his help with the title. I also thank my informants, who generously contributed their time.

1 An operating system is the set of basic programs and utilities that makes computers run. At the core of an operating system is the kernel. The kernel is the most fundamental program on the computer that manages demands on system resources. It is

what allows you to start other programs. A Linux distribution is a complete operating system built on the Linux kernel.

2 Corporate-initiated open source and free software projects are a more recent phenomenon and may follow a different model.

3 The ability to allocate specific rights to access the code base to specific people.

4 Such projects include GNU, Perl, Apache, BIND, Sendmail, Linux, Samba, Python, Fetchmail, GNOME, KDE, Qt, php, MYSQL.

5 See http://www.linux.org/groups/ for a list of Linux user groups around the world.

6 Permission was granted to tape interviews in all cases. In some cases, informants allowed their names to be used, but anonymity was maintained in the writing of the study.

7 Some developers engage in wage-earning activities that allow them to work on Debian as part of their paid work; they are what I define as sponsored contributors. Others are volunteer. Participation in the project is always voluntary. GNU is a recursive acronym that represents the phrase "GNU is Not Unix." The GNU system developed by Richard Stallman was designed in opposition to the proprietary restrictions associated with Unix.

8 GNU Linux, or Linux, commonly refers to the kernel of an operating system and is often packaged with other software to form a complete distribution. The kernel serves as an intermediary between user applications and the system hardware by managing system resources. There are more than a hundred different Linux and GNU/Linux distributions that build off stable versions of the Linux kernel. See http://www.lwn.net/2001/0322/dists.php3 for the most complete listing of Linux distributions available. The Debian GNU/Linux version is the only known Linux distribution that is managed by a nonprofit group.

9 Project documentation (http://www.debian.org/devel/join/nm-step2).

10 This reference to other Linux distributions managed by one person likely refers to the Linux kernel managed by Linus Torvalds.

11 In introducing the concept of value rationality, I am not addressing the implicit or explicit factors that might affect individual motivations for contributing to open source projects (for more information, see Lakhani and Wolf, 2005; Lerner and Tirole, 2002). I am merely characterizing a type of rationality that might account for these project goals.

12 As is well documented elsewhere (Moody 2001; Moon and Sproull, 2002; Raymond, 1999), the Linux project attracted a worldwide base of contributors that improved this operating system to the point where it became commercial-grade and attracted the attention of firms.

13 The project's name stems from a combination of the names of the founder and his wife.

14 The Free Software Foundation is the primary organization that represents the free software movement and "is dedicated to promoting computer users' right to use, study, copy, modify, and redistribute computer programs. The FSF promotes the development and use of free (as in freedom) software—particularly the GNU operating system (used widely today in its GNU/Linux variant)" (www.gnu.org). The FSF supported the project by hiring the founder from 1994 to 1995.

15 This informant is referring to Linux distributions that are sold by firms who also develop proprietary code.

16 It is likely that this rate of growth in contributors would not have been possible without the Internet.

17 Although the Internet was not a viable medium in Goffman's time, he did consider phone and mail to include presence, and I extend this to include electronic mediums such as mailing lists.

18 The effect of such participation on wage-earning work activities is unknown. It should be pointed out, however, that many Debian developers do wage-earning work that may be related to their Debian activities and that this may potentially have a synergistic effect with their wage-earning work activities.

19 Because participants are distributed across time and space, members encourage all project-relevant discussions to happen on the appropriate list so that all members have equal access to that information. Although members may meet occasionally, off-list discussions are not encouraged as they may create inequities in the information available to other project members.

20 The founder left the project for personal reasons, and a second leader was informally appointed to replace him.

21 The Linux kernel is managed very differently from the Debian project, as write access, or the ability to commit code directly to the code base, is not distributed but rests in one or two final decision makers.

22 Red Hat and Caldera are two for-profit corporations that sell distributions of Linux.

23 The exact percentage of voter participation among members is unknown but is likely large as there were a little more than 400 project members at that time.

24 Whereas skills and tasks may be highly differentiated in the package system, it is always possible for members to maintain awareness of what others are doing.

25 This is not to say that the Debian project does not have sponsors. Of the 105 vendors who sell Debian distributions, 55 percent of them will collect donations for Software in the Public Interest (SPI) and the Debian community. Other companies provide hardware or support contributors to the project. However, all contributors work on a volunteer basis, and there is no one single corporation who sponsors the group.

26 See www.debian.org/distrib/vendors. Of these vendors, 57 percent donate or provide an option for customers to make a donation to the Debian project.

27 Examples include alternative schools, food cooperatives, and nonprofit organizations providing pro bono legal counsel, medical services, or counseling (Rothschild and Russell, 1986).

28 This project is not supported by any one physical location.

Jean Comaroff and John Comaroff

REFLECTIONS ON YOUTH, FROM
THE PAST TO THE POSTCOLONY

PROLEGOMENON

> Philosophy does not concern itself with children. It leaves them to pedagogy, where they're
> not in very good hands. Philosophy has forgotten about children.
> —Bernhard Schlink, *The Reader*

There has long been a tendency in the public discourse of the West to speak of youth as a transhistorical, transcultural category, as if it has existed everywhere and at all times in much the same way. This is in spite of the fact that anthropologists and historians have insisted, for almost as long, that the cultural meanings and social attributes ascribed to "youth" have varied a great deal across time and space; recall Malinowski and Margaret Mead, not to mention Philippe Ariès. It is also an anthropological truism that the way young people are perceived, named, and represented betrays a lot about the social and political constitution of a society. Thus it is that, in nineteenth-century Britain, down-class juveniles were referred to as "nomads"; their terrains, the internal colonies of the industrial metropole, were called "Jungles," even "Africas" (Hebdige, 1988, 20). Similarly, in late twentieth-century North America and South Africa (Seekings, 1993, xii, citing David Everatt), white preadults are typically termed "teenagers," while their black counterparts are "youth"—adolescents with attitude, so to speak. In this manner, language racializes and demonizes difference without explicitly marking it. "Words," Joseph Conrad (1911/1957, 11) once said, are "the great foes of reality." But they also open a window onto its secrets.

Far from constituting a universal category—a social status generated by the abstract sociological principle of generation—youth, as we speak of them here, are the historical offspring of modernity: modernity, that is, as the ideological formation that arose during the Age of Revolution, 1789–1848 (see Hobsbawm, 1962), and was honed in the fraught dialectics of empire, modernity as an ideological formation that naturalized its own telos in a model of human development (Lukose, 2000), casting youth as both the essential precondition and the indefinite postponement of maturity.[1] Industrial capitalist society has been more or less unique in making childhood into a site of self-conscious cultural reproduction, releasing its young from the workplace so that they might enter the rarified world of education, the latter being the space in which the nation-state seeks to husband its potential, in which it invests in its human capital, in which, says Foucault (1976, 81), it "hides its dreams." Yet juveniles are also the creatures of our nightmares, of our social impossibilities and our existential angst.

It is in this latter sense that, for Hebdige (1988, 17), youth enter modernist narratives only when they stand for trouble. But the matter is more ambiguous than he suggests. Trouble, Butler (1990, vii) insists, need not merely be cast in the negative. It can also imply the productive unsettling of dominant epistemic regimes under the heat of desire, frustration, or anger. Youth, in other words, are complex signifiers, the stuff of mythic extremes (Blanch, 1980, 103), simultaneously idealizations and monstrosities, pathologies and panaceas. This has been true for a very long time. Witness the ambivalent appearance of the young in Dickensian London, on one hand as orphans and artful dodgers, yet also as the bearers of Great Expectations. Or the discordant images of juvenile activists in late-twentieth-century Africa: contrast, for example, the preternatural child soldiers of Mozambique or Sierra Leone, the very epitome of civil disintegration (Honwana, 1999), with the heroic "young lions" of South Africa, who were the harbingers of democracy and the end of apartheid. Such contrasts are likely to persist: in Brazil, homeless children have come to symbolize both the collective shame of the nation-state and its future resurrection through proper planning and legal intervention (Veloso, 1998).

In short, youth stands for many things at once: for the terrors of the present, the errors of the past, the prospect of a future. For old hopes and new frontiers (see De Boeck, 2005). In all of these tropic guises, of course, they are figures of a popular imagination far removed from more nuanced social realities.[2] This is crucial to keep in mind as we interrogate the place of young people in the late-twentieth-century nation-state—especially those neoliberal nation-states currently in difficulty—in Africa and elsewhere.

The meaning of globalization, at least as an analytic concept, might still be in dispute in some circles. But few would deny that one global feature of the contemporary world—from Chicago to Cape Town, Calcutta to Caracas—is a sense of crisis surrounding the predicament of juveniles. Although it is always locally mediated and modulated, that predicament appears to arise out of the workings of neoliberal capitalism and the changing planetary order of which it is part. It takes many forms, patently. But it seems everywhere to be founded on a counterpoint, a doubling, a contradiction perhaps. On one hand is the much remarked exclusion of the young from national economies, especially from their shrinking, metamorphosing productive sectors. As the frenzied expansion of the free market runs up against the demise of the welfare state, a process that manifests itself in an ever widening gulf between rich and poor, the commonweal of all but a few sovereign polities has been drastically eroded. In the upshot, most are unable or unwilling to sustain previous levels of social services and benefits, to afford the cost of infrastructural reproduction, or to underwrite a labor market in which there is regular or secure employment in any abundance. Even in advanced industrial societies, the modernist dream of infinite progress—a narrative according to which each generation does better than its predecessor—is constantly mocked by conditions that disenfranchise many people, disproportionately the young and unskilled of the inner city and the countryside, from full-waged citizenship in the nation-state.[3] This despite the claims by some that the current generation of mainstream American "kids" is more compliant, less cynical than those who came before them (Howe and Strauss, 2000). To be sure, patterns of polarization and exclusion, among youth and across the age spectrum at large, are ever more palpable.

On the other hand is the recent rise of assertive, global youth cultures of desire, self-expression, representation; also, in some places, of potent, if unconventional, forms of politicization to go along with them. In the cyberspace age, juveniles have an enhanced capacity to communicate in, and act effectively on, the world at large. Generation has become a concrete, quotidian principle of social mobilization, inflecting other dimensions of difference, notably, race, gender, ethnicity, and class.[4] Transnational youth activism, and the mutually comprehensible signifying practices on which it is based, are facilitated by planetary flows—of currencies, people, value—across old sovereign boundaries (see Appadurai, 1990; Venkatesh, n.d., 6). The young have taken to the Internet and to the streets in growing numbers as post-Fordist economics recast relations between capital and labor, profoundly altering global geographies of production. More of this below.

In the late twentieth century, in sum, youth have gained unprecedented autonomy as a social category *an und für sich*, both in and for themselves. This is in spite of, or perhaps because of, their relative marginalization from the normative world of work and wage. In many Western contexts, they, along with other disenfranchised persons,[5] add up to an incoherent counternation with its own illegal economies of ways and means, its own spaces of production and recreation, its own parodic patriotisms. Elsewhere (Comaroff and Comaroff, 1999a), we use the term "alien-nation" to describe the phenomenon; in like vein, Žižek (1997, 127) treats these disenfranchised persons as the "symptoms" of late capitalist universalism, whose imminent logic ensures that their equivalent deprivations never find unified voice in some "rainbow coalition, notwithstanding progressivist liberal hopes and expectations." As this suggests, youth embody the sharpening contradictions of the contemporary world in especially acute form. Take South Africa, for example. Here, in the apartheid years, the juvenile black counternation had a palpable opponent in the racist state. With the demise of the ancien régime, the dispossessed won the right to enter the workplace as "free" individuals. But, in a tragic irony, this occurred just as the global impact of neoliberal capitalism began to kick in. Now large-scale privatization, the loss of blue-collar employment, and the erosion of working-class identities vitiate the prospects of building an inclusive social democracy. Young people of color, would-be citizens of the "new" millennial order, must find their place in a society whose hard-won nationhood is already subverted by forces that compromise the sovereignty of its political economy.

But we are running ahead of ourselves. To push our understanding of the contemporary predicament of youth beyond the merely superficial, to explore further the doubling—the ambiguous threat and promise—inherent in its formation, it is necessary to dig a little deeper into the modernist archaeology of the category. For it is here that we are likely to find the source of contemporary generation troubles. Or, at least, our apprehension of them.

A BRIEF HISTORY OF YOUTH

Foucault (1976, 80) may or may not have been correct in claiming that modern Western society is unique in accentuating the gulf between children and adults. But we do appear to have romanticized and commodified that space, making it a site wherein immature carelessness confronts full-grown desire, wherein an irrepressible sense of invincibility seems to drive precocious power. Of course, the nation-states of Europe were not alone in marking out youth as a life phase whose liminal force could be tapped for the collective good. Age-based societies in Africa mobilized premarital warriorhood to this end as well; indeed, those who languish between corporeal and social maturity, debarred from marrying or establishing families, have become the foot soldiers of adult hegemony in many places. Youth, from this perspective, is everywhere a potential category of exclusion and exploitation, a source of surplus value.

It is arguable that twentieth-century European polities—with their technologies of mass production, communication, and coercion—have been singularly well positioned to idealize and utilize the physical and imaginative resources of the young. Yet one of the hallmarks of the present moment, of the age of globalization and postcoloniality, has been a diminishing of the capacity of governments—if not of the market forces they foster—to control adolescent bodies, energies, or intentions. From the spread of global youth cultures and environmental politics to the sprouting of urban gangs, soccer armies, and neo-Nazi cadres, the nation-state plays host to forces that it can no longer adequately rein in. Often, moreover, the more radical of these forces name themselves—Hip Hop Nation, Gay Nation—in ways that both mimic and mock it, all the better to trouble its sovereignty. Thus the phalanxes of football supporters in the new Europe, who savage people and property, assault police, and transgress barriers and borders at home and abroad—all in the name of national pride (Buford, 1993). Likewise the rise of libertarian militias, whose youthful troops declare war on established government in the name of purer forms of patriotism, albeit often at the behest of more cynical, less visible father figures.

How has this come to be? Whatever its resemblance to comparable usages in other periods and places, the Euroconstruction of youth, we repeat, is the outworking of a specific set of social conditions; its evolution, still ongoing, bespeaks a submerged history of modernity and its imperial underbelly. While those covered by the term have long had their deviant identity thrust upon them (see below)—and, since World War II, sold to them—they have increasingly made it their own. A brute deus ex machina propels this unfolding story: the complex relationship between capital and the nation-state. Industrial capitalist economies were capricious in the ways they, Janus-faced, both begat and undermined equalities of citizenship and entitlement; their postindustrial counterparts have cumulatively subverted national sovereignty and the substantive rights of subjects. The sanguine expectations that once framed bourgeois cultures of progress and their civilizing missions abroad—ideals that vouchsafed the young a future under the sign of "development"—are, as we have already said, sorely compromised by the growing inequalities wrought in the name of neoliberal capitalism. Postmodernity is often characterized as modernism bereft of its hopeful, utopian thrust.

Concomitantly, the new age of globalism might be seen as one in which the worldwide fabrication of desire, of the promise of infinite possibility, meets the impossibilities occasioned by widening disparities of wealth, itself a corollary of the devolution and decommissioning of economies of manufacture. In the face of all this, many youthful entrepreneurs, having been raised in advanced commodity cultures, find their own ways and means. Sometimes these involve the supply of hitherto unimagined "services"; sometimes the recommissioning of the detritus of consumer society; sometimes the resale of purloined property of the state; sometimes the short-circuiting of existing networks of exchange. For a burgeoning number, they entail entry into the lower reaches of the transnational trade in drugs, and/or into a netherworld in which the deployment of violence becomes a routine mode of production and redistribution—often in a manner that replicates the practices of international business. And visibly corrodes the authority of the state. But more of this in due course.

If, to return to the earlier moment, it was the rise of industrial capitalism that first created the conditions for the emergence of a semiautonomous category of youth, it was in the exploding cities of modern Europe that this category first took on a manifest sociological reality. Hebdige (1988, 19; see earlier reference) has argued that the young first showed their insolent face across modern Britain in the "delinquent" crowds that gathered in manufacturing towns, where the offspring of the rising working-class were often left to survive and to create their own social worlds, independent of paternal or patrician control (Blanch, 1980; Gillis, 1974; G. S. Jones, 1971/1984). Observers were particularly disturbed by children and adolescents in urban slums, by the "wandering tribes" or "young Arabs" who inhabited the internal colonies at the heart of London and Manchester (Mayhew, 1851, 277). These were the artful dodgers of the Dickensian inner city, to whom we alluded earlier, the mutant citizens of its alien-nation. They inspired a civilizing crusade, prompting the founding of Ragged Schools and Reformatories and, in due course, a compulsory system of state education; also a pedagogic mission to "the dark places" of the earth. One might note, with the hindsight of history (Willis, 1977), not least South African history, that state education would not so much eradicate the alien-nation as reproduce it by different means. The South African Broadcasting Corporation, in collaboration with the Department of Education, recently commissioned a team of the country's most gifted young filmmakers to make a docudrama on postapartheid schooling.[6] They painted a chilling portrait of endemic frustration and routine violence, prompting widespread and anguished national debate.

Youth as a sign of contradiction, as the figuration of mythic bipolarity, is enshrined in the foundations of the modern collective imaginary. In the abstract, the term congeals pure, utopic potential. In everyday reality, however, "youth" is a collective noun that has all too often indexed a faceless mass of persons who are alike underclass, unruly, male, challengingly out of place—and at once morally immature and physically powerful enough to seize the initiative from their elders and betters. They personify the failure of moral reproduction, the dangerous obverse of capitalist optimism, the limits of a meliorist, bourgeois social vision. The tensions embodied in this pre-adult population, exacerbated where differences of race or creed color those of generation, have peaked in periods of economic slump. For, as surplus citizens, youth are not born; they are made by historical circumstances. And rarely as they like.

But if these young people have embodied the threat of civil disorder, they can also be harnessed for state projects of organized violence; in particular, for mobilization as soldiers. Often, those not yet deemed ready to live as full citizens of the nation-state have been called upon to die for it. (Remember, in this respect, the Africans who served the colonial powers in both World Wars; see, e.g., Bent, 1952.) This is the flip side of the story of youth and modernity: adolescence as the infantry of adult statecraft, as the ever more reluctant blood and bone of national aspiration. At the core of the making of "modern" youth, then, has been the role of the state in naturalizing, exploiting, and narrating the relationship between juveniles and violence, a relationship all too neatly eclipsed in the disciplinary logic of peacetime discourses about adolescent deviance.

Thus it is that the association of juveniles with the threat of precocious, uncontained physicality—sexual, reproductive, combative—has haunted popular and scholarly perceptions alike in the twentieth century. In the 1920s, a rapidly professionalizing sociology (first in America, then in Europe) depicted youth as a disruptive masculine force in the city, as purveyors of violent crime and ready recruits to the barbarities of life in gangs. Functionalist sociology turned historical contradiction into social pathology and took these youth to be its epitome. They were tribal, feral beings who hunt in packs, anticitizens, an affront to bourgeois family values and social order. Delinquent, down-class, male, and violent, they were also increasingly black. Nor is this true only in the northern and western hemispheres. Recent South African history is another instance. In the final years of struggle against apartheid, the category of youth expanded to include diverse classes of freedom fighters: students, workers, even criminals. In this story, it is true, not all young blacks are youth. But all youth are black. Also overwhelmingly, if not exclusively, male. And if some people never become youth, others seem unable to outgrow the label, even in middle age (see Buford, 1993; Seekings, 1993, 11). Shades here again of Mannheim's foundational insight, recalled by Bundy (1987, 304) in the African context, that generation is a social, not a chronological, category. It is also a political one. With deep material roots.

THE RISE OF GLOBAL "YOUTH CULTURE"

The rise of neoliberal capitalism on a planetary scale has further complicated the modernist construction of youth. Often associated with the events of 1989, this epochal transformation was heralded by the thoroughgoing shifts in global power, economy, and modes of communication set in motion in the wake of World War II, shifts that would reshape the structure of international capital and intensify its workings. As we shall see, those shifts would not merely reconstruct colonial relations, national economies, and international markets in goods, services, and signs. They would also globalize the division of labor, remake human subjects, alter the relationship between production and consumption, and reform identities and citizenships across the world. Though in no sense homogenizing, this process involved novel forms of space-time compression, as well as the reformulation of boundaries and localities everywhere. It also ushered in a new moment in the history of youth; to be sure, as we noted earlier, an electronically mediated "youth culture" was one of its earliest, most expansive cultural expressions, providing a lexicon for the ever more explicit assertion of juveniles across the globe as agents in and for themselves.

It is significant, in this respect, that the United States—"the only victor" of the Great War (Fussell, 1975, 317)—emerged as the major economic and cultural force on the international scene after 1945. For here, where postwar affluence and pronatalism combined to usher in a fresh phase of expansionist capitalism, the "teenager" became the new model consumer-citizen, the term itself an invention of the marketing industry (D. Cook, 1998). Equipped with disposable wealth to spend on commodities and "leisure" (Cohn, 1969; Hebdige, 1988, 30), this was the first generation set loose to craft itself in large part through consumption. Capitalists for the first time saw youth as a market with its own infinitely cultivable needs. "Fawning like mad" (Cohn, 1969, 15), they manufactured the means—clothes, music, magazines, dances—for creating age-based collectivities with unprecedented self-awareness, visibility, and translocal potential.

The capacity of the languages of youth culture to mark emergent identities and consciousness was shown when the "rebels without a cause" of the 1950s became rebels with causes aplenty, from the romance of white hippy flower power to militant Black Panther antiracism. And although the naïve self-absorption of lifestyle politics and rock resistance might have been evident from its roots in Haight Ashbury, the mass protests against the Vietnam War demonstrated that a self-conscious youth counterculture could engage mainstream politics. Artful dodgers became draft dodgers, and the right of states to commandeer the means of violence, especially in the bodies and purposes of youth, was seriously challenged. Neither was this a purely parochial struggle; that much was attested by simultaneous upheavals among restive students in many parts of the world. The historical significance of these youth uprisings remains an open question. But one thing about them is clear: they were a precursor of new sorts of social movements, movements born of the creative refiguring of local means and ends in light of global, media-driven identities, ideologies, and vocabularies. The sounds of the 1960s, perhaps the true Age of Youth, traversed a multicentered, electronically unified planet, fueled by transnational commercial interests. Amid a rapidly proliferating flow of signs and values (Appadurai, 1990; Hannerz, 1989), youth culture began to construct an "elsewhere"—a universe-wide, alienated age grade—that gave preadults the language for an identity apart from the "soiled and compromised parent culture" (Hebdige, 1988, 30).

This age grade, purely a figurative community, of course, was inherently tenuous and virtual. Its imagining could seldom fully transcend the limitations imposed by the commodity-dependence of mass cultural forms. As actors-through-consumption, teenagers bought—literally—into mainstream interests at the same time as they contested them. In so doing, they typified the predicament of would-be subversives in advanced capitalist contexts, of those who struggle to seize control of commodified signs and practices, thus to use them in ways that do more than merely reaffirm the status quo. Located far from sites of primary production, theirs is often a politics of style.

Its iconoclasm is effected on camera-ready bodies, or, more recently, along digital frontiers where hackers and "cyberpunks" protest freedoms lost as computer technology becomes ever more subject to corporate control (E. G. Coleman, n.d.). To the critically minded, like Hebdige (1988, 35), their exertions appear ambiguous, as "neither affirmation nor refusal." Their iconoclastic play with mainstream commodity forms often signals subversion, as in the case of punk and rap, and may discomfort the guardians of property and propriety. But it must always struggle to remain ahead of encroaching market forces, forces that threaten to neutralize its effects by reducing its creativity to bland consumer goods.

BEYOND THE POLITICS OF METAPHOR

Still, we mistake the possibilities of the moment if we see youth culture simply as a "politics of metaphor" (Hebdige, 1988, 35). It is a mistake that flows from focusing more on the products of that culture, on its disembodied images and texts, than on their situated production and use. The potential of its signs and objects to be (re)deployed, to be "cut and mix[ed]," have made them easily available for the fashioning of a wide variety of identities and projects—identities and projects whose sometimes subversive strain, itself often acted out rather than spoken out, underlies the ambivalences endemic to the late-twentieth-century representation of the young, sui generis. Also, perhaps, endemic to the political spirit of the age writ large. For the productive aspect of youth culture has expanded as juveniles have come to participate on a global scale in shaping their own markets, both legal and illegal, as their signifying practices have connived with those species of post-Fordist capital that owe little loyalty to local establishments or economies. Youth have been integral to the opening up of new economic spaces of profitability: fertile Silicon Valleys, where young "nerds," eschewing academic credentials and professional regulation, have become multimillionaires. The childlike insouciance that typifies this field, in image if not in terms of real control, is legible in the bespectacled boyishness of an aging Bill Gates.

The libertarian possibilities of electronic technologies that simultaneously privatize and globalize the means of communication are intrinsic to the effects of capitalism in its neoliberal guise and have generated new openings for juvenile adventurers, ostensibly unfettered by a gerontocratic establishment. This is captured in the equivocal figure of the "hacker," an underage outlaw bent on maintaining the freedom of the information highway and redeeming his (more rarely her) creative potential from the grasp of "evil" corporations and imperious governments (E. G. Coleman, n.d.). A string of American movies (such as *Hackers, Wargames,* and *Johnny Mnemonic*) rehearse popular nightmares of electronic whiz kids breaking into top security enclaves and threatening to hold the state and its guardians for ransom. Recent reports in the U.S. media, interestingly, tell of teenage e-traders amassing huge fortunes in their bedrooms while putatively doing their school homework.

But suburban cyberbrats are hardly unique in their capacity to mine the potential of new economic frontiers. Every bit as inspired and ingenious have been the ventures of less advantaged young people from the inner cities, from postcolonial and postrevolutionary societies, and from other terrors incognita, who seek to make good the promise of worldwide laissez-faire. Here, too, liberalization has created room for youthful entrepreneurs to maneuver beyond the confines of modernist modes of production, polity, legitimacy. Take the burgeoning "bush economies" of Cameroon and Chad, where "market boys" cross borders, change passports, trade currencies, and traffic in high-risk cargo like guns and drugs; in so doing, they invent fresh ways of getting rich on the margins of global markets (Roitman, n.d.). Or consider the ferociously escalating teenage diamond trade—another amalgam of danger, desire, and deregulation—that provisions armies in West and Central Africa, setting up innovative configurations of libertarian commerce, violence, and profit (De Boeck, 2000). Or observe the young Mouride men from Senegal who have taken to translocal enterprise with such energy that they talk of New York as "a suburb of Dakar"; their remittances finance major reconstruction of urban neighborhoods at home, transform local power relations, and, concomitantly, highlight the dwindling capacity of the nation-state to sustain its infrastructure (Buggenhagen, 2001; Mamadou Diouf, personal communication, 2000). These fluid economies are usually not altogether free of gerontocratic control, of course. Nor do they supplant all formal political and economic arrangements, with which they have complex and multiple interconnections. But they do circumscribe and relativize them in significant ways, thereby challenging their exclusive sovereignty.

In sum, youth culture, in an epoch of liberalization, has shown itself uniquely able to link locales across transnational space—and to motivate the kinds of material practices that, in turn, have redrawn the maps of high modernism. Contemporaneity is its essence. In this, it echoes present-day pop, whose fast-moving "sampling" distends the normative by juxtaposing sounds in startlingly labile ways, not least when it cannibalizes ethno-musics from across the planet. Small wonder that our nightmare adolescent—wearing absurdly expensive sports shoes, headphones blaring gangsta rap, beeper tied to a global underground economy—is a synthesis of street child and corporate mogul.

A qualification here. The marginalization of young people, at least in its present-day form, may be a very general structural consequence of the rise of neoliberal capitalism. And youth culture may be increasingly global in its reach. But this does not mean that the predicament of juveniles, or their experience, is everywhere the same, everywhere homogenized. Neither in its social nor in its cultural dimensions is this the case. It takes highly spe-cific forms, and has very different material implications, in Los Angeles and Dakar, London and Delhi. Hip hop, Air Jordans, and Manchester United colors might animate youthful imaginations almost everywhere, often serv-ing as a poignant measure of the distance between dream and fulfillment, between desire and impossibility, between centers of great wealth and periph-eries of crushing poverty. But these signs are always domesticated to some degree. Otherwise, they would have very little density of meaning. Appropri-ated and recontextualized, they are translated into hybrid languages capable of addressing local concerns. Thus it is that rap music is inflected in one way on the Cape Flats, another on the streets of Bombay or Havana. Writes Richard Ssewakiryanga (1999, 26): "Today in Uganda, rap music is not only received in its American form, but repackaged by borrowing from some of the traditional folklore to fill in the incomprehension . . . suffered by the audience listening to the poetics of American rappers." Imported images, he notes, quickly penetrate local repertoires of humor, irony, anger. At the same time, these media remain points of intersection, points of connection be-tween here and elsewhere, between sameness and difference, between re-ceived identities and a global imaginary.

Partly as a result of all this, youth tend everywhere to occupy the innova-tive, uncharted borderlands in which the global meets the local, this often being audible in the elaboration of creolized argots, such as Street Setswana and Kwaito in South Africa, that give voice to imaginative worlds very dif-ferent from those of the parental generation.[7] These frontiers are also sites of tension, particularly for young people who confront the contradictions of modernity as they try to make good on the millennial promise of democracy and the free market in the newly liberalized states of Africa and Eastern Europe. In the late twentieth century, we have suggested, the image of youth-as-trouble has gained an advanced capitalist twist as impatient adolescents try to "take the waiting out of wanting," thus to lessen the gulf between hope and fulfillment. In the process, they have felt their power, power born of a growing willingness and ability to turn to the use of force, to garner illicit wealth, to hold polite society to ransom. Bill Buford (1993, 264) has said that it is only in moments of concerted violence that riotous British soccer fans experience a real sense of community, a point others have extended to gangland wars in U.S. cities, to witch burning in the northerly provinces of South Africa, and to cognate social practices elsewhere. Is it surprising, then, that so many juveniles see themselves as ironic, mutant citizens of alien-nations, finding scant reflection of themselves in the rites and rhetoric, the provisions and entitlements, of a liberal democratic civic order?

ENDNOTE

It was the ANC manifesto that proclaimed "jobs for all at a living wage." . . .

Where are the promised youth brigades? Where are the jobs? Where is the living wage?

Now is the time.

—Shaheed Mohamed, *Cape Times* (South Africa), July 29, 1999

Elsewhere (Comaroff and Comaroff, 2000a), we explore the (onto)logic of neoliberal capitalism, or "millennial capitalism," as we refer to it, thus to index not merely its epochal rise at the end of the century, but also the fact that it has become invested with an almost magical, salvific capacity to yield wealth without work, money without manufacture. There we seek to show that structural transformations in the material, moral, and signal relationship of production to consumption have altered the very essence of labor and social reproduction, also the essence of—and mutual bleeding into each other—of class, race, gender, and generation.[8] In the final analysis, it is this epochal history, this analytic ur-narrative, that holds the key to any understanding of the present and future predicament of youth, even of its unfolding construction as a category *an und für sich.* Here we have sought to lay out, somewhat cavalierly, bits and pieces of the genealogy of that ur-narrative.

In so doing, we have sought to complicate current talk, at least in populist discourses, of "the crisis of youth," talk that portrays the predicament of the younger generation in monochromatically bleak terms.[9] As if all were entropy, all catastrophe, all impossibility in this Age of Futilitarianism, this age in which rampant self-interest meets rampant pessimism (Comaroff and Comaroff, 1999b). It is not that these terms are inaccurate, nor that deep concern is unwarranted. To the contrary. The metamorphosis of the global economy is marginalizing many people before they grow to full maturity, excluding them from the prospect of regular employment, treating them increasingly as adults before the law when they transgress the bounds of the normative, demonizing them as they turn to crime in the absence of any other means of livelihood. The young of today, it seems, are more than ever enfranchised as consumers—welcomed into the marketplace in the immediate interests of corporate capital—often then to be excluded from the benefits of mainstream economic participation, political acknowledgment, and civic responsibility (see Venkatesh and Murphy, forthcoming).

But this is only a part of the story.

For one thing, as we have said, the attribution to unruly youth of the standardized nightmares of polite society—not unlike the witch in precolonial and colonial Africa (Wilson, 1951)—goes back to the genesis of industrial capitalism and its bourgeois sensibilities. It is on the back of those situated in the liminal space between childhood innocence and adult responsibility that modernist sociomoral anxieties have tended to be borne. For another thing, it is crucial, if we are to make any real sense of the contemporary predicament of youth, of its neomodern construction as a category in and for itself, that we stress its intrinsic bipolarity, its doubling. Youth is not only a signifier of exclusion, of impossibility, of emasculation, denigration, and futility. Nor, by all accounts, is it experienced as such. Although they may not, for the most part, have captured the mainstream—and may, indeed, constitute an infinitely exploitable market, an inexhaustible reservoir of consumers, an eternal font of surplus value to be extracted—the young remain a constant source of creativity, ingenuity, possibility, empowerment. A source of alternative, yet-to-be-imagined futures.

NOTES

1 Constructs such as "racial adolescence," deployed by civilizing missions abroad to measure the (lack of) "progress" of colonized peoples toward "modernity," demonstrate the ideological uses of this form of developmentalism; see Willoughby (1923, 239) for a South African instance.

2 Apart from all else, youth are always only a fraction of those not yet adult, that fraction whose anomalous agency asserts itself in honor or breach of communal order. Often, they are the mutant citizens of the modern nation, purveyors of its violent undersides. This is a point to which we shall return.

3 The theme of disenfranchisement was sounded repeatedly by proponents of Ralph Nader's Green Party in the U.S. elections of 2000. Michael Moore, radical filmmaker

and anticorporate activist, described Nader as the champion of "young people, who feel disenfranchised and dispossessed by mainstream American politics" (special election report, 848, National Public Radio, November 6, 2000).

While it might be argued that, constitutionally, citizenship in liberal democracies has never included a right to work, the provision of unemployment benefits, worker's compensation, and pensions to the nationals of welfare states has implied entitlement to an income. Such benefits are widely under threat in this neoliberal age, but the obligation to sustain the highest possible levels of employment continues to be one of the taken-for-granted expectations of government everywhere, notwithstanding the ferocious realpolitik of market competition. In this essay, we use the notion of "waged citizenship" to imply social and moral membership in the national commonweal.

4 This is not to imply that youth forms a "homogeneous, sociological category of people which thinks, organizes and acts" in coherent ways (Seekings, 1993, xiv); but the same may be said of "working class politics" (pace Seekings). Youth, like the working class, is a politically constructed category; both are rooted in their relationship to production and consumption. Increasingly, moreover, they are entailed in each other (see Comaroff and Comaroff, 2000a; Corrigan and Frith, 1976).

5 Most notably, immigrant workers and nonautochthonous minorities; see Comaroff and Comaroff (2000b).

6 *Yizo Yizo*, a thirteen-part series, aired on SATV3 in 1998. It was created and written by Mtutuzeli Matshoba and Angus Gibson and directed by Angus Gibson and Teboho Mahlatsi.

7 For an excellent study of Street Setswana in the North West Province of South Africa, see S. Cook (1999).

8 Age and generation, as the Marxist anthropology of precapitalist societies has long pointed out, may coalesce in self-reproducing structures of exploitation. In many of these societies, youthful cadres provided labor power, and hence surplus value, for their elders. The parallel with neoliberal capitalism is obvious. Increasingly, "youth" and "underclass," both ever more racinated and ethnicized, run together; note, here, Abdullah's (1998) suggestive use of the term "lumpen youth culture."

9 No less problematic are statements of unqualified optimism about a new and undifferentiated "millennial generation" in the United States, bereft of the cynicism and rebelliousness of their parents (Howe and Strauss, 2000).

Paul A. Silverstein

GUERRILLA CAPITALISM AND GHETTO-CENTRIC COSMOPOLITANISM ON THE FRENCH URBAN PERIPHERY

After the mid-1970s, France experienced repeated waves of de-industrialization and corporate flight, processes that particularly affected the major urban peripheries (*banlieues*)[1] that house large lower-class, multiethnic populations and currently witness unemployment rates upwards of 30 percent. In response to the dismantling of automobile and manufacturing concerns as the motor of the local economy, the French state established a framework for increased corporate penetration into the service sectors of the housing projects, thus obviating the need for direct state investment and suturing the future of the banlieues to the anticipated utopia of the "New Economy." This essay focuses on two such industries, sports and music, as sites for the negotiation of the banlieues' integration into a new economics of global corporate production, marketing, and distribution. Although the banlieue New Economy was clearly dependent on the limited capacities of residents to consume the sportswear and CDs being marketed to them, increasingly present corporations like Sony and Nike operated as if such realities were irrelevant, as if each *banlieusard* was a potential rap or soccer star, or at least could be convinced to consume like one.

Beyond being global industries, music and sports function in the banlieues as spaces of expressive politics that outline a specifically "ghettocentric" social imaginary.[2] Since the 1970s, the postindustrial peripheries of urban France have developed a healthy "second society" consisting of both a number of "guerrilla capitalist" ventures (from gray market vending to the informal provision of services) as well as a set of stylistic practices that appropriate technological innovation associated with the larger New Economy to articulate a critique of the larger political and economic structures of "exclusion."[3] In discussing the guerrilla commercialization and consumerist fantasies of sports and music, I explore how the marketing and technological transformations of the New Economy are appropriated for the construction and reinforcement of localized identities and solidarities, how the practices and ideas of the New Economy are remade on the French urban periphery. The result, I argue, is an ambivalent role for musical and sports artists emerging from the banlieues as simultaneously urban guerrillas and icons of a new, cosmopolitan citizenry—an ambivalence that is reflected not only in their explicit political discourse, but also in the state's multifarious responses.

URBAN CIVILIZING PROCESSES

A starting point for this essay is to recognize the incompletion of what Norbert Elias (1994) has referred to as the "civilizing process": the progressive normalization of bourgeois economic, political, and social practices (i.e., *civilisation*) throughout the French empire since the end of the eighteenth century. This incompletion stems from two parallel antagonisms: first, the simultaneous structural necessities for both an underclass of laboring populations and a burgeoning consuming public; second, an ideological ambivalence attached to the category of "civilized" that can serve as a mark of distinction and a justification of meritocratic privilege only through the maintenance of a set of classed, raced, and ethnicized "others" (i.e., the "uncivilized" or "not-yet-civilized"). These antagonisms were particularly acute in the establishment of French colonial policy and the maintenance of control abroad, and have likewise resurfaced in postcolonial metropolitan France in the guise of "suburban problems" (*les problèmes de banlieue*). To address these enduring "problems," the French state has adopted a set of new economic practices that market ethnoracial difference to banlieue consuming publics.

Thinking historically, a rich literature has emerged detailing the French "civilizing mission" as a justifying myth for France's colonial expansion into North Africa, West Africa, Indochina, and the South Pacific under the period of the Third Republic (1871–1940; Bowlan, 1998; Bullard, 2000; Guilhaume, 1992; Lorcin, 1995; Rosenblum, 1988; Silverstein, 2002a). As previous studies have shown, French colonial officials, using education and urban planning policies, endeavored to disenchant the territory and chronology of the natives encountered, to integrate these spaces and times into a centralized, uniform structure of politics, economics, and culture (Çelik, 1997; Colonna,

1975; Mitchell, 1988; Rabinow, 1989; Wright, 1991). Although these policies were often inscribed with philanthropic notions of universal human progress, they emerged more directly from realpolitik concerns over maintaining racial hierarchies between settler and native, between ruler and ruled, necessitated by the structures of exploitation of territory and labor.

However, as has become increasingly clear, such concerns were not limited to the colonial frontier; indeed, they reflect a more general set of bourgeois ideologies and fears. Civilizing the "savages" encountered in North Africa always operated in parallel with urban practices designed to civilize the underclass in the metropolis (see Elias, 1994; Stoler and Cooper, 1997; Thorne, 1997). As Jean and John Comaroff (1997, 321) have argued with reference to the British colonial venture in South Africa:

> Cultural colonialism was a reflexive process, a double gesture, whereby "others" abroad, the objects of the civilizing mission, were put to the purposes of reconstructing the "other" back home. The two sites, the two impulses, went hand in hand. British colonialism was always as much about making the center as it was about making the periphery. The colony was not a mere extension of a modern society. It was one of the instruments by which that society was made modern in the first place.

This dialectical relation between colony and metropole as sites of civilizing processes, whereby colonial and metropolitan underclasses served as mimetic representations of each other, became all the more tautly construed with the immigration of colonial laborers to the metropole. Although the first major recruitment of African men to serve as laborers and soldiers in metropolitan France occurred as early as World War I, an African immigrant underclass did not develop in France until the *Trente Glorieuses*, the thirty-year period of economic expansion in France following World War II.[4] On the eve of Algerian independence in 1962, more than half a million North African men worked in France, primarily on temporary labor contracts in the construction, manufacturing, and mining industries, often of seasonal duration. Although the Evian Accords that ended the Algerian War reaffirmed the free circulation of Algerians to France, an increasingly settled community of North African men, women, and children developed in France in response to the wartime and immediate postwar political and economic instability in North Africa. As such, when limits were finally imposed on labor migration to France after the economic slowdown following the 1973 oil embargo, more than a million North Africans had settled in France. Today, this population has increased to an estimated 1.5 million, as policies of family reunification and political asylum allowed settled immigrants to bring their immediate relatives to France.

Although North African immigrants and their children have inserted themselves into every aspect of French metropolitan life, they have nonetheless primarily entered the ranks of the urban poor and intensified the racial orderings to which the latter have been historically subjected. Originally following patterns of chain migration (whereby new migrants followed pioneering relatives and covillagers), early North African male laborers in France tended to occupy either temporary dormitories established by their employers or transit hotels in the working-class neighborhoods of Paris, Lyon, and Marseille. In the latter case, veritable "urban villages," of the type described by Herbert Gans (1962) for Italian communities in Boston, tended to develop, with older migrants opening shops and cafés that underwrote local community life (providing informal postal and banking services) and served to reproduce the social structures and organizations of the migrants' natal villages.[5] This relative isolation was reinforced in the late 1950s and 1960s, when many of these migrants relocated with their newly arrived families to the large shantytowns (*bidonvilles*) that had been established after World War II on the outskirts of major cities. The larger of these shantytowns (particularly those in Nanterre, Champigny, and Saint-Denis) were veritable cities unto themselves, with their own grocery stores, cafés, *halal* butcheries, repair shops, and a variety of other services.

By the 1970s, this relative spatial isolation of North African families had largely come to an end. Government orders tore down the bidonvilles and forcibly relocated their residents to a set of public housing projects (*cités*) built primarily in suburban peripheral areas. Most of these cités were constructed in the 1960s with the utopian ideal of relieving the congestion of urban metropolises by enticing underclass and lower-middle-class residents to experience the benefits of self-sufficient living in more pastoral landscapes (Soulignac, 1993).[6] Built with a minimum of 500 units in a combination of high-rise towers and low-rise blocks, they contained their own commercial, educational, and recreational facilities. As a result, these projects have tended to be incredibly multiethnic and multiracial, with "foreigners" rarely making up a majority of the local population. However, racial and ethnic "minorities" are, for a variety of historical and structural reasons, relatively overrepresented in comparison to other urban areas (Boumaza, de Rudder, and de Maria, 1989; de Rudder, 1992; Desplanques and Tabard, 1991; A. Hargreaves, 1995). Indeed, the construction of this public low-rent housing was significantly financed through the sale of apartments to manufacturing concerns, who utilized them to house their workers, many of whom were immigrants. In the heyday of the Trente Glorieuses economic boom, buses from Renault, Talbot, and other companies would shuttle workers from housing projects such as Val-Fourré in Mantes-la-Jolie (50 km outside of Paris) to their factories (Boubekeur and Daoud, 1993, 22–23).

In more recent years, however, the utopian fantasies of self-sufficient worker communities have broken down as France, like many other nation-states in both the "developed" and "developing" world, struggles with a set of socioeconomic challenges associated with the accelerated, global constitution of the New Economy.[7] As has been well-studied, this macroprocess takes on myriad forms throughout the world, as late capitalism (like all of its previous manifestations) is indigenized in each local cultural environment.[8] In the French case, the movement to European economic and monetary union has both opened the country to job and capital flight and necessitated (in the name of currency stabilization) a reduction of state expenditures that has meant the gradual dismantling of the public sector. Both factors contribute to the creation of a postindustrial economy, with ongoing high levels of unemployment that have nationally reached 13 percent and up to triple that in the working-class areas that previously relied on the manufacturing sector (Daoud, 1993b, 75).[9] Indeed, these statistics are even more disheartening when broken down by "nationality," particularly among populations historically employed in factory work.[10] As of 1990, unemployment figures for "foreigners" (étrangers) were twice that of the national average (Institut National de la Statistique et des Etudes Economiques [INSEE], 1992, 19, cited in A. Hargreaves 1995, 40; see Talha, 1989). Based on a slightly earlier household survey, Michèle Tribalat (1991, 165) discovered that the unemployment rate for 21-year-old men and women whose mothers were Algerian was 39 percent and 49 percent, respectively, or about three times that of the children of mothers with French nationality.[11] In certain housing projects, these figures can reach as high as 85 percent (Daoud, 1993b, 75).

Today, with many of the factories closed or not hiring, the cités have been marked by significant physical dilapidation and the flight of local commerce, creating an atmosphere of depressed sterility and an experience of social exile and "feeling distraught" (galère; Dubet and Lapeyronnie, 1992). The concomitant stigmatizing effects of this dilapidation and impoverishment have made residence in certain cités an impediment to being hired for a job, thus reproducing the very conditions of unemployment that inaugurated processes of marginalization and prejudice in the first place. Indeed, one resident of Val-Fourré informed me that he always uses his sister's address in Paris whenever applying for a job.

Given these structural conditions, it is not surprising that French housing projects have developed a healthy informal economy—including a series of gray market institutions revolving around the drug trade or the fencing of stolen consumer items—for the provision of employment as well as goods and services not otherwise available or affordable.[12] Cultural and religious associations in the cités constitute themselves as a parallel education system, attempting to make up for the depressed learning conditions (poor facilities, overcrowded classrooms, teachers not knowledgeable about or flexible toward the students' multicultural needs) in the local schools through afterschool tutoring, preparation for the baccalaureate exam, or cultural/religious training. Daily open-air markets operate in the shadow of boarded-up shopping centers, providing the quotidian requirements of food, clothing, and school supplies. And those residents with vehicles have created an informal taxi service to carry neighbors to and from transportation centers or places of work, commerce, or entertainment.

Alternative economic ventures such as these generate increased state scrutiny and lead to a large police presence in the cités. This police presence ironically increases tensions with inhabitants, tensions that often have escalated since the mid-1980s into full-scale incidents of violent popular unrest, termed "riots" (*émeutes*) by the national media, particularly when security forces arrested or killed young residents. The violence associated with these clashes with police often exceeds the interpersonal, targeting those state and economic institutions (notably police stations, shopping malls, and municipal centers) symbolically associated by residents with their exclusion. Moreover, this violence and property destruction, when portrayed by the media as riots, tend to underwrite the negative stereotypes of these areas and contribute to the infernal spiral of social marginalization and the racialization of their residents as "other" (Silverstein, 2004, chap. 3).

The government's response to this urban socioeconomic crisis developing since the early 1980s, and often referred to as *fracture sociale* (or "social fracture"), has been twofold. On the one hand, it unleashed a series of urban renewal plans—leading to the creation of a complex network of national commissions, urbanization laws, educational priority zones, and funding programs—designed to reintegrate the cités in question into national and global new economies and transform their inhabitants into productive citizens. These plans reached perhaps their most elaborated form in Gaullist prime minister Alain Juppé's 1995–1996 "Marshall Plan" (which included the National Urban Integration Plan and the Urban-Revival Pact).[13] With the goal of luring young residents from the street economy into the formal economy, the plan originally delimited 546 "sensitive urban zones" (*zones urbaines sensibles*) in which local associations would receive state subsidies to hire young residents to work in paid internships.[14] At the same time, the plans established twenty "enterprise zones" (*zones franches*) in especially "hot areas" (*quartiers chauds*) throughout the country to provide tax incentives to encourage the return of commercial ventures scared away by the rise in suburban violence. As such, like the original Marshall Plan designed to re-construct war-torn Europe, Juppé's plan depended on an insertion of capital into de-capitalized areas, though this time, with a New Economy twist, with local associations and multinational corporations acting as the prime agents of change.

On the other hand, the French government has responded to the "crisis" of the cités with increased police intervention, predicating urban renewal on social and political quiescence. Reacting to the growth of "lawless zones [*zones de non-droit*] in which the law of the Republic is totally absent" (*Le Monde*, September 7, 1995), the 1995–1996 plans added 200 plainclothes in-spectors to the already expanded suburban security forces to "penetrate the milieus of delinquency" (*L'Express*, November 9, 1995). In 1999, Socialist prime minister Lionel Jospin took these surveillance measures one step fur-ther, mobilizing 13,000 additional riot police and 17,000 military gendarmes to patrol these same sensitive urban zones, and thus effectively completing the militarization of the French suburbs.[15]

In this sense, France's adoption of ideas and practices associated with the New Economy along its urban periphery has been necessarily equivocal. Nearly every euro it has saved by "tightening the belt" on the public sector— and for which it has incurred severe electoral wrath, including periodic general strikes by public servants (*fonctionnaires*)—has been redeployed into the forces of security.[16] The banlieue Marshall Plan, according to former Gaullist minister of integration Eric Raoult, has meant first and foremost the "reinforcement of the presence of the State" (*Le Monde*, October 28, 1995). In other words, rather than implying the retraction of government from the economic sphere, as New Economy ideologues would have us believe, the liberation of capital flows has actually required increased state intervention (R. Martin, 1999, 4).

France's response to the socioeconomic implications of a new, postindus-trial economy thus registers a profound ambivalence. Although the state, in alliance with multinational corporations, tends to encourage the expansion of new economic policies of consumerism and technological innovation throughout its internal peripheries, it nonetheless seeks to regulate the practices engendered by such expansionism. Every attempt at "integrating" (or "civilizing") underclass residents of the cités to national political, economic, and social norms is balanced by heavy-handed urbanization practices that continue to demarcate these populations as racially and spatially "other," as structurally distant from the metropolis and its symbolics of power. As the remainder of this essay will demonstrate, the French state historically has played an active role in defining the legitimate forms of cultural and political expression emerging from the cités, as well as the commercial means through which these forms are disseminated.

THE NEW ECONOMY OF SPORTS AND MUSIC

This ambivalence of state protectionism and retraction has had the paradoxical effect of actually underwriting the growth of musical and sports subcultures in the cités. It is not surprising, perhaps, that music and sports should constitute privileged cultural practices of residents of the French suburban cités. A wealth of sociological and historical literature, drawing primarily on the American case, has underlined these two fields as privileged avenues of mobility for underclass and ethnoracial "minority" populations (see Bloom, 2000; Cronin and Mayall, 1998; Eisen and Wiggins, 1994; Elias, 1971; Franks, 2000; R. Martin and Miller, 1999). Historically, music and sports have offered fewer class and racial barriers to entry than other professions, being more subject to volatile, high-risk market and meritocratic demands and less dependent on the relatively stable structures of "inheritance" and "reproduction" that Pierre Bourdieu and Jean-Claude Passeron (Bourdieu, 1979/1984; Bourdieu and Passeron, 1964, 1970) have identified as characterizing many other French professional worlds. Not requiring the successful completion of the rigorous national high school examination (*baccalauréat*) or more advanced university degrees, music and sports remain open to cité youth hampered by premature tracking to vocational diplomas and a nationally organized school system ill-equipped to accommodate the diversity of cultural backgrounds and educational habitus encountered in the cités (Aïssou, 1987). In a postindustrial context characterized by the contraction of manufacturing and construction concerns in which the previous generation had for the most part earned financial independence, music and sports thus remain among the few legal sources of potential wealth for many cité residents.

These privileged avenues of legitimate social mobility have been reinforced through processes of commodity fetishism by which previously successful musicians and athletes have been transformed into celebrities. Multinational sportswear and record companies have invested large sums of capital
in branding their sponsored artists and athletes, creating rags-to-riches images for cité youth to identify. As I discuss below, successful musicians and
athletes from the cités have more often than not eschewed any claim to being
role models; they have nonetheless proved complicit in the fetishism of their
success. In particular, they have generally maintained close ties to their natal
areas both in terms of their explicit identity diacritics and avowals in their
lyrics or public statements and in terms of their incorporation of family and
childhood friends into their retinues and "posses." Drawing on these explicit
connections, local youth recount fictive (genealogical or other) ties to various
celebrities or inscribe celebrities' signs on their bodies through wearing jer-
seys and other logo-laden clothing. This identification not only produces the
desire for the particular products sold, but also encourages the continued
production of cité athletes and musicians whose successes will lead to further
sportswear and record sales, and hence the reproduction of the structures of
capital accumulation as enabled under the New Economy.

However, it would be wrong to understand musical and sports subcultures as the natural product of a postindustrial New Economy. In fact, violat-
ing the tenets of neoclassical market theory, the French state has more often
than not taken an active role in underwriting the music and sports industries
in the cités. As early as 1983, the socialist government under François Mit-
terrand began directly promoting the multicultural identity of French housing projects, funding local cultural associations and sponsoring a variety of
musical, dance, and theater groups. In one instance, the Ministry of Culture
funded an exhibit at the Georges Pompidou Center, "Children of North African Immigrants," dedicated to the celebration of "Beur" (Franco-Maghrebi)
cultural hybridity. The exhibit focused on the growth of Berber theater (e.g.,
the Kahina ensemble) and Oranais raï popular music (e.g., Carte de Séjour)
among "second-generation" Algerian immigrants living in the cités of Paris
and Lyon, and the catalogue (CCI, 1984) included an adulatory preface by
Yannick Noah, the French Cameroonian tennis player who had gained great
notoriety by winning the French Open the previous year.

In more recent years, state support for cité music and sports subcultures
has increased in scope. One of the consistent features of the variety of urban
revitalization projects since the late 1980s is the construction of social centers
and sports facilities. Housing projects designed by chief architect Roland Cas-

tro under the "Banlieues 89" plan (actually created in 1983) include central courtyards with soccer fields and basketball courts, as well as indoor gymnasiums and boxing rings. Moreover, sports figured high in the twenty measures proposed by Prime Minister Michel Rocard in 1990 in response to the youth riots in the working-class suburbs of Vaulx-en-Velin and Mantes-la-Jolie. In September 1992, the Ministry of Urbanization, headed by entrepreneur and then owner of the Olympique Marseille soccer club Bernard Tapie, launched a "Youth and Sports" program which invested 40 million francs (approximately US$8 million) over the next several years in the construction of 1,000 sports installations and 100 fields in 120 different municipalities.

One Youth and Sports activity was the "Summer Prevention" operation (originally experimented with in 1982), which in 1992 alone sponsored more than 1,500 cité youth on weekend excursions and summer camps (Daoud, 1993, 141; Sakhoui, 1996, 82–83). The camps had as their goal not only to prevent violence, delinquency, and drug abuse, but also to defuse the "communitarianism" supposedly created in the parallel summer camps organized by Muslim cultural associations for cité youth, camps that would become popularized in the media as training bases for jihad (see Pujadas and Salam, 1995). In this sense, the Youth and Sports plans treated sport as a "privileged remedy for contemporary social dysfunction" (Sakhoui, 1996, 81), as a means to "integrate" (or "civilize") cité youth into moral French subjects defined by secular attitudes, a sense of fair play, and a strong work ethic.[17]

Moreover, these programs receive direct support from the sports industry and from many professional athletes who were raised in immigrant or cité environments. Yannick Noah, the light-heavyweight boxer Anaclet Wamba, and the world kickboxing champion Khalid el-Khandali, among other hybrid French sports stars, have participated directly in these state-sponsored programs for cité youth. Along similar lines, the Paris Saint-Germain professional soccer club offered thousands of free tickets to young residents of the neighborhoods targeted by the Youth and Sports operation. Also joining in the promotion of these sports programs have been large multinational sports companies like Nike, Reebok, Adidas, and Puma. The former two sponsored playground basketball tournaments and slam-dunk competitions in 1995 and 1996, and the latter, with further support from Coca-Cola and Orangina as well as the French Soccer Federation, initiated soccer challenge matches for banlieue youth in 1996 (*Le Monde*, April 14, 1995, 16; Sakouhi, 1996, 93). Through projects of socioeconomic reconstruction, the French state thus enabled the corporate penetration of suburban economic spaces.

If sports have functioned as a privileged tool in recent French urban civilizing processes, the cité music scene, particularly the burgeoning hip hop/rap industry, has likewise ironically benefited from a situational alliance of state and multinational capital. Not surprisingly, the French state has regarded the rap music emerging from the cités with suspicion, censoring and even arresting certain hardcore ("gansta") rap groups such as Ministère Amer and Suprême NTM when their lyrics or stage antics are seen to threaten the public and moral order (*l'ordre morale*; Silverstein, 2002c).[18] Moreover, the cultural globalization that French hip hop—with its continual musical and symbolic exchanges with genres and styles from across Europe, the Mediterranean, and the Atlantic—represents has engendered a backlash of French protectionism. Linguistically, this has translated into an increased legal surveillance (including the 1994 Toubon Law) of the French language against Americanisms, Arabisms, and a variety of word plays (such as syllabic inversion [*verlan*]) that mark the everyday language of the cités and the base of French rap discourse.[19] Musically, pressure for protectionism has led to establishment of legal quotas (the 1994 Carignon Law) requiring a minimum of 40 percent of musical programming on radio stations to be in French and 20 percent by contemporary artists.[20]

However, given the paucity of successful mainstream musical production by French artists, these efforts at cultural protection have actually encouraged the growth and commercialization of Francophone rap (*Le Monde*, January 10, 1996). Whereas during the late 1980s, rap was relegated to underground and independent Parisian radio stations such as Radio-Nova (Cannon, 1997, 157), today it dominates the French FM band and has become the mainstay of megastations such as Fun-Radio, Sky-Rock, and NRJ, all previously organized along the Anglophone-dominated pop/contemporary rock format. This state-created demand not only constituted the condition of possibility for the financial success of already established rap groups like MC Solaar, Suprême NTM, IAM, Alliance Ethnik, and Assassin, but it further encouraged major record labels such as Sony, BMG, and EMI-Virgin to expand their hip hop portfolios. Using local middlemen as recruiters, these multinational concerns have penetrated further into the cités—the exact environments that have been historically productive of the "hate" (*la haine*) against the "system" that gives much of French rap its power and (presumed) authenticity, and thus the logical birthplace of the genre—in search of new local musical talent. As such, state protectionism of the French music market has ironically abetted the corporate colonization of cité space and the commoditization—and hence the increased visibility and profitability—of its "hate."

As much as contemporary rap artists and athletes emerging from the cités have profited both from the multinational marketing of the New Economy and from state protectionism, they have been explicitly critical of the means of their success. Residents of suburban housing projects are painfully aware of the intimate connection between sports development programs and state surveillance procedures. On more than one occasion, violent struggles of cité youth with security forces have destroyed sports facilities along with schools and police commissariats. Although the newspapers, following police reports, have classed these riots (émeutes) in the category of juvenile delinquency, the conflicts have in fact been relatively well-organized displays of resistance targeting the particular state structures imposed on the neighborhoods. In Vaulx-en-Velin in 1991 and again in Bron in 1994, residents destroyed the gymnasiums and climbing walls that had been recently unveiled through one of the government's sports programs.

Furthermore, when cité youth do utilize the facilities, they do not necessarily do so in the ways envisioned by the projects' builders. Rather, residents have appropriated these public spaces for their own, alternative practices of "integration." Local Berber and Islamic associations have incorporated soccer and judo teams into their activities, in part to attract younger members, in part to foster loyalty to a political or religious cause via the medium of sports play. Some Islamic associations have gone as far as to invest in local sports facilities to recruit membership, taking over financially in many cases where government programs leave off.[21] In addition, resident youth have utilized cité sports facilities for informal sports based on their own revised sets of rules; they have in effect privatized the public spaces and created what critics of government sports projects have bewailed as "ghetto-sports" (see Sakhoui, 1996, 92–95). For example, a single soccer field may be used for multiple games played simultaneously, with book bags and jackets used to demarcate alternate goals and the boundary lines, and the formal rules varying to meet the playing conditions. Far from constituting an unruly chaos, these practices reveal an internal organization and permissive creativity that, while flexible with the field and player constraints, allow for self-organized challenge matches and tournaments that parallel if not replace the corporate-sponsored competitions described earlier.[22]

Likewise, hip hop artists emerging from the cités have generally displayed an ambivalent attitude toward the state neoliberal structures at the basis of their own riches and fame. MC Solaar, the most successful commercial French hip hop artist worldwide, has famously deformed "capitalist" into *caca-pipi-caca-pipitaliste* ("shit-piss-shit-pisstalist"; "Matière grasse contre matière grise" [Fat Matter against Gray Matter], 1991) and portrayed the New Economy as a "new Far West" where "credit cards replace Remingtons" ("Nouveau western," 1994). Likewise, Assassin, whose logo appears on T-shirts and hoodies (*sweat-capuches*) sold throughout France, has likened international trade to drug trafficking ("Légal ou illégal" [Legal or Illegal], 1995), accused the International Monetary Fund and the World Bank of promoting a war between a (developed) North and (underdeveloped) South and causing the death of hundreds of thousands of children through its structural adjustment policies ("Guerre Nord-Sud" [North-South War], 1995), and generally declared war on capitalist "Babylon," where a Porsche "demands more love than a mother nursing her children" ("Shoota Babylone," 1995). Suprême NTM has criticized money's tendency to "rot people" and perpetuate global inequality ("L'argent pourrit les gens" [Money Rots People], 1991), at the same time embracing New Economy commercialism with a multirecord contract with Epic-Sony since 1991 and a concomitant sportswear deal with Adidas. In other words, French rap, while utilizing the expressive styles—from gangwear (sports pants, hoodies, bandanas, baseball caps, chunk jewelry, etc.) to colloquial (if not vulgar) forms of address and gesturing—of outlaw resistance, clearly also embraces the rapacious possibilities enabled by capital accumulation.[23] In other words, the marketing and technological innovations of the New Economy outline a New France rappers love to hate.

One response that rap artists in particular have adopted in the face of this dilemma has been to infiltrate the "system" to capture its fruits more directly, thus attempting to circumvent the financial exploitation accompanying corporate penetration. While continuing to depend on the multinational record corporations for the manufacturing of their recordings, they have often taken over the production, management, and marketing ends themselves. IAM established its own record label, Côté Obscur, which produced gold albums for groups 3e Oeil and Fonky Family. Likewise, Suprême NTM's Kool Shen and Joey Starr each established their own production companies (IV My People and BOSS, respectively), which not only underwrote the careers of younger artists (including Bustaflex and Zoxea), but also tended to cross corporate lines, with IV My People allied with Warner and NTM with Sony. Further, the intermediaries (often rappers themselves) established by the corporate record labels to procure new artists have begun more and more to act as entrepreneur-agents, demanding such increased control and profit sharing that mainstream producers are likening them to a mafia (*Libération*, January 26, 1999).

French rappers have attempted to garner control of the marketing end of the recording business as well, establishing alternative networks of distribution. Realizing that television and radio advertisements failed to reach their target consumers (primarily suburban youth), rap groups have adopted a number of "street marketing techniques," from massive leafleting to local appearances.[24] Moreover, they have produced a number of inexpensive fanzines, with Anglophone titles such as *Down With This, Get Busy*, and *Authentik*, which promote the associated artists and their dependent groups (Cannon, 1997, 159), most of which are increasingly available and accessed online at the artists' respective Web sites. This increasing use of the Internet as a tool of marketing and distribution has likewise affected the song tracks themselves, which previously primarily had circulated among cité residents in the form of pirated cassettes, but now increasingly change hands as MP3 files. Although not necessarily encouraged by rap artists, this pirated circulation constitutes a fundamental means, in the absence of expensive corporate marketing campaigns, for French hip hop artists to gain a listening public. In these various ways, French rappers, rather than taking a revolutionary stance against the commercial system, have sought to infiltrate it directly, becoming "guerrilla capitalists," as it were. As IAM rapper Imhotep remarked, "[Rappers] are understanding younger and younger. They hear talk of money, and they want a piece of it. They want to profit from the system, screw it over. That's what motivates them" (*Libération*, January 26, 1999).

GHETTOCENTRIC COSMOPOLITANISM

These sports and hip hop formations based on guerrilla capitalism have underwritten particular practices of cosmopolitanism in France's suburban peripheries. A burgeoning literature has explored the relationship between conceptualizations of "cosmopolitan citizenship" and the social formations allied with the New Economy in the context of the putative breakdown of the nation-state as the hegemonic site for the enactment of politics. In this light, much of the literature, drawing on Kantian notions, emphasizes the "flexible" and "borderless" qualities of cosmopolitan political participation and belonging (see Appiah, 1999; Cheah and Robbins, 1999; Hutchings and Dannreuther, 1999; Mignolo, 2000; Ong, 1999; Pollock et al., 2000). The sports and hip hop formations examined here certainly outline a set of vernacular citizenship practices in the cités, but their embeddedness in the structures of the New Economy places severe limits on any envisioned collective action. In other words, it is necessary to understand "cosmopolitanism" as a potentially enabling discourse, but one that finds itself currently colonized by state national and consumer capitalist concerns.

On the one hand, as direct actors in the New Economy, banlieue rappers and athletes have in effect affirmed themselves as "global citizens" (see Joseph, 1999, 8). Soccer stars hailing from the French cités such as Zinedine Zidane and Mustapha Hajji are truly mobile agents, with Zidane playing professionally in Italy and Spain while participating on the French national team for the World Cup, and Hajji playing professionally in France and England while competing internationally for Morocco.[25] Zidane, whose contract with Turin-based Juventus was bought in 2001 for a record amount by the Spanish Real Madrid side, is married to a Spanish woman, Veronica, and has a son named after Enzo Francescoli, the Uruguayan forward of Italian descent who played for the French Olympique Marseille club that Zidane cheered for as a child. Zidane and Hajji are global fetish objects, being both popular spokesmen for a variety of multinational firms and powerful sources of identification for North Africans in the Maghreb and the diaspora.

French hip hop artists to a certain extent participate in a similar transnational existence. In becoming unmediated interlocutors with multinational firms and active participants in the global circulations of commodities and styles that instantiate the New Economy, they exist as full-fledged members of new spheres of cosmopolitanism that link musical publics worldwide (see Appadurai 1996, 64). With reciprocal musical and ideological exchanges between Gangstarr (U.S.) and MC Solaar (France), between Wu Tang Clan (U.S.) and IAM (France), and trans-Atlantic collaboration albums like *Le Flow* (Various Artists, 2000), rappers emerging from the cités have charted new spaces of belonging and contestation that traverse official political borders.[26]

On the other hand, rappers and athletes have been adamant in affirming their commitment to local constituencies, to "their people" of the cités from which they emerged. Zidane, while publicly speaking on behalf of Algerian victims of the civil war and denouncing the ongoing racism in Europe, has remained firmly rooted in his boyhood Marseille cité of La Castellaine, a neighborhood that remains both a reference point and a site of ongoing solidarity (Vinocur, 1999). Indeed, his unrelenting support for boyhood friend and fellow soccer star Christophe Dugarry has become legendary (see Zidane, 1998), even leading to speculation that Zidane unduly influenced the inclusion of Dugarry on the national team in spite of the existence of potentially better players.

As mentioned earlier, French rap artists have similarly underlined local over national or international ties, organizing themselves around posses of fellow residents of their natal housing projects who often serve the groups as managers, promoters, security guards, and back-up singers.[27] They invoke locality in tags, album titles, and song lyrics that reference their particular cité. For example, NTM constantly references their native Saint-Denis and the larger administrative unit (*département*) of Seine-Saint-Denis, and its short-hand postal code 93, in song (e.g., "Seine-Saint-Denis Style," 1998) as well as in the name of their posse and tag, "93 NTM." For Ministère Amer, the reference is Sarcelles, or "95200" (the name of their 1994 album).[28]

This "ghettocentricity" (Kelley, 1996, 136) is further evidenced not only in the themes of French rap focusing on life on the streets (including realistic portrayals of violence and drug dealing), but also in the musical and linguistic tropes used in the songs. Indeed, the vocal style of the rapping (e.g., their "flow") mimics everyday speech by youth in the cités not only in word choice (i.e., the use of various slang expressions and *verlan*), but also in rhythm, enunciation, scansion, and prosody that can denote very specific localities and origins. By alternating their flow, rappers can even play particular characters of everyday cité life, from the hardcore gangster (*caillera*; e.g., NTM's "Plus jamais ça" [Never Again], 1995) to the just off-the-boat immigrant (e.g., Alliance Ethnik's "Intro," 1999) to the bourgeois Frenchman (e.g., Zebda's "Je crois que ça va pas être possible" [I Think It Won't Be Possible], 1998) to the police officer (e.g., NTM's "Police," 1993). Moreover, in utilizing samples from other expressive genres, such as the journalist's report in NTM's "On est encore là" (We're Still Here, 1998) track, or president Jacques Chirac's infamous 1991 "Noise and Smell" racist political speech (Zebda, "Le bruit et l'odeur" [The Noise and the Smell], 1995), French rap groups effectively normalize the argot of the cités as unmarked in contrast to the contextually marked speech forms of mainstream France. They thus establish a normative musical soundscape whose auditory center is the suburban housing project rather than the Parisian metropolis.

The respatialization of the cité as the center of the athletes' and musicians' cognitive maps and auditory geographies entails particular political ramifications. The rappers' primary loyalty to these neighborhoods is manifest not only in the composition of their posses, but also in their dedications, credits, and acknowledgments that always "shout out" to their native cités. Moreover, their treatment of inhabitants of the project as "family"—a characteristic of everyday life in the housing estates where generational cohorts are called "brothers" and neighbors look out for each others' children (Aïchoune, 1991;

Duret, 1996; Silverstein, 2004, chap. 5)—emerges clearly in many French rap songs that invoke kinship ties to the song's imagined audience or referent, most notably in NTM's "That's My People" (1998). Assassin has taken this invocation of fictive kinship to its logical genealogical end, extending local solidarity to political belonging: "My only nation is my posse. . . . The flag of unity is planted in the 18th [arrondissement of Paris, from where the group hails]" ("Kique ta merde" [Kick Your Shit], 1993).

This politics of locality expressed in rap discourse is paralleled by a ghetto-centrism of sports practice in the cités. Pascal Duret (1996, 149–173) has examined how older residents (known colloquially as "big brothers" [grands frères]) have utilized participation in sports clubs to foster a sense of community spirit (often glossed in the language of kinship) and local citizenship among younger banlieue residents. This sense of local identity can mark a given cité, or even an individual building within the project, and games tend to be organized along such nested divisions. Moreover, these processes of recursive appropriation can engender spatially based rivalries and conflicts, and indeed municipal sports structures often serve as spaces of contestation between residents and deemed "others." During my fieldwork in the north-eastern Parisian suburb of Pantin in 1996, I witnessed one of these conflicts between youth of housing projects of Quatre Chemins and those more bour-geois residents of the Petit Pantin neighborhood over a municipal weight room that was located on the border of the two spaces (Silverstein, 2002b, 45–48). Even more dramatically, a skating rink in Mantes-la-Jolie has been the source and location of pitched battles between young residents of the paired housing estates of Val-Fourré and Chanteloup-les-Vignes (Daoud, 1993c, 27).

These localisms have frustrated French state efforts to instrumentalize athletes and rap artists as agents of the various civilizing processes. Govern-ment officials charged with combating the socioeconomic exclusion of im-migrants, such as former Minister of Integration Eric Raoult, have repri-manded rap artists for not taking a more active role in various antiracist and anti-AIDS movements and for inciting violence through their calls to "fuck the police" (nique la police; Le Monde, November 17–18, 1999). Some groups, such as Assassin, espouse radical agendas of transformative politics; most simply see themselves as street journalists, as "loudspeakers" for the extant rage in the cités.[29] Joey Starr of Suprême NTM has claimed in an interview, "It's not up to me to explain what there is to do. . . . We're just a reflection of what's happening. . . . We don't throw stones at cops, only words. . . . Some people think we exaggerate; I'd say we tend to understate" (Le Monde, No-vember 16, 1999).[30]

These attitudes point to the ways the structural conditions associated with the New Economy have produced a generalized sentiment of political power-lessness. As Marxist critics Richard Burbach, Orlando Núñez, and Boris Kagarlitsky (1997, 144) have argued, "Throughout the world, neo-liberalism has generated a palpable feeling that participation in any movement or pro-test is futile. Voting does no good, since one set of politicians is the same as another." Joey Starr echoes this evaluation, infamously likening voting to "pissing in the wind": "For people like me, a government of the Left or the Right is the same" (*Libération*, January 26, 1999).

However, this general apathy with regard to formal or revolutionary poli-tics should not necessarily imply the complete de-politicization of the cités. Indeed, one musical group, Zebda, entered into the formal political arena, using the proceeds from its platinum album sales to finance a grassroots development association, Tactikollectif, and a political party, Motivé-e-s, in its native Toulouse. Running on a far-left, antiglobalization platform that emphasized local investment, racial equality, and civic participation in the cités, Motivé-e-s garnered a surprise 12.4 percent of the vote in the first round of the 2001 municipal elections before allying with other leftist parties in hopes of unseating Toulouse's rightist mayor. Inspired by their success, other "alternative lists" were organized in Rennes, Marseille, Grenoble, Lille, and Strasbourg, cities with significant housing projects (*Les Echos*, February 26, 2001; *Le Monde*, March 16, 2001).

Although Zebda may be exceptional in its entry into formal, participant politics, sports and musical practices in the cités nonetheless retain a general political character. Music and sports, as iconic industries of the New Econ-omy that are played out in the banlieues, outline spaces of expressive politics that bypass the nation-state and collapse distinctions between the global and the local, spaces that I have elsewhere characterized as "transpolitical" (Sil-verstein, 2004). For Joey Starr, the quality of his citizenship is clear: "Without going to vote, I am more of a citizen than most people. I do my civic duty in talking about what's going on around me, in keeping up-to-date and also being an outlet [*exutoire*] for some. . . . I fulfill my obligations as a citi-zen everyday, in writing my raps" (*Libération*, January 26, 1999).[31] His self-ascribed political role is to recount accurately the structural conditions of his cité (to represent his "people") and relate it to the larger conditions of in-equality and racism elsewhere. Indeed, although NTM adamantly denied any leadership or role-model capacity, their 1998 album had a distinct pedagogi-cal quality to it, with songs instructing parents to "not let their kids wander" ("Laisse pas trainer ton fils" [Don't Let Your Son Wander], 1998) and imploring "bad boys" to "put down their guns" ("Pose ton gun" [Put Down Your Gun], 1998). In these ways, the musical and sports worlds of the cités outline a distinct arena of ghettocentric cosmopolitanism, determinedly placing local practice at the center of global processes of consumption and commercialization.

CONCLUSION

In this respect, viewing the civilizing process through the lens of incompletion, as I suggested in the beginning of this essay, provides an important means to understand how the ideas and practices of the New Economy are remade on state peripheries. Under both colonial and postcolonial regimes, civilizing processes—in the form of education policy, urban planning, and commodity circulation—have outlined particular classed, raced, and ethnicized localities as simultaneously inside and outside the social, political, and economic norms of the French metropole. The urban revitalization plans developed by the French state to "integrate" (i.e., "civilize") cité residents into the national and global political economies have simultaneously fostered the penetration of multinational capital and reinforced the state's military presence in these areas. Responding to both sets of violence, local inhabitants (celebrity or otherwise) have engaged in guerrilla capitalist ventures that appropriate the commercial techniques of the New Economy for the articulation and reinforcement of forms of cosmopolitanism that are simultaneously global in reach while remaining unremittingly ghettocentric.

In this context, French musicians and athletes directly participate in a corporate world they despise, yet on which they depend for both their professional lives and their ideological influence, for their ability to escape the cité physically while still remaining attached to it. Enabled by the French state's opening of French housing projects to the marketing interests of multinational capital, rappers and soccer players draw on their ongoing embeddedness in the landscape of the cités to claim "authenticity." From this privileged position, they can articulate a critique of the very state policing apparatus and corporate structures of the New Economy that allows for their continued success and ability to have a public voice. While generally disengaged from formal (or revolutionary) politics, they nonetheless outline a particular form of cosmopolitanism where ghetto identity is fetishized as a globally fungible, marketable, and explicitly resistant category of political engagement.

I am arguing that this ghettocentric cosmopolitanism represents a new mode of transnational solidarity that functions in parallel with both formal state political processes and the corporate structures of the New Economy. If Paris to one degree or another remains the capital of a certain form of *civilisation*, the music and sports practices of the suburban cités present themselves as an alternative, neighboring space of anti*civilisation*, though one largely dependent on larger capital structures that provide a larger market access to global consuming publics.[32] In this respect, the French state's progressive corporatization and militarization of the banlieues can be read as an attempt to recapture the economic and political innovativeness of the cités, to recenter ghettocentric practices on Paris proper. Evading such capture, banlieue rappers and athletes have increasingly adopted the role of guerrilla capitalists, or at least pirate capitalists, progressively grabbing control of various aspects of the management and marketing of their musical and sports talent. It is this unanticipated and largely unintended collusion between state policy, corporate marketing, and cité entrepreneurship that underlines one important aspect of the New Economy as explored in this volume: namely, that global economic processes are always and everywhere locally instantiated phenomena and require ethnographic description as such.

NOTES

1 Although *banlieue* can be glossed in English as "suburb," the term is used in French popular discourse to cognitively map the "limit-place" of French *civilisation*—outlying areas supposedly beyond the pale of French civility and rampant with violence, criminality, and socioeconomic "exclusion." To reflect this powerful image, I use the term to reference those postindustrial suburbs of Paris and Lyon characterized by large housing projects (*cités*) inhabited by lower-class, multiethnic populations. Such banlieues include, for Paris, Argenteuil, Asnières, Aubervilliers, Aulnay-sous-Bois, Bobigny, Créteil, La Courneuve, Mantes-la-Jolie, Montfermeil, Nanterre, Saint-Denis, Sarcelles, Sartrouville, and Vitry; and for Lyon, Vaulx-en-Velin, Vénissieux, and Villeurbanne.

2 Robin D. G. Kelley (1996, 1997) has discussed the construction of "ghettocentric" imaginaries in the context of American hip hop formations. In using this term to describe certain forms of political and social practices of the French banlieues, I by no means wish to imply an equivalence between French and American urban peripheral forms. Indeed, French housing projects (cités) are not "ghettos" in an ethnic or racial sense. For a thoroughgoing critique of the application of the American category of ghetto to the French cités, see Wacquant (1992).

3 For a discussion of the "second society," particularly its relation to the "second economy" of state socialist Eastern Europe, see Gal (1991), Hankiss (1988), and Verdery (1996). I borrow the term "guerrilla capitalism" from the work of Josephine and Alan Smart (1999) on Hong Kong investment in China, though my use of the term

departs from their interpretation of the practice as one of risk minimization. For the rich literature on "exclusion" (and its twin, "social fracture" [*fracture sociale*]) in the French banlieue context, see Begag (1995), Clavel (1998), Ferréol and Autès (1992), Schnapper (2001), Wieviorka and Bataille (1999), Wihtol de Wenden and Daoud (1993).

4 For histories and statistics of African immigration to France, see Bernard (1998), Liauzu (1996), Macmaster (1993), Noiriel (1988), Talha (1989).

5 Early, government-sponsored studies of these enclaves by Louis Massignon in 1921 and by Robert Montagne in 1950–1953 underlined these aspects of social life that reflected North African village institutions (Direche-Slimani, 1992, 54).

6 This construction was facilitated by the institution of two legal mechanisms: first, the creation of a National Corporation for the Construction of Housing for Algerian Workers in 1952 that earmarked funds for the relocation of shantytown residents; second, the establishment of a category, Urban Priority Zone that would target urban renewal projects to specific suburban localities.

7 The literature on globalization and the New Economy is vast and varied. For the spatiocultural effects of accelerated capital and labor mobility, see Appadurai (1990), Burbach et al. (1997), Castells (1996, 1997), Hannerz (1987), Harvey (1989), Inda and Rosaldo (2001), Jameson (1991), A. D. King (1997), Sassen (1998). For an extended discussion of the ramifications of New Economy theorizing, see the introduction to this volume.

8 On the indigenization of (global) capitalism, see Sahlins (1988).

9 To a certain extent, these figures are not inherently new. France has witnessed periodic double-digit unemployment percentages since the general economic slowdown of the mid-1970s.

10 Note that French surveying bodies officially do not keep data on ethnicity or race, so socioeconomic figures for variously hyphenated, "minority" French men and women can only be estimated.

11 As of 1990, North Africans constituted nearly 40 percent of the foreign population in France, with Algerians a significant majority among them (INSEE, 1992, R6).

12 Although many residents have procured employment in service sector jobs outside of the projects, the informal economy in many ways monopolizes the economic life of the cités proper. For ethnographic and statistical discussions of the economic organization of the French banlieue, see de Rudder (1992), Petonnet (1982), Silverstein (2004), Wihtol de Wenden and Daoud (1993). For comparative perspectives on violence, segregation, and the informal economy in the parallel postindustrial context of Chicago's housing projects, see Venkatesh (2000), Wacquant (1994).

13 President Jacques Chirac promised a "Marshall Plan for the banlieues" during his April 1995 election campaign.

14 These numbers would increase by the June 1996 re-presentation of the plan before the National Assembly, from twenty duty-free zones to thirty-five, and from 546 sensitive urban areas to 744 (*Le Monde*, June 19, 1996).

15 For a similar discussion of how state investment has abetted de facto urban segregation in postindustrial Los Angeles, see Davis (1990, 223–263).

16 Eric Raoult estimates that over 12 billion francs have been reinvested into the various banlieue plans. Interview in *Authentik* 1(1), 1998.

17 On the role of sports in global civilizing processes, see Dunning and Rojek (1992), J. Hargreaves (1992), Hoberman (1984), MacClancy (1996), Magdalinski and Chandler (2002). On sports and Islam as putatively opposed models of integration in 1990s France, see Silverstein (2000).

18 For general histories and analyses of French hip hop, see Bazin (1995), Cachin (1996), Durand (2002).

19 Law 94–665 of August 4, 1994, sponsored by Minister of Culture Jacques Toubon, which declared the French language to be "a fundamental element of the personality and heritage of France," mandated the use of French language in the French public sphere. The regulation applied to language used in all public gatherings and audiovisual contexts, but not in the musical works themselves.

20 The law, which went into effect on January 1, 1996, and was named after the minister of communication, Alain Carignon, did not apply to "communitarian" radio stations, such as Beur-FM or Radio Latina, which represent particular immigrant communities.

21 Séverine Labat, interview in *Le Monde*, October 13, 1995.

22 See Chantelat, Fodimbi, and Camy (1996) for a discussion of the differences between street sports and club sports and the flexible usage of the housing project terrains.

23 Hip hop artists in particular are well-known for their ambivalent disavowal of capitalism and avowal of consumerism (see Kelley, 1997, 44–45; Quinn, 1996, 81–83; T. Rose, 1994, 40–41). See Gilroy (1991, 199–211) for one such argument regarding the emphasis of Afrodiasporic music (soul, reggae, hip hop) on nonproductive pleasure.

24 These practices, like rap itself, tend to be transnationally organized, as French street marketing concerns (e.g., Double-H Productions, founded by DJ Cut Killer) have learned directly from American marketing firms such as Wicked and III Trendz (*Libération*, January 26, 1999).

25 European professional football sides have become increasingly diverse, as players from Latin America, Africa, and Asia have ventured to Europe in search of higher salaries. This migration actually has many of the characteristics of earlier colonial labor migration, with both active recruitment abroad by the clubs in question and a chain migration character in the ways movement from particular countries to particular national leagues reproduces itself. The French national team (les Bleus) that won the World Cup in 1998 and the European Championships in 2000 was renowned for its racial and ethnic diversity, with the majority of starting players from immigrant families. On sports labor migration, see Maguire and Bale (1994). For the French case, see Lanfranchi (1994).

26 This is not to say that the nation-state has become in any way politically irrelevant, but only that it is no longer necessarily the only game in town, and that questions of "representation" are being decided outside as well as inside national borders. See Sassen (1998), Glick Schiller, Basch, and Szanton-Blanc (1994).

27 In the U.S. case, posses better define the cultural producers than the rappers themselves, as in KRS-One's Boogie Down Productions, Public Enemy's The Bomb Squad,

and Ice Cube's The Lench Mob. Avowals of locality include Boogie Down Productions' "South Bronx" (1987) and NWA's "Straight Outta Compton" (1988). See T. Rose (1994, 10) for a discussion of the place of the "hood" in American rappers' self-presentation.

28 Crossover hip hop groups likewise explicitly reference their particular native localities in their oeuvres, including Zebda's "Toulouse" (1995), Alliance Ethnik's "Creil City" (1999), and Cheb Mami and K-Mel's "Parisien du Nord" (Parisian from the North, 1998).

29 See Suprême NTM's "Le Monde de Demain" (Tomorrow's World, 1991). This assessment of their role dovetail with American gangsta rap artist Ice Cube's own self-portrayal: "We call ourselves underground street reporters. We just tell it how we see it, nothing more, nothing less" (quoted in Mills, 1990, 32, cited in Kelley 1996, 121).

30 See interviews with NTM in *Authentik* 1(1), 1998: 31–36, and on their Internet homepage, http://www.supreme-ntm.com.

31 See also his interview in *Authentik* 1(1), 1998: 32.

32 I want to thank Greg Downey for suggesting this line of argument.

DISCOGRAPHY

Alliance Ethnik, *Fat Comeback*. Delabel, 1999.

Assassin. *Le futur que nous réserve-t-il?* Delabel, 1993.

Assassin. *L'homocide volontaire*. Delabel, 1995.

Boogie Down Productions. *Criminal Minded*. Jive, 1987.

Cheb Mami and K-Mel. *Parisien du Nord*. Virgin France, 1998.

MC Solaar. *Prose combat*. Polydor, 1994.

Ministère Amer. *95200*. Hostile/Delabel, 1994.

NWA. *Straight Outta Compton*. Priority, 1989.

Suprême NTM. *Authentik*. Sony/Epic, 1991.

Suprême NTM. *J'appuie sur la gachette*. Sony/Epic, 1993.

Suprême NTM. *Paris sous les bombes*. Sony/Epic, 1995.

Suprême NTM. *Suprême NTM*. Sony/Epic, 1998.

Various Artists. *Le flow*. Ultra, 2000.

Zebda. *Le bruit et l'odeur*. Barclay, 1995.

Zebda. *Essence ordinaire*. Barclay, 1998.

Saskia Sassen

AFTERWORD:
KNOWLEDGE PRACTICES AND
SUBJECT MAKING AT THE EDGE

The editors asked me to reflect on the future of an anthropology of the New Economy. With them, I take the latter as a construct that captures a moment of unsettlement: technoexuberance and sharp boom and bust cycles. To respond to the editors' request, I single out one particular issue to which the different essays make substantive contributions even though it is not a central aim of this volume: how to conceptualize the new information and communication technologies (ICTs). This choice also resolves my problem with the notion of the New Economy. The research and interpretive strategies used by the authors to examine the New Economy provide one angle into the larger question of how to study these technologies. Notwithstanding highly diverse objects of study and interpretive strategies, these essays all engage the question of the new ICTs. Yet these never become an object of study nor the occasion for a heuristic about research and interpretation in this realm.

It is difficult to do justice in a short afterword to this volume's rich contribution. And it is a daunting task since these essays arise from several complex research fields. Finally, in a volume so aware of knowledge practices, including those of the authors themselves, I should identify the particular and inevitably partial stance from which I write this afterword. It is centered in efforts that have organized my research over the last twenty years. These efforts include grounding technical and abstract systems in thick environments; deciphering the need for cultures of interpretation by users of complex mathematical financial instruments; detecting the social logics that organize electronic interactive domains and "distort" the technical logics of engineers' designs; apprehending the emergence of "blurred" subjects not easily represented through conventional categories. These concerns help me understand and situate the particular contributions of each essay.

DOING RESEARCH AT THE EDGE

The essays in this volume focus on types of sites where we can capture existing arrangements and knowledge practices in their moment of unsettlement, whether because of crises in the economy, sharp innovations, or unexpected uses of the new technologies by marginalized actors. It is in this sense that I think of these as sites at the edge—at the edge of economic operation, the edge of systems of social inclusion, the edge of technology. The edge is in key ways an extreme condition, even when this is not always evident because of the cultural work of building agreement and shared norms, and even when the extreme condition is microscopic or hermetic, thus not easily coded as extreme.

In these sites we can detect types of knowledge practices and subject making that go into constituting the global and the technical, both in their moment of unsettlement and in the producing of (new) meanings that have come to be stabilized. This also suggests that what typically gets interpreted as economic and technological change is actually social change and cultural laboring.

A focus on these knowledge practices and forms of subject making, then, grounds what has come to be thought of as hypermobile, seamless, and placeless. This grounding takes many different forms. The essays in this volume capture this variability as it is present in that mix of global economic and technical trends that came to be called the New Economy. And they show us that at the heart of this variety of global technico-economic conditions is the fact that localized social relations and utilities feed and even constitute these knowledge practices, no matter how global the capabilities involved: the new information and communication technologies, the Internet, global firms, internationally traded financial instruments, central bank policy. Global currency transactions are shown to be constituted and enabled by trust systems among traders on an exchange floor (Zaloom). The new ICTs are shown to be used by marginalized actors for purposes other than engineers may have designed for (Silverstein) or international development professionals may aim for (Simone); they are shown to have the potential to sharpen intergenerational conflict (Comaroff and Comaroff); electronic networks are shown to need social connectivity for their effective functioning (O'Mahony) and to function as ways of negotiating unsettlement (Fisher).

Global management technologies are shown to depend on concrete connections and adaptations by local actors (Ong). International financial markets and instruments are shown to need specific legal changes and, even in their most technical version, the cultural work of creating consensus around the notion of value involved (Riles). They are also shown to be constituted through technical academic narrations (Holmes and Marcus). An electronic medium is used to capture bodily knowledge (Downey). Global capital is shown to need specific types of places and whatever interventions it takes to execute the transfer of these territories into new uses (Smith).

The analytics developed in these chapters and their empirical specifications bring with them an elaboration of the meaning of ethnographic research. The sites for research are frontier zones of novel systems—in this case, various components of the so-called New Economy and the new ICTs. Highly technical instruments and systems are decoded so that we can understand how site-specific social and cultural capabilities construct the "technical" outcome. And scaled-up instantiations are thereby shown to be constituted, at least partly, by these site-specific capabilities. These local moments are found to be at the center of the global, rather than being the nonglobal. As a result, the global and the technical are shown to vary across locations; that is, they comprise the variability arising out of multiple locations. Studying the global and the technical thus requires ethnographies of various local moments: trading pits, networks of computer programmers, global marketing firms, particular types of urban places, the utilities that different types of actors (marginalized users, women professionals, traders) can extract from the new technologies. Each of these local moments comprises specific knowledge practices. And each comprises specific subjects: bankers, lawyers, traders, professional women, marginalized actors, entrepreneurial managers. The focus on self-reflexive practices by various knowledge-producing actors perhaps inevitably raises the issue of the knowledge-producing practices of the ethnographers themselves, a question addressed in several of the essays. This mix of features in the volume contributes to a new type of ethnography.

KNOWLEDGE PRACTICES AND SUBJECT MAKING
IN ELECTRONIC SITES

A volume on the New Economy perhaps inevitably makes the new ICTs a central presence, albeit not always a central focus.[1] More substantively, a critical positioning of these technologies actually requires considering the kinds of social and cultural issues these essays raise. Yet, because these technologies are not the focus of these essays, in what follows I want to develop such a critical positioning, elaborating on what is mostly left unexamined in the volume, even though often implied and present in a somewhat diffuse manner. What follows, then, is in the spirit of extending the critical apparatus developed in this volume.[2]

Three analytic foci that capture various features developed in this volume and move us toward a more general set of analytic strategies for doing research and interpreting the new interactive digital technologies are (1) the imbrications between digital and nondigital conditions, (2) scaling, and (3) the mediating cultures connecting users and the technologies. The next three sections develop these issues and signal how various aspects discussed in this volume are instances of this type of analytic practice.[3]

Digital/Nondigital Imbrications

As the authors in this volume recognize and criticize, the hypermobility characteristic of New Economy transactions is usually seen as a mere function of the new technologies. This understanding erases the fact that it takes multiple nondigital conditions to achieve this outcome, conditions examined in several chapters (Zaloom, Holmes and Marcus, Riles, Ong, O'Mahony). Once we recognize that this hypermobility had to be *produced*, we introduce nondigital variables into our analysis of a digital domain. The digital domain is shown to require, for instance, certain types of places with state-of-the-art built environments, well-housed talent, and conventional infrastructure—from highways to airports and railways (Smith). Or it is shown to require the thick environment of the trading floor for screen-based traders (Zaloom).

The hypermobility gained by an object, a transaction, or capital through digitization is but one moment of a more complex condition, one that includes the knowledge practices of key actors. Representing that digital moment is, then, a partial representation as it includes only some of the components at work. Much of what is liquefied and circulates in digital networks and is marked by hypermobility remains nondigital in some of its components.[4]

Second, the nature of this place-boundedness differs from what it may have been even twenty years ago, when place-boundedness was far more likely to be a form of immobility. Today it is a place-boundedness that is inflected or inscribed by the hypermobility of some of its components, products, and outcomes. Both capital fixity and mobility are located in a temporal frame where speed is ascendant and consequential. This type of capital fixity cannot be fully captured through a description confined to its material and locational features, that is, through a topographical description. The real estate industry illustrates some of these issues. Financial services firms have invented instruments that liquefy real estate, thereby facilitating investment and circulation of these instruments in global markets. Yet, part of what constitutes real estate remains very physical. At the same time, however, that which remains physical has been transformed by the fact that it is represented through highly liquid instruments that can circulate in global markets. It may look the same, it may involve the same bricks and mortar, it may be new or old, but it is a transformed entity.

Thus, the partial representation of real estate through liquid financial instruments produces a complex imbrication of the digital and the nondigital moments of that which we continue to call real estate. And so does the fact that physical infrastructure and traders' experience are partly endogenized in electronic financial markets.

I see in the essays by Simone and Silverstein a similar dynamic, albeit constituted in very different terms: the material environments of the disadvantaged or marginalized users they each examine are inflected by their use of digital networks. They can enter into whole new worlds of interactions at various scales other than that of their local environments. In this process, those local material environments are themselves altered; they become, besides all the other things they are, microenvironments with global span. In O'Mahony's examination of an open source software network, its largely, almost exclusively electronic transactions are deeply imbricated with various forms of social connectivity.

Third, much of what happens in electronic space is inflected by the cultures, the material practices, the imaginaries that take place outside electronic space. Much of the digital composition of financial markets is inflected by the agendas that drive global finance. Much of what we think of when it comes to cyberspace would lack any meaning or referents if we were to exclude the world outside cyberspace. The networks examined by Fisher capture this clearly, as do those examined by Simone, Zaloom, and Silverstein. Perhaps in a more intermediated way, one might see this type of imbrication of the digital and the nondigital also in some of the other essays. In brief, interactive digital space is not an exclusive condition that stands outside the nondigital. Digital interactive domains are partly constituted by the larger societal, cultural, subjective, economic, imaginary structurations of lived experience and the systems within which users exist and operate.[5]

The Destabilizing of Older Conceptions of Scale

Recognizing the imbrications between the digital and the nondigital brings with it a destabilizing of conceptions that posit the scalar as hierarchical. Older conceptions of scaling date from the period that saw the ascendance of the nation-state. They are typically organized in terms of institutional size and territorial scope: from the international, down to the national, the regional, the urban, to the local. As the national scale loses some of its significance along with various policy and organizational transformations, other scales can gain strategic importance. Most especially among these are subnational scales such as the global city and supranational scales such as global markets. Today's rescaling dynamics cut across institutional size and across the institutional encasements of territory produced by the formation of national states. This does not mean that the old hierarchies disappear, but rather that rescalings emerge alongside the old ones that can often trump the latter.

One outcome is that the emergence of global electronic networks alters the meaning of the local. For example, much of what we might still experience as the local (an office building or a house or an institution right there in our neighborhood or downtown) actually is something I would rather think of as a microenvironment with global span insofar as it is deeply internetworked. Such a microenvironment is in many senses a localized entity, but it is also part of global digital networks, which give it immediate far-flung span. More important, the juxtaposition between the condition of being a sited materiality and having global span captures the imbrication of the digital and the nondigital and illustrates the inadequacy of a purely technological reading of the technical properties of digitization that would lead us to posit the neutralization of the place-boundedness of that which precisely makes possible the condition of being an entity with global span. A version of this trend is evident in this volume, where even digital formations that need not be transboundary, such as those examined by Silverstein and by Simone, wind up being so directly or indirectly.

A second instance is the bundle of conditions and dynamics that marks the model of the global city. Just to single out one key dynamic: the more globalized and digitized the operations of firms and markets, the more their central management and coordination functions (and the requisite spatial agglomerations and material structures) become strategic. It is precisely because of digitization that simultaneous worldwide dispersal of operations (whether factories, offices, or service outlets) and system integration can be achieved. And it is precisely this combination that raises the importance of central functions. Global cities are, among other components, strategic sites for the combination of resources necessary for the production of these central functions. The cross-border network of global cities emerges as one of the key components in the architecture of "international relations," a realm once exclusive to national states.

The essays in this volume make an important contribution to this analytic effort in that they situate the local at the heart of the global and show the global to be partly constituted by a variety of forms of the local. Although this is present throughout the volume, some essays address it more explicitly in terms of electronic networks. The essays by Smith and Zaloom show us how, respectively, global firms and vast global electronic markets require grounding in specific local environments (trading pits and state-of-the-art built environments). Simone shows us how virtualized geographies emerge from their grounding in specific locales. And Ong shows us that the negotiations of disparate cultural and scalar standards by entrepreneurial managers in Shanghai are a way of articulating that place with global markets.

Cultures of Use

There are multiple ways of examining the interactions between these digital technologies and their users. A strong tendency in the literature is to conceptualize the matter of use as an unmediated event, as unproblematized activity, one merely conditioned by access and technical competence and, perhaps, interface design. In contrast, the essays in this volume are not concerned with the purely technical features of digital networks and what these might mean for users, nor simply with its impact on users. The concern is with an in-between zone that constructs the articulations of digital space and users—whether as social, political, or economic actors. These articulations are constituted in terms of mediating cultures; it is not simply a question of access and understanding how to use the hardware and the software. Use—to be distinguished from access—is constructed or constituted in terms of specific cultures and practices through and within which users articulate the experience and/or utility of digital technology.[6] The importance of the contributions that this volume makes to the analytics of cultures of use becomes evident from a quick review of the dominant trends in the pertinent literature.

One particular culture of use, that of "techies," has become naturalized and thereby has rendered invisible the whole question of cultures of use. Beyond this thick computer-centered culture of use, there is a tendency to flatten the practices of users to questions of competence and utility. From the perspective of the social sciences, use of the technology should be problematized rather than simply seen as shaped by technical requirements and the necessary knowledge, even as this might be the perspective of the computer scientist and engineer who designed it. A second trend is a considerable simplification of "modern" versus "traditional" users, where the former are assumed to be the better users or more disposed to become users. Finally, it has also led to a variety of assertions about the increased dominance of English. Each one of these can be shown to be problematic at best and simply incorrect at worst.[7]

Let me take some freedoms in interpreting some of the contributions several essays in the volume make to an elaboration of cultures of use. I see elements of such an elaboration most clearly in the already discussed essays by Simone, Silverstein, and Downey. Albeit concerned with a different technology (cable television), Downey shows us a particular culture of use: televised fighting that serves a network of athletes to extract knowledge about fighting techniques. A distinct culture of use is also clear in Fisher's examination of Wall Street professional women setting up a digital network of colleagues to negotiate changing norms and opportunities in their work world. Though far more intermediated, I also see such an elaboration of a culture of use in Riles's examination of how experts think they need to produce a fiction, a narrative, represented as changes of the law in order to enable entry of Japanese financial instruments into global electronic financial markets. Even more intermediated—and perhaps not quite there—is Holmes and Marcus's examination of self-reflexive experts using high-tech capabilities (a far broader concept than digital networks and an invocation that does not entail use by the experts themselves) to construct a policy outcome (high growth that can avoid inflation by raising productivity) that has the effect of overriding a foundational economic proposition (high growth will bring inflationary pressures).

The constructing of the using subject is also a critical dimension in the elaboration of cultures of use. This is clearly present in several of the essays, with those by Simone, Fisher, O'Mahony, and Silverstein perhaps the most explicitly focused on this question. Jean and John Comaroff touch on this question in their examination of youth and how use of these technologies can intensify the intergenerational differences between the adults and youth, that is, producing youth as an even more distinct subject than has been typical in the past. Riles's self-reflexive experts also are a distinct type of using subject, as are Holmes and Marcus's central bankers (albeit with the above cited qualifications). Finally, the problematic assumption of a traditional versus modern user, where the latter is seen as the superior user, is confronted by

Simone and Silverstein. In both of their essays, disadvantaged people, easily construed as more traditional than, let's say, middle-class Westerners, are shown to have highly innovative uses of the technology.[8]

CONCLUSION: TOWARD A NEW OBJECT OF ETHNOGRAPHIC STUDY

The essays in this volume can be seen as contributing critical conceptual and empirical elements to the constructing of digital space as an object of study. A focus on this particular aspect is one possible way of responding to the editors' concern with moving forward. The new technologies need to be deciphered given misrepresentation in much of the literature and abuses by powerful actors. This deciphering matters if we are to use the New Economy notion as a heuristic that allows us to understand something about the unsettling of powerful arrangements and what it takes to ensure stabilized meanings.

Although not the object of study, several of the essays actually signal the existence of distinct and variable interactive electronic domains. As developed in this afterword, electronic interactive domains are digitized structures that contain endogenized social logics. They are partly shaped and given meaning by social, political, economic, ideational, and often visual conditions that exist typically outside of, or, at a minimum, transcend the technology as such. These digitized domains assume multiple forms and involve diverse actors. One feature in some of the networks examined in this volume is the possibility of capturing the weight of the social and the cultural in the actual digital interactive domain.

Several of the essays show us how these technologies can rescale social relations. What has tended to operate or be nested at local scales can now move to global scales, and global relations and domains can now, in turn, more easily become directly articulated with thick local settings. As a result of the growing presence and use of these technologies, an increasing range of social relations and domains have become de facto transboundary. It need not be this way, and indeed many of these digital formations are not, but the trend is definitely toward expanding the world of transboundary relations and domains. Actors we have thought of as stuck in nested hierarchies of scale can now participate in transboundary domains. These trends contain a number of theoretical and political implications when it comes to specifying the global, the local, the cultural, and the technical—four key presences throughout this volume.

Much of the vast literature on the new ICTs fails to capture these dynamics. The conventional categories for analysis make the digital and non-digital mutually exclusive and thereby tend to evict the local and the cultural from the analysis. The essays in this volume contribute, albeit often unwittingly, to unsettling these dualities and showing us the imbrications between knowledge practices and the variable meanings of these technologies, and how these in turn produce specific subjects.

The central concern in the volume is with knowledge practices and subject making that show us that the local and the cultural are present in realms —global electronic markets, open source networks, and so on—typically represented as technical and as global. The effort in this brief afterword was to focus on knowledge practices and subject making that show us that interactive electronic domains, also usually represented as technical and global, are shaped and partly constituted by the local and the nontechnical. At issue here is the constructing of an object of study that is an electronic domain with endogenized social/cultural logics. This type of domain is proliferating, engaging a growing range of actors and processes. Its examination will require the types of ethnographic and interpretive work evident in this volume.

NOTES

1 I do not assume that technology and society are actually separate entities, and accept many of the propositions in the critical social science literature about technology as one particular instantiation of society—society frozen, that is, one moment in a trajectory that once might have been experienced as simply social (Latour, 1987). Without losing this critical stance, I want, nonetheless, to capture the specifics of these technical domains. A growing number of scholars, including Karin Knorr Cetina and Urs Bruegger (2002a), are bringing both dimensions together.

2 I see several of the essays in this volume as working against a profuse scholarship on the technical properties of the new ICTs and their capacities for producing change. These technologies increasingly dominate explanations of contemporary change and development, with technology seen as the impetus for the most fundamental social trends and transformations. Such explanations tend to understand these technologies exclusively in terms of technical properties and to construct the relation to the social world as one of applications and impacts. (I have developed this critique in Sassen, 2002.) Several anthropologists and sociologists have formulated critiques coming from diverse angles (e.g., Maurer, 2002b; Wajcman, 2002, 2004).

3 Although not specifically recognized or defined, the essays in this volume mostly deal with a very specific component of the new ICTs, even though the more general term is used. It is computer-centered interactive technologies (for short, digital technologies). Further, the focus is on actual interactive domains, not on virtual environments or game-theoretic domains. What matters to these authors is sociality, not the precise technical attributes involved. The one reference to a noninteractive

condition—the digitization of financial instruments—is not really an object of attention here, but more like a passing recognition. In my own research (see Sassen, 2005), I see the digitization of complex financial instruments as very significant, and I interpret it as greatly enabling some of the social and cultural infrastructure in finance that is also examined in this volume.

4 Much of my work on global cities has been an effort to conceptualize and document the fact that the global digital economy requires massive concentrations of material conditions in order to be what it is. Finance is an important intermediary in this regard: it represents a capability for liquefying various forms of nonliquid wealth and for raising the mobility (i.e., hypermobility) of that which is already liquid.

5 In a just completed multiyear project, we (Latham and Sassen, 2005) focused on electronic interactive domains: electronic markets, Internet-based large-scale conversations, knowledge spaces arising out of NGO networks, open source software development networks, and early conflict warning systems, among others. Such structures result from various mixes of computer-centered technologies and the broad range of social contexts that provide the utility logics, substantive rationalities, and cultural meanings for much of what happens in these digital spaces. In that project we developed a category for analysis—digital formation—to capture digital spaces that evince not only the endogenous technical capabilities of such networks, but also endogenized social logics (Latham and Sassen, 2005, introduction). The endogenizing of social logics that marks digital formations sets limits to technical logics in that these intersect with social logics that can inhibit technical capacities or produce frictions and obstacles. But social logics can also produce whole new possibilities and push technical advances, as has clearly been the case in electronic financial markets, for instance. The multiplication of digital formations over the past decade means that these can, in turn, begin to function as social, albeit digitized, conditionings of the technology. Digital formations are, then, to be distinguished from digital technology tout court; further, not all digital networks are digital formations. They are mixed outcomes in that they result from endogenous technical properties and endogenized social logics. There are elements of such a configuration in the electronic networks identified by Simone, Silverstein, O'Mahony, and Fisher.

6 A long-standing concern with what I have called "analytic borderlands" has led me to try to detect the mediations in the act of using the technologies. (For a more detailed explanation of these issues concerning how use is constructed or constituted in terms of specific cultures and practices through and within which users articulate the experience/utility of electronic space, see e.g., Sassen, 2002, 2005.)

7 The practices through which use is constituted partly derive their meanings from the aims, values, cultures, power systems, and institutional orders of the users and their settings. These mediating cultures also can produce a subject and a subjectivity that become part of the mediation. For instance, in open source networks (S. Weber, 2005), much meaning is derived from the fact that these practitioners contest a dominant economic-legal system centered in private property protections; participants become active subjects in a process that extends beyond their individual work and produces a culture. The kinds of rural-user-oriented networks examined by Garcia (2005) partly result from an awareness of long-term historical and institu-

tional disadvantages of rural areas compared to urban areas and an orientation toward overcoming this disadvantage. There are multiple ways of examining the mediating cultures organizing use. Among others, these can conceivably range from small-scale ethnographies to macrolevel surveys, from descriptive to highly theorized accounts, from a focus on ideational forms to one on structural conditions.

8 A study by the anthropologist Jon Anderson (Anderson and Gonzales-Quijano, 2004) on Internet use among Muslims in the Middle East found that "modern Muslim youth" use the Internet to shop, to visit favorite sites, in brief, constitute the same somewhat elementary consumer culture that Western youth do. In contrast, very "traditional users," readers of the Qur'an, had a far more elaborate and active culture of use: they hyperlinked their way through a variety of interpretive annotations at the margins of the text and introduced their own. In my own research (e.g., Sassen, 2004), I have been very concerned with this question of how what we might easily think of as the "disadvantaged, traditional" using subject might actually be the one with a more elaborate culture of use.

BIBLIOGRAPHY

Abdullah, Ibrahim. 1998. Bush Path to Destruction: The Origin and Character of the Revolutionary United Front/Sierra Leone. *Journal of Modern African Studies* 36 (2): 203–235.

Abelson. 1999. "A Network of Their Own: From an Exclusive Address, a Group for Women Only," *New York Times*, October 27, section C, p. 1.

Abolafia, Mitchel Y. 1998. Markets as Cultures. In *The Laws of the Markets*, edited by Michael Callon. Oxford: Blackwell.

———. 2004. Framing Moves: Interpretive Politics at the Federal Reserve. *Journal of Public Administration Research and Theory* 14 (3): 349–370.

———. Forthcoming. Making Sense of Recession. In *The Economic Sociology of Capitalism*, edited by Victor Nee and Richard Swedberg. Princeton, N.J.: Princeton University Press.

Africa Regional Office. 1999. Project Appraisal Document in a Proposed Credit in the Amount of SDR 12.9 Million (U.S. 18 Million Equivalent) to the Republic of Guinea for a Third Urban Development Project in the Support of the First Phase of the Third Urban Development Program. Washington, D.C.: World Bank.

African Research Bulletin: Economic Series. 1998. Vol. 35 (July).

Agger, Ben. 1989. *Fast Capitalism: A Critical Theory of Significance*. Urbana: University of Illinois Press.

Aglietta, Michel, and Régis Breton. 2001. Financial Systems, Corporate Control and Capital Accumulation. *Economy and Society* 30 (4): 433–466.

Aïchoune, Farid. 1991. *Nés en banlieue*. Paris: Editions Ramsay.

Aïssou, Abdel. 1987. *Les Beurs, l'école et la France*. Paris: Harmattan/CIEMI.

Alcaly, Roger. 2003. *The New Economy: What It Is, How It Happened, and Why It Is Likely to Last*. New York: Farrar, Straus and Giroux.

Al-Kenz, A. 1995. Youth and Violence. In *Africa Now: People, Places and Institutions*, edited by Stephen Ellis. The Hague: DGIS.

Allen, John. 2002. Symbolic Economies: The "Culturalization" of Economic Knowledge. In *Cultural Economy: Cultural Analysis and Commercial Life*, edited by Paul du Gay and Michael Pryke. London: Sage.

Allison, Anne. 1994. *Nightwork: Sexuality, Pleasure, and Corporate Masculinity in a Tokyo Hostess Club.* Chicago: University of Chicago Press.

———. 1996. *Permitted and Prohibited Desires: Mothers, Comics, and Censorship in Japan.* Boulder, Colo.: Westview Press.

Amin, Aloysius, and Jean-Luc Dubois. 1999. *A 1999 Update of the Cameroon Poverty Profile.* Washington, D.C.: World Bank.

Amin, Ash, and Nigel Thrift, eds. 2004. *The Blackwell Cultural Economy Reader.* Malden, Mass.: Blackwell.

Anderson, David M., and Richard Rathbone. 2000. Urban Africa: Histories in the Making. In *Africa's Urban Past,* edited by David M. Anderson and Richard Rathbone. Portsmouth, N.H.: Heinemann.

Anderson, Jon, and Yves Gonzales-Quijano. 2004. Technological Mediation and the Emergence of Transnational Muslim Publics. In *Public Islam and the Common Good,* edited by Dale F. Eickelman and Armando Salvatore. Leiden: E. J. Brill.

Andersson, J. 2001. Reintegrating the Rural-Urban Connection: Migration Practices and Sociocultural Dispositions of Buhera Workers in Harare. *Africa* 71 (1): 81–111.

Angelini, Paolo. 1998. An Analysis of Competitive Externalities in Gross Settlement Systems. *Journal of Banking and Finance* 22 (1): 1–18.

Antonio, Robert, and Alessandro Bonanno. 1996. Post-Fordism in the United States: The Poverty of Market Centered Democracy. *Current Perspectives in Social Theory* 16:3–32.

Appadurai, Arjun. 1990. Disjuncture and Difference in the Global Cultural Economy. *Public Culture* 2 (2): 1–24.

———. 1996. *Modernity at Large: Cultural Dimensions of Globalization.* Minneapolis: University of Minnesota Press.

Appiah, Kwame Anthony. 1999. Cosmopolitan Patriots. In *Cosmopolitics: Thinking and Feeling beyond the Nation,* edited by Pheng Cheah and Bruce Robbins. Minneapolis: University of Minnesota Press.

Apter, Andrew. 1999. IBB=419: Nigerian Democracy and the Politics of Illusion. In *Civil Society and the Political Imagination in Africa,* edited by John L. Comaroff and Jean Comaroff. Chicago: University of Chicago Press.

Arendt, Hannah. 1976. *The Origins of Totalitarianism.* New York: Harcourt Brace Jovanovich.

Armstrong, Peter. 2001. Science, Enterprise and Profit: Ideology in the Knowledge-driven Economy. *Economy and Society* 30 (4): 524–552.

Aryeety, E., and M. Nissanke. 1998. Asia and Africa in the Global Economy: Economic Policies and External Performance in South-East Asia and Sub-Saharan Africa 1998. Paper presented at the United Nations University–African Economic Research Consortium Conference on Asia and Africa in the Global Economy, Tokyo, August 3–4.

Asenso-Okyere, W. K., George Benneh, and Wouter Tims. 1997. *Sustainable Food Security in West Africa.* Dordrecht: Kluwer Academic.

Atkinson, Michael. 2002. Fifty Million Viewers Can't Be Wrong: Professional Wrestling, Sports-Entertainment, and Mimesis. *Sociology of Sport Journal* 19 (1): 47–66.

Baba, Marietta L. 2003. Afterword: Looking Forward, Looking Back. In *Advertising Cultures,* edited by Timothy Malefyt and Brian Moeran. Oxford: Berg.

Bach, Donald C. 1999. *Regionalization in Africa: Integration and Disintegration.* Bloomington: Indiana University Press.

Badcock, B. A. 1992. Adelaide's Heart Transplant. 1970–88. I: Creation, Transfer and Capture of "Value" within the Built Environment. *Environment and Planning A* 24:215–241.

Bagli, C. V. 1991. "De-gentrification" Can Hit When Boom Goes Bust. *New York Observer*, August, 5–12.

Baker, Wayne E. 1984a. Floor Trading and Crowd Dynamics. In *The Social Dynamics of Financial Markets*, edited by Peter A. Adler and Patricia Adler. Greenwich, Conn.: JAI Press.

——. 1984b. The Social Structure of a National Securities Market. *American Journal of Sociology* 89 (4): 775–811.

Bale, John, and Joseph Maguire, eds. 1994. *The Global Sports Arena: Athletic Talent Migration in an Interdependent World*. London: Frank Cass.

Ball, Michael R. 1990. *Professional Wrestling as Ritual Drama in American Popular Culture*. Lewiston, N.Y.: Edwin Mellen.

Balnaves, Mark, James Donald, and Stephanie Hemelryk Donald. 2001. *The Penguin Atlas of Media and Information: Key Issues and Global Trends*. New York: Penguin Putnam.

Bangura, Y. 1994. Economic Restructuring, Coping Strategies and Social Change: Implications for Institutional Development in Africa. *Development and Change* 25:785–827.

Bank of Japan. 1996. *Nihon Ginko touza yokin kessai no "RTGS-ka ni tsuite"* (About the move to RTGS for the settlement of deposits at the Bank of Japan). Tokyo: Bank of Japan.

——. 1998. *The Framework for Restructuring BOJ-NET JGB Services*. Tokyo: Bank of Japan.

——. 2003. *Payment and Settlement Statistics*. Tokyo: Bank of Japan.

Barlow, John Perry. 1996. A Declaration of the Independence of Cyberspace. Electronic Freedom Foundation, http://www.eff.org/7Ebarlow/Declaration-Final.html.

Barnett, Steven. 1990. *Games and Sets: The Changing Face of Sport on Television*. London: British Film Institute.

Baron, Neil D. 1996. The Role of Rating Agencies in the Securitization Process. In *A Primer on Securitization*, edited by Leon T. Kendall and Michael J. Fishman. Cambridge, Mass.: MIT Press.

Barry, Andrew, and Don Slater. 2002. Introduction: The Technological Economy. *Economy and Society* 31 (2): 175–193.

Barthes, Roland. 1957/1972. The World of Wrestling. In *Mythologies*. Translated by A. Lavers. New York: Noonday Press.

Bastian, Misty L. 1993. Bloodhounds Who Have No Friends: Witchcraft and Locality in the Nigerian Popular Press. In *Modernity and Its Malcontents: Ritual and Power in Postcolonial Africa*, edited by Jean Comaroff and John L. Comaroff. Chicago: University of Chicago Press.

Bayart, Jean-François. 2000. Africa in the World: A History of Extraversion. *African Affairs* 99:217–267.

Bazin, Hugues. 1995. *La culture hip-hop*. Paris: Desclée de Brouwer.

Beck, Ulrich. 1992. *Risk Society: Towards a New Modernity*. London: Sage.

Beck, Ulrich, Anthony Giddens, and Scott Lash. 1994. *Reflexive Modernization: Politics, Tradition and Aesthetics in the Modern Social Order*. Stanford: Stanford University Press.

Becker, Charles M., Andrew M. Hamer, and Andrew R. Morrison. 1994. *Beyond Urban Bias in Africa: Urbanisation in an Era of Structural Adjustment.* Portsmouth, N.H.: Heinemann.

Beech, Mark. 2002. In Need of a Fix. *Sports Illustrated* 97 (September 30): 25.

Begag, Azouz. 1995. *Espace et exclusion: Mobilités dans les quartiers péripheriques d'Avignon.* Paris: Harmattan.

Behlendorf, Brian. 1999. Open Source as a Business Strategy. In *Open Sources: Voices from the Open Source Revolution*, edited by Chris DiBona, Sam Ockman, and Mark Stone. Sebastopol, Calif.: O'Reilly.

Belkin, Lisa. 2003. The Opt-Out Revolution. *New York Times Magazine*, October 26, section 6, p. 42.

Ben Hammouda, Hakim. 1999. Guerriers et marchands: Éléments pour une économie politique des conflits en Afrique. *Africa Development* 24(3/4): 1–18.

Bennis, Warren. 1966. Changing Organizations. *Journal of Applied Behavioral Science* 2(3): 247–263.

Benston, George J., and Al L. Hartgraves. 2002. Enron: What Happened and What We Can Learn from It. *Journal of Accounting and Public Policy* 21(2): 105–127.

Bent, Alan R. 1952. *Ten Thousand Men of Africa: The Story of the Bechuanaland Pioneers and Gunners, 1941–1946.* London: HMSO.

Bernard, Philippe. 1998. *L'immigration: Les enjeux de l'intégration.* Paris: Le Monde.

Bernault, Florence. 2000. The Political Shaping of Sacred Locality in Brazzaville, 1959–97. In *Africa's Urban Past*, edited by David M. Anderson and Richard Rathbone. Portsmouth, N.H.: Heinemann/James Currey.

Bernstein, Peter. 1986. *Capital Ideas: The Improbable Origins of Modern Wall Street.* New York: Free Press.

Berry, Sara. 1993. *No Condition Is Permanent: The Social Dynamics of Agrarian Change in Sub-Saharan Africa.* Madison: University of Wisconsin Press.

——. 1997. Stable Prices, Unstable Values: Some Thoughts on Monetization and the Meaning of Transactions in West African Economies. In *Money Matters: Instability, Values, and Social Payments in the Modern History of West African Communities*, edited by Jane Guyer. Portsmouth, N.H.: Heinemann/James Currey.

Bessen, James. 2001. Open Source Software: Free Provision of a Complex Public Good. Working paper, http://www.researchoninnovation.org/opensrc.pdf.

Best, Steven, and Douglas Kellner. 1991. *Postmodern Theory: Critical Interrogations.* New York: Guilford Press.

Beunza, Daniel, and David Stark. 2002. A Sociology of Arbitrage: Market Instruments in a Trading Room. Paper presented at the New York Conference on the Social Studies of Finance, Columbia University and the Social Science Research Council, New York, May 3–4.

Beynon, John, and David Dunkerley, eds. 2000. *Globalization: The Reader.* New York: Routledge.

Bijker, Wiebe, Thomas P. Hughes, and Trevor Pinch. 1999. *The Social Construction of Technological Systems.* Cambridge, Mass.: MIT Press.

Billetoft, Jørgen. 1996. *Between Industrialisation and Poverty Alleviation: The Dilemma of Support to Micro-Enterprises.* Copenhagen: Centre for Development Research.

Blanch, Michael. 1980. Imperialism, Nationalism and Organised Youth. In *Working Class Culture: Studies in History and Theory*, edited by John Clark, Chas Critcher, and Richard Johnson. New York: St. Martin's Press.

Blinder, Alan S. 1998. *Central Banking in Theory and Practice*. Cambridge, Mass.: MIT Press.

———. 2004. *The Quiet Revolution*. New Haven: Yale University Press.

Bloom, John. 2000. *To Show What an Indian Can Do: Sports and Native American Boarding Schools*. Minneapolis: University of Minnesota Press.

Blumenthal, Howard J., and Oliver R. Goodenough. 1998. *This Business of Television*. New York: Billboard/Watson-Guptill.

Board of Governors of the Federal Reserve System. 1994. *Federal Reserve System: Purposes and Functions*. Washington, D.C.: Federal Reserve System.

Bockman, Johanna, and Gil Eyal. 2002. Eastern Europe as a Laboratory of Economic Knowledge. *American Journal of Sociology* 108 (2): 310–352.

Boden, Deidre. 2000. Worlds in Action: Information, Instantaneity and Global Futures Trading. In *The Risk Society and Beyond: Critical Issues for Social Theory*, edited by Barbara Adam, Ulrich Beck, and Joost Van Loon. Thousand Oaks, Calif.: Sage.

Boies, John, and Harland Prechel. 2002. Capital Dependence, Business Political Behavior, and Change to the Multilayered Subsidiary Form. *Social Problems* 49 (3): 301–326.

Boubekeur, Ahmed, and Zakya Daoud. 1993. Radiographie de la plus grande ZUP de France. In *Banlieues . . . intégration ou explosion?*, edited by Catherine Wihtol de Wenden and Zakya Daoud. Special issue, *Panoramiques* 2 (12): 21–24.

Boumaza, Nadir, Véronique de Rudder, and Marie France de Maria. 1989. *Banlieues, immigration, gestion urbaine*. Grenoble: Institut de Géographie Alpine.

Bourdieu, Pierre. 1977. *Outline of a Theory of Practice*. Cambridge: Cambridge University Press.

———. 1979/1984. *Distinction: A Social Critique of the Judgement of Taste*. Cambridge, Mass.: Harvard University Press.

Bourdieu, Pierre, and Jean-Claude Passeron. 1964. *Les héritiers: Les étudiants et la culture*. Paris: Minuit.

———. 1970. *La reproduction: Eléments pour une théorie du système d'enseignement*. Paris: Minuit.

Bourne, L. S. 1993. The Demise of Gentrification? A Contemporary and Prospective View. *Urban Geography* 14:95–107.

Bowlan, Jeanne. 1998. Civilizing Gender Relations in Algeria: The Paradoxical Case of Marie Bugéja, 1919–39. In *Domesticating the Empire: Race, Gender, and Family Life in French and Dutch Colonialism*, edited by Julia Clancy-Smith and Frances Gouda. Charlottesville: University of Virginia Press.

Boyer, Dominic. 2003. The Dilemma of the Anthropology of Experts. Paper presented at the 102nd annual meeting of the American Anthropological Association, Chicago November 19–23.

Braathen, Einar, Morten Bøås, and Gjermund Sæther, eds. 2000. *Ethnicity Kills: The Politics of War, Peace and Ethnicity in Sub-Saharan Africa*. New York: Macmillan.

Brams, Steven J., and Peter C. Fishburn. 1978. Approval Voting. *American Political Science Review* 72 (3): 831–847.

Brash, J. 2000. Gentrification in Harlem? A Second Look. Master's thesis, Columbia University.

Brenner, Robert. 2002. *The Boom and the Bubble: The U.S. in the World Economy.* London: Verso.

Brooke, James. 1995. Modern-Day Gladiators Head for Denver, but the Welcome Mat Is Rolled Up. *New York Times*, December 10, section 1, p. 22.

Brooks, John. 1973. *The Go-Go Years.* New York: Weybright and Talley.

Brown, John S., and Paul Duguid. 2000. *The Social Life of Information.* Boston: Harvard University Business School Press.

Buck-Morss, Susan. 1994. The Cinema Screen as Prosthesis of Perception: A Historical Account. In *The Senses Still: Perception and Memory as Material Culture in Modernity*, edited by C. Nadia Seremetakis. Chicago: University of Chicago Press.

Buford, Bill. 1993. *Among the Thugs.* New York: Vintage Departures.

Buggenhagen, Beth Anne. 2001. Prophets and Profits: Gendered and Generational Visions of Wealth and Value in Senegalese Murid Households. *Journal of Religion in Africa* 31 (4): 373–401.

Bullard, Alice. 2000. *Exile to Paradise: Savagery and Civilization in Paris and the South Pacific, 1790–1900.* Stanford: Stanford University Press.

Bundy, Colin. 1987. Street Sociology and Pavement Politics: Aspects of Youth and Student Resistance in Cape Town, 1985. *Journal of Southern African Studies* 13: 303–330.

Burawoy, Michael. 2000. Introduction. In *Global Ethnography*, by Michael Burawoy, Joseph A. Blum, Sheba George, Zsuzsa Gille, Teresa Gowan, Lynne Haney, Maren Klawiter, Steve H. Lopez, Seán Ó Riain, and Millie Thayer. Berkeley: University of California Press.

Burawoy, Michael, Joseph A. Blum, Sheba George, Zsuzsa Gille, Teresa Gowan, Lynne Haney, Maren Klawiter, Steve H. Lopez, Seán Ó Riain, and Millie Thayer. 2000. *Global Ethnography: Forces, Connections, and Imaginations in a Postmodern World.* Berkeley: University of California Press.

Burbach, Roger, Orlando Núñez, and Boris Kagarlitsky. 1997. *Globalization and Its Discontents: The Rise of Postmodern Socialisms.* London: Pluto Press.

Burstein, Daniel, and Arne de Keijzer. 1998. *Big Dragon: The Future of China; What it Means for Business, the Economy, and the Global Order.* New York: Simon and Schuster.

Butler, Judith. 1990. *Gender Trouble: Feminism and the Subversion of Identity.* New York: Routledge.

Cachin, Olivier. 1996. *L'offensive rap.* Paris: Gallimard.

Calder, Kent E. 1989. Elites in an Equalizing Role: Ex-Bureaucrats as Coordinators and Intermediaries in the Japanese Government-Business Relationship. *Comparative Politics* 21 (4): 379–403.

Calhoun, Craig. 1995. "New Social Movements" of the Early Nineteenth Century. In *Repertoires and Cycles of Collective Action*, edited by Mark Traugott. Durham, N.C.: Duke University Press.

Callon, Michel. 1998. Introduction: The Embeddedness of Economic Markets in Economics. In *The Laws of the Markets*, edited by Michel Callon. Malden, Mass.: Blackwell.

Callon, Michel, and Koray Caliskan. 2005. New and Old Directions in the Anthropology of Markets. Paper presented at *New Directions in the Anthropology of Markets: A Workshop*, Wenner-Gren Foundation, New York, April 9.

Callon, Michel, Cécile Méadel, and Vololona Rabeharisoa. 2004. The Economy of Qualities. In *The Blackwell Cultural Economy Reader*, edited by Ash Amin and Nigel Thrift. Malden, Mass.: Blackwell.

Campbell, Colin. 1987. *The Romantic Ethic and the Spirit of Capitalism.* Oxford: Blackwell.

Canclini, Néstor García. 2001. *Consumers and Citizens: Globalization and Multicultural Conflicts.* Minneapolis: University of Minnesota Press.

Cannon, Steven. 1997. Paname City Rapping: B-Boys in the *Banlieues* and Beyond. In *Post-Colonial Cultures in France*, edited by Alec G. Hargreaves and Mark McKinney. London: Routledge.

Cappelli, Peter. 1999. *The New Deal at Work: Managing the Market-Drive Workforce.* Boston: Harvard Business School Press.

Carrier, James G. 1998. Introduction. In *Virtualism: A New Political Economy*, edited by James G. Carrier and Daniel Miller. Oxford: Berg.

Carruthers, Bruce G. 1995. Accounting, Ambiguity, and the New Institutionalism. *Accounting, Organizations and Society* 20 (4): 313–328.

Carruthers, Bruce G., and Arthur L. Stinchcombe. 1999. The Social Structure of Liquidity: Flexibility, Markets, and States. *Theory and Society* 28 (3): 353–382.

Carter, Michael R., and Julian May. 1999. Poverty, Livelihoods and Class in Rural South Africa. *World Development* 27 (1): 1–20.

Castel, Robert. 1991. From Dangerousness to Risk. In *The Foucault Effect: Studies in Governmentality. With Two Lectures by and an Interview with Michel Foucault*, edited by Graham Burchell, Colin Gordon, and Peter Miller. London: Harvester Wheatsheaf.

Castells, Manuel. 1996. *The Rise of the Network Society.* Vol. 1 of *The Information Age.* New York: Blackwell.

——. 1997. *The Power of Identity.* Vol. 2 of *The Information Age.* New York: Blackwell.

——. 1998. *End of Millennium.* Vol. 3 of *The Information Age.* New York: Blackwell.

——. 2000. Toward a Sociology of the Network Society. *Contemporary Sociology* 29 (4): 693–699.

Castronova, Edward. 2001. Virtual Worlds: A First-Hand Account of Market and Society on the Cyberian Frontier. CESifo Working Paper No. 618, http://papers.ssrn.com/abstract=294828.

CCI/Centre Georges Pompidou. 1984. *Enfants d'immigrés maghrébins.* Paris: Centre de Création Industrielle.

Cefkin, Melissa. 2003. Business and Anthropological Intermediations in the New Economy. Paper presented at the national meeting of the American Anthropological Association, Chicago.

Çelik, Zeynep. 1997. *Urban Forms and Colonial Confrontations: Algiers under French Rule.* Berkeley: University of California Press.

Chabal, Patrick, and Jean-Pascal Daloz. 1999. *Africa Works: The Political Instrumentalization of Disorder.* Bloomington: Indiana University Press/James Currey.

Chantelat, Pascal, Michel Fodimbi, and Jean Camy. 1996. *Sports de la cité: Anthropologie de la jeunesse sportive.* Paris: Harmattan.

Cheah, Pheng, and Bruce Robbins, eds. 1999. *Cosmopolitics: Thinking and Feeling beyond the Nation.* Minneapolis: University of Minnesota Press.

Chicago Board of Trade. 1993. *Floor Practice Handbook.* Chicago: Board of Trade of the City of Chicago.

——. 1997. *Action in the Marketplace.* Chicago: Board of Trade of the City of Chicago.

Child, John, and Rita Gunther McGrath. 2001. Organizations Unfettered: Organizational Form in an Information-Intensive Economy. *Academy of Management Journal* 44:1135–1148.

China Europe International Business School (CEIBS). 1998. *China Expatriate Programme,* June 5–9 and November 8–12, Shanghai: 1.

Chukwuezi, Barth. 2001. Through Thick and Thin: Igbo Rural-Urban Circularity, Identity and Investment. *Journal of Contemporary African Studies* 19 (1): 55–66.

Clarke, Lee. 1999. *Mission Improbable: Using Fantasy Documents to Tame Disaster.* Chicago: University of Chicago Press.

Clavel, Gilbert. 1998. *La société d'exclusion: Comprendre pour en sortir.* Paris: Harmattan.

Cohen, Phil. 1981. Policing the Working-Class City. In *Crime and Society: Readings in History and Theory,* edited by Mike Fitzgerald, Gregor McLennan, and Jennie Pawson. London: Routledge and Kegan Paul.

Cohn, Nik. 1969. *Rock from the Beginning.* New York: Stein and Day.

Coleman, Enid Gabriella. n.d. The Politics of Survival and Prestige: Hacker Ideology and the Global Production of an Operating System. Master's thesis, Department of Anthropology, University of Chicago.

Coleman, James S. 1974. *Power and the Structure of Society.* New York: Norton.

Collier, Paul, and Jan Willem Gunning. 1998. Explaining African Economic Performance. Working Paper WPS/97.2.2, Centre for the Study of African Economies, University of Oxford.

Collier, Stephen, and Aihwa Ong. 2003. Oikos/Anthropos: Rationality, Technology, Infrastructure. *Current Anthropology* 44 (3): 421–426.

——. 2005. Global Assemblages, Anthropological Problems. In *Global Assemblages: Technology, Politics, and Ethics as Anthropological Problems,* edited by Aihwa Ong and Stephen J. Collier. London: Blackwell.

Colonna, Fanny. 1975. *Instituteurs Algériens, 1883–1939.* Paris: Presses de la Fondation Nationale des Sciences Politiques.

Colyer, Edwin. 2003. Taking a Close Look at Your Customers. Brandchannel.com, http://www.brandchannel.com/features—effect.asp?pf—id=167.

Comaroff, Jean, and John L. Comaroff. 1997. *Of Revelation and Revolution.* Vol. 2. Chicago: University of Chicago Press.

——. 1999a. Alien-nation: Zombies, Immigrants and Millennial Capitalism. *CODESRIA Bulletin* (3/4): 17–28. Reprinted in *Forces of Globalization,* edited by Gabrielle Schwab. New York: Columbia University Press, 2002.

——. 1999b. Occult Economies and the Violence of Abstraction: Notes from the South African Postcolony. *American Ethnologist* 26 (3): 279–301.

——. 2000a. Millennial Capitalism: First Thoughts on a Second Coming. In *Millennial Capitalism and the Culture of Neoliberalism,* edited by John L. Comaroff and Jean Comaroff. Special issue, *Public Culture* 12 (2): 291–343.

——. 2000b. Naturing the Nation: Aliens, Apocalypse and the Postcolonial State. *Hagar: International Social Science Review* 1 (1): 7–40.

Conrad, Joseph. 1911/1957. *Under Western Eyes.* Harmondsworth, England: Penguin.

Constantin, F. 1996. L'informal international ou le subversion de la territorialité. *Cultures and Conflicts* (21/22): 311–346.

Cook, Daniel. 1998. The Commoditization of Childhood: Personhood, the Children's Wear Industry and the Moral Discourses of Consumption, 1917–1967. Ph.D. dissertation, University of Chicago.

Cook, Susan. 1999. *Street Setswana: Evidence for the Double Bind of Class and Ethnicity in the New South Africa.* Ph.D. dissertation, Yale University.

Cooper, Frederick. 1994. Conflict and Connection: Rethinking African Colonial History. *American Historical Review* 99 (5): 1516–1545.

Cooper, Michael J., Orlin Dimitrov, and P. Raghavendra Rau. 2001. A Rose.com by Any Other Name. *Journal of Finance* 56 (6): 2371–2388.

Corrigan, Paul, and Simon Frith. 1976. The Politics of Youth Culture. In *Resistance through Rituals: Youth Subcultures in Post-War Britain*, edited by Stuart Hall and Tony Jefferson. London: Hutchinson.

Coval, Joshua D., and Tyler Shumway. 1998. *Is Noise Just Sound?* CBOT Working Paper Series.

Cronin, Mike, and David Mayall, eds. 1998. *Sporting Nationalism: Identity, Ethnicity, Immigration, and Assimilation.* London: Frank Cass.

Cronon, William. 1991. *Nature's Metropolis: Chicago and the Great West.* New York: Norton.

Crook, Tonyn. 2004. Transactions in Perpetual Motion. In *Transactions and Creations: Property Debates and the Stimulus of Melanesia*, edited by Eric Hirsch and Marilyn Strathern. New York: Berghahn.

Czarniawska, Barbara. 2004. Women in Financial Services: Fiction and More Fiction. In *The Sociology of Financial Markets*, edited by Karin Knorr Cetina and Alex Preda. New York: Oxford University Press.

Daft, Richard L., and Arie Y. Lewin. 1993. Where Are the Theories for the "New" Organizational Forms? An Editorial Essay. *Organization Science* 4: i–vi.

Daoud, Zakya. 1993a. Brève histoire de la politique de la ville. In *Banlieues... intégration ou explosion?*, edited by Catherine Wihtol de Wenden and Zakya Daoud. Special issue, *Panoramiques* 2 (12): 136–139.

——. 1993b. Le chomage? Brève histoire de la politique de la ville. In *Banlieues... intégration ou explosion?*, edited by Catherine Wihtol de Wenden and Zakya Daoud. Special issue, *Panoramiques* 2(12): 72–75.

——. 1993c. Mantes, ma jolie! In *Banlieues... intégration ou explosion?*, edited by Catherine Wihtol de Wenden and Zakya Daoud. Special issue, *Panoramiques* 2 (12): 25–28.

Davis, Mike. 1990. *City of Quartz.* London: Verso.

Dawson, Jonathan. 1992. The Relevance of Flexible Specialization Paradigm for Small-Scale Industrial Restructuring in Ghana. *DS Bulletin* 23 (2): 34–38.

De Boeck, Filip. 1998a. Beyond the Grave: History, Memory and Death in Postcolonial Congo/Zaire. In *Memory and the Postcolony: African Anthropology and the Critique of Power*, edited by Richard Werbner. London: Zed.

———. 1998b. Domesticating Diamonds and Dollars: Identity, Expenditure, and Sharing in Southwestern Zaire (1984–1997). *Development and Change* 29:777–810.

———. 2000. Borderland Breccia: The Mutant Hero in the Historical Imagination of a Central-African Diamond Frontier. *Journal of Colonialism and Colonial History* 1(2): http://muse.jhu.edu/journals/journal—of—colonialism—and—colonial—history/voo1/1.2boeck.html.

———. 2005. Children and Witchcraft in the Democratic Republic of Congo. In *Makers and Breakers: Children and Youth in Postcolonial Africa*, edited by Alcinda Honwana and Filip De Boeck. Oxford: James Currey.

De Garis, Laurence. 1999. Experiments in Pro Wrestling: Toward a Performative and Sensuous Sport Ethnography. *Sociology of Sport Journal* 16 (1): 65–74.

De Goede, Marieke. 2005. *Virtue, Fortune, and Faith: A Geneaology of Finance*. Minneapolis: University of Minnesota Press.

Deleuze, Gilles, and Felix Guattari. 1972/1983. *Anti-Oedipus: Capitalism and Schizophrenia*. Translated by Robert Hurley, Mark Seem, and Helen R. Lane. Minneapolis: University of Minnesota Press.

de Rudder, Véronique. 1992. Immigrant Housing and Integration in French Cities. In *Immigrants in Two Democracies: French and American Experience*, edited by Donald L. Horowitz and Gérard Noiriel. New York: New York University Press.

DeSanctis, Gerardine, and Peter Monge. 1999. Introduction. In *Communication Processes for Virtual Organizations*. Special issue, *Organization Science* 10 (6): 693–703.

Desplanques, Guy, and Nicole Tabard. 1991. La localisation de la population étrangère. *Economie et statistique* 242:51–62.

Devisch, René. 1996. Frenzy, Violence and Ethical Renewal in Kinshasa. *Public Culture* 7:593–629.

Diez, Fermin. 1980. The Popularity of Sports in America: An Analysis of the Values of Sports and Role of the Media. *Michigan Discussions in Anthropology* 6 (1): 161–165.

Dimock, Marshall Edward. 1968. *Japanese Technocracy: Management and Government in Japan*. New York: Walker/Weatherhill.

Diouf, Mamadou. 1996. Urban Youth and Senegalese Politics: Dakar 1988–1994. *Public Culture* 8 (2): 225–249.

———. 2000. The Senegalese Murid Trade Diaspora and the Making of Vernacular Cosmopolitanism. *Public Culture* 12 (3): 679–702.

Direche-Slimani, Karima. 1992. *Histoire de l'émigration kabyle en France au XXe siècle: Réalités culturelles et reappropriations identitaires*. Diplôme de troisième cycle, Université de Provence-Aix-Marseille.

Domhoff, G. William. 1974. *The Bohemian Grove and Other Retreats*. New York: Harper and Row.

Dore, Ronald. 1999. Japan's Reform Debate: Patriotic Concern or Class Interest? Or Both? *Journal of Japanese Studies* 25 (1): 65–89.

Douglas, Mary, and Aaron B. Wildavsky. 1982. *Risk and Culture: An Essay on the Selection of Technical and Environmental Dangers*. Berkeley: University of California Press.

Drucker, Peter. 1998. In Defense of Japanese Bureaucracy. *Foreign Affairs* 77 (5): 68–80.

Dubet, François, and Didier Lapeyronnie. 1987. *La galère: Jeunes en survie*. Paris: Seuil.

———. 1992. *Les quartiers d'exil*. Paris: Seuil.

Dubresson, Alain. 1997. Abidjan: From the Public Making of a Modern City to the Urban Management of a Metropolis. In *The Urban Challenge in Africa: Growth and Management of Its Large Cities*, edited by Carole Rakodi. Tokyo: United Nations University Press.

Dudley, William, ed. 1999. *Media Violence: Opposing Viewpoints*. San Diego: Greenhaven Press.

Duffield, Mark. 1998. Post-Modern Conflict: Warlords, Post-Adjustment States and Private Protection. *Civil Wars* 1(1): 66–102.

du Gay, Paul, and Michael Pryke, eds. 2002a. *Cultural Economy: Cultural Analysis and Commercial Life*. London: Sage.

——. 2002b. Cultural Economy: An Introduction. In *Cultural Economy: Cultural Analysis and Commercial Life*, edited by Paul du Gay and Michael Pryke. London: Sage.

Dunning, Eric, and Chris Rojek, eds. 1992. *Sport and Leisure in the Civilizing Process*. Toronto: University of Toronto Press.

Durand, Alain-Philippe, ed. 2002. *Black, Blanc, Beur: Rap Music and Hip Hop Culture in the Francophone World*. Lanham, Md.: Scarecrow.

Duret, Pascal. 1996. *Anthropologie de la fraternité dans les cités*. Paris: Presses Universitaires de France.

Eastman, Susan Tyler, and Timothy P. Meyer. 1989. Sports Programming: Scheduling, Costs, and Competition. In *Media, Sports, and Society*, edited by Lawrence A. Wenner. Newbury Park, Calif.: Sage.

Eccles, Robert, and Dwight Crane. 1988. *Doing Deals: Investment Banks at Work*. Cambridge, Mass.: Harvard Business School Press.

Eco, Umberto. 1986. *Travels in Hyperreality*. Translated by William Weaver. San Diego: Harcourt Brace Jovanovich.

Economic Commission for Africa. 1999. *Economic Report on Africa 1999: The Challenges of Poverty Reduction and Sustainability*. Addis Ababa, Ethiopia: Economic Commission for Africa.

Economic Development Institute/World Bank. 1998. Global Connectivity for Africa. Conference report. Addis Ababa, Ethiopia, June 2–4.

Egg, J., and H. J. Herera, eds. 1998. *Echanges Transfrontaliers et Integration Regional en Afrique Subsaharienne*. Paris: Eds. De L'Aube, ORSTOM.

Ehrenreich, Barbara. 1989. *Fear of Falling: The Inner Life of the Middle Class*. New York: Pantheon.

Eisen, George, and David Kenneth Wiggins. 1994. *Ethnicity and Sport in North American History*. Westport, Conn.: Greenwood Press.

Eisenbeis, Robert A. 1997. International Settlements: A New Source of Systemic Risk? *Federal Reserve Bank of Atlanta Economic Review* (2nd quarter): 44–50.

Elias, Norbert. 1971. The Genesis of Sport as a Sociological Problem. In *The Sociology of Sport*, edited by Eric Dunning. London: Frank Cass.

——. 1994. *The Civilizing Process*. Oxford: Blackwell.

Ellis, Stephen, and Janet MacGaffey. 1996. Research on Sub-Saharan Unrecorded International Trade: Some Methodological and Conceptual Problems. *African Studies Review* 39:10–41.

Elvin, Mark, and G. William Skinner, eds. 1972. *The Chinese City between Two Worlds.* Stanford: Stanford University Press.

Englund, Harri. 2002. The Village in the City, the City in the Village: Migrants in Lilongwe. *Journal of Southern African Studies* 28 (1): 137–159.

Ericson, Edward, Jr. 2001. Tough Guys: Ultimate Fighting Is a Battle for Bloody Glory. *Hartford Advocate* 28 (October 18–24): 16–19.

Espeland, Wendy. 1994. Legally Mediated Identities: The National Environmental Policy Act and the Bureaucratic Construction of Interests. *Law and Society Review* 28 (5): 1149–1179.

Fafchamps, Marcel. 1996. Market Emergence, Trust and Reputation. Working Paper, wopstanec 96016, Stanford University.

Fainstein, Susan. 1994. *City Builders: Property, Politics and Planning in London and New York.* Oxford: Basil Blackwell.

Fainstein, Susan, and David Gladstone. 1997. Tourism and Urban Transformations: Interpretations of Urban Tourism. In *Cities in Transformation—Transformation in Cities: Social and Symbolic Change of Urban Space,* edited by O. Källtorp et al. Aldershot, Hants, UK: Avebury.

Faloon, William D. 1998. *Market Maker: A Sesquicentennial Look at the Chicago Board of Trade.* Chicago: Board of Trade of the City of Chicago.

Farvacque-Vitkovic, Catherine, and Lucien Godin. 1998. *The Future of African Cities: Challenges and Priorities for Urban Development.* Washington, D.C.: World Bank.

Ferguson, James. 1990. *The Anti-politics Machine: Development, Depoliticization, and Bureaucratic Power in Lesotho.* Cambridge: Cambridge University Press.

——. 1999. *Expectations of Modernity: Myth and Meanings of Urban Life on the Zambian Copperbelt.* Berkeley: University of California Press.

Ferguson, Robert. 1998. Stand-Up Grappling and Close-Range Striking: A Prescription for Curing Brazilian Jujitsu's Biggest Ailments. *Black Belt Magazine,* December, http://www.blackbeltmag.com/archives/blackbelt/1998/dec98/stn.html (accessed July 19, 2002).

Ferrell, David. 1997. A Brutal Sport Fights for Its Life. *Los Angeles Times,* November 1, p. A1. Lexis-Nexis (accessed September 21, 2000).

Ferréol, Gilles, and Michel Autès. 1992. *Intégration et exclusion dans la société française contemporaine.* Lille: Presses Universitaires de Lille.

Fineman, Martha A. 1995. *The Neutered Mother, the Sexual Family and Other Twentieth Century Tragedies.* New York: Routledge.

Fischer, Claude S. 1992. *America Calling: A Social History of the Telephone to 1940.* Berkeley: University of California Press.

Fischer, Frank. 1990. *Technocracy and the Politics of Expertise.* Newbury Park, Calif.: Sage.

Fisher, Melissa. 2003. Wall Street Women: Gender, Culture and History in Global Finance. Ph.D. dissertation, Columbia University, Department of Anthropology.

——. 2004. Wall Street Women's "Herstories." In *Constructing Corporate America: History, Politics, Culture,* edited by Kenneth Lipartito and David Sicilia. New York: Oxford University Press.

——. 2005. Performing Business Anthropology in the New Consumer Economy. Paper presented at the Society for Applied Anthropology, Santa Fe, N.M.

Fitzpatrick, Eileen. 1994. Does New Vidmark Release Stand a "Fighting" Chance? *Bill-board* 106 (14): 57.

———. 1995. Wrestling Pinned as Video Contender. *Billboard* 107 (38): 88.

Fligstein, Neil. 1996. Markets as Politics: A Political-Cultural Approach to Market Institu-tions. *American Sociological Review* 61 (4): 656–673.

———. 2001. *The Architecture of Markets: An Economic Sociology of Twenty-First-Century Capitalist Societies.* Princeton, N.J.: Princeton University Press.

Fligstein, Neil, and Iona Mara-Drita. 1996. How to Make a Market: Reflections on the Attempt to Create a Single Market in the European Union. *American Journal of Sociology* 102 (1): 1–33.

Folkerts-Landau, David, Peter Garber, and Dirk Schoemaker. 1996. The Reform of Wholesale Payment Systems and Its Impact on Financial Markets. Occasional Paper 51. Washington, D.C.: Group of Thirty.

Fortun, Kim. 2001. *Advocacy after Bhopal: Environmentalism, Disaster, New Global Or-ders.* Chicago: University of Chicago Press.

Foster, Ed. 1997. Best Technical Support Award: Linux Community. *Infoworld*, http://ww1.infoworld.com/cgi-bin/displayTC.pl?97poy.supp.htm.

Foucault, Michel. 1976. *Mental Illness and Psychology.* Translated by Alan Sheridan. New York: Harper Colophon.

———. 1991. Governmentality. In *The Foucault Effect: Studies in Governmentality. With Two Lectures by and an Interview with Michel Foucault,* edited by Graham Burchell, Colin Gordon, and Peter Miller. London: Harvester Wheatsheaf.

Frank, Thomas. 2000. *One Market under God: Extreme Capitalism, Market Populism and the End of Economic Democracy.* London: Secker and Warburg.

Franks, Joel S. 2000. *Crossing Sidelines, Crossing Cultures: Sport and Asian Pacific Ameri-can Cultural Citizenship.* Lanham, Md.: University Press of America.

Freedman, Jonathan L. 2002. *Media Violence and Its Effects on Aggression: Assessing the Scientific Evidence.* Toronto: University of Toronto Press.

Friess, Steve. 2002. Homeless *Fight Club* Miffs Critics. *Wired News,* June 5, http://www.wired.com/news/culture/0,1284,52971,00.html.

Fussell, Paul. 1975. *The Great War and Modern Memory.* New York: Oxford University Press.

Gadrey, Jean. 2003. *New Economy, New Myth.* London: Routledge.

Gal, Susan. 1991. Bartok's Funeral: Representations of Europe in Hungarian Political Rhetoric. *American Ethnologist* 18(3): 440–458.

Gandel, Stephen. 2002. Women Losing out in Wall St. Downsizing: 20% Job Drop, Top Execs Disappearing. *Crain's New York Business* 18(41): 1, 41.

Gans, Herbert. 1962. *The Urban Villagers.* New York: Free Press.

Garcia, Linda. D. 2005. Cooperative Networks and the Rural-Urban Divide. In *Digital Formations: Information Technology and New Architectures in the Global Realm,* edited by Robert Latham and Saskia Sassen. Princeton, N.J.: Princeton University Press.

Garcia Herera, Luz Marina. 2001. Gentrification in Tenerife. Paper presented at the ISA Group 21 Conference, Amsterdam, June.

Garside, J. 1993. Inner-city Gentrification in South Africa: The Case of Woodstock, Cape Town. *GeoJournal* 30:29–35.

Garsten, Christina, and Monica Lindh De Montoya, eds. 2005. *Market Matters: Exploring Cultural Processes in the Global Market Place.* New York: Palgrave Macmillan.

Geertz, Clifford. 1960. *Peddlers and Princes.* Princeton, N.J.: Princeton University Press.

——. 1973. Deep Play: Notes on the Balinese Cockfight. In *The Interpretation of Cultures.* New York: Basic Books.

Geisst, Charles. 1997. *Wall Street: A History.* New York: Oxford University Press.

Gentry, Clyde, III. 2001. *No Holds Barred. Evolution: The Truth behind the World's Most Misunderstood Sport!* Richardson, Texas: Archon.

Gerth, H. H., and C. Wright Mills, eds. 1946. *From Max Weber.* New York: Oxford University Press.

Geschiere, Peter. 1997. *The Modernity of Witchcraft: Politics and the Occult in Postcolonial Africa.* Charlottesville: University Press of Virginia.

Gibbens, Robert. 2002. U.S. Women's Business Group Sets Up Quebec Chapter. *National Post* (Toronto), May 17, p. 1.

Giddens, Anthony. 1984. *The Constitution of Society.* Berkeley: University of California Press.

——. 1991. *Modernity and Self-Identity: Self and Society in the Late Modern Age.* Cambridge, England: Polity Press.

Gillis, John R. 1974. *Youth and History: Tradition and Change in European Age Relations, 1770–Present.* New York: Academic Press.

Gilroy, Paul. 1991. *"There Ain't No Black in the Union Jack": The Cultural Politics of Race and Nation.* Chicago: University of Chicago Press.

Ginzburg, Carlo. 1980. Morelli, Freud and Sherlock Holmes: Clues and Scientific Method. *History Workshop* 9:5–36.

Glaser, Barney G., and Anselm L. Strauss. 1967/1999. *The Discovery of Grounded Theory: Strategies for Qualitative Research.* New York: Aldine De Gruyter.

Glass, Ruth. 1964. *London: Aspects of Change.* London: Centre for Urban Studies/ MacGibbon and Kee.

Glick, Ira O. 1957. A Social Psychological Study of Futures Trading. Ph.D. dissertation. Department of Sociology, University of Chicago.

Glick Schiller, Nina, Linda Basch, and Cristina Szanton-Blanc. 1994. *Nations Unbound: Transnational Projects, Postcolonial Predicaments, and Deterritorialized Nation-States.* Langhorne, Penna.: Gordon and Breach.

Goffman, Erving. 1961. *Asylums: Essays on the Social Situation of Mental Patients and Other Inmates.* Garden City, N.Y.: Anchor Books.

——. 1983. The Interaction Order: American Sociological Association, 1982 Presidential Address. *American Sociological Review* 48 (1): 1–17.

Gold, Joel. 2001. The Time Has Come: The New Face of the UFC. *No Holds Barred News,* March 12, http://www.fcfighter.com/newstemplhtm (accessed March 18, 2001).

Goldstein, Jeffrey, ed. 1998. *Why We Watch: The Attractions of Violent Entertainment.* New York: Oxford University Press.

Goodall, Keith, and Willem Burgers. 1998. Frequent Fliers? Chinese Managers in a Turbulent Job-Market. China Europe International Business School, Shanghai, http://www.ceibs.edu/business—in—china/human—resource.

Gordon, Colin. 1991. Government Rationality: An Introduction. In *The Foucault Effect:*

Studies in Governmentality. With Two Lectures by and an Interview with Michel Foucault, edited by Graham Burchell, Colin Gordon, and Peter Miller. London: Harvester Wheatsheaf.

Graeber, David. 2002. The Anthropology of Globalization (with Notes on Neomedievalism, and the End of the Chinese Model of the Nation-State). Book review essay. *American Anthropologist* 104 (4): 1222–1227.

Granovetter, Mark. 1985. Economic Action and Social Structure: The Problem of Embeddedness. *American Journal of Sociology* 91 (3): 481–510.

Greenhouse, Carol J. 2002. Introduction: Altered States, Altered Lives. In *Ethnography in Unstable Places: Everyday Lives in Contexts of Dramatic Political Change*, edited by Carol J. Greenhouse, Elizabeth Mertz, and Kay B. Warren. Durham, N.C.: Duke University Press.

Gross, Josh. 2001. It's Unanimous: MMA Is Vegas Bound; UFC to Take Place September 28th at the Mandalay Bay. *Maxfighting.com*, July 24, http://www.maxfighting.com/Gross/gross—07–24–01.asp (accessed February 7, 2002).

Guilhaume, Jean-François. 1992. *Les mythes fondateurs de l'Algérie française*. Paris: Harmattan.

Guillaumont, Patrick, Silviane Guillaumont-Jeanneney, and Aristomène Varoudakis. 1995. *Economic Policy Reform and Growth Prospects in Emerging African Economies*. OECD Development Centre Technical Paper No. 145. Paris: OECD.

Gupta, Akhil. 1995. Blurred Boundaries: The Discourse of Corruption, the Culture of Politics, and the Imagined State. *American Ethnologist* 22 (2): 375–402.

Guthey, Eric. 2004. New Economy Romanticism: Narratives of Corporate Personhood, and the Antimanagerial Impulse. In *Constructing Corporate America: History, Politics, Culture*, edited by Kenneth Lipartito and David Sicilia. New York: Oxford University Press.

Guthrie, Douglas. 1998. The Declining Significance of *Guanxi* in China's Economic Transition. *China Quarterly* 154:31–62.

Guttmann, Allen. 1986. *Sports Spectators*. New York: Columbia University Press.

Haan, Hans. 1995. Informal Sector Associations in Africa. TOOLConsult Working Paper No. 1. Amsterdam: TOOLConsult, B.V.

Haas, Ernst. 1964. Technocracy, Pluralism and the New Europe. In *A New Europe?*, edited by Stephen R. Graubard. Boston: Houghton Mifflin.

——. 1968. *The Uniting of Europe: Political, Social, and Economic Forces, 1950–1957*. Stanford: Stanford University Press.

Hackworth, Jason. 2000. The Third Wave. Ph.D. dissertation, Rutgers University.

Hackworth, Jason, and Neil Smith. 2001. The State of Gentrification. *Tijdschrift voor Economische en Sociale Geografie* 92 (4): 464–477.

Hahnel, Robin. 1999. *Panic Rules! Everything You Need to Know about the Global Economy*. Cambridge, Mass.: South End Press.

Haley, John O. 1987. Governance by Negotiation: A Reappraisal of Bureaucratic Power in Japan. *Journal of Japanese Studies* 13 (2): 343–357.

Halfani, Mohamed. 1996. Marginality and Dynamism: Prospects for the Sub-Saharan African City. In *Preparing for the Urban Future: Global Pressures and Local Forces*, edited by Michael A. Cohen, Blair A. Ruble, and Joseph S. Tulchin, with Allison Garland. Washington, D.C.: Woodrow Wilson Center Press.

Hall of Fame: Royce Grace, 1994 Competitor of the Year. 1994. *Black Belt Magazine*, http://w3.blackbeltmag.com/halloffame/html/184.html (accessed July 7, 2002).

Hankiss, Elemér. 1988. The "Second Society": Is There an Alternative Social Model Emerging in Contemporary Hungary? *Social Research* 55 (1–2): 13–45.

Hannerz, Ulf. 1987. The World in Creolization. *Africa* 57 (4): 546–559.

——. 1989. Notes on the Global Ecumene. *Public Culture* 1 (2): 66–75.

——. 1990. Cosmopolitans and Locals in World Culture. In *Global Culture: Nationalism, Globalization, and Modernity*, edited by Mike Featherstone. London: Sage.

——. 2004. *Foreign News: Exploring the World of Foreign Correspondents*. Chicago: University of Chicago Press.

Hanson, Janet Tiebout. 2000. Broad's-EyeView. *Working Woman* (September): 64–70.

Hanson, Janet Tiebout, and Rebecca John. 2000. Cyberspace Mentors. Women Working 2000 + Beyond, http://www.womenworking2000.com/feature/index.php?id=42.

Haraway, Donna Jeanne. 1991. *Simians, Cyborgs, and Women: The Reinvention of Nature*. New York: Routledge.

——. 1997. *ModestWitness@SecondMillennium.FemaleManMeetsOncoMouse: Feminism and Technoscience*. New York: Routledge.

Harding, James. 1998. When Expats Should Pack Their Bags: Management Job Localization. *Financial Times* (U.S. ed.), September 1.

Hardt, Michael, and Antonio Negri. 2000. *Empire*. Cambridge, Mass.: Harvard University Press.

Hargreaves, Alec. 1995. *Immigration, "Race," and Ethnicity in Contemporary France*. London: Routledge.

Hargreaves, Jennifer. 1992. Sex, Gender and the Body in Sport and Leisure: Has There Been a Civilizing Process? In *Sport and Leisure in the Civilizing Process*, edited by Eric Dunning and Chris Rojek. Toronto: University of Toronto Press.

Harootunian, Harry D. 2000. *Overcome by Modernity: History, Culture, and Community in Interwar Japan*. Princeton, N.J.: Princeton University Press.

Harrison, Bennett. 1994. *Lean and Mean: The Changing Landscape of Corporate Power in the Age of Flexibility*. New York: Basic Books.

Hart, Keith. 1988. Kinship, Contract and Trust: The Economic Organization of Migrants in an African City Slum. In *Trust: The Making and Breaking of Cooperative Relations*, edited by Diego Gambetta. London: Basil Blackwell.

——. 2001. *Money in an Unequal World*. New York: Texere.

Harts-Broekhuis, Annelet. 1997. How to Sustain a Living: Urban Households and Poverty in a Sahelian Town of Mopti, Africa. *Africa* 67 (1): 106–131.

Harvey, David. 1989. *The Condition of Post-Modernity: An Enquiry into the Origins of Cultural Change*. Cambridge, Mass.: Blackwell.

Hashim, Yahaya, and Kate Meagher. 2000. Cross Border Trade and the Parallel Currency Market: Trade and Finance in the Context of Structural Adjustment. Research Report 113. Uppsala, Sweden: Nordic Africa Institute.

Haugerud, Angelique, M. Priscilla Stone, and Peter D. Little, eds. 2000. *Commodities and Globalization: Anthropological Perspectives*. Lanham, Md.: Rowman and Littlefield.

Haveman, Heather A., and Hayagreeva Rao. 1997. Structuring a Theory of Moral Sentiments: Institutional and Organizational Co-evolution in the Early Thrift Industry. *American Journal of Sociology* 102 (6): 1606–1651.

Hayek, Friedrich August von. 1952. *The Counter-revolution of Science*. Glencoe, Ill.: Free Press.

——. 1975. *The Rule of Law*. Menlo Park, Calif.: Institute for Human Studies.

He Qinglian. 1997. *China's Pitfall*. Hong Kong: Mingjing Chubanshe.

——. 2000. China's Listing Social Structure. *New Left Review* 5 (September–October): 69–100.

Hebdige, Dick. 1988. *Hiding in the Light: On Images and Things*. London: Routledge.

Heelas, Paul. 2002. Work Ethics, Soft Capitalism and the "Turn to Life." In *Cultural Economy*, edited by Paul du Gay and Michael Pyrke. London: Sage.

Hein, Laura. 2003. Statistics for Democracy: Economics as Politics in Occupied Japan. *positions: east asia cultures critique* 11 (3): 765–778.

Held, David, Anthony G. McGrew, David Goldblatt, and Jonathan Perraton. 1999. *Global Transformations: Politics, Economics, and Culture*. Stanford: Stanford University Press.

Henricks, Thomas. 1974. Professional Wrestling as Moral Order. *Sociological Inquiry* 44(3): 177–188.

Henwood, Doug. 2003. *After the New Economy*. New York: New Press.

Hertz, Ellen. 1998. *The Trading Crowd: An Ethnography of the Shanghai Stock Market*. New York: Cambridge University Press.

Herzfeld, Michael. 1993. *The Social Production of Indifference: Exploring the Symbolic Roots of Western Bureaucracy*. Chicago: University of Chicago Press.

——. 1997. *Cultural Intimacy: Social Poetics in the Nation-State*. London: Routledge.

Heydebrand, Wolf W. 1989. New Organizational Forms. *Work and Occupations* 16: 323–357.

Hibou, Béatice. 1999. The Social Capital of the State as an Agent of Deception. In *The Criminalization of the State in Africa*, edited by Jean François Bayart, Stephen Ellis, and Béatice Hibou. London: James Currey/Indiana University Press.

Hoberman, John M. 1984. *Sport and Political Ideology*. Austin: University of Texas Press.

Hobsbawm, Eric J. 1962. *The Age of Revolution, 1789–1848*. New York: New American Library.

Hoffman, Lisa. 2000. The Art of Becoming an Urban Professional: The State, Gender, and Subject Formation in "Late-Socialist" China. Ph.D. dissertation, Department of Anthropology, University of California at Berkeley.

Holland, Heidi. 1989. *The Struggle: A History of the African National Congress*. New York: G. Braziller.

Holmes, Douglas R. 1993. Illicit Discourse. In *Perilous States: Conversations on Culture, Politics and Nation*, edited by George E. Marcus. Chicago: University of Chicago Press.

——. 2000. *Integral Europe: Fast-Capitalism, Multiculturalism, Neofascism*. Princeton, N.J.: Princeton University Press.

Holmes, Douglas R., and George E. Marcus. 2005a. Cultures of Expertise and the Management of Globalization: Toward the Re-functioning of Ethnography. In *Global Assemblages*, edited by Aihwa Ong and Stephen J. Collier. Oxford: Blackwell.

——. 2005b. Refunctioning Ethnography: The Challenge of an Anthropology of the Contemporary. In *Handbook of Qualitative Research*, 3rd ed., edited by Norman Denizen and Yvonna Lincoln. Thousand Oaks, Calif.: Sage.

Honwana, Alcinda. 1999. Negotiating Post-War Identities: Child Soldiers in Mozambique and Angola. *CODESRIA Bulletin* (1/2): 4–13.

Hopkins, Anthony G. 1973. *An Economic History of West Africa*. New York: Columbia University Press.

Howe, Neil, and William Strauss. 2000. *Millennials Rising: The Next Great Generation*. New York: Vintage Books.

Hull, John C. 1997. *Options, Futures, and Other Derivatives*. Upper Saddle River, N.J.: Prentice Hall.

Humphrey, John. 1995. Industrial Reorganization in Developing Countries: From Models to Trajectories. *World Development* 23 (1): 149–162.

Hutchings, Kimberly, and Roland Dannreuther. 1999. *Cosmopolitan Citizenship*. New York: St. Martin's Press.

Hutton, Will, and Anthony Giddens, eds. 2001. *On the Edge: Living with Global Capitalism*. New York: Verso.

Inda, Jonathan Xavier, and Renato Rosaldo, eds. 2001. *The Anthropology of Globalization: A Reader*. Malden, Mass.: Blackwell.

Institut National de la Statistique et des Etudes Economiques. 1992. *Recensement de la population de 1990: Nationalités, résultats du sondage au quart*. Paris: INSEE.

Is There a Private Global Central Bank in Your Future? 1997. *American Banker*, May 12.

Ivy, Marilyn 1995. *Discourses of the Vanishing: Modernity, Phantasm, Japan*. Chicago: University of Chicago Press.

Jackall, Robert. 1988. *Moral Mazes: The World of Corporate Managers*. New York: Oxford University Press.

Jamal, Vali, and John Weeks. 1993. *Africa Misunderstood, or, Whatever Happened to the Rural-Urban Gap?* Basingstoke, England: Macmillan.

Jameson, Fredric. 1991. *Postmodernism, or, the Cultural Logic of Late Capitalism*. Durham, N.C.: Duke University Press.

——. 1997. Culture and Finance Capital. *Critical Inquiry* 24:246–265.

Jean-Klein, Iris E. F. 2002. Alternative Modernities, or Accountable Modernities? The Palestinian Movement(s) and Political (Audit) Tourism during the First Intifada. *Journal of Mediterranean Studies* 12 (1): 43–80.

Jenkins, Craig J. 1977. Radical Transformation of Organizational Goals. *Administrative Science Quarterly* 22 (4): 568–586.

Jensen, Mike. 1999. The Status of African Information Infrastructure. Paper presented at the first meeting of the Committee on Development Information (CODI), Economic Commission for Africa, Addis Ababa, Ethiopia, June 28–July 2.

Johnson, Ana Gutierrez, and William Foote Whyte. 1977. The Mondragon System of Worker Production Cooperatives. *Industrial Labor Relations Review* 31:18–30.

Johnson, Justin Pappas. 2001. Economics of Open Source Software. Working paper, Open Source Research Community, http://opensource.mit.edu/papers/johnson opensource.pdf.

Johnson, Omotunde E. G. 1998. *Payment Systems, Monetary Policy, and the Role of the Central Bank*. Washington, D.C.: International Monetary Fund.

Jones, Gareth A., and Ann Varley. 1999. The Reconquest of the Historic Centre: Urban Conservation and Gentrification in Puebla, Mexico. *Environment and Planning A* 31:1547–1566.

Jones, Gareth Stedman. 1971/1984. *Outcast London: A Study in the Relationship between Classes in Victorian Society*. New York: Pantheon.

Jorgenson, Dale W. 2001. Information Technology and the U.S. Economy. *American Economic Review* 91 (1): 1–32.

Joseph, May. 1999. *Nomadic Identities: The Performance of Citizenship*. Minneapolis: University of Minnesota Press.

Kafka, Peter. 2002. Brothers in Arms. *Forbes Magazine*, November 11, http://www.forbes.com/forbes/2002/1111/154.html.

Kahn, Charles M., and William Roberds. 1998. Federal Reserve Bank of Atlanta: Real-Time Gross Settlement and the Costs of Immediacy. Working Paper 98–21, Federal Reserve Bank of Atlanta.

Kanji, Nazneen. 1995. Gender, Poverty and Economic Adjustment in Harare, Zimbabwe. *Environment and Urbanization* 7:37–55.

Kanter, Rosabeth Moss. 1977. *Men and Women of the Corporation*. New York: Basic Books.

Kaufman, George G. 1996. Comment by George G. Kaufman. *Journal of Money, Credit, and Banking* 28 (4): 825–831.

Kaufman, Henry. 2000. *On Money and Markets: A Wall Street Memoir*. New York: McGraw Hill.

Kelley, Robin D. G. 1996. Kickin' Reality, Kickin' Ballistics: Gangsta Rap and Postindustrial Los Angeles. In *Droppin' Science: Critical Essays on Rap Music and Hip Hop Culture*, edited by William Eric Perkins. Philadelphia: Temple University Press.

——. 1997. *Yo' Mama's Disfunktional! Fighting the Culture Wars in Urban America*. Boston: Beacon Press.

Kelly, William. 1986. Rationalization and Nostalgia: Cultural Dynamics of New Middle-Class Japan. *American Ethnologist* 13(4): 603–618.

Kelsall, Tim. 2000. Subjectivity, Collective Action and the Governance Agenda in Animeru East (Tanzania). Queen Elizabeth House Working Paper QEHWPS42. Oxford University, Oxford, England.

Kendall, Leon T. 1996. Securitization: A New Era in American Finance. In *A Primer on Securitization*, edited by Leon T. Kendall and Michael J. Fishman. Cambridge, Mass.: MIT Press.

Kenny, Charles. 1998. Senegal and the Entropy Theory of Development. *European Journal of Development Research* 10 (1): 160–188.

Kiesler, Sara, Jane Siegel, and Timothy W. McGuire. 1984. Social Psychological Aspects of Computer-Mediated Communication. *American Psychologist* 39 (10): 1123–1124.

King, Anthony D., ed. 1997. *Culture, Globalization and the World-System*. Minneapolis: University of Minnesota Press.

King, Kenneth. 1996. *Jua Kali Kenya: Change and Development in an Informal Economy*. London: Villiers.

King, Rodney. n.d. The Evolution of NHB: What You Need to Know. *Grapplers' World*, http://www.grapplersworld.com/nhb—drive—thru3.thm (accessed April 11, 2001).

Klatell, David A., and Norman Marcus. 1988. *Sports for Sale: Television, Money, and the Fans.* New York: Oxford University Press.

Klein, Naomi. 2000. *No Logo: Taking Aim at the Brand Bullies.* Toronto: Knopf Canada.

Knight, Frank. 1922/1971. *Risk, Uncertainty and Profit.* Chicago: University of Chicago Press.

Knorr Cetina, Karin, and Urs Bruegger. 2000. The Market as an Object of Attachment: Exploring Post-Social Relations in Financial Markets. *Canadian Journal of Sociology* 25 (2): 141–168.

——. 2002a. Global Microstructures: The Virtual Societies of Financial Markets. *American Journal of Sociology* 107 (4): 905–950.

——. 2002b. Traders' Engagement with Markets: A Postsocial Relationship. *Theory, Culture and Society* 19 (5/6): 161–185.

Kodres, Laura E. 1996. Foreign Exchange Markets: Structure and Systemic Risks. *Finance and Development* 33 (4): 22.

Koh, B. C. (Byung Chul). 1989. *Japan's Administrative Elite.* Berkeley: University of California Press.

Kolker, Robert. 2003. Down and Out on Wall Street. *New York Magazine,* March 17, 22–28.

Kole, Ellen. 2000. Topics for the AFTIDEV Electronic Debate on ICT Transfer to Africa. Africa, Technology, Information and Development, http://www.aftidev.net/en/ressources/documents/html/kole.html.

Kondo, Dorinne K. 1990. *Crafting Selves: Power, Gender and Discourses of Identity in a Japanese Workplace.* Chicago: University of Chicago Press.

Koschmann, Victor J. 2002. Tekunorojii no shihai/shihai no tekunorojii (Rule by technology, technologies of rule). In *Sāryokusenka no chi to seido, 1935–55* (Knowledge and Institutions Under National War Mobilization) (Iwanami kôza kindai Nihon no bunkashi 7), 7–1, Juanami, Modern Japanese Cultural History Series, edited by Komori Yôichi, Sakai Naoki, Shimazono Susumu, Nanta Ryjhcki, Chino Kaon, and Yashim Shun'ya. Tokyo: Iwanami Shoten.

KPMG Consulting. 2000. The Impact of the New Economy on Poor People in Developing Countries. A report for the Department of International Development, United Kingdom, July 7.

Kynaston, David. 1997. *LIFFE: A Market and Its Makers.* Cambridge, England: Granta Editions.

Laakso, Liisa, and Adebayo Olukoshi. 1996. The Crisis of the Post-Colonial Nation-State Project in Africa. In *Challenges to the Nation State in Africa,* edited by Adebayo Olukoshi and Liisa Laakso. Uppsala, Sweden: Nordic Africa Institute/Helskinki Institute of Development Studies.

Lakhani, Karim, and Eric von Hippel. 2000. How Open Source Software Works: "Free" User-to-User Assistance. Unpublished manuscript, MIT Sloan School of Management, Cambridge, Mass.

Lakhani, Karim R., and Robert G. Wolf. 2005. Why Hackers Do What They Do: Understanding Motivation and Effort in Free/Open Source Software Projects. In *Perspec-*

tives on Free and Open Source Software, edited by Joseph Feller, Brian Fitzgerald, Scott A. Hissam and Karim R. Lakhani. Cambridge, Mass.: MIT Press.

Lane, Randall. 1995. It's Live, It's Brutal. *Forbes* 155 (11): 48.

Lanfranchi, Pierre. 1994. The Migration of Footballers: The Case of France, 1932–1982. In *The Global Sports Arena: Athletic Talent Migration in an Interdependent World*, edited by John Bale and Joseph Maguire. London: Frank Cass.

Lapassade, Georges, and Philippe Rousselot. 1990. *Le rap, ou le fureur de dire*. Paris: Loris Talmart.

Larkin, Brian. 2002. Bandiri Music, Globalization, and Urban Experience in Nigeria. *Cahiers D'Etudes Africaines* 168:739–762.

Lash, Scott, and John Urry. 1994. *Economies of Signs and Space*. London: Sage.

Latham, Robert, and Saskia Sassen. 2005. Introduction: Digital Formations: Constructing an Object of Study. In *Digital Formations: Information Technology and New Architectures in the Global Realm*, edited by Robert Latham and Saskia Sassen. Princeton, N.J.: Princeton University Press.

Latour, Bruno. 1987. *Science in Action: How to Follow Scientists and Engineers through Society*. Cambridge, Mass.: Harvard University Press.

——. 1988. Drawing Things Together. In *Representation in Scientific Practice*, edited by Michael Lynch and Steve Woolgar. Cambridge, Mass.: MIT Press.

——. 1993. *We Have Never Been Modern*. Translated by Catherine Porter. Cambridge, Mass.: Harvard University Press.

——. 1996. *Aramis, or, The Love of Technology*. Cambridge, Mass.: Harvard University Press.

Leadbeater, Charles. 1999. *Living on Thin Air: The New Economy*. Harmondsworth, England: Viking.

Lebra, Takie Sugiyama. 1984. *Japanese Women: Constraint and Fulfillment*. Honolulu: University of Hawaii Press.

Lee, Benjamin, and Edward LiPuma. 2002. Cultures of Circulation: The Imaginations of Modernity. *Public Culture* 14 (1): 191–213.

Lee, Gwendolyn K., and Robert E. Cole. 2003. From a Firm-Based to a Community-Based Model of Knowledge: The Case of the Linux Kernel Development. *Organization Science* 14 (6): 633–649.

Lees, Loretta, and Liz Bondi. 1995. De-Gentrification and Economic Recession: The Case of New York City. *Urban Geography* 16:234–253.

Lefebvre, Henri. 1970. *La Revolution Urbaine*. Paris: Gallimard.

Lemarchand, René. 1997. Patterns of State Collapse and Reconstruction in Central Africa: Reflections on the Great Lakes Region. *Afrika Spectrum* 32:173–194.

Lépinay, Vincent-Antonin. 2002. Finance as Circulating Formulas. Paper presented at the New York Conference on Social Studies of Finance, Columbia University, May 3–4.

Lerner, Josh, and Jean Tirole. 2002. Some Simple Economics of Open Source. *Journal of Industrial Economics* 50 (June 2002): 197–234.

Levin, Carol E., Marie T. Ruel, Saul S. Morris, Daniel G. Maxwell, Margaret Armar-Klemensu, and Clement Ahiadeke. 1999. Working Women in an Urban Setting: Traders, Vendors, and Food Security in Accra. *World Development* 27 (11): 1977–1996.

Lewellen, Ted C. 2002. *The Anthropology of Globalization: Cultural Anthropology Enters the 21st Century*. Westport, Conn.: Bergin and Garvey.

Ley, David. 1992. Gentrification in Recession: Social Change in Six Canadian Inner Cities, 1981–1986. *Urban Geography* 13:230–256.

Leyshon, Andrew, and Nigel Thrift. 1997. *Money/Space: Geographies of Monetary Transformation*. London: Routledge.

Liauzu, Claude. 1996. *Histoire des migrations en méditerranée occidentale*. Brussels: Editions Complexe.

Lincoln, Bruce. 1989. *Discourse and the Construction of Society*. Oxford: Oxford University Press.

Lipartito, Ken, and David Sicilia, eds. 2004. *Constructing Corporate America: History, Politics, Culture*. New York: Oxford University Press.

Lipgens, Walter. 1985. *Continental Plans for European Union 1939–1945*. Vol. 1 of *Documents on the History of European Integration*. Berlin: Walter de Gruyter.

Liu, Xin. 2002. *The Otherness of Self: A Genealogy of the Self in Contemporary China*. Ann Arbor: University of Michigan Press.

Liu Binyan and Perry Link. 1998. A Great Leap Backward? Review of *Zhongguo de Xianjing* [*China's Pitfall*] by He Qinglian. *New York Review of Books*, October 8.

Lodge, Tom. 1983. *Black Politics in South Africa Since 1945*. London: Longman.

Löfgren, Ovar. 2003. The New Economy: A Cultural History. *Global Networks* 3 (3): 239–254.

Lorcin, Patricia M. E. 1995. *Imperial Identities: Stereotyping, Prejudice and Race in Colonial Algeria*. London: I.B. Tauris.

Lowenstein, Roger. 2000. *When Genius Failed: The Rise and Fall of Long-Term Capital Management*. New York: Random House.

Lukose, Ritty. 2000. Learning Modernity: Youth Culture in Kerala, South India. Ph.D. dissertation, University of Chicago.

MacClancy, Jeremy, ed. 1996. *Sport, Identity and Ethnicity*. London: Berg.

MacGaffey, Janet, and Remy Bazenguissa-Ganga. 2000. *Congo-Paris: Transnational Traders on the Margins of the Law*. International African Institute in association with Bloomington: Indiana University Press/James Currey.

MacKenzie, Donald. 2001. Physics and Finance: S-Terms and Modern Finance as a Topic for Science Studies. *Science, Technology and Human Values* 26 (2): 115–144.

——. 2003. An Equation and Its Worlds: Bricolage, Exemplars, Disunity and Performativity in Financial Economics. *Social Studies of Science* 33 (6): 831–868.

MacKenzie, Donald, and Yuval Millo. 2001. Negotiating a Market, Performing Theory: The Historical Sociology of a Financial Derivatives Exchange. Paper presented at the European Association for Evolutionary Political Economy, Siena, Italy.

MacKenzie, Donald, and Judy Wajcman. 1999. Introductory Essay: The Social Shaping of Technology. In *The Social Shaping of Technology*, 2nd ed., edited by Donald MacKenzie and Judy Wajcman. Buckingham, England: Open University Press.

Macmaster, Neil. 1993. Patterns of Emigration, 1905–1954: "Kabyles" and "Arabs." In *French and Algerian Identities from Colonial Times to the Present*, edited by Alec Hargreaves and Michael J. Hefferman. Lewiston, N.Y.: Edwin Mellen Press.

Magdalinski, Tara, and Timothy J. L. Chandler. 2002. With God on Their Side: An Introduction. In *With God on Their Side: Sport in the Service of Religion*, edited by Tara Magdalinski and Timothy J. L. Chandler. London: Routledge.

Maguire, Joseph, and Frank Bale. 1994. Introduction: Sports Labour Migration in the Global Arena. In *The Global Sports Arena: Athletic Talent Migration in an Interdependent World*, edited by John Bale and Joseph Maguire. London: Frank Cass.

Mahieu, François Régis. 1995. Variable Dimension Adjustment in the Côte D'Ivoire: Reasons for Failure. *Review of African Political Economy* 22 (63): 9–26.

Malefyt, Timothy deWaal, and Brian Moeran. 2003. Introduction: Advertising Cultures— Advertising, Ethnography, and Anthropology. In *Advertising Cultures*, edited by Timothy Malefyt and Brian Moeran. Oxford: Berg.

Malkiel, Burton Gordon. 1996. *A Random Walk down Wall Street*. New York: Norton.

Malone, Thomas W., and Robert J. Laubacher. 1998. The Dawn of the E-Lance Economy. *Harvard Business Review* (September–October): 145–152.

Manning, Peter K., and Mahendra P. Singh. 1997. Violence and Hyperviolence: The Rhetoric and Practice of Community Policing. *Sociological Spectrum* 17 (3): 339–361.

Marcus, George E. 1983. *Elites: Ethnographic Issues*. Albuquerque: University of New Mexico Press.

——. 1995. *Technoscientific Imaginaries: Conversations, Profiles and Memoirs*. Chicago: University of Chicago Press.

——, ed. 1998a. *Corporate Futures: The Diffusion of the Culturally Sensitive Corporate Form*. Chicago: University of Chicago Press.

——. 1998b. Introduction. In *Corporate Futures: The Diffusion of the Culturally Sensitive Corporate Form*, edited by George E. Marcus. Chicago: University of Chicago Press.

——. 1999a. Critical Anthropology Now: An Introduction. In *Critical Anthropology Now: Unexpected Contexts, Shifting Constituencies, Changing Agendas*, edited by George E. Marcus. Santa Fe, N.M.: School of American Research Press.

——. 1999b. *Ethnography through Thick and Thin*. Princeton, N.J.: Princeton University Press.

——. 1999c. What Is At Stake—and Not—in the Idea and Practice of Multi-Sited Ethnography. *Canberra Anthropology* 22 (2): 6–14.

——. 2001. From Rapport under Erasure to the Theater of Complicit Reflexivities. *Qualitative Inquiry* 7:519–528.

——. 2002a. Beyond Malinowski and after *Writing Culture*: On the Future of Cultural Anthropology and the Predicament of Ethnography. *Australian Journal of Anthropology* 13:191–199.

——. 2002b. On the Problematic Contemporary Reception of Ethnography as the Stimulus for Innovations in Its Forms and Norms in Teaching and Research. *Anthropological Journal on European Cultures* 11:191–206.

——. 2003. The Unbearable Slowness of Being an Anthropologist Now: Notes on a Contemporary Anxiety in the Making of Ethnography. *Xcp* 12:7–20.

Marcuse, Herbert. 1964. *One Dimensional Man: Studies in the Ideology of Advanced Industrial Society*. Boston: Beacon Press.

Marks, John. 1997. Whatever It Takes to Win. *U.S. News and World Report* 122 (February 24): 46.

Martin, Emily. 1995. *Flexible Bodies*. Boston: Beacon Press.

Martin, Randy. 1999. Globalization? The Dependencies of a Question, *Social Text* 17 (3): 1–14.

Martin, Randy, and Toby Miller. 1999. *SportCult*. Minneapolis: University of Minnesota Press.

Marx, Karl. 1967. *Capital: A Critique of Political Economy*. Vol. 1. New York: International Publishers.

Marx, Karl, and Friedrich Engels. 1848/1978. Manifesto of the Communist Party. In *The Marx-Engels Reader*, by Robert C. Tucker. New York: Norton.

Maurer, Bill. 1995. Complex Subjects: Offshore Finance, Complexity Theory, and the Dispersion of the Modern. *Socialist Review* 25:113–145.

——. 1999. Forget Locke? From Proprietor to Risk-Bearer in New Logics of Finance. *Public Culture* 11:47–67.

——. 2002a. Anthropological and Accounting Knowledge in Islamic Banking and Finance: Rethinking Critical Accounts. *Journal of the Royal Anthropological Institute* 8:645–667.

——. 2002b. Repressed Futures: Financial Derivatives' Theological Unconscious. *Economy and Society* 31 (1): 15–36.

——. 2005. Introduction to "Ethnographic Emergences." *American Anthropologist* 107 (1): 1–4.

Mauss, Marcel. 1935/1973. Techniques of the Body. Trans. B. Brewster. *Economy and Society* 2 (1): 70–87.

Mayhew, Henry. 1851. *London Labour and the London Poor: A Cyclopaedia of the Condition of Those that Will Work, Those that Cannot Work, and Those that Will not Work*. Vol. 1. London: G. Woodfall.

McAdam, Doug. 1995. "Initiator" and "Spin-off" Movements: Diffusion Processes in Protest Cycles. In *Repertoires and Cycles of Collective Action*, by Mark Traugott. Durham, N.C.: Duke University Press.

McCarthy, Helen. 2004. *Girlfriends in High Places: How Women's Networks Are Changing the Workplace*. London: Demos.

McCarthy, John D., and Mayer N. Zald. 1977. Resource Mobilization and Social Movements: A Partial Theory. *American Journal of Sociology* 82 (6): 1212–1241.

McChesney, Robert W. 1998. The Political Economy of Global Communications. In *Capitalism and the Information Age: The Political Economy of the Global Communication Revolution*, edited by Robert W. McChesney, Ellen Meiksins Wood, and John Bellamy Foster. New York: Monthly Review Press.

McConnell, Scot. 1999. A Champion in Our Midst: Lessons Learned from the Impacts of NGOs' Use of the Internet. TeleCommons Development Group, http://www.telecommons.com.

McCormick, Dorothy. 1998. Enterprise Clusters in Africa: On the Way to Industrialisation? IDS Discussion Paper 366. Sussex, England: Institute of Development Studies.

McCulloch, Neil, Milasoa Cherel-Robson, and Bob Baulch. 2000. Growth, Inequality and Poverty in Mauritania 1987–1996. Working paper of the Poverty Dynamics in Africa Program. Washington, D.C.: World Bank.

McDowell, Christopher, and Arjan de Haan. 1998. Migration and Sustainable Livelihoods: A Critical Review of the Literature. IDS Working Paper 65. Sussex, England: Institute of Development Studies.

McDowell, Jim. 1996. Extreme Controversy and Violence. *Alberta Report, Newsmagazine* 23 (May 13): 35.

McDowell, Linda. 1997. *Capital Culture: Gender at Work in the City*. Oxford: Blackwell.

McEachern, Tim, and Chris O'Brien. 2002. The New New Economy. New York, AMACOM.

McKinley, Brunson. 2000. Statement of Brunson McKinley, Director General, International Organization for Migration in Africa. Globalization and Prospects for Regional Mechanisms Conference, Addis Ababa, Ethiopia, October 18.

McLean, Bethany. 2000. Inside the World's Weirdest Family Business. *Fortune* 142 (October 16): 292–312.

McRobbie, Angela. 2002. From Holloway to Hollywood: Happiness at Work in the New Cultural Economy? In *Cultural Economy*, edited by Paul du Gay and Michael Pyre. London: Sage.

McVeigh, Brian J. 1998. *The Nature of the Japanese State: Rationality and Rituality*. London: Routledge.

Meli, Francis. 1989. *A History of the ANC: South Africa Belongs to Us*. Bloomington: Indiana University Press.

Metcalf, Peter. 2001. Global "Disjuncture" and the "Sites" of Anthropology. *Cultural Anthropology* 16 (2): 165–182.

Meyer, Laurence H. 2004. *A Term at the Fed: An Insider's Account: People and Politics in the World's Most Powerful Institution*. New York: HarperCollins.

Meynaud, Jean. 1969. *Technocracy*. New York: Free Press.

Mhone, Guy C. Z. 1995. *The Impact of Structural Adjustment on the Urban Informal Sector in Zimbabwe*. Geneva: International Labor Office.

Michels, Robert. 1949. *Political Parties: A Sociological Study of the Oligarchical Tendencies of Modern Democracy*. Glencoe, Ill.: Free Press.

Michigan Judge Refuses to Enjoin Ultimate Fighting Challenge. 1996. *Entertainment Litigation Reporter*, June 30, Lexis-Nexis (accessed April 8, 2001).

Mignolo, Walter D. 2000. The Many Faces of Cosmo-polis: Border Thinking and Critical Cosmopolitanism. *Public Culture* 12 (3): 721–748.

Mikuni, Akio, and R. Taggart Murphy. 2002. *Japan's Policy Trap: Dollars, Deflation, and the Crisis of Japanese Finance*. Washington, D.C.: Brookings Institution Press.

Miles, Raymond E., and Charles C. Snow. 1986. Organizations: New Concepts for New Forms. *California Management Review* 28 (3): 62–73.

Miller, Daniel. 1998. Conclusion: A Theory of Virtualism. In *Virtualism: A New Political Economy*, edited by James G. Carrier and Daniel Miller. Oxford: Berg.

Miller, Peter. 1998. The Margins of Accounting. In *The Laws of the Markets*, edited by Michael Callon. Oxford: Blackwell.

Millo, Yuval, Fabian Muniesa, Nikiforos S. Panourgias, and Susan V. Scott. 2003. *Detaching Trades: Clearing and Settlement as a Calculative Space*. Paper presented at the Constance Conference on Social Studies of Finance, Constance, Switzerland, May 16–18.

Mills, C. Wright. 1956. *The Power Elite*. New York: Oxford University Press.

Mills, David. 1990. The Gangsta Rapper: Violent Hero or Negative Role Model? *The Source* 16 (December): 32.

Misser, François, and Olivier Vallée. 1997. *Les gemmocraties: L'economie politique du diamant africain.* Paris: Desclee de Brouwer.

Mitchell, Timothy. 1988. *Colonising Egypt.* Cambridge: Cambridge University Press.

———. 2002. *Rule of Experts: Egypt, Techno-politics, Modernity.* Berkeley: University of California Press.

Mitullah, Winnie V. 1996. Collective Efficiency in the Fish Industry: Lesson from Uhanya Beach Census. IDS Working Paper No. 509. Nairobi, Kenya: Insitute for Development Studies, University of Nairobi.

Miyazaki, Hirokazu. 2003. The Temporalities of the Market. *American Anthropologist* 105 (2): 255–265.

Miyazaki, Hirokazu, and Annelise Riles. 2005. Failure as an Endpoint. In *Global Assemblages: Technology, Politics, and Ethics as Anthropological Problems,* edited by Aihwa Ong and Stephen J. Collier. Malden, Mass.: Blackwell.

Mkandawire, Thandika. 1999. The Political Economy of Financial Reform in Africa. *Journal of International Development* 11 (3): 321–347.

Molla, Alemayehu. 2000. *Africa and the Information Economy: Foundations, Opportunities, Challenges and Research Agenda.* Addis Ababa, Ethiopia: United Nations Economic Commission for Africa.

Monga, Célestin. 1996. *The Anthropology of Anger: Civil Society and Democracy in Africa.* Boulder, Colo.: Lynne Rienner.

Monnet, Jean. 1978. *Jean Monnet: Memoirs.* Translated by Richard Mayne. Garden City, N.Y.: Doubleday.

Moody, Glyn. 2001. *Rebel Code: Inside Linux and the Open Source Revolution.* New York: HarperCollins.

Moon, Jae Yun, and Lee Sproull. 2002. Essence of Distributed Work: The Case of the Linux Kernel. In *Distributed Work,* edited by Pamela Hinds and Sara Kiesler. Cambridge, Mass.: MIT Press.

Moore, Robert. E. 2003. From Generic to Viral Marketing: On "Brand." *Language and Communications* 23:331–357.

Morris-Suzuki, Tessa. 1994. *The Technological Transformation of Japan: From the Seventeenth to the Twenty-first Century.* Cambridge: Cambridge University Press.

Moser, Caroline, and Jeremy Holland. 1997. Confronting Crisis in Chawama, Lusaka, Zambia: Household Responses to Poverty and Vulnerability. Urban Management Policy Paper No. 24, United Nations Development Programme, United Nations Centre for Human Settlements, World Bank.

Municipal Development Program. 1998. Pour une gestion efficient des déchets dans les villes africaines: Les mutations à conduire. Cahiers du PDM No. 1. Cotonou, Benin: PDM.

Muniesa, Fabian. 2000a. Performing Prices: The Case of Price Discovery Automation in the Financial Markets. In *Facts and Figures: Economic Representations and Practices.* Vol. 16 of *The Economy and Society Yearbook,* edited by Herbert Kalthoff, Richard Rottenberg, and Hans-Jürgen Wagener. Marburg: Metropolis.

———. 2000b. Un robot walrasien: Cotation electronique et justesse de la decouverte des prix. *Politix* 13 (52): 121–154.

——. 2002. L'automatisation de la cotation a la Bourse de Paris: La Machine au Coeur de la Reforme des Annees 80. Paper presented at Place Financiere, Ecole des Mines, Paris, May 17.

Murakami, Yasusuke, and Thomas P. Rohlen. 1987. Social-Exchange Aspects of the Japanese Political Economy: Culture, Efficiency, and Change. In *The Political Economy of Japan*, vol. 3, edited by Sumpei Kumon and Henry Rosovsky. Stanford: Stanford University Press.

Murdock, Ian. 1994. A Brief History of Debian: Appendix A—The Debian Manifesto. http://www.debian.org/doc/manuals/project-history/ap-manifesto.en.html.

Murphy, John. 1999. *Technical Analysis of the Financial Markets.* New York: New York Institute of Finance.

Nakane, Chie. 1967. *Kinship and Economic Organization in Rural Japan.* London: University of London Athlone Press.

——. 1970. *Japanese Society.* Berkeley: University of California Press.

Nath, Vikas. 2000. ICT Enabled Knowledge Societies for Human Development. *Information Technology in Developing Countries* (newsletter of IFIP Working Group 9.4) 10 (2), http://www.iimahd.ernet.in/egov/ifip/aug2000.htm.

Neff, Gina, and David Stark. 2003. Permanently Beta: Responsive Organization in the Internet Era. In *Society Online: The Internet in Context*, edited by Phillip E. N. Howard and Steve Jones. Thousand Oaks, Calif.: Sage.

Nesbitt, Jim. 1997. Battling for Respect: Bad Reputation Haunting Ultimate Fighters. *New Orleans Times-Picayune*, December 14, section C, p.1.

Niang, Demba, Bouna Warr, Laurent Bossard, and Jean-Marie Cour. 1997. The Local Economy of St. Louis and the Senegal River Delta: Case Study for the Program Enhancing Local Economies in West Africa. Paris: Club du Sahel, OECD/Cotonou Municipal Development Program.

Noiriel, Gérard. 1988. *Le creuset français: Histoire de l'immigration XIXe-XXe siècle.* Paris: Seuil.

Nolte, Sharon H., and Sally Ann Hastings. 1991. The Meiji State's Policy toward Women, 1890–1910. In *Recreating Japanese Women, 1600–1945*, edited by Gail Lee Bernstein. Berkeley: University of California Press.

Norris, Floyd. 2001. An Exaggerated Productivity Boom May Soon Be a Bust. *New York Times*, May 11, section C, p. 1.

Okimoto, Daniel I. 1989. *Between MITI and the Market: Japanese Industrial Policy for High Technology.* Stanford: Stanford University Press.

Olds, Kris. 2000. Globalizing Cities and the "Global Intelligence Corps": A Cautionary Note from Asia. Paper presented at the Globalizing Architecture conference, Berkeley, Calif., October 20.

Olds, Kris, and Nigel Thrift. 2005. Cultures on the Brink: Re-Engineering the Soul of Capitalism—on a Global Scale. In *Global Assemblages: Oikos and Anthropos Information*, edited by Aihwa Ong and Stephen J. Collier. New York: Blackwell.

O'Mahony, Siobhán. 2002. Community Managed Software Projects: The Emergence of a New Commercial Actor. Ph.D. dissertation, Stanford University.

O'Mahony, Siobhán, and Stephen R. Barley. 1999. Do Digital Telecommunications Affect

Work and Organization? The State of Our Knowledge. *Research in Organizational Behavior* 21:125–161.

O'Malley, Pat. 2000. Uncertain Subjects: Risks, Liberalism and Contract. *Economy and Society* 29:460–484.

Ong, Aihwa. 1999. *Flexible Citizenship: The Cultural Logics of Transnationality*. Durham, N.C.: Duke University Press.

———. 2001. Modernity: Anthropological Aspects. In *International Encyclopedia of the Social and Behavioral Sciences*, vol. 15, edited by N. J. Smelser and Paul B. Baltes. Oxford: Pergamon.

———. 2005. Ecologies of Expertise: Governmentality in Asian Knowledge Societies. In *Global Assemblages: Technology, Politics, and Ethics as Anthropological Problems*, edited by Aihwa Ong and Stephen J. Collier. Malden, Mass.: Blackwell.

Onzuka, Chris. 2001. "The Survivor" of Arm-Bar-Getting-It: Jason Walls. *Full Contact Fighter* 6 (4): 19, 45–46.

Opara, Anthony. 2000. Organized Crime and Democracy in Nigeria. Working Paper, Centre for Law Enforcement Education, Lagos, Nigeria.

Organisation Geopolitique des Drogues. 1999. *Africa Report*. Paris: OGD.

Orlikowski, Wanda J. 2000. Using Technology and Constituting Structures: A Practice Lens for Studying Technology in Organizations. *Organization Science* 11 (4): 404–428.

Orlikowski, Wanda J., and JoAnne Yates. 1994. Genre Repertoire: The Structuring of Communicative Practices in Organizations. *Administrative Science Quarterly* 39 (4): 541–574.

Orlikowski, Wanda J., JoAnne Yates, Kazuo Okamura, and Masayo Fujimoto. 1995. Shaping Electronic Communication: The Metastructuring of Technology in the Context of Use. *Organization Science* 6 (4): 423–444.

Ortner, Sherry B. 1996. Gender Hegemonies. In *Making Gender: The Politics and Erotics of Culture*, edited by Sherry B. Ortner. Boston: Deacon Press.

———. 1999. Generation X: Anthropology in a Media Saturated World. In *Critical Anthropology Now*, edited by George Marcus. Santa Fe, N.M.: School of American Research Press.

———. 2003. *New Jersey Dreaming: Capital, Culture, and the Class of '58*. Durham, N.C.: Duke University Press.

Ostrower, Francie. 1995. *Why the Wealthy Give: The Culture of Elite Philanthropy*. Princeton, N.J.: Princeton University Press.

Pearson, Margaret M. 1997. *China's New Business Elite: The Political Consequences of Reform*. Berkeley: University of California Press.

Peck, Jamie, and Nik Theodore. 2001. Contingent Chicago: Restructuring the Space of Temporary Labor. *International Journal of Urban and Regional Research* 25 (3): 471–496.

Pedersen, Paul Ove. 1997. Clusters of Enterprises within Systems of Production and Distribution: Collective Efficiency and Transaction Costs. In *Enterprise Clusters and Networks in Developing Countries*, edited by Meine Pieter van Dijk and Roberta Rabelloti. London: Frank Cass.

Pempel, T. J., and Michio Muramatsu. 1995. The Japanese Bureaucracy and Economic Development: Structuring a Proactive Civil Service. In *The Japanese Civil Service and Economic Development: Catalysts for Change*, edited by Hyung-ki Kim, Nishio Muramatsu, T. J. Pempel, and Kozo Yamamura. Oxford: Clarendon Press.

Peters, Pauline E. 1994. *Dividing the Commons: Politics, Policy and Culture in Botswana.* Charlottesville: University Press of Virginia.

Petonnet, Colette. 1982. *Ethnologie des banlieues.* Paris: Editions Galilée.

Piepenbrink, Brian. 2002. Style vs. Style Is Officially Dead. Part II: Finance and Footlocks: Thinking in New Directions. *Sherdog.com*, http://www.sherdog.com/interviews/lister—01/lister—04.htm (accessed January 17, 2002).

Platteau, Jean-Philippe. 2000. Order, the Rule of Law and Moral Norms. Paper presented at UNCTAD X—High Level Roundtable on Trade and Development: Directions for the 21st Century, Bangkok, February 12.

Pohjola, Matti. 2002. The New Economy: Facts, Impacts, and Policies. *Information Economics and Policy* 14:133–144.

Pollock, Sheldon, Homi K. Bhabha, Carol A. Breckenridge, and Dipesh Chakrabarty. 2000. Cosmopolitanisms. *Public Culture* 12 (3): 577–589.

Poovey, Mary. 1998. *A History of the Modern Fact: Problems of Knowledge in the Sciences of Wealth and Society.* Chicago: University of Chicago Press.

Porter, Michael E., and Hirotaka Takeuchi. 1999. Fixing What Really Ails Japan. *Foreign Affairs* 78 (3): 66–81.

Porter, Theodore. 1995. *Trust in Numbers: The Pursuit of Objectivity in Science and Public Life.* Princeton, N.J.: Princeton University Press.

Powell, Walter W. 1990. Neither Market nor Hierarchy: Network Forms of Organization. In special issue, edited by Barry M. Staw and L. L. Cummings, *Research in Organizational Behavior* 12:295–336.

Power, Michael. 1997. *The Audit Society: Rituals of Verification.* New York: Oxford University Press.

Preda, Alex. Forthcoming. Socio-Technical Agency in Financial Markets: The Case of the Stock Ticker. *Social Studies of Science.*

Pryke, Michael, and J. Allen. 2000. Monetized Time-Space: Derivatives—Money's "New Imaginary"? *Economy and Society* 29 (2): 329–344.

Pryke, Michael, and R. Lee. 1995. Place Your Bets: Towards an Understanding of Globalization, Socio-Financial Engineering, and Competition without a Financial Centre. *Urban Studies* 32 (2): 329–344.

Pujadas, David and Ahmed Salam. 1995. *La tentation du Jihad.* Paris: J.C. Lattès.

Quadros, Stephen. 1999. Fightsport: Mark Kerr and Frank Shamrock Ranked No. 1 in an Evolving Sport. *Black Belt Magazine* (March), http://www.blackbeltmag.com/archives/blackbelt/1999/mar99/fig.html (accessed July 19, 2002).

——. 2002. The Female Perspective: *Fightsport* Talks with Fox Sports Net's Lisa Guerrero about Media, Men and Mixed Martial Arts. *Fightsports* 1(2): 60–63.

Quinn, Michael. 1996. "Never Shoulda Been Let Out the Penitentiary": Gangsta Rap and the Struggle over Racial Identity. *Cultural Critique* 34:65–89.

Rabinow, Paul. 1989. *French Modern: Norms and Forms of the Social Environment.* Cambridge, Mass.: MIT Press.

——. 2003. *Anthropos Today: Reflections on Modern Equipment.* Princeton, N.J.: Princeton University Press.

Rader, Benjamin G. 1984. *In Its Own Image: How Television Has Transformed Sports*. New York: Free Press.

Ranieri, Lewis S. 1996. The Origins of Securitization, Sources of Its Growth, and Its Future Potential. In *A Primer on Securitization*, edited by Leon T. Kendall and Michael J. Fishman. Cambridge, Mass.: MIT Press.

Rao, Hayagreeva, Calvin Morrill, and Mayer N. Zald. 2000. Power Plays: How Social Movements and Collective Action Create New Organizational Forms. *Research in Organizational Behavior* 22:237–281.

Raymond, Eric S. 1999. *The Cathedral and the Bazaar: Musings on Linux and Open Source by an Accidental Revolutionary*. Sebastopol, Calif.: O'Reilly.

Reich, Robert B. 1992. *The Work of Nations: Preparing Ourselves for Twenty-first Century Capitalism*. New York: Vintage.

Reno, William. 1998. *Warlords, Politics and African States*. Boulder, Colo.: Lynne Rienner.

Richardson, Ingrid, and Carly Harper. 2002. Corporeal Virtuality: The Impossibility of a Fleshless Ontology. *Body, Space and Technology* 2 (2), http://wwwmcc.murdoch.edu.au/ReadingRoom/VID/corporeal.html.

Riles, Annelise. 2000. *The Network Inside Out*. Ann Arbor: University of Michigan Press.

——. 2001. Real-Time: Governing the Market after the Failure of Knowledge. Paper presented at the University of California at Berkeley, Department of Anthropology, January 18.

——. 2004a. Property as Legal Knowledge: Means and Ends. *Journal of the Royal Anthropological Institute* (N.S.) 10:773–793.

——. 2004b. Real Time: Unwinding Technocratic and Anthropological Knowledge. *American Ethnologist* 31 (3): 392–405.

——. 2006. Introduction. In *Documents: Artifacts of Modern Knowledge*, edited by Annelise Riles. Ann Arbor: University of Michigan Press.

Rinehart, Robert E. 1998. *Players All: Performances in Contemporary Sport*. Bloomington: Indiana University Press.

Roberts, Susan. 1998. Global Strategic Vision: Managing the World. In *Globalization under Construction: Governmentality, Law, and Identity*, edited by Richard Perry and Bill Maurer. Minneapolis: University of Minnesota Press.

Robertson, Claire C. 1998. Women Entrepreneurs? Trade and Gender Division of Labor in Nairobi. In *African Entrepreneurship: Theory and Reality*, edited by Anita Spring and Barbara E. McDade. Gainesville: University of Florida Press.

Robertson, Roland. 1995. Glocalization: Time-Space and Homogeneity-Heterogeneity. In *Global Modernities*, edited by Mike Featherstone, Scott Lash, and Roland Robertson. London: Sage.

Rogerson, Christian M. 1997. Globalization or Informalization? African Urban Economies in the 1990's. In *The Urban Challenge in Africa: Growth and Management of Large Cities*, edited by Carole Rakodi. Tokyo: United Nations University Press.

Rohlen, Thomas P. 1974. *For Harmony and Strength: Japanese White-Collar Organization in Anthropological Perspective*. Berkeley: University of California Press.

Roitman, Janet. 1998. Garrison-Entrepôt. *Cahiers d'Ètudes africaines* 150–152, xxxvii–2–4:297–329.

———. 2004. *Fiscal Disobedience: An Anthropology of Economic Regulation in Central Africa.* Princeton, N.J.: Princeton University Press.

Romanelli, Elaine. 1991. The Evolution of New Organizational Forms. *Annual Review of Sociology* 17:79–103.

Rose, Dan. 2002. The Midweek Grind: The Efforts of Many Result in Gains for All. *Sherdog*, June 27, http://www.sherdog.com/viewnews.cfm?newsid=EpkVkukuFziLX EntJy (accessed September 20, 2002).

Rose, Tricia. 1994. *Black Noise: Rap Music and Black Culture in Contemporary America.* Hanover, N.H.: University Press of New England.

Rosenblum, Mort. 1988. *Mission to Civilize: The French Way.* New York: Anchor Press.

Ross, Andrew. 2003. *No-Collar: The Hidden Costs of the Humane Workplace.* New York: Basic Books.

Roszak, Theodore, and Burton I. Weiss. 1969. *The Making of a Counter Culture: Reflections on the Technocratic Society and Its Youthful Opposition.* Garden City, N.Y.: Doubleday.

Rothschild, Joyce, and Raymond Russell. 1986. Alternatives to Bureaucracy: Democratic Participation in the Economy. *Annual Review of Sociology* 12:307–328.

Rothschild, Joyce, and J. Allen Whitt. 1986. *The Cooperative Workplace: Potentials and Dilemmas of Organizational Democracy and Participation.* New York: Cambridge University Press.

Rothschild-Whitt, Joyce. 1979. The Collectivist Organization: An Alternative to Rational-Bureaucratic Models. *American Sociological Review* 44:509–527.

Rowe, David. 1999. *Sport, Culture and the Media: The Unruly Trinity.* Buckingham, England: Open University Press.

Rowe, David, Geoffrey Lawrence, Toby Miller, and Jim McKay. 1994. Global Sport? Core Concern and Peripheral Vision. *Media, Culture and Society* 16 (4): 661–675.

Sage, George. 1998. *Power and Ideology in American Sport: A Critical Perspective.* 2nd ed. Champaign, Ill.: Human Kinetics.

Sagna, Oliver. 1999. From Community to African Unity. *Africa Recovery*, United Nations, Economic Development Institute/World Bank, 13 (4): 24.

Sahlins, Marshall. 1988. Cosmologies of Capitalism: The Trans-Pacific Sector of the "World System." *Proceedings of the British Academy* 74:1–51.

———. 1996. The Sadness of Sweetness: The Native Anthropology of Western Cosmology. *Current Anthropology* 37(3): 395–428.

Sakhoui, Fethi. 1996. L'insertion par le sport des jeunes d'origine maghrébine des banlieues en difficulté. *Migrations Société* 8(45): 81–100.

Sassen, Saskia. 1996. *Losing Control? Sovereignty in an Age of Globalization.* New York: Columbia University Press.

———. 1998. *Globalization and Its Discontents.* New York: New Press.

———. 2001. *The Global City: New York, London, Tokyo.* Princeton, N.J.: Princeton University Press (new updated edition; originally published in 1991).

———. 2002. Introduction: Locating Cities on Global Circuits. In *Global Networks: Linked Cities*, edited by Saskia Sassen. New York: Routledge.

———. 2005. Electronic Markets and Online Activist Networks: The Variable Outcomes of

Technology. In *Digital-Formations: IT and New Architectures in the Global Realm*, edited by Robert Latham and Saskia Sassen. Princeton, N.J.: Princeton University Press.

——. 2006. *Territory, Authority, Rights: From Medieval to Global Assemblages*. Princeton, N.J.: Princeton University Press.

Sastry, Anjali, and Fiona Lee. 2000. Pairing Stability with Change: Rules, Operations, and Structures in an Enduring Organization. Paper presented at the ICOS Seminar, University of Michigan, January 28.

Sato, Makoto. 1998. Central Bank Targets Financial System Risk: Plan to Introduce Real-Time Settlement Forces Restructuring. *Nikkei Weekly*, September 21, p. 1.

Satow, Roberta Lynn. 1975. Value-Rational Authority and Professional Organizations: Weber's Missing Type. *Administrative Science Quarterly* 20:526–531.

Schaede, Ulrike. 1995. The Old Boy Network and Government-Business Relationships in Japan. *Journal of Japanese Studies* 21 (2): 293–317.

Schivelbusch, Wolfgang. 1986. *The Railway Journey: The Industrialization of Time and Space in the 19th Century*. Berkeley: University of California Press.

Schlink, Bernhard. 1998. *The Reader*. Translated by Carol Brown Janeway. New York: Vintage Books.

Schmitz, Hubert. 1997. Collective Efficiency and Increasing Returns. IDS Working Paper 50. Sussex, England: Institute of Development Studies.

Schnapper, Dominique. 2001. *Exclusions au coeur de la Cité*. Paris: Anthropos.

Schuyler, Ed, Jr. 2001. Ultimate Fighting Is for Athletes. *Associated Press*, Sports News, July 12, Lexis-Nexis (accessed July 5, 2002).

Schwartz, Frank J. 1998. *Advice and Consent: The Politics of Consultation in Japan*. Cambridge: Cambridge University Press.

Seekings, Jeremy. 1993. *Heroes or Villains? Youth Politics in the 1980's*. Johannesburg, South Africa: Ravan Press.

Seidel, Marc-David L., and Stewart, Katherine J. 2001. An Initial Description of the C-form Organization. Unpublished working paper.

Sender, John, and Sheila Smith. 1990. *Poverty, Class, and Gender in Rural Africa: A Tanzanian Case Study*. London: Routledge.

Sennett, Richard. 2000. The New Political Economy and Culture. *Hedgehog Review* 12 (1): 1–13, http://www.virginia.edu/iasc/hh/ThrTocsVol2-1.html.

Sethuraman, S. V. 1997. *Africa's Informal Economy*. Geneva: International Labor Office.

Shamrock, Ken, and Richard Hanner. 1997. *Inside the Lion's Den: The Life and Submission Fighting System of Ken Shamrock*. Boston: Charles E. Tuttle.

Shaw, Rosalind. 1996. The Politician and the Diviner: Divination and the Consumption of Power in Sierra Leone. *Journal of Religion in Africa* 26 (1): 30–55.

Sherry, John F., Jr., Robert V. Kozinets, Diana Storm, Adam Duhachek, Krittinee Nuttavuthisit, and Benét DeBerry-Spence. 2001. Being in the Zone: Staging Retail at ESPN Zone Chicago. *Journal of Contemporary Ethnography* 30 (4): 465–510.

Silverstein, Paul A. 2000. Sporting Faith: Islam, Soccer and the French Nation-State. *Social Text* 65:25–53.

——. 2002a. The Kabyle Myth: The Production of Ethnicity in Colonial Algeria. In *From the Margins: Historical Anthropology and Its Futures*, edited by Brian Keith Axel. Durham, N.C.: Duke University Press.

——. 2002b. Stadium Politics: Sport, Islam, and Amazigh Consciousness in France and North Africa. In *With God on Their Side: Sport in the Service of Religion*, edited by Tara Magdalinski and Timothy Chandler. London: Routledge.

——. 2002c. "Why Are We Waiting to Start the Fire?": French Gangsta Rap and the Critique of State Capitalism. In *Black, Blanc, Beur: Rap Music and Hip Hop Culture in the Francophone World*, edited by Alain-Philippe Durand. Lanham, Md.: Scarecrow Press.

——. 2004. *Algeria in France: Transpolitics, Race, and Nation*. Bloomington: Indiana University Press.

Simmel, Georg. 1907/1990. *The Philosophy of Money*. New York: Routledge.

Singer, Linda. 1993. *Erotic Welfare: Sexual Theory and Politics in the Age of Epidemic*. New York: Routledge.

Skidelsky, Robert. 2000. *Fighting for Freedom, 1937–1946*. Vol. 3 of *John Maynard Keynes*. New York: Penguin.

Slater, Don. 2002. Capturing Markets from the Economists. In *Cultural Economy*, edited by Paul du Gay and Michael Pyre. London: Sage.

Sloan, Mike. 2002. One on One with Frank Shamrock! *Sherdog.com*, April 15, http://www.sherdog.com/interviews/fshamrock—01/shamrock—01.htm (accessed August 14, 2002).

Smart, Josephine, and Alan Smart. 1999. Personal Relations and Divergent Economies: A Case of Hong Kong Investment in South China. In *Theorizing the City*, edited by Setha M. Low. New Brunswick, N.J.: Rutgers University Press.

Smith, Charles W. 1999. *Success and Survival on Wall Street*. New York: Rowman and Littlefield.

Smith, Neil. 1979. Toward a Theory of Gentrification: A Back to the City Movement by Capital not People. *Journal of the American Planning Association* 45:538–548.

——. 1992. Contours of a Spatialized Politics: Homeless Vehicles and the Production of Geographical Space. *Social Text* 33:54–81.

——. 1996. *New Urban Frontier: Gentrification and the Revanchist City*. New York: Routledge.

Smith, Neil, and J. DiFilippis. 1999. The Reassertion of Economics: 1990s Gentrification in the Lower East Side. *International Journal of Urban and Regional Research* 23:638–653.

Smith, Neil, and Peter Williams. 1986. From Renaissance to Restructuring: The Dynamics of Contemporary Urban Development. In *Gentrification of the City*, edited by Neil Smith and Peter Williams. Boston: Allen and Unwin.

Smith, Vicki. 1997. New Forms of Work Organization. *Annual Review of Sociology* 23:315–339.

Snow, David A., and Robert D. Benford. 1992. Master Frames and Cycles of Protest. In *Frontiers of Social Movement Theory*, edited by Aldon D. Morris and Carol M. Mueller. New Haven: Yale University Press.

Soja, Edward. 1997. Six Discourses on the Post Metropolis. In *Imagining Cities: Scripts, Signs, Memory*, edited by Sallie Westwood and John Williams. London: Routledge.

Soulignac, François. 1993. *La banlieue parisienne*. Paris: La Documentation Française.

Sproull, Lee, and Sara Kiesler. 1995. *Connections: New Ways of Working in the Networked Organization*. Cambridge, Mass.: MIT Press.

Squires, Michael. 2002. Film Cashes in on Street Scenes: Video Selling Fast, but Advocates for Homeless Critical. *Las Vegas Review-Journal*, May 5, http://www.lvrj.com/lvrj—home/2002/May-05-Sun-2002/news/18662641.html.

Ssewakiryanga, Richard. 1999. New Kids on the Blocks: African-American Music and Uganda Youth. *CODESRIA Bulletin* (1/2): 24–27.

Stallman, Richard. 1999. The GNU Operating System and the Free Software Movement. In *Open Sources*, edited by Chris DiBona, Sam Ockman, and Mark Stone. Sebastopol, Calif.: O'Reilly.

Stark, David, A. 1999. Heterarchy: Distributing Authority and Organizing Diversity. In *The Biology of Business: Decoding the Natural Laws of Enterprise*, edited by John Clippinger III. San Francisco: Jossey-Bass.

——. 2001. Value, Values, and Valuation: Work and Worth in the New Economy. Paper presented at "The New Economy" ssrc conference, Atlanta.

Stiegler, Bernard. 1998. *Technics and Time, 1. The Fault of Epimetheus*. Translated by Richard Beardsworth and George Collins. Stanford: Stanford University Press.

Stinchcombe, Arthur L. 2001. *When Formality Works: Authority and Abstraction in Law and Organizations*. Chicago: University of Chicago Press.

Stokes, Martin. 1996. "Strong as a Turk": Power, Performance and Representation in Turkish Wrestling. In *Sport, Identity and Ethnicity*, edited by Jeremy MacClancy. Oxford: Berg.

Stoler, Ann Laura, and Frederick Cooper. 1997. Between Metropole and Colony: Rethinking a Research Agenda. In *Tensions of Empire: Colonial Cultures in a Bourgeois World*, edited by Frederick Cooper and Ann Laura Stoler. Berkeley: University of California Press.

Strathern, Marilyn. 1988. *The Gender of the Gift: Problems with Women and Problems with Society in Melanesia*. Berkeley: University of California Press.

——. 2000. *Audit Cultures: Anthropological Studies in Accountability, Ethics, and the Academy*. London: Routledge.

Strauss, Anselm L. 1987. *Qualitative Analysis for Social Scientists*. New York: Cambridge University Press.

Suchman, Lucy. 1987. *Plans and Situated Actions: The Problem of Human-Machine Communication*. New York: Cambridge University Press.

——. 2003. Anthropology as "Brand": Reflections on Corporate Anthropology. Center for Science Studies, Lancaster University, http://www.lancs.ac.uk/fss/sociology/papers/suchman-anthropology-as-brand.pdf.

Swidler, Ann. 1979. *Organization without Authority: Dilemmas of Social Control in Free Schools*. Cambridge, Mass.: Harvard University Press.

——. 1986. Culture in Action: Symbols and Strategies. *American Sociological Review* 51 (2): 273–286.

Swyngedouw, Eric. 1998. Territories of Innovation: Innovation as a Collective Process and the Globalization of Competition. Oxford University Economics Working Paper 99–4. Oxford: Oxford University.

Tabb, William. 1982. *The Long Default*. New York: Monthly Review Press.

Talha, Larbi. 1989. *Le salariat immigré devant la crise*. Paris: Editions du cnrs.

Temple, Jonathan. 2002. The Assessment: The New Economy. *Oxford Review of Economic Policy* 18 (3): 241–264.

Thomas, Gerald A. 1991. The Gentrification of Paradise: St. John's, Antigua. *Urban Geography* 12:469–487.

Thorne, Susan. 1997. "The Conversion of Englishmen and the Conversion of the World Inseparable": Missionary Imperialism and the Language of Class in Early Industrial Britain. In *Tensions of Empire: Colonial Cultures in a Bourgeois World*, edited by Frederick Cooper and Ann Laura Stoler. Berkeley: University of California Press.

Thrift, Nigel. 1996. Shut Up and Dance, or, Is the World Economy Knowable? In *The Global Economy in Transition*, edited by Peter W. Daniels and William F. Lever. Essex, England: Longman.

———. 1999. The Globalization of the System of Business Knowledge. In *Globalization and the Asia-Pacific: Contested Territories*, edited by Kris Olds, Peter Dicken, Philip F. Kelly, Lily Kong, and Henry Wai-Chung Yeung. London: Routledge.

———. 2000. Performing Cultures in the New Economy. *Annals of the Association of American Geographers* 90 (4): 674–692.

———. 2001. "It's the Romance, Not the Finance, that Makes the Business Worth Pursuing": Disclosing a New Market Culture. *Economy and Society* 30 (4): 412–432.

Tobioka, Ken. 1993. Japan's Matrix of Nature, Culture, and Technology. In *Japanese Business: Cultural Perspectives*, edited by Subhash Durlabhji and Norton E. Marks. Albany: State University of New York Press.

Todreas, Timothy. 1999. *Value Creation and Branding in Television's Digital Age.* Westport, Conn.: Quorum Books.

Torvalds, Linus. 1999. The Linux Edge. In *Open Sources*, edited by Chris Ockman, Sam Stone, and Mark DiBona. Sebastopol, Calif.: O'Reilly.

Traube, Elizabeth. 1992. *Dreaming Identities: Class, Gender, and Generation in 1980s Hollywood Movies.* Boulder, Conn.: Westview Press.

Traweek, Sharon. 1999. Faultlines. In *Doing Science + Culture*, edited by Roddey Reid and Sharon Traweek. New York: Routledge Press.

Tribalat, Michèle. 1991. *Cent ans d'immigration: Etrangers d'hier, Français d'aujourd'hui.* Paris: Presses Universitaires de France/INED.

Tripp, Aili Mari. 1997. *Changing the Rules: The Politics of Liberalization and the Urban Informal Economy in Tanzania.* Berkeley: University of California Press.

Tsutsui, William M. 1998. *Manufacturing Ideology: Scientific Management in Twentieth-Century Japan.* Princeton, N.J.: Princeton University Press.

Tuomi, Ilkka. 2000. Internet, Innovation, and Open Source: Actors in the Network. SITRA, the Finnish National Fund for Research and Development Working Paper, Helsinki.

———. 2002. *Networks of Innovation: Change and Meaning in the Age of the Internet.* New York: Oxford University Press.

Turkle, Sherry. 1995. *Life on the Screen: Identity in the Age of the Internet.* New York: Simon and Schuster.

———. 1999. Identity in the Age of the Internet. In *The Media Reader: Continuity and Transformation*, edited by Hugh Mackay and Tim O'Sullivan. London: Sage.

Tushman, Michael, and Charles O'Reilly. 1996. Ambidextrous Organizations: Managing Evolutionary and Revolutionary Change. *California Management Review* 38 (4): 8–30.

Ueno, Chizuko. 1988. The Japanese Women's Movement: The Counter-values to Industrialism. In *The Japanese Trajectory: Modernization and Beyond*, edited by Gavan McCormack and Yoshio Sugimoto. Cambridge: Cambridge University Press.

———. 1994. *Kindai kazoku no seiritsu to shåuen* (The Rise and Fall of the Modern American Family). Tokyo: Iwanami Shūen.

UFC President Dana White: UFC London Press Conference Interview. 2002. *SFUK: Submission Fighting UK*, April 17, http://sfuk.tripod.com/interviews—02/ufcukprss—dana.html.

UFC and LMNO Ready to "Get It on Primetime." 2002. *Variety*, April 24, http://www.ufc.tv/news/unique.asp?articleID=206 (accessed July 17, 2002).

UK Department of the Environment, Transport and the Regions. 1999. Towards an Urban Renaissance: Report of the Urban Task Force.

Uno, Kathleen S. 1999. *Passages to Modernity: Motherhood, Childhood, and Social Reform in Early Twentieth Century Japan*. Honolulu: University of Hawaii Press.

Valverde, Mariana. 2003. *Law's Dream of a Common Knowledge*. Princeton, N.J.: Princeton University Press.

Van Arkadie, Brian. 1995. The State and Economic Change in Africa. In *The Role of the State in Economic Change in Africa*, edited by Ha-Joon Chang and Robert Rowthorn. Oxford: Clarendon.

Van Dijk, Meine Pieter. 1998. The Urban Informal Sector as New Engine for Development: Theoretical Developments Since 1972. Working paper of the Institute for Housing and Urban Studies, Rotterdam.

VanHoose, David D. 1991. Bank Behavior, Interest Rate Determination, and Monetary Policy in a Financial System with an Intraday Federal Funds Market. *Journal of Banking and Finance* 15:343–365.

Van Maanen, John. 1998. *Qualitative Studies of Organizations*. Thousand Oaks, Calif.: Sage.

Vargo, Keith. 1999. Way of the Warrior: Royce Gracie Is Only Human. *Black Belt Magazine*, April, http://www.blackbeltmag.com/archives/blackbelt/1999/apr99/way.html (accessed July 19, 2002).

Veloso, Leticia Medeiros. 1998. "Children are the Future of the Nation": Law, the State, and the Making of Tomorrow's Citizens in Brazil. Doctoral research proposal, University of Chicago.

Venkatesh, Sudhir. 2000. *American Project: The Rise and Fall of a Modern Ghetto*. Cambridge, Mass.: Harvard University Press.

———. n.d. Robert Taylor, the Problem of Order, and the General Crisis of Governability. Dissertation outline, Department of Sociology, University of Chicago.

Venkatesh, Sudhir, and Alexandra Murphy. Forthcoming. Policing Ourselves: Law and Order in the American Ghetto. In *Youth, Law, and Globalization*, edited by Sudhir Venkatesh and Ronald Kassimir. Stanford: Stanford University Press.

Verdery, Katherine. 1996. *What Was Socialism, and What Comes Next?* Princeton, N.J.: Princeton University Press.

Vine, D. 2001. Development or Displacement? The Brooklyn Academy of Music and Gentrification in Fort Greene. Paper presented at the Gotham History Festival, CUNY Graduate Center, New York, October.

Vinocur, John. 1999. Just a Soccer Star, After All. *New York Times*, March 14, sect. 6, p. 32.

Von Hippel, Eric. 2001. Open Source Shows the Way: Innovation by and for Users—No Manufacturer Required. *Sloan Management Review* 42 (4): 82–85.

Von Hippel, Eric, and Georg von Krogh. 2003. Exploring the Open Source Software Phenomenon: Issues for Organization Science. *Organization Science* 14 (2): 209–223.

Wacquant, Loïc. 1992. Pour en finir avec le mythe des "cités-ghettos." *Annales de la Recherche Urbaine* 54 (March): 21–30.

——. 1994. Urban Outcasts: Color, Class and Place in Two Advanced Societies. Ph.D. dissertation, Department of Sociology, University of Chicago.

Wajcman, Judy. 2002. Addressing Technological Change: The Challenge to Social Theory. *Current Sociology* 50:347–363.

——. 2004. *Technofeminism*. Cambridge. England: Polity Press.

Walder, Andrew. 1995. China's Transitional Economy: Interpreting Its Significance. *China Quarterly* 144 (December): 963–979.

Walshe, Peter. 1971. *The Rise of African Nationalism in South Africa: The African National Congress, 1912–1952*. Berkeley: University of California Press.

Walzer, Michael. 1984. Welfare, Membership and Need. In *Liberalism and Its Critics*, edited by Michael Sandel. New York: New York University Press.

Washington Post. 1998. In China, the Pitfalls of a Bestseller. October 20.Watts, Michael J. 1993. Idioms of Land and Labour: Producing Politics and Rice in Senegambia. In *Land in African Agrarian Systems*, edited by Thomas J. Basset and Donald E. Crummey. Madison: University of Wisconsin Press.

Webb, Sidney, and Beatrice Webb. 1920. *A Constitution for the Socialist Commonwealth of Great Britain*. London: Longmans.

Weber, Max. 1925/1966. *Max Weber on Law in Economy and Society*. 2nd ed. Translated by Edward Shils. Cambridge, Mass.: Harvard University Press.

——. 1930/1998. *The Protestant Ethic and the Spirit of Capitalism*. Translated by Talcott Parsons. Revised introduction by Randall Collins. Los Angeles: Roxbury.

——. 1978. *Economy and Society: An Outline of Interpretive Sociology*. Edited by Guenther Roth and Claus Wittich. Translated by Ephraim Fischoff et al. Berkeley: University of California Press.

Weber, Max, and Samuel N. Eisenstadt. 1968. *Max Weber on Charisma and Institution Building: Selected Papers*. Chicago: University of Chicago Press.

Weber, Steven. 2005. The Political Economy of Open Source Software and Why It Matters. In *Digital Formations: Information Technology and New Architectures in the Global Realm*, edited by Robert Latham and Saskia Sassen. Princeton, N.J.: Princeton University Press.

Webley, Irene A. 1986. Professional Wrestling: The World of Roland Barthes Revisited. *Semiotica* 58 (1/2): 59–81.

Weiss, Todd. 2001. HP Adopting Debian Linux for Internal R&D. May 11, http://www.computerworld.com/softwaretopics/os/story/0,10801,60507,00.html (accessed November 5, 2005).

Werna, Edmundo. 1998. Urban Management in the Provision of Public Services and Intra-urban Differentials in Nairobi. *Habitat International* 22 (1): 15–26.

West, Harry G., and Todd Sanders. 2003. *Transparency and Conspiracy: Ethnographies of Suspicion in the New World Order.* Durham, N.C.: Duke University Press.

Westbrook, David A. 2003. *The City of Gold: An Apology for Global Capitalism in a Time of Discontent.* New York: Routledge.

Weston, Kath. 2002. *Gender in Real Time: Power and Transience in a Visual Age.* New York: Routledge.

Whittel, Andreas. 2001. Toward a Network Sociality. *Theory, Culture and Society* 18 (6): 51–76.

Whyte, William Foote. 1982. Social Inventions for Solving Human Problems. *American Sociological Review* 47 (1): 1–13.

Whyte, William Foote, and Kathleen King Whyte. 1988. *Making Mondragon: The Growth and Dynamics of the Worker Cooperative Complex.* Ithaca, N.Y.: ILR Press/New York State School of Industrial Labor Relations, Cornell University.

Wieviorka, Michel, and Philippe Bataille. 1999. *Violence en France.* Paris: Seuil.

Wihtol de Wenden, Catherine, and Zakya Daoud, eds. 1993. *Banlieues . . . intégration ou explosion?* Special issue of *Panoramiques* 2(12).

Willer, David E. 1967. Max Weber's Missing Authority Type. *Sociological Inquiry* 37:231–39.

Willis, Paul. 1977. *Learning to Labor: How Working Class Kids Get Working Class Jobs.* New York: Columbia University Press.

Willoughby, William C. 1923. *Race Problems in the New Africa: A Study of the Relation of Bantu and Briton in Those Parts of Africa under British Rule.* Oxford: Clarendon Press.

Wilson, Monica. 1951. Witch Beliefs and the Social Structure. *American Journal of Sociology* 56:307–313.

Winner, Langdon. 1977. *Autonomous Technology: Technics-out-of-Control as a Theme in Political Thought.* Cambridge, Mass.: MIT Press.

World Bank. 2000a. *Can Africa Claim the 21st Century?* Washington, D.C.: World Bank.

———. 2000b. World Development Report: *Series: Workers' Remittances, Receipts.* Washington, D.C.: World Bank.

———. 2001a. *Aid and Reform in Africa.* Washington, D.C.: World Bank.

———. 2001b. Economic Toolkit for African Policy Makers. *World Bank Findings* 192 (October), http://www.worldbank.org/afr/findings/english/find192.pdf.

———. 2001c. Poverty Reduction Strategy Reports from Tanzania and Ethiopia. Washington, D.C.: World Bank.

Wright, Gwendolyn. 1991. *The Politics of Design in French Colonial Urbanism.* Chicago: University of Chicago Press.

Yang, Mayfair. 1994. *Gifts, Favors, and Banquet: The Art of Guanxi in Chinese Society.* Ithaca, N.Y.: Cornell University Press.

———, ed. 2000. *A Space of Their Own.* Minneapolis: University of Minnesota Press.

Yates, JoAnne, and Wanda J. Orlikowski. 1992. Genres of Organizational Communication: A Structurational Approach to Studying Communication and Media. *Academy of Management Review* 17 (2): 299–326.

Yates, JoAnne, Wanda J. Orlikowski, and Kazuo Okamura. 1995. Constituting Genre Repertoires: Deliberate and Emergent Patterns of Electronic Media Use. *Best Papers Proceedings*. Special issue of *Academy of Management Journal*, 353–357.

Zaloom, Caitlin. 2003. Ambiguous Numbers: Trading Technologies and Interpretation in Financial Markets. *American Ethnologist* 30:258–272.

——. 2005. The Discipline of Speculators. In *Global Assemblages: Technology, Politics, and Ethics as Anthropological Problems*, edited by Aihwa Ong and Stephen J. Collier. London: Blackwell.

Zidane, Zinedine. 1998. *Zidane-Dugarry, mes copains d'abord*. Paris: Mango-Sport.

Žižek, Slavoj. 1997. *The Plague of Fantasies*. London: Verso.

Zukin, Sharon. 1982. *Loft Living: Culture and Capital in Urban Change*. Baltimore: Johns Hopkins University Press.

——. 2004. *Point of Purchase: How Shopping Changed American Culture*. New York: Routledge Press.

CONTRIBUTORS

JEAN COMAROFF is the Bernard E. and Ellen C. Sunny Distinguished Service Professor of Anthropology and of Social Sciences in the College and the Clinical Scholars Program at the University of Chicago, and honorary professor at the University of Cape Town. Her fieldwork in southern Africa and Great Britain has focused especially on colonialism, modernity, ritual, power, and consciousness. Among other works, she is the author of *Body of Power, Spirit of Resistance: The Culture and History of a South African People* (1985).

JOHN L. COMAROFF is the Harold H. Swift Distinguished Service Professor of Anthropology and of Social Sciences in the College of the University of Chicago, senior research fellow at the American Bar Foundation, and honorary professor at the University of Cape Town. His areas of interest include social theory, modernity, neoliberalism, politics, and law, especially among the Tswana peoples of southern Africa. His many works include *Rules and Processes: The Cultural Logic of Dispute in an African Context* (with S. A. Roberts, 1981).

Together, John and Jean Comaroff have authored or edited a number of landmark volumes, including *Of Revelation and Revolution* (2 volumes, 1991 and 1997), *Ethnography and the Historical Imagination* (1992), *Modernity and Its Malcontents: Ritual and Power in Africa* (1993), *Civil Society and the Political Imagination in Africa: Critical Perspective, Problems, Paradoxes* (1999), and *Millennial Capitalism and the Culture of Neoliberalism* (2000).

GREG DOWNEY is a Lecturer in Anthropology at Macquarie University. He received his Ph.D. from the University of Chicago in 1998. He is the author of *Lessons in Cunning: Learning Capoeira, an Afro-Brazilian Art* (2005) and has published articles on sports and performance in a range of journals. He is currently continuing his research on the relationships among gender, violence, media, popular culture, and culturally induced physiological change. His nonacademic experience includes a brief stint as a design consultant for a Chicago-based design-planning firm.

MELISSA S. FISHER is an Assistant Professor of Anthropology in the Department of Sociology and Anthropology at Georgetown University. Currently she is writing a book about the career, networking, and mentoring practices of the first generation of Wall Street women. This work draws attention to the ways women's experiences are grounded in larger historical frameworks of various sorts, including generational cultures (the 1960s and 1970s), social movements (feminism), and epochal shifts (the globalization of financial capitalism). She received her Ph.D. in Cultural Anthropology from Columbia University in 2003 and was a Visiting Summer Fellow at the Institute for Advanced Social and Management Studies at Lancaster University in the United Kingdom. She also has experience working as a freelance corporate anthropologist specializing in consumer research for Fortune 500 companies.

DOUGLAS R. HOLMES is a Professor of Anthropology at Binghamton University. During the past decade his research has focused on the social and cultural dynamics of advanced European integration. His current research project examines the Deutsche Bundesbank and the European Central Bank as they experiment with the formulation and communication of monetary policy. His published works include *Integral Europe: Fast-Capitalism, Multiculturalism, Neofascism* (2000) and *Cultural Disenchantment: Worker Peasantries in Northeast Italy* (1989).

GEORGE E. MARCUS is the Chancellor's Professor of Anthropology at the University of California, Irvine. He is the founding editor of the journal *Cultural Anthropology* and creator of the fin de siècle series Late Editions at the University of Chicago Press. His many influential works include *Anthropology as Cultural Critique* (coauthored with Michael Fischer, 1986) and *Writing Culture* (coedited with James Clifford, 1986). His recent works include *Ethnography through Thick and Thin* (1998) and the edited volume *Critical Anthropology Now* (1999).

Together, Professors Douglas Holmes and George Marcus are collaborating on an ongoing attempt to reinvent the norms and forms of ethnographic research to adjust to its changing circumstances of production. In particular, they are examining the theoretical and methodological challenges posed by the study of cultures of expertise. They have proposed a series of strategies by which the production of knowledge in domains of science, politics, business, and art can be investigated ethnographically.

SIOBHÁN O'MAHONY is an Assistant Professor at the Harvard Business School in the Negotiation, Organizations, and Markets Unit. Her research examines the organization and governance of community forms of enterprise, the management of common information platforms, and the factors affecting cumulative innovation. She has written and cowritten articles for *Research in Organization Behavior*, *Research Policy*, and the *Academy of Management Journal*.

AIHWA ONG is Head of Socio-Cultural Anthropology at the University of California, Berkeley. She is the author of *Spirits of Resistance and Capitalist Discipline: Factory Women in Malaysia* (1987) and *Flexible Citizenship: The Cultural Logics of Transnationality* (1999), and her edited volumes include *Ungrounded Empires: The Cultural Politics of Modern Chinese Transnationalism* (1995) and (with Stephen J. Collier) *Global*

Assemblages: Technology, Politics, and Ethics as Anthropological Problems (2005). Her new book is *Neoliberalism as Exception: Mutations in Citizenship and Sovereignty* (2006).

ANNELISE RILES is Professor of Law and Professor of Anthropology at Cornell University. Her work focuses on the character of legal and technocratic knowledge and the challenges it poses for cultural analysis and critique. Her first book, *The Network Inside Out* (2000), concerned the knowledge practices of international human rights organizations. A forthcoming edited collection, *Documents: Artifacts of Modern Knowledge,* brings together essays by lawyers, anthropologists, sociologists, and historians of science. She is currently completing a book, based on her anthropological fieldwork in the United States and Japan, about the knowledge practices of lawyers engaged in the private economic realm.

SASKIA SASSEN is the Ralph Lewis Professor of Sociology at the University of Chicago and Centennial Visiting Professor at the London School of Economics. Her new book is *Territory, Authority, Rights: From Medieval to Global Assemblages* (2006). She has just completed for UNESCO a five-year project on sustainable human settlement for which she set up a network of researchers and activists in more than thirty countries. Her most recent books are the edited *Global Networks, Linked Cities* (2002) and the coedited *Socio-Digital Formations: New Architectures for Global Order* (2005). *The Global City* is out in a new fully updated edition in 2001. Her comments have appeared in the *Guardian,* the *New York Times, Le Monde Diplomatique,* the *International Herald Tribune, Vanguardia, Clarin,* and the *Financial Times,* among others.

PAUL A. SILVERSTEIN is Associate Professor of Anthropology at Reed College and a member of the editorial committee of *Middle East Report.* His work on migration, cultural production, transnational politics, and racialization processes across the western Mediterranean has appeared in a number of disciplinary and area studies journals and edited volumes. He is the author of *Algeria in France: Transpolitics, Race, and Nation* (2004) and editor (with Ussama Makdisi) of *Memory and Violence in the Middle East and North Africa* (2006).

ABDOUMALIQ SIMONE is an urbanist holding joint academic appointments at the Graduate Program in International Affairs, New School University, and the Institute of Social and Economic Research, University of Witwatersrand. He has taught at five African universities and worked for a range of African NGOs and regional institutions. Key publications include *In Whose Image: Political Islam and Urban Practices in the Sudan* (1994) and *For the City Yet to Come: Changing Urban Life in Four African Cities* (2004).

NEIL SMITH is Distinguished Professor of Anthropology and Geography and directs the Center for Place, Culture, and Politics at City University of New York. He has written extensively about the broad intersection between space, nature, social theory, and history. His most recent books are *The Endgame of Globalization* (2005) and *American Empire: Roosevelt's Geographer and the Prelude to Globalization* (2003), which won the *Los Angeles Times* Book Prize in biography. Among his earlier books are *New Urban Frontier: Gentrification and the Revanchist City* (1996) and *Uneven Development: Nature, Capital, and the Production of Space* (1984). He is a co-organizer of the International Critical Geography Group.

CAITLIN ZALOOM is an Assistant Professor in the Department of Social and Cultural Analysis at New York University. Her book, *Out of the Pits: Traders and Technology from Chicago to London*, (2006) examines technological rationalization, emerging social formations, and economic subjectivity in financial futures markets. She received a Ph.D. in Anthropology from the University of California, Berkeley, in 2002.

central banks (*continued*)
95–96, 98; liquidity needed by, 98, 99; motherhood metaphor and, 101–3, 107nn14–15; payment systems of, 87–88, 89–91, 99, 104–5, 106n4 (*see also* Designated Time system; Real Time system); powerlessness of bankers, 33–34, 88; significance of, 47; systemic risk in, 90–92, 94–95. *See also* Bank of Japan *and other specific banks*

Cetina, Karin Knorr, 314n1

Chad, 136

Chambers, John T., 44

Champigny (France), 285

Chanteloup-les-Vignes, 298

charity, 219, 232, 234

chartists, 66

Cheb Mami and K-Mel, 304n28

Chicago Board of Trade. *See* CBOT

Chicago group (numbers players), 79–80

Chicago Mercantile Exchange, 68, 84n16

Child, John, 264

childhood. *See* youth

"Children of North African Immigrants" (Georges Pompidou Center), 290

child soldiers, 139, 268, 273

China: Chinese employees, as self-interested/disloyal, 172–73, 174, 175, 181; Chinese employees, business ethics taught to, 174–75, 184–85; "company men" in, creation of, 173–75; democratization of, 190n15; global corporations in, influx of, 166; GPCR generation in, 174–75, 177, 188–89 (*see also* Communist Party); guanxi in, 164, 165, 167, 173, 178, 181–82, 184–87; international knowledge class in, 174, 180, 187–88; management evolution in, 176–78, 189n11; market reforms in, 181–82; membership in WTO, 57n6; rationalizing effects of market reforms in, 164; social communications in, 177–78 (*see also* guanxi); as socialist state, 171–72; social norms of, vs. American managerial expectations, 178–80; SOEs in,

185–86; subjectivities/management technologies in, 12–13, 188; television in, 110; transitional economy of, 163–64; Western vs. Chinese managers in, 173; Western vs. Chinese culture and, 173, 186–87. *See also* Shanghai

China Europe International Business School. *See* CEIBS

China's Pitfall (He), 181

chipmakers, 37

Chirac, Jacques, 302n13

Citibank, 167

cities, 24–25, 133, 135, 191–93, 200–201, 213, 229–30, 284, 310–11. *See also* London; New York City; Shanghai; Tokyo

citizenship, waged, 281n3

citizenship/disenfranchisement: of immigrant workers, 281n5; of non-autochthonous minorities, 281n5; of youth, 17, 269, 270, 280–81n3

City of Gold (Westbrook), 34, 38, 53–54, 55–57nn5–6

civilizing process, incompletion of, 283–89, 300

Clarke, Lee, 106n1

class: elites, 232; knowledge, 188; middle, upper middle, and professional-managerial, 199–201, 204, 206, 214–17; social mobility and, 212–13, 218, 234, 278–79, 289–90; underclass, 273, 298–300; working, 4, 25, 191–94, 280–81n4

Clinton, Bill, 201

Coca-Cola, 167, 291

collectivist organizations, 252–53, 259, 260–61, 262–63. *See also* Debian project

colonialism, French, 283–84

Colyer, Edwin, 19

Comaroff, Jean, 17, 284

Comaroff, John, 17, 284

communes, 261

Communist Party (China), 181, 182, 187–88

Computer Literacy (San Jose), 240

computer programmers, 16. *See also* Debian project

Estonia, 57n6

Ethiopia, 136

ethnography: anecdotal data in, 36, 40;
of bureaucracy, 94; business, in New
Economy, 18–22, 306–7; on the "edge,"
306; ethnology vs., 23–24; global
assemblages investigated by, 34, 55n1;
importance of, 22–26, 101; knowledge
production in, 11, 88–89; New Economy study, 5; refunctioning of, 35–36;
research methods in, 19–22, 36, 45,
103–4, 239–41, 263–64, 316n7; of technocracy, 87; thin vs. thick data in, 36.
See also anthropology/anthropologists;
para-ethnography

ethnology, 23

E-trader Graphic User Interface (GUI),
72–74, 85n18

EU (European Union), 51–52, 57n6, 205

Eurex, 73, 74, 85n18

European gentrification, 204–7

European institutions, 34, 47–48, 51–52,
53

European Union. *See* EU

Evian Accords, 284

exchange rates, 9

experts, 11, 100–101

extended families, 137–39

The eXtreme Games (X Games), 113, 114

face, 178

face-to-face activity, 13–14

family dynamics, 17

family relations in Africa, 137–39, 151

fantasy documents, 106n1

fast capitalism: anecdotal data/reports
and, 36, 40–42, 43–44; derivatives as
hallmark of, 9 (*see also* derivatives);
FOMC and, 34, 36–38, 39–40, 42–47;
global polity/supranational markets
and, 34, 47, 53–54, 55–57nn5–6 (*see also*
globalization); knowledge creation
and, 34; less than perfect knowledge
and, 39–40; markets' constitution and,
47–54; para-ethnography and (*see*

para-ethnography); as performance,
30n9; symbolic analysts and, 34, 47–54

Federal Open Market Committee (FOMC),
34, 36–38, 39–40, 42–47

Federal Reserve (New York District
branch), 46–47

Federal Reserve Banks, 40–42

Federal Reserve System, 1–7n10, 34, 43–
44, 55n2. *See also* Federal Open Market
Committee; Federal Reserve Banks

feedback, resistance to, 179

feminism, 211, 225–28, 230, 231, 232, 233–
34, 235n2

Ferguson, James, 87

Ferguson, Robert, 123

Ferrell, David, 114

Fertitta, Frank, 119, 126, 131n20

Fertitta, Lorenzo, 119, 126, 128, 131n20

fiber-optic capacity, 7

fieldwork, 35, 89, 101–2, 165, 264, 298

FightSport, 126

finance: conceptions of "financial," 214,
216; constitutive role of, 8; deregulation
of, 216

financescapes/space of flows, 60

financial markets: informational transparency and, 62–64; liquidity in, 15;
virtual capital in, 22–23. *See also* banks;
futures trading

financial services: employment expansion in, 229; liquid instruments of,
309; social relations' importance in,
13–14

Financial Women's Association of New
York. *See* FWA

Fischer, Claude, 82n2

Fischer, Frank, 86

Fishburn, Peter C., 259

Fisher, Melissa, 14, 26, 309, 312

Le Flow, 296

FOMC. *See* Federal Open Market
Committee

Fonky Family, 294

football, 111, 113, 125, 271, 303n25

Fort Greene (Brooklyn), 198

General Public License. *See* GNU GPL

generation, 267, 269–79

gentrification, 191–208; in "blighted" neighborhoods, 194, 196, 208n2; causes of, 195; class nature of, 193, 199–200, 204, 206; degentrification and, 198; as discrete process, 191; in Europe, 204–7; global capital's role in, 202; as global urban strategy, 200–204; homelessness and, 197, 199–200, 202–3, 206–7; in New York City, 192, 193–201; opposition to, 197, 202–3, 207–8; outward diffusion of, 203; in Paris, 192; public-private partnerships for, 24–25, 192, 201–2; redlining/greenlining and, 196; scope/spread of, 192–93, 197, 198–99, 205; sectoral generalization of, 198–99, 201, 203–4; social balance and, 206; state's role in, 201–2; in United Kingdom, 191–92, 193, 194; as urban regeneration, 192, 204–7; as urban renaissance, 191–92; urban renewal of 1950s–1970s vs., 192, 194, 203

Gentry, Clyde, 123, 125

"geobribes," 202

Germans (numbers players), 79

Geschiere, Peter, 138

Get Busy, 295

Ghana, 140, 142

gi (jujitsu uniform), 125, 131n16

Gibson, Angus, 281n6

Giddens, Anthony, 52–53

GIS Goorgoorlu, 143

Glass, Ruth, 191–92, 193

Glick, O., 84n16

global assemblages, 34

global cities, 24, 167, 189n6, 229, 310–11

Global Crossing, 2

global financial sites, 11–12, 228. *See also* Japan; London; New York City

globalization: binary opposites of, 163; citizens, 310; cultural, 129, 269–70, 275, 277–78, 292, 300–301; of gentification discourse, 192–93, 200; history of, 34, 47–54; individual actors/specific pro-

cesses vs. anonymous global flows and, 25–26, 307, 309; localization, 184, 239–40; markets, 165, 188; of media, 110, 114; as mimetic transmission of bodily techniques, 129; studies of, 25–26, 302n7; of Wall Street women's networks, 229–30. *See also* management, global

global localization/indigenization, 168–71, 189n7

global polity/supranational markets, 34, 47, 53–54, 55–57nn5–6. *See also* globalization

GNU GPL (General Public License), 247, 248, 254, 255

GnuPG (GPG) keys, 250–51

goal transformation, 254

Goffman, Erving, 248, 266n17

Goldman Sachs, 210, 222, 224. *See also* 85 Broads

gold reserves, 136

Goodenough, Oliver R., 116

GPCR (Great Proletarian Cultural Revolution), 174–75, 177, 188–89. *See also* Communist Party

GPG (GnuPG) keys, 250–51

GPL. *See* GNU GPL

Gracie, Rorian, 115, 120–21, 130n12

Gracie, Royce, 120, 121, 125

Gracie family history, 115

Gracie Jiu-Jitsu Academy (California), 115, 127, 130n11

Graeber, David, 26

Great Britain: colonial venture in South Africa, 284; gentrification in, 191–92, 193, 194; on Lend-Lease Agreement, 48–49; urban regeneration in, 204–7. *See also* London

Greater Abidjan, 158n1

Greater Nairobi, 145

Great Proletarian Cultural Revolution. *See* GPCR

Green, Joan, 231

Greenhouse, Carol, 101

Green Party, 280–81n3

Greenspan, Alan, 4–5, 11, 39–40

skill and, 59, 82–83n2; variability in uses of, 306–7; work from home enabled by, 15. *See also* electronic trading

130n12; cable television and extreme sports, 108, 113–14; clothing of fighters, 125, 131n16; fighting technique transmitted by television, 109–10, 124–28, 131n17, 312; importance of televised sports, 110–12, 130n4; instructional videos on, 127–28, 129, 131–32n21; international nature of, 122–23; on Internet, 125; local competitions in, 131n19; martial arts, deregulation of, 109, 120–24; opposition to, 118; participant-fans of, 125–27, 131n19; publications on, 126; rituals in, 124, 131n15; scandals surrounding, 109, 117–19; sportsmanship in, 131n15; styles/techniques in, 121–24; UFC, 7, 108–10, 114–24, 125–26, 129n1, 130n12, 131n14; U.S. vs. Japanese, 119, 131n14; violent spectacle vs. painful truth, 109, 120, 124, 128–29, 130n7

nongovernmental organizations (NGOs), 14, 143

North Africa: emigration to France from, 284–85, 296, 302n5, 302n11; French colonial expansion into, 283–84; youth's use of technologies in, 6–7

NRJ (France), 292

NTM. See Suprême NTM

numbers: bid/ask, 61–62, 64, 66–67, 83n6; key players of, 77–81; physicality of, 68–71; psychological significance of, 66; role in futures trading, 61–62, 63, 64–67, 82, 84n14, 85nn18–19

Núñez, Orlando, 299

NWA, 304n27

NYSE (New York Stock Exchange), 202, 217

Observatory on Information Systems, Networks and Information Highways (Dakar), 141

occupational subjectivity, 216

Ogilvy & Mather, 167

oil production, 136

Okamura, Kazuo, 248–49

Olds, Kris, 189n6

Olympic broadcasting, 113, 114, 117

Olympique Marseille soccer club (France), 291, 296

O'Mahony, Siobhán, 16, 22

O'Malley, Pat, 84n13

Ong, Aihwa, 6, 9, 12–13, 22

online trading. See electronic trading

on-screen trading. See electronic trading

open-outcry markets. See pit trading

Oranais raï music, 290

Orangina, 291

organizational forms, emergence of, 238, 262–63. See also Debian project

organizational studies, 240–41

Orlikowski, Wanda J., 248–49

Ouagadougou (Burkina Faso), 152

Outward Bound, 222

Pan African Telecommunications Union, 141

pancrasse (Japanese martial art), 122

Pantin (Paris), 298

paper money, 97–98

parachute anthropology/ethnography, 19, 21

para-ethnography: as anecdotal evidence, 40; in culture of expertise, 36, 37–38; defining the contemporary and, 35–36, 38, 43, 54; as intuition, 39–40; practices of, 11, 100–101; technical knowledge's failure and, 33–34

Paris, 301n1

Park Slope (Brooklyn), 196

Parliament, Deidre, 225

Parmalat, 2

Passeron, Jean-Claude, 289

pastoralism, 102

payment systems, 87–88, 89–91, 99, 104–5, 106n4. See also Designated Time system; Real Time system

pay-per-view television, 114, 115–17, 118, 129, 130–31n13

Pearl Harbor, 48

Pentagon, attack on. See September 11 attacks (2001)

urban regeneration/renewal, 166, 192,
204–7, 287–88, 290–91, 300. *See also*
gentrification
Urban-Revival Pact, 287–88
Urban Task Force (U.K.), 191–92
U.S. Central Bank, 36, 39, 40
USAID Leland Initiative, 141
USA Today, 130n4

Val-Fourré, 298
value: Black-Scholes pricing formula, 10–
11; of ".com," perceived, 30n9; consensus on, 10–11; of production vs.
guanxi, 186–87; social/cultural aspects
of, 7, 8; virtual, 22–23
value rationality, 245, 254, 257, 258, 265n11
Van Maanen, John, 240–41
Vargo, Keith, 121
Vaulx-en-Velin uprisings, 291, 292
Vietnam War protests, 275
virtual environments, 314–15n3
virtualism, 22, 30n11
virtuality, conceptions of, 133–34, 156
virus writers, 17
voting, 258–59, 299

Wagner, Rachel, 228
Walder, Andrew, 164
Wallerstein, Immanuel, 131n14
Walls, Jason, 127
Wall Street, 10, 209, 211, 231–32
Wall Street women's networks, 209–34,
312; diversity/philanthropy in, 212, 219,
231–32, 234; 85 Broads, 210, 212–13, 220–
24, 225, 232, 233, 234; FWA, 209–10, 211–
13, 214–20, 225–28, 229–31, 232, 233–34,
235n2, 235n5; glass ceilings and, 235n5;
habitus making in, 219–20; logic of, 213,
229–30; membership categories/goals/
subjects of, 214–20, 225; mentoring in,
221; New Economy and, 212; as New
Economy elite, 217–18, 232; self-
management and, 223–24; sexual
harassment and, 211; success/work
ethics and, ideologies/narratives of, 213,

221, 223, 233–34; support from, during
economic uncertainty, 235n5
Wamba, Anaclet, 291
Warner, 294
Weber, Max, 83n3, 88, 164, 245, 257
West Africa, 283–84
Westbrook, David: *City of Gold*, 34, 38,
53–54, 55–57nn5–6
White, Dana, 126–27
White, Harry Dexter, 47, 49, 50–51
Whyte, William Foote, 240–41
Wide World of Sports, 113
Williams, Jones, 209–10
Williamsburg (Brooklyn), 198
Windows operating system, 240
Winfrey, Oprah, 222
women. *See* Wall Street women's
networks
"Workshop on the New Global Economy"
(Goizueta Business School, Emory
University, 2001), 26
World Bank, 294
World Championship Wrestling, 114
WorldCom, 2
World Trade Center. *See* September 11
attacks (2001)
World Wildlife Fund (WWF), 114
worth. *See* value
wrestling: freestyle, 123; Olympic-style,
122; professional, televised, 109, 114,
130n8; sambo, 122; sumo, 113
Wu Tang Clan, 296
WWE (World Wrestling Entertainment),
114, 130n8
WWF (World Wildlife Fund), 114

X Games, 113, 114
Xintiandi ("New Heaven and Earth";
Shanghai), 182–83

Yang, Mayfair, 181–82
Yates, JoAnne, 248–49
Yizo Yizo, 281n6
Young Women's Investment Association
(YWIA). *See* FWA

youth, 267–80; activism of, 268, 270, 271, 274, 275–76; adults vs., 270–71, 312; autonomy as social category, 269–70; citizenship/disenfranchisement of, 17, 269, 270, 280–81n3; clubs/gangs, 247; crisis of, 17, 269, 279–80; educating/ civilizing of, 272–73; employment of, 269; as entrepreneurs, 276–77; expulsion of, in Africa, 139; generation trouble and, 269–70; global youth culture, rise of, 271, 274–76; history of, 270–74; Internet use by, 143, 269–70, 316n8; marginalization of, 278, 280, 281n8; meanings/conceptions of, 267–68, 273, 280; modernist construction of, 267–68, 271, 274, 280n1; Muslim, 316n8; optimism about, 280, 281n9; production/consumption and, 269–70, 274–75, 280, 281n4; as soldiers, 139, 268, 273; summer camps for, 291; technological change mastered by, 17; transnational activism by, 269–70; violence by, 272, 273–74, 279, 280n2; youth culture as politics of metaphor, 276–79, 281n8

Youth and Sports program (France), 291

Youth Network for Development, 143

Yuppies, 197

YWIA (Young Women's Investment Association). *See* FWA

Zaloom, Caitlin, 5–6

Zebda, 297, 299, 304n28

Zidane, Zinedine, 296

Zimbabwe, 136, 140

Zoxea, 294

Zuffa, 119, 126, 131n14, 131n20

Zukin, Sharon, 196

Žižek, Slavoj, 270

Melissa S. Fisher is an assistant professor of anthropology at Georgetown University. Greg Downey is a lecturer in anthropology at Macquarie University.

An earlier version of Jean Comaroff and John Comaroff's chapter was published as "Reflections on Youth: From the Past to the Postcolony," in *Makers and Breakers: Children and Youth in Postcolonial Africa*, edited by Alcinda Honwana and Filip de Boeck (Oxford: James Currey, 2005). Reprinted with permission.

An earlier version of Annelise Riles's chapter was published in *American Ethnologist* 31.3 (2004): 392–405. © University of California Press. Reprinted with permission.

An earlier version of Neil Smith's chapter was published as "New Globalism, New Urbanism: Gentrification as Global Urban Strategy" in *Antipode* 34.3 (2002): 427–420. © Blackwell Publishing. Reprinted with permission.

An earlier version of Caitlin Zaloom's chapter was published as "Ambiguous Numbers: Trading Technologies and Interpretation in Financial Markets," in *American Ethnologist* 30.2 (2003): 259–272. © University of California Press. Reprinted with permission.

Library of Congress Cataloging-in-Publication Data
Frontiers of capital : ethnographic reflections on the new economy / edited by Melissa S. Fisher and Greg Downey.
p. cm.
Includes bibliographical references and index.
ISBN-13: 978-0-8223-3727-0 (cloth : alk. paper)
ISBN-10: 0-8223-3727-4 (cloth : alk. paper)
ISBN-13: 978-0-8223-3739-3 (pbk. : alk. paper)
ISBN-10: 0-8223-3739-8 (pbk. : alk. paper)
1. Information technology—Social aspects. 2. Information society—Economic aspects. 3. Capitalism—Social aspects. 4. Culture—Economic aspects. 5. Social change—Economic aspects. I. Title: Ethnographic reflections on the new economy. II. Fisher, Melissa S. (Melissa Suzanne), 1962– III. Downey, Greg.
HC79.I55F76 2006
306.3—dc22   2006004918